Canon EOS M: From Snapshots to Great Shots

Jeff Carlson

Peachpit Press

Canon EOS M: From Snapshots to Great Shots
Jeff Carlson

Peachpit Press
www.peachpit.com

To report errors, please send a note to errata@peachpit.com
Peachpit Press is a division of Pearson Education.

Senior Editor: Susan Rimerman
Production Editor: Lisa Brazieal
Copyeditor/Proofreader: Scout Festa
Composition: Jeff Carlson
Indexer: Karin Arrigoni
Cover Image: Jeff Carlson
Cover Design: Aren Straiger
Interior Design: Riezebos Holzbaur Design Group
All photography © Jeff Carlson

ISBN-13: 978-0-321-90748-6
ISBN–10: 0-321-90748-5

9 8 7 6 5 4 3 2 1
Printed and bound in the United States of America

DEDICATION

For Patty and Robert

The camera used while writing this *From Snapshots to Great Shots* book was generously provided by B&H Photo.

B&H

PHOTO - VIDEO - PRO AUDIO

www.bhphotovideo.com

ACKNOWLEDGMENTS

I'm a pretty self-contained author. I write and package my books, which generally means I hand Peachpit a completed manuscript that they can take to the printer. I'm never alone of course—editors, copyeditors, proofers, indexers, and others contribute to the finished product.

I'm saying this not to boast, but to help you understand that there's no way I could have been a self-contained author on this book. Without the incredibly hard work of the people listed here, I'd be standing in a field somewhere hoping for golden late afternoon sunlight and making lists of all the photos yet to be shot. My sincere thanks go out to:

Nancy Peterson, for getting the project rolling.

Susan Rimerman, for making sure the project didn't roll right over me.

Scout Festa, for crack copyediting skills and quick turnaround times.

Karin Arrigoni, for creating the index (a task I happily turn over to the professionals).

Lisa Brazieal, for getting on my case about every misaligned pixel ("for having truly excellent design and production eyes," I mean) and making me laugh.

Jeff Revell, for starting the From Snapshots to Great Shots series and providing the foundation on which to build this book.

Laurence Chen, for his invaluable assistance back when I first started to take photography seriously.

Glenn Fleishman, for early lunches, afternoon coffees, and reality checks as deadlines began looming.

Katie Lacey, Krystal Townsend, Joey Bates, Lara Hamilton, and **Sandro Menzel** for modeling.

Glenn, Lynn D. Warner, Dana Bos, David Bos, Steve Horn, and **Jill Thompson** for permission to include their lovely children in the book.

Ellie Carlson, for being a patient and frequent model, and charming me in ways I can't describe.

Kimberly Carlson, for laughter and patience and support and love.

Contents

Introduction

Walk into any bookseller and you will see countless books on the subject of photography. Look a little further and you will locate the camera-specific books. It is this divide between the camera-specific and instructional photography books that inspired this book. A lot of books sort of miss the mark—especially when it comes to combining actual photographic instruction with the use of a specific brand and model of camera. So with that, this book on the Canon EOS M is not a rehash of the owner's manual but is a resource to teach photography with the wonderful technology present in the EOS M. I have put together a short Q&A to help you get a better understanding of just what it is that you can expect from this book.

Q: IS EVERY CAMERA FEATURE GOING TO BE COVERED?

A: Nope, just the ones I felt you need to know about in order to start taking great photos. Believe it or not, you already own a great resource that covers every feature of your camera: the owner's manual. Writing a book that just repeats this information would have been a waste of my time and your money. What I did want to write about was how to harness certain camera features to the benefit of your photography. As you read through the book, you will also see callouts that point you to specific pages in your owner's manual that are related to the topic being discussed. For example, in Chapter 5 I discuss the Continuous shooting mode, but there is more information available on this feature in the manual. I cover the function as it applies to our specific needs, but I also give you the page numbers in the manual so you can explore it even further.

Q: SO IF I ALREADY OWN THE MANUAL, WHY DO I NEED THIS BOOK?

A: The manual does a pretty good job of telling you how to use a feature or turn it on in the menus, but it doesn't necessarily tell you *why* and *when* you should use it. If you really want to improve your photography, you need to know the whys and whens to put all of those great camera features to use at the right time. To that extent, the manual just isn't going to cut it. It is, however, a great resource on the camera's features, and it is for that reason that I treat it like a companion to this book. You already own it, so why not get something of value from it?

Q: WHAT CAN I EXPECT TO LEARN FROM THIS BOOK?

A: Hopefully, you will learn how to take great photographs. My goal, and the reason the book is laid out the way it is, is to guide you through the basics of photography as they relate to different situations and scenarios. By using the features of your EOS M and this book, you will learn about aperture, shutter speed, ISO, lens selection, depth of field, and many other photographic concepts. You will also find plenty of full-page photos that include captions, shooting data, and callouts so you can see how all of the photography fundamentals come together to make great images. All the while, you will be learning how your camera works and how to apply its functions and features to your photography.

Q: WHAT ARE THE ASSIGNMENTS ALL ABOUT?

A: At the end of most of the chapters, you will find shooting assignments, where I give you some suggestions as to how you can apply the lessons of the chapter to help reinforce everything you just learned. Let's face it—using the camera is much more fun than reading about it, so the assignments are a way of taking a little break after each chapter and having some fun.

Q: SHOULD I READ THE BOOK STRAIGHT THROUGH OR CAN I SKIP AROUND FROM CHAPTER TO CHAPTER?

A: Here's the easy answer: yes and no. No, because the first four chapters give you the basic information that you need to know about your camera. These are the building blocks for using the camera. After that, yes, you can move around the book as you see fit because the later chapters are written to stand on their own as guides to specific types of photography or shooting situations. You can bounce from portraits to shooting landscapes and then maybe to a little action photography. It's all about your needs and how you want to address them. Or, you can read it straight through. The choice is up to you.

Q: IS THAT IT?

A: One last thought before you dive into the first chapter. My goal in writing this book has been to give you a resource that you can turn to for creating great photographs with your Canon EOS M. Take some time to learn the basics and then put them to use. Photography, like most things, takes time to master and requires practice. Always remember that it's not the camera that makes beautiful photographs—it's the person using it. Have fun, make mistakes, and then learn from them. In no time, I'm sure you will transition from a person who takes snapshots to a photographer who makes great shots.

LATE-BREAKING NEWS

As you may have discovered by now, the EOS M's autofocus is often slow (I also mention this in Chapter 5). It's one of the few items that disappoint me in an otherwise excellent camera. As this book goes to press, rumors are swirling that Canon will release a firmware update that might address the issue. Hopefully, by the time you read this an update will be available; see "Updating the EOS M's Firmware" in Chapter 2 to learn how to apply it.

I've also read rumors that Canon plans to release an additional EOS M body that includes a viewfinder. Normally I'm skeptical of rumors—I believe things when I see them. However, the realities of publishing mean that this book had to go to press on a specific date, before either of these rumored events occurred. But that doesn't leave you out in the cold. To stay apprised of these and other issues, register your book at peachpit.com/canoneosm, where I'll post updated information. After you've registered the book, go to the Registered Products tab in your account and click the Access Bonus Content link.

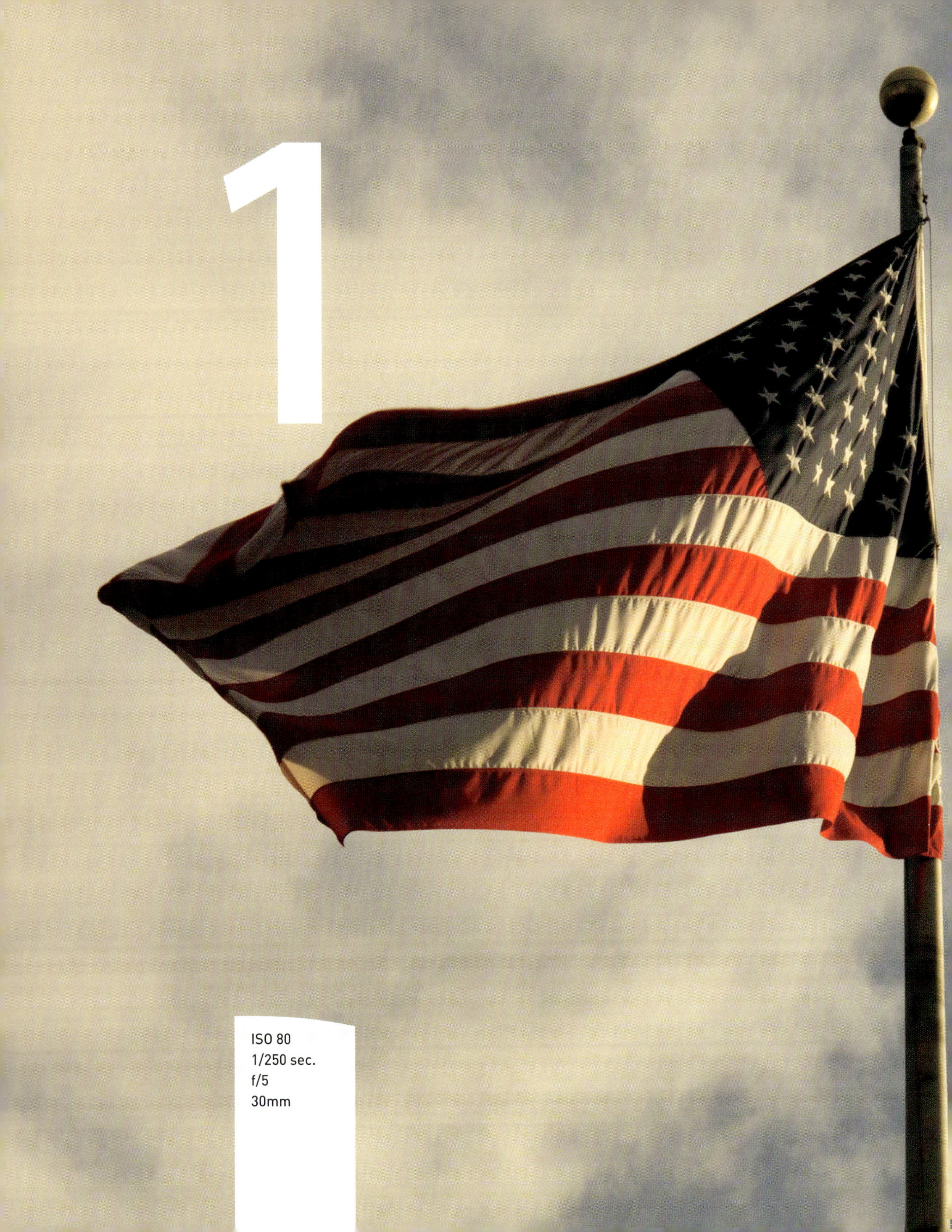

1

ISO 80
1/250 sec.
f/5
30mm

The EOS M Top Ten List

TEN TIPS TO MAKE YOUR SHOOTING MORE PRODUCTIVE RIGHT OUT OF THE BOX

First, I want to thank you for leaving your new camera in its box until you've had a chance to start reading the instruction manual… Oh, I can't even finish that sentence with a straight face. I'm sure you've already started snapping exposures! Yes, we know that we should read the manual to learn how to use the camera's features, but what fun is that?

Of course, this route often leads to frustration—there are always issues that would have been easily addressed had I known about them before I started shooting. Maybe if I had a Top Ten list of things to know, I could be more productive without having to spend countless hours with the manual. So this is where we begin.

The following list will get you up and running without suffering many of the "gotchas" that come from not being at least somewhat familiar with your new camera. So let's take a look at the top ten things you should know before you start taking pictures with your Canon EOS M.

CAMERA FRONT

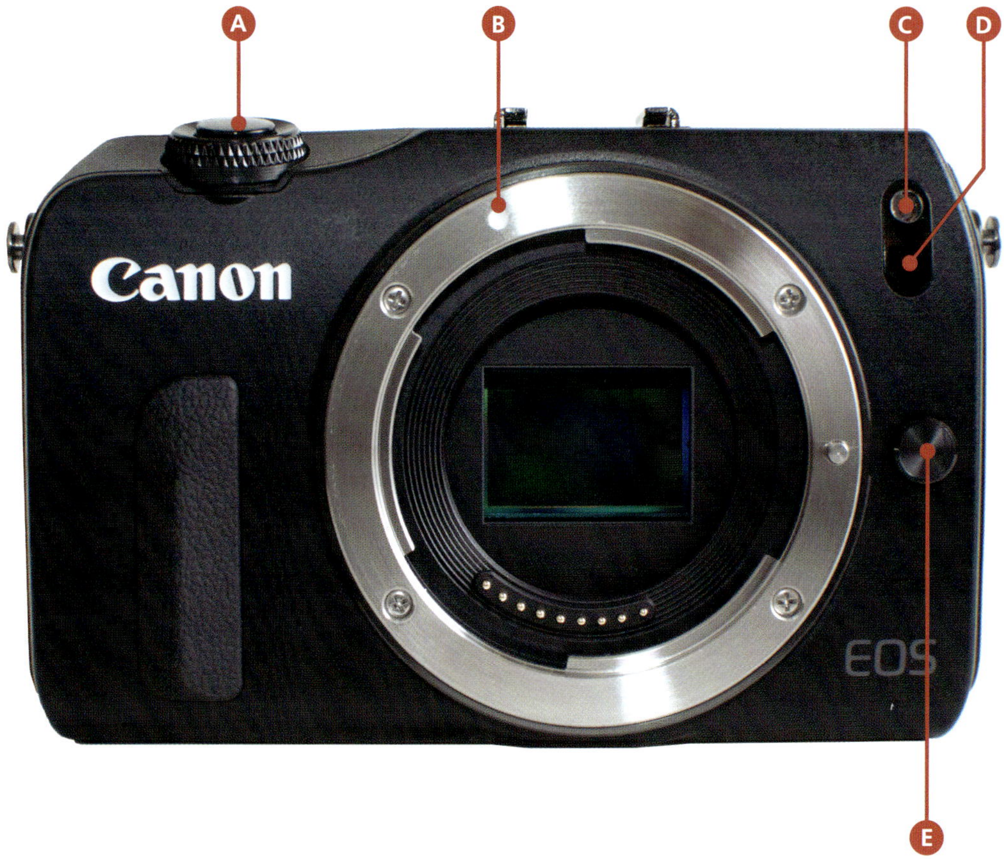

A Shutter Release Button
B Lens Align Mark
C Red-Eye Reduction/Self-Timer Lamp
D Remote Control Sensor
E Lens Release

CAMERA BACK

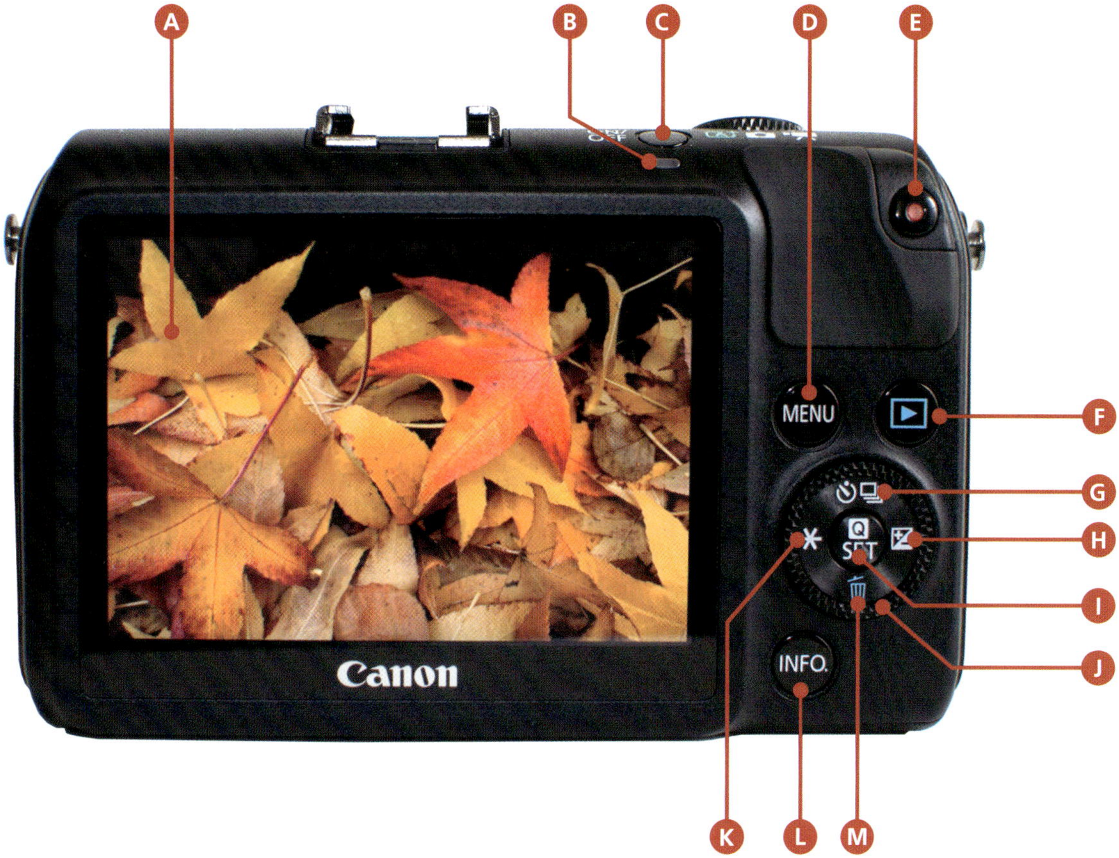

A LCD
B Power/Access Lamp
C On/Off Button
D Menu Button
E Movie Start/Stop Button
F Playback Button
G Drive Mode Selection/Up Cross Key
H Exposure Compensation/
Right Cross Key
I Quick Control/Set Button
J Main Dial
K AE/FE Lock/Left Cross Key
L INFO Button
M Erase Button/Down Cross Key

PORING OVER THE CAMERA

CAMERA TOP

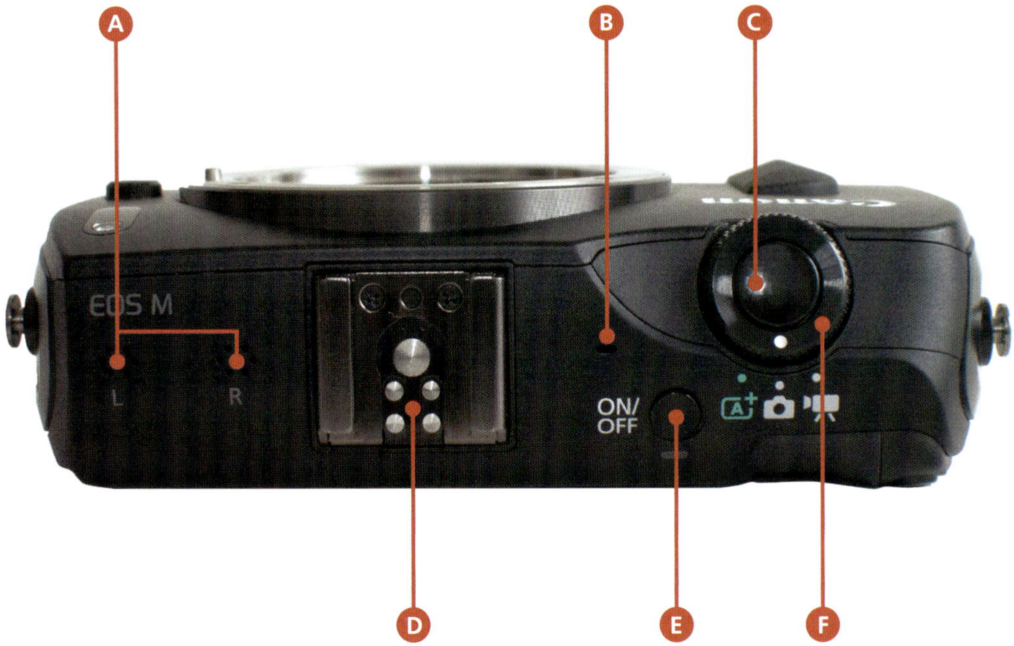

A Microphone
B Speaker
C Shutter Release
D Speedlite Hot Shoe
E On/Off Button
F Mode Dial

1. CHARGE YOUR BATTERY

I know this will be one of the hardest things for you to do because you really want to start shooting, but a little patience will pay off later.

When you first open your camera and slide the battery into the battery slot, you will be pleased to find that there is probably juice in the battery and you can start shooting right away. Resist the temptation, and instead get out the battery charger and give that power cell a full charge. Not only will this give you more time to shoot later on, but it will also start the battery off on the right foot. No matter what claims the manufacturers make about battery life and battery memory, I always find I get better life and performance when I charge my batteries fully and then use them right down to the point where they have nothing left to give. To check your battery's level, insert it into the camera, turn on the camera, and look for the battery indicator on the LCD. You might have to press the shutter release button to wake up the camera. This will activate the LCD and allow you to see the battery-level indicator, located in the upper-left portion of the display panel (**Figure 1.1**).

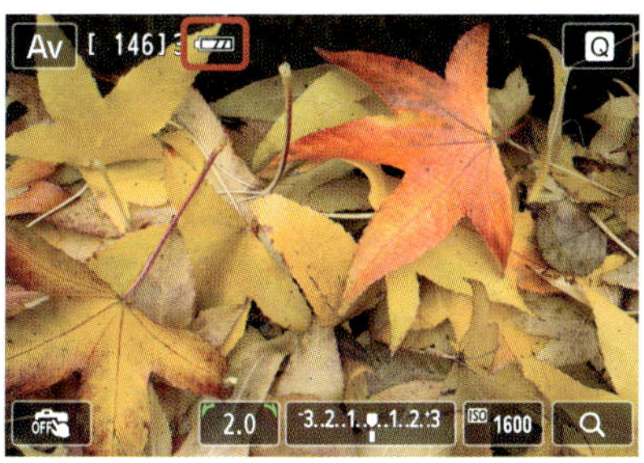

FIGURE 1.1
The LCD screen shows how much charge is left on your battery.

KEEPING A BACKUP BATTERY

If I were to suggest just one accessory that you should buy for your camera, it would probably be a second battery. Nothing stinks more than being out in the field and having your camera die. Keeping a fully charged battery in your bag gives you the confidence that you can keep on shooting without fail. Not only will this extend your shooting time, but alternating between batteries helps lengthen their lives. Using batteries half as much increases their usefulness.

2. TURN OFF THE RELEASE SHUTTER WITHOUT CARD SETTING

If you really want to ruin your day, try shooting for a couple of hours only to find that you didn't put a memory card in your camera and thus didn't save any of the pictures you took. This was always a concern with film shooters, and it hasn't gone away with digital cameras. You see, camera manufacturers want to give prospective buyers a way to test out the camera without having to keep a memory card in it, so they came up with a setting called Release Shutter Without Card. When your camera is set up in this mode, it will act and shoot just as it would when you have a memory card inserted. It will even display your shot on the LCD. Unfortunately, this is where most photographers get fooled into thinking they are saving their images. If they were to look at the LCD, they would see that Canon was nice enough to overlay a message on the display that clearly says No Card. If you are shooting without looking at the display, you could easily be fooled.

Unfortunately, there is no visual clue within the viewfinder to alert you to this No Card status. So here is the simple solution.

TURNING OFF THE RELEASE SHUTTER WITHOUT CARD SETTING

1. Turn the camera on.
2. Press the Menu button on the back of the camera to bring up the menu list.
3. Use the Main dial to select the far-left menu tab.
4. Now use the cross keys to scroll down to the Release shutter without card option, and press the Set button (**A**).
5. Use the cross keys to select the Disable option, and then press the Set button once again (**B**).
6. Press the Menu button again to return to shooting mode.

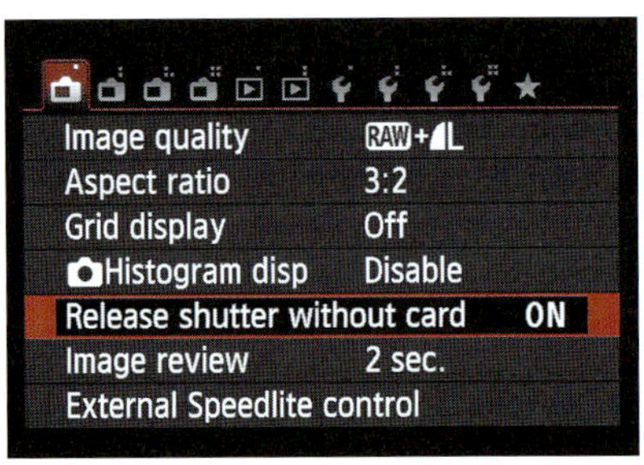

A

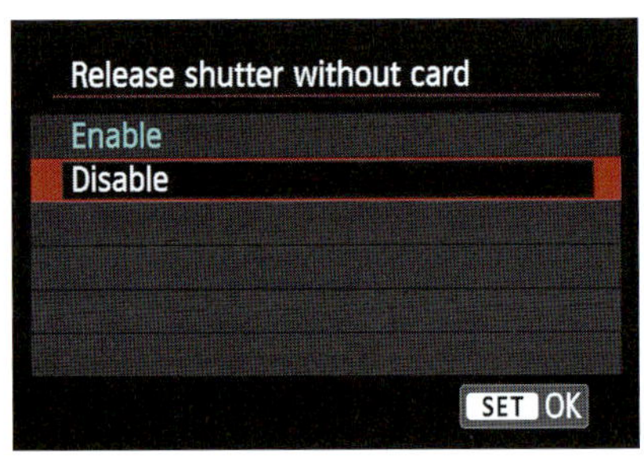

B

Now when you try to take a photo without a memory card inserted in the camera, you will see the phrase No Card in Camera across the top of the LCD; the word *Card* also appears in the lower-left corner when you press the shutter release button. This is your clue that you need to insert your memory card before the camera will fire. We will have an in-depth discussion on memory cards and proper formatting in Chapter 2.

3. KEEP A BACKUP MEMORY CARD

True story: I grabbed my camera, went to the beach, and just when my daughter was doing something especially cute, I discovered I had left the camera's memory card in the card reader attached to my computer.

Cards are relatively inexpensive, so consider not only picking up one or two spares, but also storing them in a convenient place: a wallet, a purse, or a car's glove compartment. I'll discuss memory cards and proper formatting in more depth in Chapter 2.

4. SET YOUR JPEG IMAGE QUALITY

Your new EOS M has a number of image-quality settings to choose from, and you can adjust them according to your needs. Most people shoot with the JPEG option (versus RAW) because it allows them to capture a large number of photos on their memory cards. The problem is, unless you understand how JPEG works, you might be degrading the quality of your images without realizing it.

The JPEG (Joint Photographic Experts Group) format has been around since about 1994 and was developed as a method of reducing large file sizes while retaining the original image information. (Technically, JPEG isn't even a file format—it's a mathematical equation for reducing image file sizes—but to keep things simple, we'll just refer to it as a file format.) The problem with JPEG is that, in order to reduce file size, it has to throw away some of the information. This is referred to as "lossy compression." This is important to understand, because while you can fit more images on your memory card by choosing a lower-quality JPEG setting, you also reduce the quality of your image. This effect becomes more apparent as you enlarge your pictures.

The JPEG file format also has one other characteristic: To apply the compression to the image before final storage on your memory card, the camera has to process the image first. Image processing involves such factors as sharpening, color adjustment, contrast adjustment, noise reduction, and so on. Many photographers now prefer to use the RAW file format to get greater control over the image processing. We will take a closer look at RAW in Chapter 2, but for now let's just make sure we're using the best-quality JPEG possible.

> ## Manual Callout
> For a chart that shows the image quality settings with the number of possible shots for each setting, turn to page 105 in your user manual.

The EOS M has eight quality settings for the JPEG format. There are two settings each for the Large, Medium, and Small settings. The two settings represent more or less image compression based on your choice. The Large, Medium, and Small settings determine the actual physical size of your image in pixels. There are also two additional settings (Small 2 and Small 3) that are even smaller in dimension than Small 1 but do not have compression options. Let's work with the highest-quality setting possible. After all, our goal is to make big, beautiful photographs, so why start the process with a lower-quality image?

SETTING THE IMAGE QUALITY

1. Press the Menu button on the back of the camera to bring up the menu list.
2. Use the Main dial to select the far-left menu tab.
3. At the top of this menu tab, locate the Image quality option (**A**).
4. Press the Set button to bring up the options screen.
5. Use the Left/Right cross keys to select the first L, which renders an 18-megapixel image with a dimension of 5184 pixels by 3456 pixels (the number in brackets after the dimensions indicates how many photos at that resolution will fit onto the current memory card) (**B**).
6. Press the Set button to lock in this change.

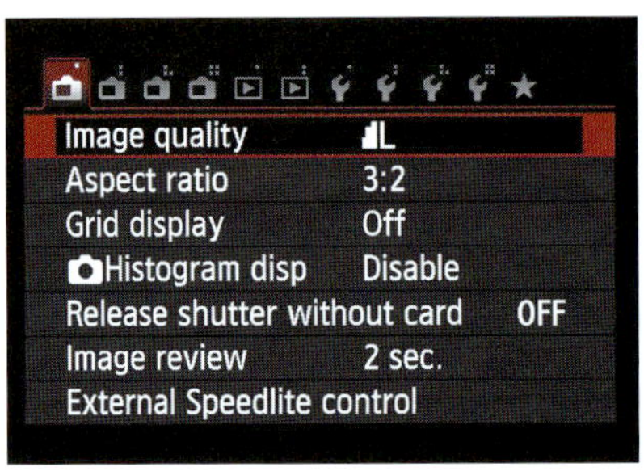

A

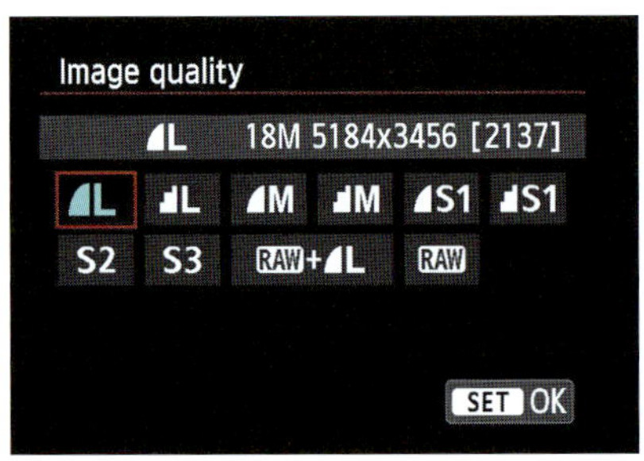

B

5. TURN OFF THE AUTO ISO SETTING

The ISO setting in your camera allows you to choose the level of sensitivity of the camera sensor to light. The ability to change this sensitivity is one of the biggest advantages to using a digital camera. In the days of film cameras, you *had* to choose the ISO by film type. This meant that if you wanted to shoot in lower light, you had to replace the film in the camera with one that had a higher ISO. So not only did you have to carry different types of film, but you also had to remove one roll from the camera to replace it with another, even if you hadn't used up the current roll. Now all we have to do is go to the menu and select the appropriate ISO.

Having this flexibility is a powerful option, but just as with the Quality setting, the ISO setting has a direct bearing on the quality of the final image. The higher the ISO, the more digital noise the image will contain. Since our goal is to produce high-quality photographs, it is important that we get control over all of the camera controls and bend them to our will. When you turn your camera on for the first time, the ISO will be set to Auto. This means that the camera is determining how much light is available and will choose what it believes is the correct ISO setting. Since you want to use the lowest ISO possible, you need to turn this setting off and manually select the appropriate ISO.

Which ISO you choose depends on your level of available or ambient light. For sunny days or very bright scenes, use a low ISO such as 100 or 200. As the level of light is reduced, raise the ISO level. Cloudy days or indoor scenes might require you to use ISO 400. Low-light scenes, such as when you are shooting at night, will mean you need to bump up that ISO to 1600 or higher. The thing to remember is to shoot with the lowest setting possible for maximum quality. Later, we will cover some other specifics of exposure so that you know just how and why to raise your ISO.

SETTING THE ISO

1. Activate the camera by lightly pressing the shutter release button.
2. Press the ISO button at the lower-right corner of the LCD.
3. Use the Main dial or swipe with your finger to select an ISO between 100 and 12800. (You can also tap once on the value you want, instead of swiping.)
4. Lightly press the shutter release button or tap the Return button (⮌) to lock in your change.

NOISE

Noise is the enemy of digital photography, but it has nothing to do with the loudness of your camera operation. It is a term that refers to the electronic artifacts that appear as speckles in your image. They generally appear in darker shadow areas and are a result of the camera trying to amplify the signal to produce visible information. The more the image needs to be amplified–e.g., raising the sensitivity through higher ISOs–the greater the amount of noise there will be.

6. SET THE FOCUS MODE TO AF+MF

Now here's an odd feature—or rather, lack of a feature—of the EOS M: There's no dedicated MF (manual focus) button. It's especially surprising on a camera that uses interchangeable lenses with manual focus rings. For those times when you want to control the focus yourself, you can switch to MF mode, but that requires digging into the menu system. Instead, put the camera into AF+MF focus mode, an odd compromise that works like this: Press the shutter button halfway to lock focus using the camera's autofocus mode, and then, while continuing to hold the shutter button, use the focus ring on the lens to manually adjust the focus.

SETTING THE FOCUS MODE TO AF+MF

1. Press the Menu button.
2. Use the Main dial or press the Right cross key to select the second menu tab.
3. Press the Down cross key to select the Focus mode option (**A**).
4. Press the Set button to view the Focus mode options.
5. Select the AF+MF item and then press the Set button to switch modes (**B**).
6. Press the Menu button or lightly press the shutter button to exit the menu.

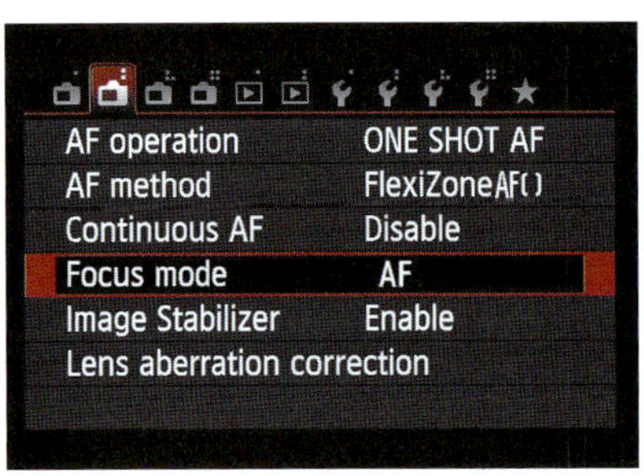

A

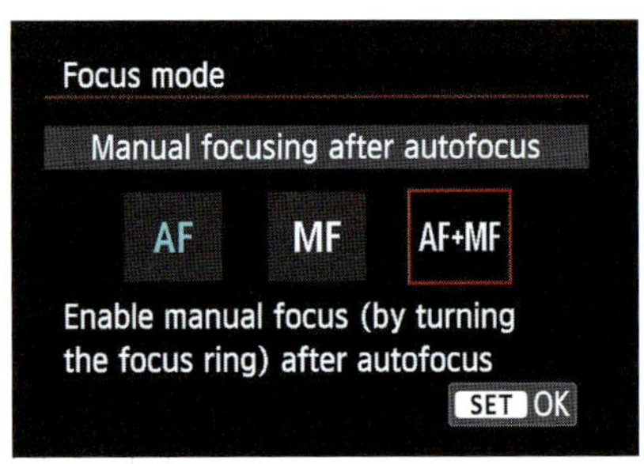

B

7. SET YOUR AUTOFOCUS METHOD AND MODE

Usually you'll rely on the camera's autofocus mode, but there's a limitation. No matter how intelligent it is, the camera is looking at all of the subjects in the scene and determining which is closest to the camera. It then uses this information to determine where the proper focus point should be. It has no way of knowing what *your* main emphasis is, so it's using a "best guess" system. To help the camera focus on the items you want, set both an autofocus method and a focus mode.

Three autofocus methods are available. Facial+Tracking identifies people's faces (or at least, shapes that appear to be faces) and focuses on them; you can also tap any object in a scene and the lens will stay focused on it, even as you move the camera. FlexiZone – Multi hands the duties over to the EOS M, identifying multiple focus points depending on what it perceives as important objects; you can also tap the screen to specify a smaller area for it to analyze. FlexiZone – Single lets you identify the focus point by tapping anywhere on the LCD.

After you choose a focus method, set the focus mode to One Shot so that you can focus on your subject and then recompose your shot while holding that point of focus. This method allows for better composition. (You may want to change one other focus feature: In the second menu screen, set Continuous AF to Disable so the camera isn't always scanning for focus.)

SETTING THE AUTOFOCUS METHOD AND FOCUS MODE

1. Press the Set button to bring up the Quick Control menu.
2. Tap the AF method button in the upper-left corner.
3. Now tap, use the cross keys, or turn the Main dial to choose one of the methods (**A**).
4. To set the focus mode, tap the AF operation button, which is just below the AF method button.
5. Select the One Shot mode by tapping or by using the cross keys or the Main dial, then press the Set button (**B**).

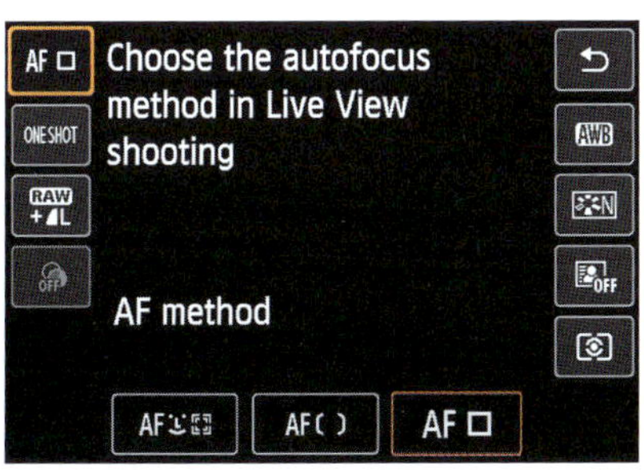

A

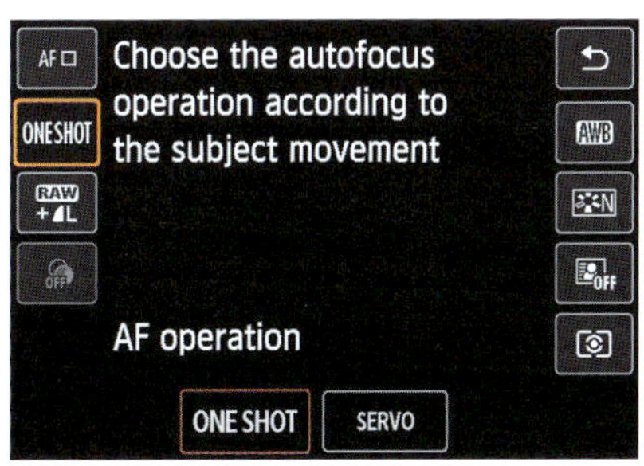

B

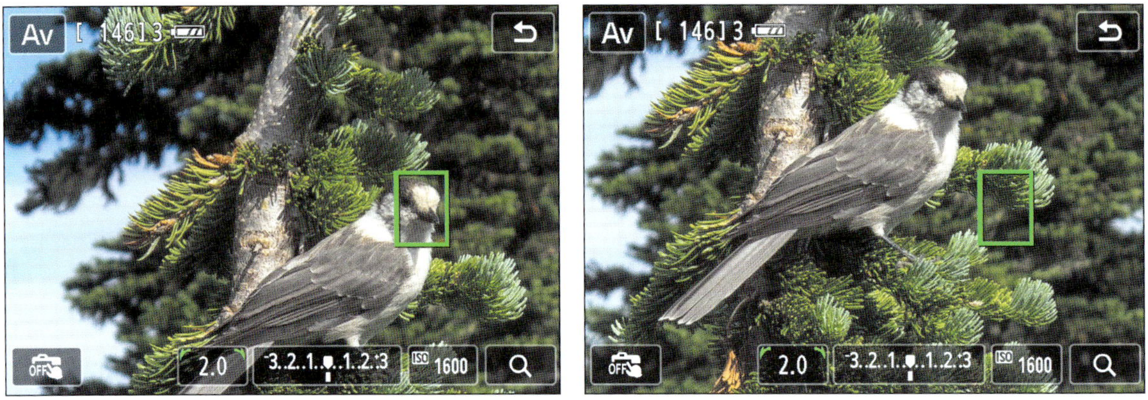

FIGURE 1.2
Using the single-focus point in One Shot mode allows you to focus on your subject in the center and then recompose your photograph for a better composition.

The camera is now ready for single focusing. The focus box turns green and you hear a chirp (if sounds are enabled) when the camera has locked in and focused. To focus on your subject and then recompose your shot, just position the focus point on your subject, depress the shutter release button halfway until the point turns green, and without letting up on the shutter button, recompose your shot and then press the shutter button all the way down to make your exposure (**Figure 1.2**).

8. SET THE CORRECT WHITE BALANCE

White balance correction is the process of rendering accurate colors in your final image. Most people don't even notice that light has different color characteristics, because the human eye automatically adjusts to changes in color temperature—so quickly, in fact, that everything looks correct in a matter of milliseconds.

When color film ruled the world, photographers would select which film to use depending on what their light source was going to be. The most common film was balanced for daylight, but you could also buy film that was color balanced for tungsten light sources. Most other lighting situations had to be handled by using color filters over the lens. This process was necessary for the photographer's final image to show the correct color balance of a scene.

Your camera has the ability to perform this same process automatically, but you can also choose to override it and set it manually. Guess which method we are going to use? You are catching on fast! Although the automatic white balance feature does a good job, some situations can befuddle it. You'll want to know how to quickly change the white balance on the spot, which saves time later so you don't have to correct the color in software on your computer. Your photography should be all about maintaining control over everything that influences the final image.

Luckily, you don't need to have a deep understanding of color temperatures to control your camera's white balance. The choices are given to you in terms that are easy to relate to and that will make things pretty simple. Your white balance choices are:

- **Auto:** The default setting for your camera. It is also the setting used by all of the Basic modes (see Chapter 3).
- **Daylight:** Most often used for general daylight/sunlit shooting.
- **Shade:** Used when working in shaded areas that are still using sunlight as the dominant light source.
- **Cloudy:** The choice for overcast or very cloudy days. This and the Shade setting will eliminate the blue color cast from your images.
- **Tungsten:** Used for any occasion where you are using regular household-type bulbs for your light source. Tungsten is a very warm light source and will result in a yellow/orange cast if you don't correct for it.
- **White Fluorescent:** Used to get rid of the green-blue cast that can result from using regular fluorescent lights as your dominant light source. Some fluorescent lights are actually balanced for daylight, which would allow you to use the Daylight white balance setting.
- **Flash:** Used whenever you're using a flash on the hot shoe. (The hot shoe is the small bracket located on the top of your camera; see Chapter 8.) Select this white balance to adjust for the slightly cooler light that comes from using a flash.
- **Custom:** Indicates that you are using a customized white balance that is adjusted for a particular light source. If you know what the color temperature of your light source is, you can manually create a white balance setting specifically for that light source.

Your camera has several different shooting modes, but it's most helpful if we break them into two "zones": Basic and Creative. All of the Basic modes (such as Portrait, Landscape, and Sports), which are identified by icons, are automatic in nature and offer fewer customization options for settings such as white balance. The Creative modes, identified by letter symbols (P, Av, Tv, and M), allow for much more control by the photographer. (We'll get into the modes in Chapters 3 and 4.)

SETTING THE WHITE BALANCE

1. Tap the Mode button in the upper-left corner of the LCD, and select one of the shooting modes in the Creative zone, such as P.
2. Press the Set button on the back of the camera or tap the Q button at the upper-right corner of the LCD to bring up the Quick Control menu.

3. Tap the White Balance button (second down on the right side).
4. Use the Left/Right cross keys or the Main dial (or tap one of the icons at the bottom of the screen) to select the proper white balance for your shooting situation (**A**).
5. Press the Set button to lock in your selection.
6. Check the camera display to ensure that the proper white balance is selected.

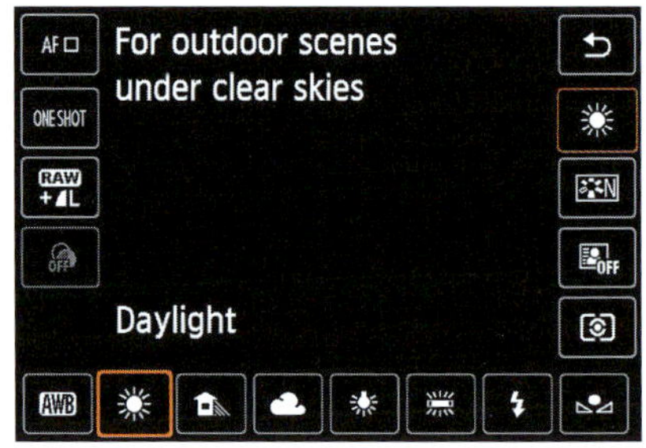

A

WHITE BALANCE AND THE TEMPERATURE OF COLOR

When you select white balances in your camera, each preset corresponds to the Kelvin temperature of the colors in the visible spectrum. The EOS M doesn't display this number, but you'll run into it when working with the photos using some image editors on the computer. The visible spectrum is the range of light that the human eye can see (think of a rainbow or the color bands that come out of a spectrum). The visible spectrum of light has been placed into a scale called the Kelvin temperature scale, which identifies the thermodynamic temperature of a given color of light. Put simply, reds and yellows are "warm," and greens and blues are "cool." Even more confusing can be the actual temperature ratings. Warm temperatures are typically lower on the Kelvin scale, ranging from 3000 degrees to 5000 degrees, while cool temperatures run from 5500 degrees to around 10000 degrees. Take a look at this list for an example of Kelvin temperature properties.

KELVIN TEMPERATURE PROPERTIES

Flames	1700K–1900K	**Daylight**	5000K
Incandescent bulb	2800K–3300K	**Camera flash**	5500K
White fluorescent	4000K	**Overcast sky**	6000K
Moonlight	4000K	**Open shade**	7000K

The most important thing to remember here is how the color temperature of light will affect the look of your images. If something is "warm," it will look reddish-yellow, and if something is "cool," it will have a bluish cast.

9. TURN OFF TOUCH SHUTTER MODE

To declutter the camera's body, Canon moved most of the controls to the touch-screen. You can interact with camera settings and menus with a touch of your finger. But the screen itself can act as a giant button—shutter button, that is. With Touch Shutter mode enabled, you tap on an area in your scene and the camera focuses and captures the image. (If it can't lock focus, it doesn't snap the shot.)

It's incredibly convenient...and I turned it off almost immediately. I often discovered that I'd brushed against the screen and snapped a shot, or I was trying to just set focus and didn't realize that Touch Shutter was on and had to wait for the camera to finish taking the picture. You also can't use continuous shooting mode to capture multiple images quickly.

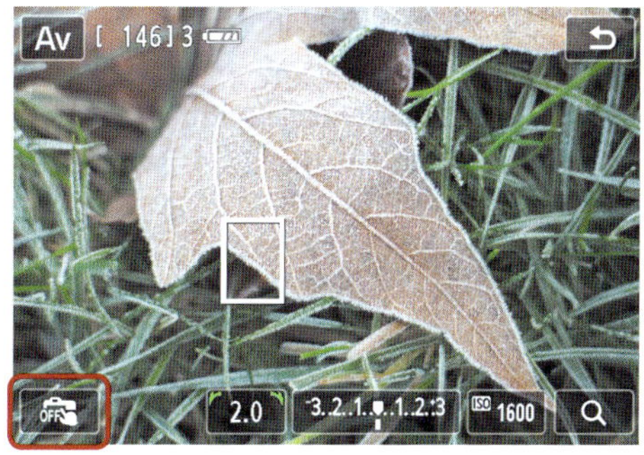

Better to just turn it off: Tap the Touch Shutter button in the lower-left corner of the screen to toggle the mode from enabled to disabled.

10. REVIEW YOUR SHOTS

One of the greatest features of digital cameras is their ability to give us instant feedback. By reviewing your images on the camera's LCD screen, you can instantly tell if you got your shot. This visual feedback allows you to make adjustments on the fly and make certain that you nailed the shot before moving on.

When you first press the shutter release button, your camera quickly processes your shot and then displays the image on the rear LCD. The default duration setting for that display is only 2 seconds. Personally, I don't find this to be nearly enough time to take in all the visual feedback I might want. Instead of using this "quick glance" method, change your display time to the Hold setting. This will keep the image on the display until you decide that you are ready to move on to your next shot. (Note that this option will drain your batteries a little faster than the default setting.)

CHANGING THE IMAGE REVIEW TIME SETTING

1. Press the Menu button and then use the Main dial to select the leftmost menu item (if it's not already selected).
2. Use the cross keys to scroll down to Image review, and press the Set button (**A**).
3. Scroll down to Hold and then press the Set button once again (**B**).
4. Press the Menu button to leave the menus and continue shooting.

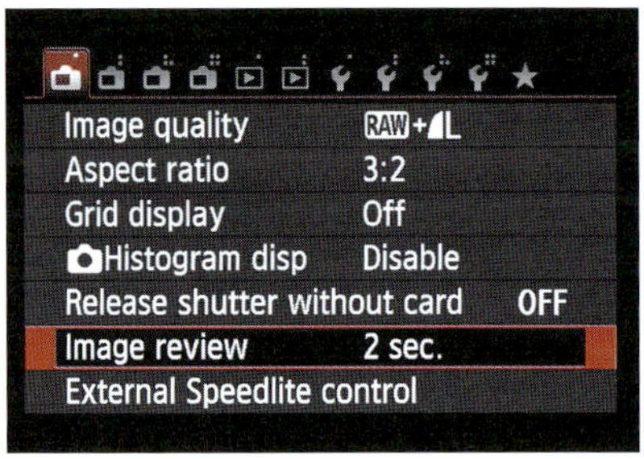

A

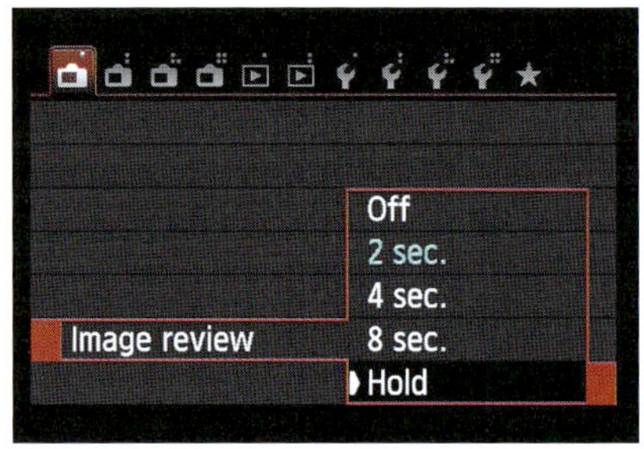

B

Now that you have the image review time set, let's check out some of the other visual information that will help you when shooting.

There are four review display modes, and each gives you a different amount of information. The default view simply displays your image (**Figure 1.3**).

To get more visual feedback, press the INFO button, located below the Main dial. Press it once to see shutter speed, aperture, file name, and the image number that you are currently viewing ("3/13" would mean that you're looking at the third image of 13 total images) (**Figure 1.4**).

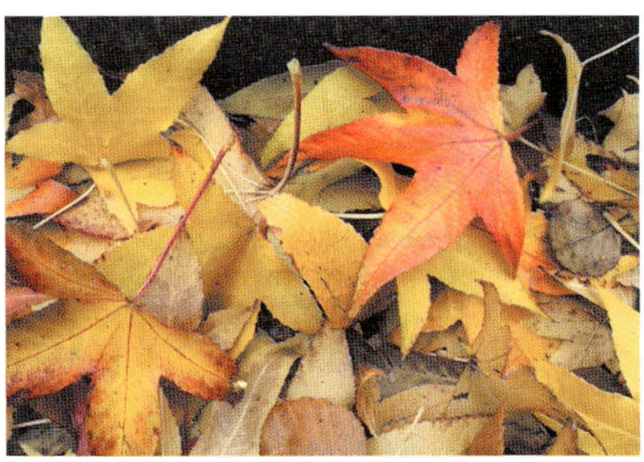

FIGURE 1.3
The default display mode on the EOS M.

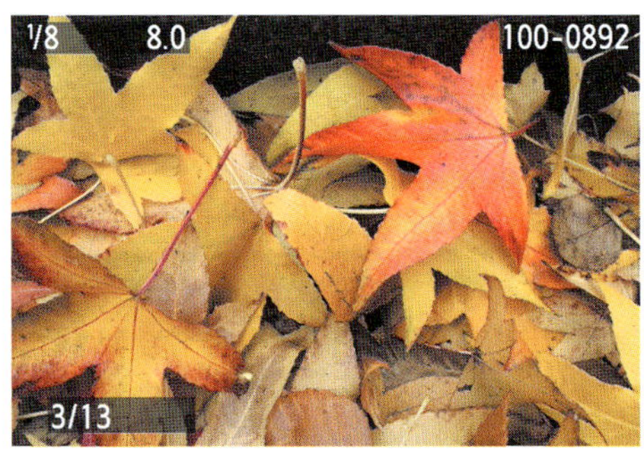

FIGURE 1.4
Press the INFO button once to see the second display option.

Pressing the INFO button a second time results in a huge amount of information displayed along with the image. You will now be able to see the following items in your display: shutter speed, aperture, exposure compensation, file name, image thumbnail, histogram, shooting mode, ISO, white balance setting, picture style, quality setting, meter mode, size of the image in megabytes, color space, image number, date, and time (**Figure 1.5**).

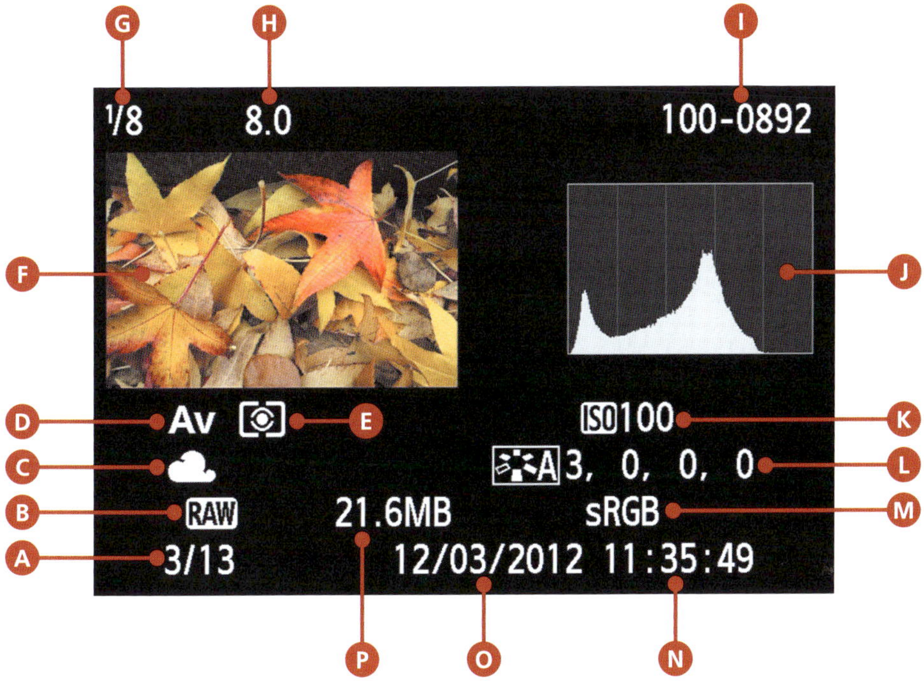

FIGURE 1.5
This display mode offers a ton of information at a glance.

A	Image Number	G	Shutter Speed	M	Color Space
B	Quality Setting	H	Aperture	N	Time
C	White Balance	I	File Name	O	Date
D	Shooting Mode	J	Histogram	P	Image Size
E	Meter Mode	K	ISO		
F	Image Thumbnail	L	Picture Style		

You probably won't want to use this display option as your default review setting, but if you are trying to figure out what settings you used or want to review the histogram (see the sidebar "The Value of the Histogram" on pages 18–19), you now have all this great information available.

Continues on page 20

THE VALUE OF THE HISTOGRAM

Simply put, histograms are two-dimensional representations of your images in graph form. There are two different histograms that you should be concerned with: luminance and color. Luminance is referred to in your manual as "brightness" and is most valuable when evaluating your exposures. In **Figure 1.6**, you see what looks like a mountain range. The graph represents the entire tonal range that your camera can capture, from the whitest whites to the blackest blacks. The left side represents black, and the right side represents white. The heights of the peaks represent the number of pixels that contain those luminance levels (a tall peak in the middle means your image contains a large number of medium-bright pixels). Looking at an image, it can be hard to determine where all of the ranges of light and dark areas are and how much of each you have. If you look at the histogram, you can see that the largest peak of the graph is in the middle and trails off as it reaches the edges. In most cases, you would look for this type of histogram, indicating that you captured the entire range of tones, from dark to light, in your image. Knowing that is fine—but here is where the information really gets useful.

A histogram that has a spike or peak riding up the far left or right side of the graph means that you are clipping detail from your image. In essence, you are trying to record values that are either too dark or too light for your sensor to accurately record. This is usually an indication of over- or underexposure. It also means that you need to correct your exposure so that the important details will not record as solid black or white pixels (which is what happens when clipping occurs). There are times, however, when some clipping is acceptable. If you are photographing a scene where the sun will be in the frame, you can expect to get some clipping, because the sun is just too bright to hold any detail. Likewise, if you are shooting something that has true blacks in it—think coal in a mineshaft at midnight—there are most certainly going to be some true blacks with no detail in your shot. The main goal is to ensure that you aren't clipping any "important" visual

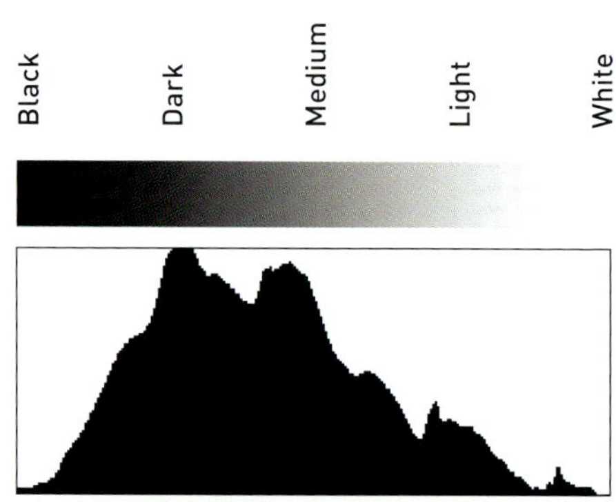

FIGURE 1.6
This is a typical histogram, where the dark-to-light tones run from left to right. The black-to-white gradient above the graph demonstrates where the tones lie on the graph and does not appear above your camera's histogram display.

information, and that is achieved by keeping an eye on your histogram. Take a look at **Figure 1.7**. The histogram displayed on the image shows a heavy skew toward the left, with no part of the mountain touching the right side. This is a good example of what an under-exposed image histogram looks like. Now look at **Figure 1.8** and compare the histogram for the image that was correctly exposed. Notice that even though there are distinct peaks on the graph, there is an even distribution across the entire histogram.

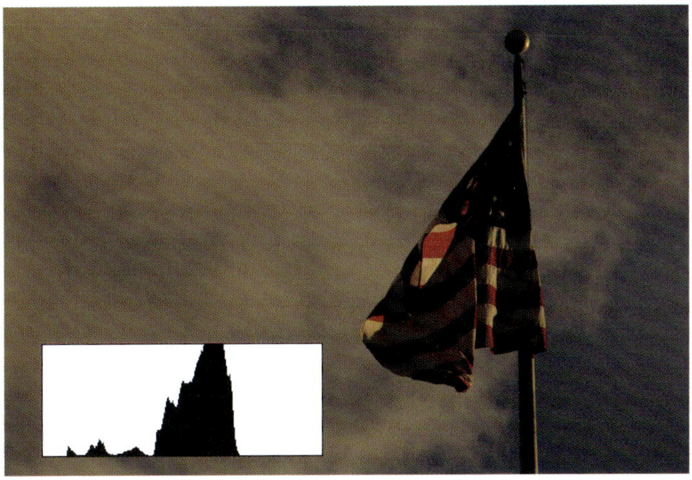

FIGURE 1.7
This image is about two stops under-exposed. Notice that the histogram is skewed to the left.

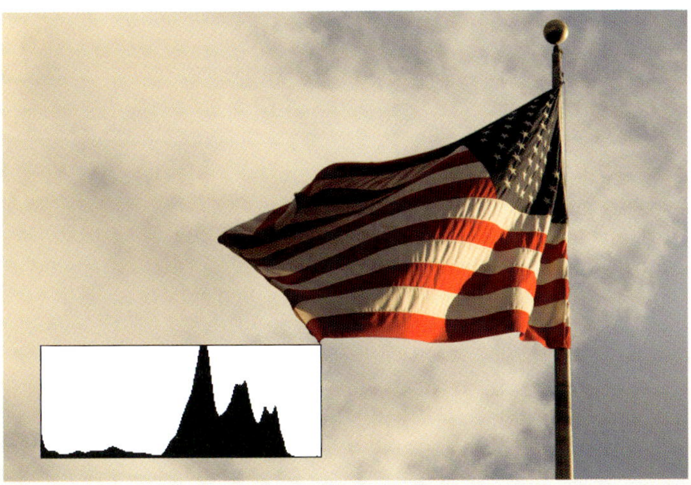

FIGURE 1.8
This histogram reflects an image with better exposure.

The fourth display option allows you to view the regular image histogram as well as a color histogram for your image. I prefer to use the standard histogram, but you may find the color histogram handy when checking to see if you were able to capture all of the information in your scene (**Figure 1.9**).

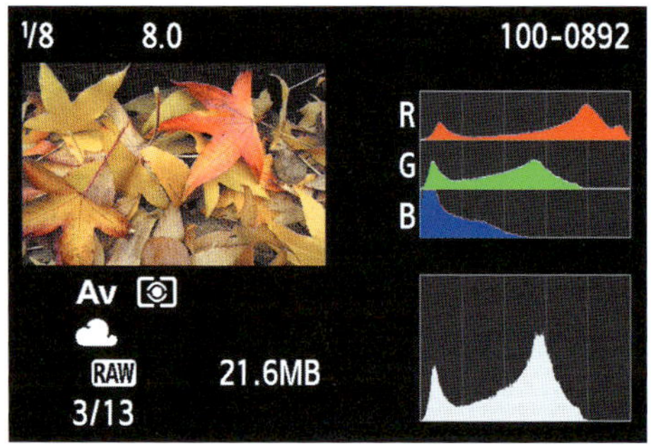

FIGURE 1.9
The fourth display option adds a color histogram that breaks out the red, green, and blue values.

Both histogram modes show your image as just a thumbnail. So while you're exposed to a lot of information concerning the camera settings, you get less visual feedback in terms of seeing the actual photo. You would probably be best served by selecting one of the first two display modes and using the histogram modes only when you need to review your shooting data.

Whichever display mode you choose, that mode will remain for all future images until you press the INFO button again. Also, pressing the shutter release or Menu button switches away from the review mode. To get your image back up on the LCD, simply press the blue Playback button on the back of the camera.

DELETING IMAGES

Deleting or erasing images is a fairly simple process. To quickly get you on your way, press the Image Review button and find the picture that you want to delete. Then press the Trash button (the Down cross key), use the Right cross key to select Erase, and press the Set button (**Figure 1.10**).

Caution: Once you have deleted an image, it is gone for good. Make sure you don't want it before you drop it in the trash.

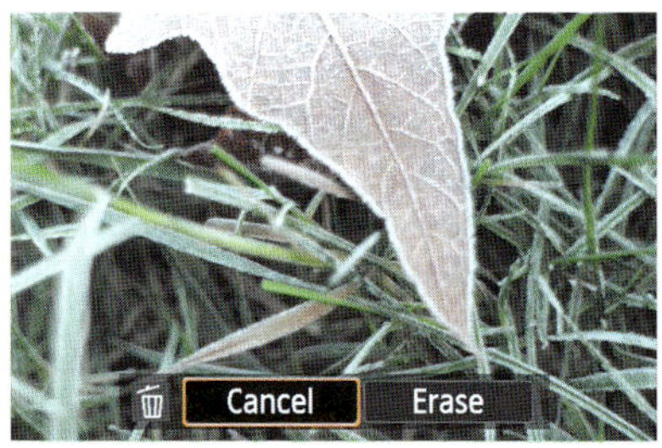

FIGURE 1.10
Deleting images on the EOS M.

Chapter 1 Assignments

Let's begin our shooting assignments by setting up and using all of the elements of the Top Ten list. Even though I have yet to cover the Creative shooting modes, you should set your camera to the P (Program) mode. This will allow you to interact with the various settings and menus that have been covered thus far.

Basic camera setup

Charge your battery to 100% to get it started on a life of dependable service. Next, using your newfound knowledge, set up your camera to address the following: shooting without a card, image quality, Auto ISO, and disabling Touch Shutter mode. And make sure you have a backup SD card!

Selecting the proper white balance

Take your camera outside into a daylight environment and photograph the same scene using different white balance settings. Pay close attention to how each setting affects the overall color cast of your images. Next, move inside and repeat the exercise while shooting in a tungsten lighting environment. Finally, find a fluorescent light source and repeat once more.

Setting up AF+MF mode for manual focusing

Switch to AF+MF focusing mode so you can switch to manual focus when you need it. Let the camera find an autofocus point, and then turn the focus ring on the lens to adjust which areas are in focus in the scene. Get familiar with how to use manual focus to achieve sharp images.

Focusing with FlexiZone

Switch between the three focus methods and see how the camera picks out faces and other items. Set the focus mode to One Shot, and practice focusing on a subject and then recomposing before actually taking the picture; also practice putting the focus frame over your subject and focusing. Try doing this with subjects at varying distances.

Evaluating your pictures with the LCD

Set up your image display properties, and then review some of your previous assignment images using the different display modes. Review your shooting information for each image, and take a look at the histograms to see how the content of your photo affects their shapes.

Share your results with the book's Flickr group!

Join the group here: flickr.com/groups/eosmfromsnapshotstogreatshots

2

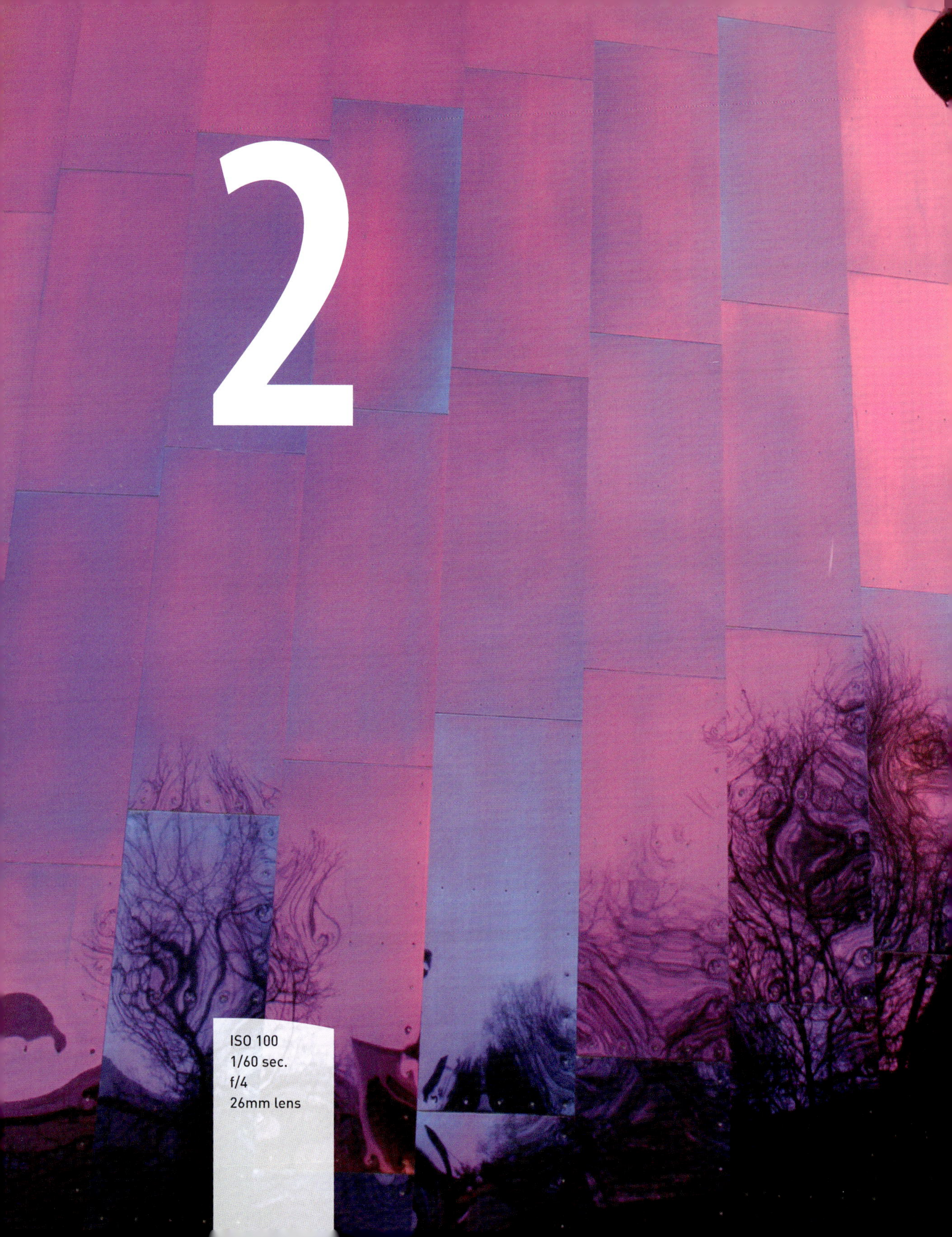

ISO 100
1/60 sec.
f/4
26mm lens

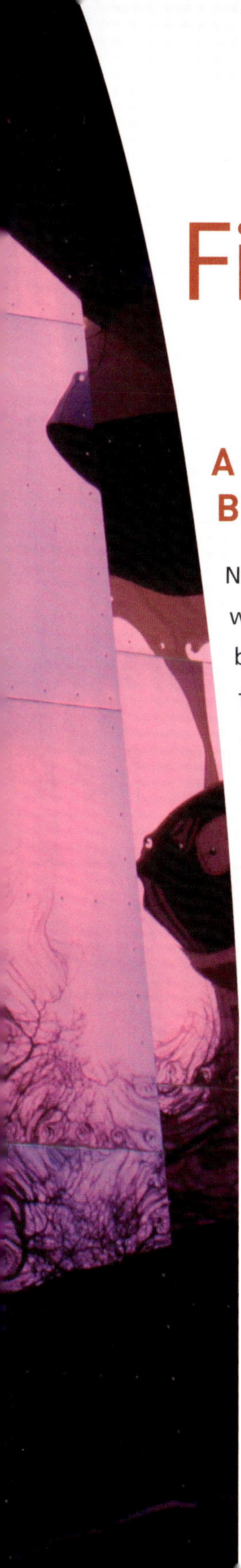

First Things First

A FEW THINGS TO KNOW AND DO BEFORE YOU BEGIN TAKING PICTURES

Now that we've covered the top ten tasks to get you up and shooting, we should probably take care of some other important details. You must become familiar with certain features of your camera before you can take full advantage of it. Additionally, we will take some steps to prepare the camera and memory card for use. So to get things moving, let's start off with something that you will definitely need before you can take a single picture: a memory card.

PORING OVER THE PICTURE

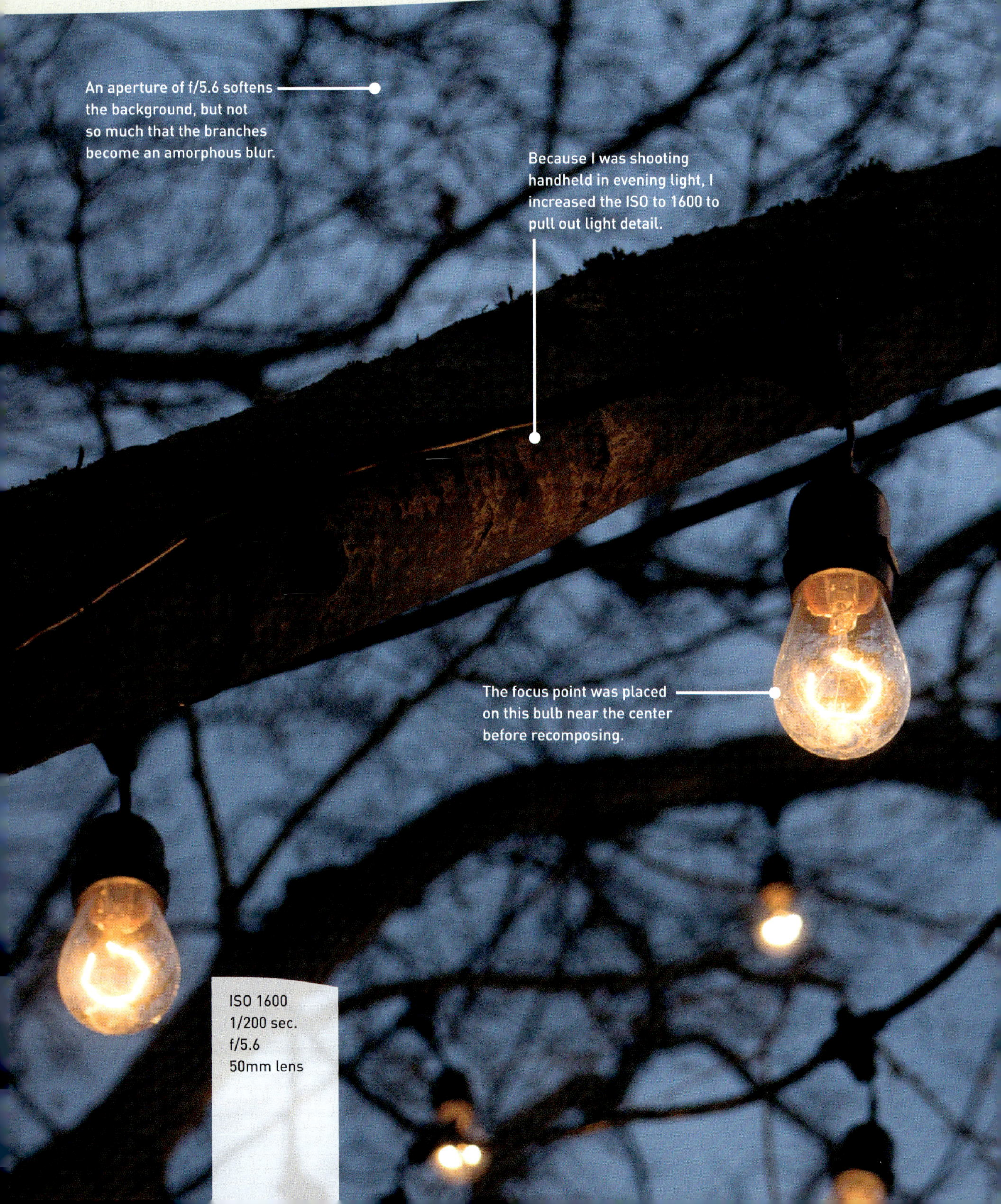

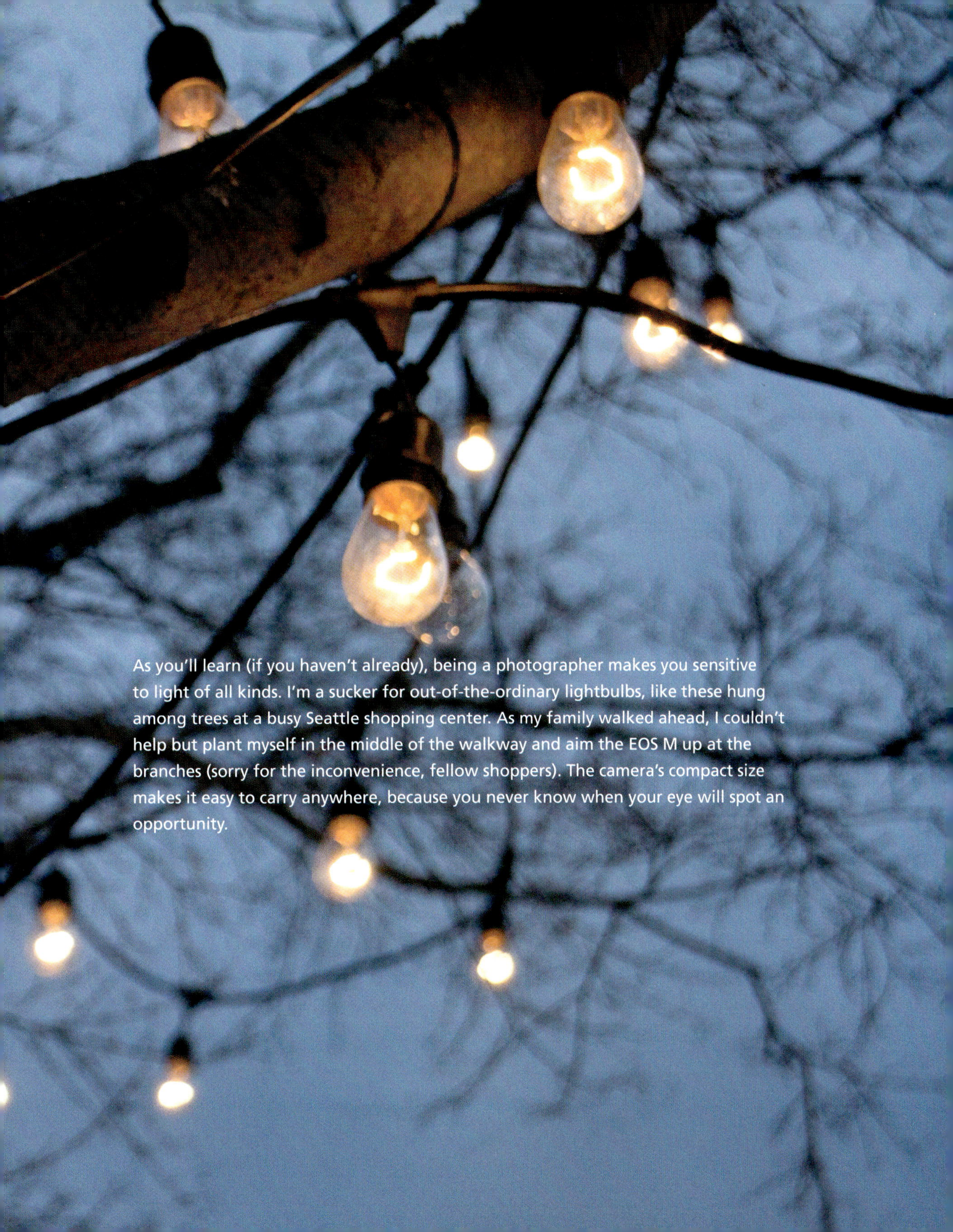

As you'll learn (if you haven't already), being a photographer makes you sensitive to light of all kinds. I'm a sucker for out-of-the-ordinary lightbulbs, like these hung among trees at a busy Seattle shopping center. As my family walked ahead, I couldn't help but plant myself in the middle of the walkway and aim the EOS M up at the branches (sorry for the inconvenience, fellow shoppers). The camera's compact size makes it easy to carry anywhere, because you never know when your eye will spot an opportunity.

PORING OVER THE PICTURE

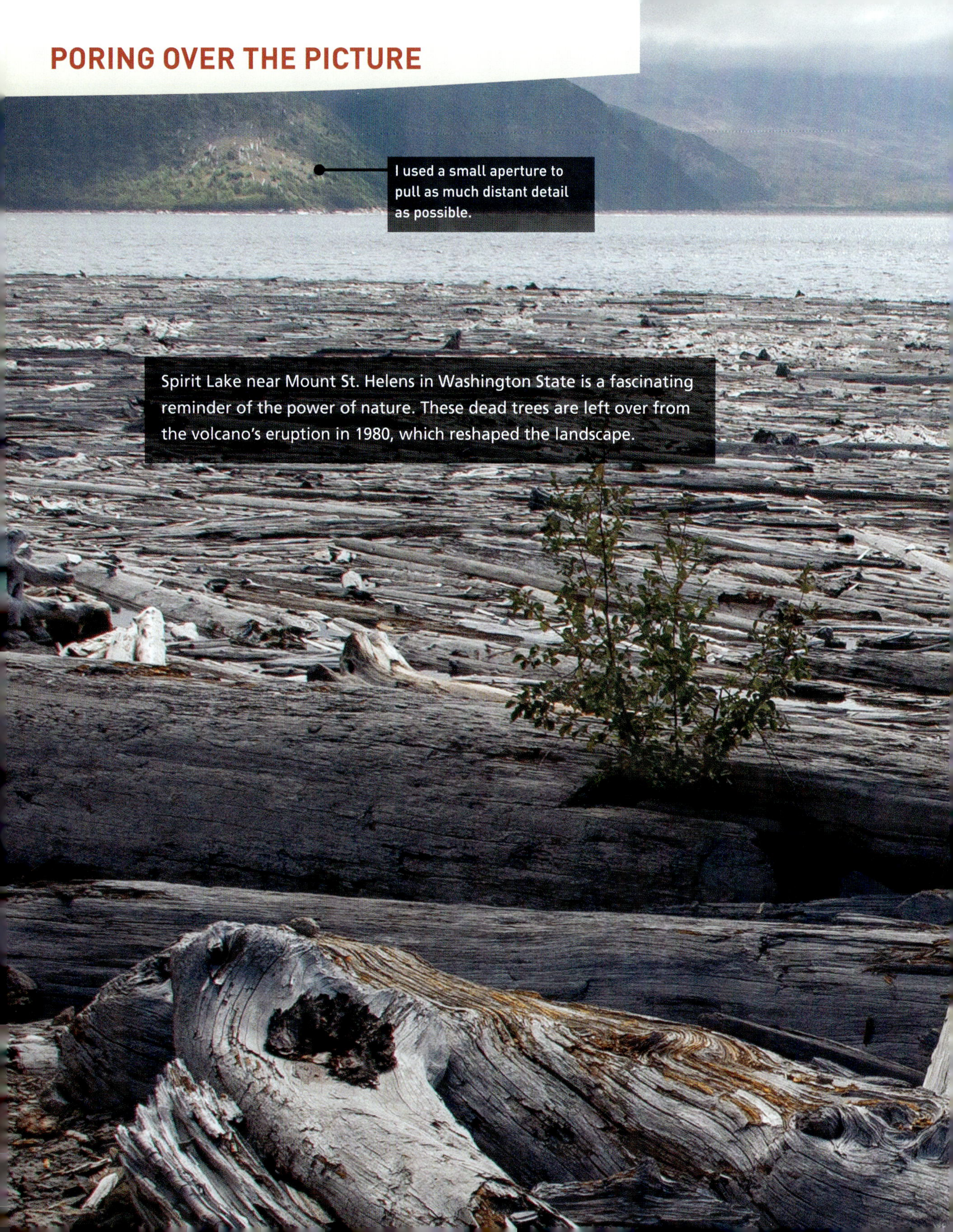

I used a small aperture to pull as much distant detail as possible.

Spirit Lake near Mount St. Helens in Washington State is a fascinating reminder of the power of nature. These dead trees are left over from the volcano's eruption in 1980, which reshaped the landscape.

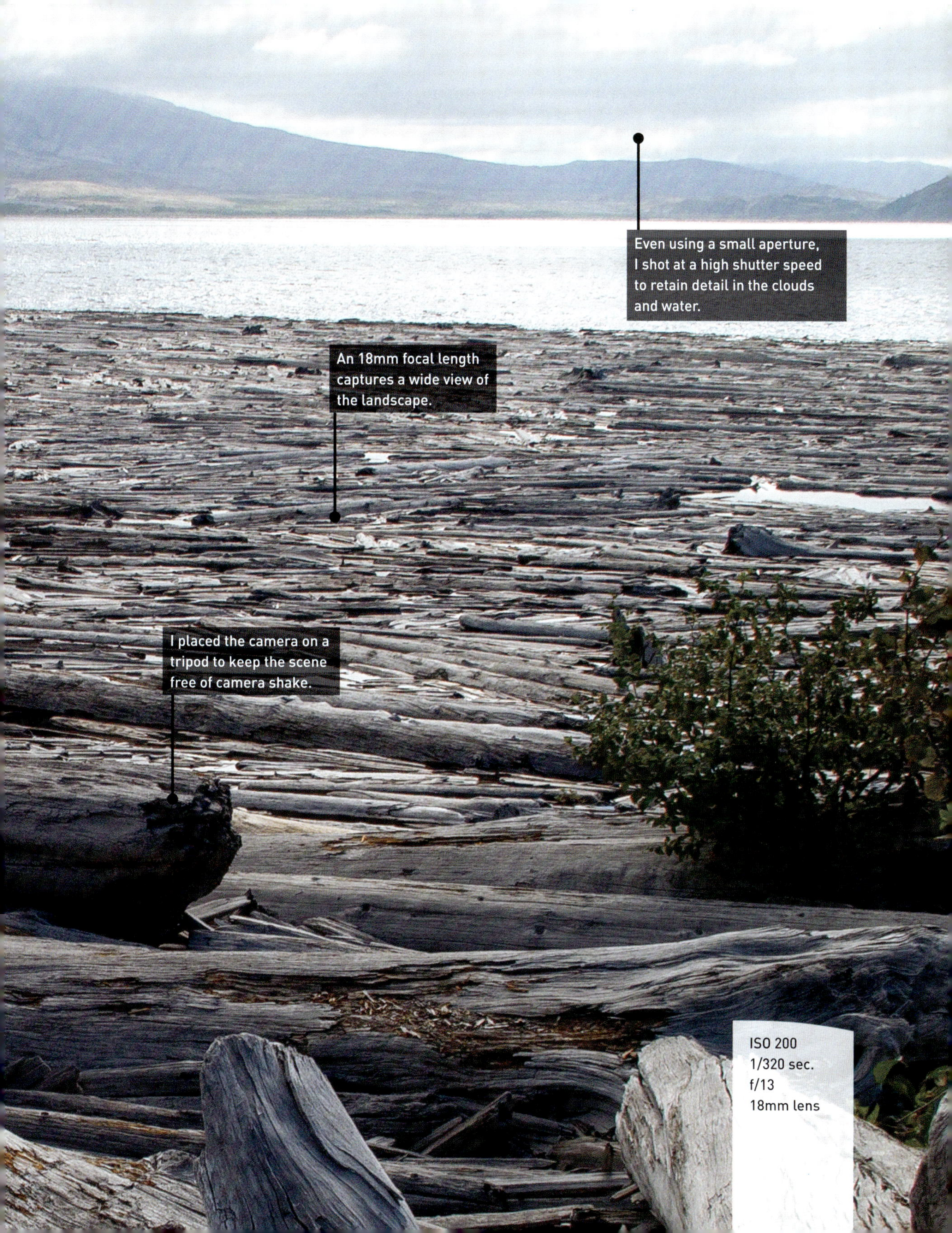
Even using a small aperture, I shot at a high shutter speed to retain detail in the clouds and water.
An 18mm focal length captures a wide view of the landscape.
I placed the camera on a tripod to keep the scene free of camera shake.
ISO 200
1/320 sec.
f/13
18mm lens

CHOOSING THE RIGHT MEMORY CARD

Memory cards are the digital film that stores every shot you take until you move them to a computer. The cards come in all shapes and sizes, and they are critical for capturing all of your photos. It is important not to skimp when it comes to selecting your memory cards. The EOS M uses Secure Digital (SD) memory cards (**Figure 2.1**).

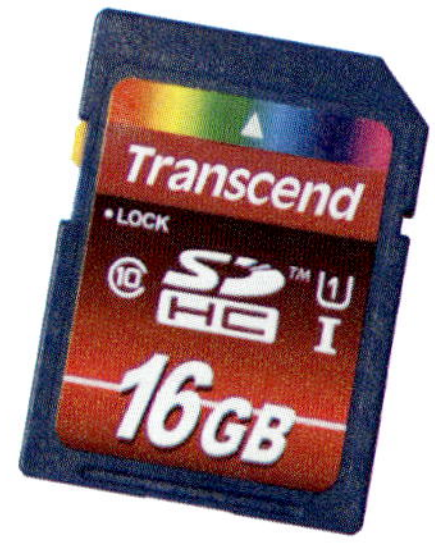

FIGURE 2.1
Make sure you select an SD card that has enough capacity and speed to handle your photography needs.

If you have been using a point-and-shoot camera, you may already own an SD media card. Which brand of card you use is completely up to you, but here is some advice about choosing your memory card:

- Size matters, at least in memory cards. At 18 megapixels each, the EOS M's photos will require a lot of storage space, especially if you shoot in the RAW or RAW+JPEG mode (more on this later in the chapter) or shoot HD video. You should definitely consider using a card with a storage capacity of at least 4 GB.
- Buy High Capacity (SDHC) cards. These cards are generally much faster, both when writing images to the card and when transferring them to your computer.
- If you are planning on using the Continuous mode (see Chapter 5) for capturing fast action, you can gain a boost in performance just by using an SDHC card with a Class rating of at least 6; Canon recommends at least that speed for shooting video. However, I've had issues with Class 6 cards that could not keep up with the demands of video recording, causing the camera to stop in the middle of a recording session. My recommendation is that, if you know you are going to be shooting video with your camera, you should use a Class 10 card to keep the pixels flowing.
- Buy more than one card. If you have already purchased a memory card, consider getting another. It's a bad day when your card is almost full and you have to either erase shots or choose a lower-quality image format so you can keep shooting. Memory cards are relatively cheap, so keeping a spare makes good sense.
- To get the fastest memory possible, you could consider purchasing an SDXC memory card. Although they appear to be the same as SD and SDHC cards, they are made to new specifications that allow memory capacities above 32 GB. Your camera is SDXC compliant, but if you plan to share SDXC cards between devices such as your EOS M and a video camera, make sure the other device is SDXC compatible too. SDXC cards will work only in SDXC devices.

FORMATTING YOUR MEMORY CARD

Now that you have your card, let's talk about formatting for a minute. When you purchase any new SD card, you can pop it into your camera and start shooting right away—and probably everything will work as it should. However, what you *should* do first is format the card in the camera. This process allows the camera to set up the card to record images in its own way. Just as with a computer hard drive, formatting your card ensures that it is properly initialized. The card may work in the camera without first being formatted, but chances of failure down the road are much higher.

As a general practice, I always format new cards or cards that have been used in different cameras. I also reformat cards after I have downloaded my images and want to start a new shooting session. Note that you should always format your card in the camera, not in your computer. Using the computer could render the card useless in your camera. You should also pay attention to the manufacturer's recommendations with respect to moisture, humidity, and proper handling procedures. The card is the only storage for the images you're going to work hard to get, so make sure it's set up correctly from the start.

So far I've referred to this process as "formatting" instead of "erasing," because there are a few important differences between the two terms. In the EOS M menus, you can choose to erase individual images or all images on the card (**Figure 2.2**). That's a quick way to make room for more photos, but it doesn't actually delete the image data from the card. Instead, it changes the file management information: The camera regards the portions of the card that contain image data as empty and writes new data over the top of the old as needed. Formatting the card also treats the card as if it were empty and ready to record new images (unless it's a "low level format," which I explain on the next page).

The advantage of this approach is that you're not permanently removing any data. If you accidentally erase or format a card before you transfer its files to your computer, you can use photo recovery software to get those images back (unless they were overwritten by new images).

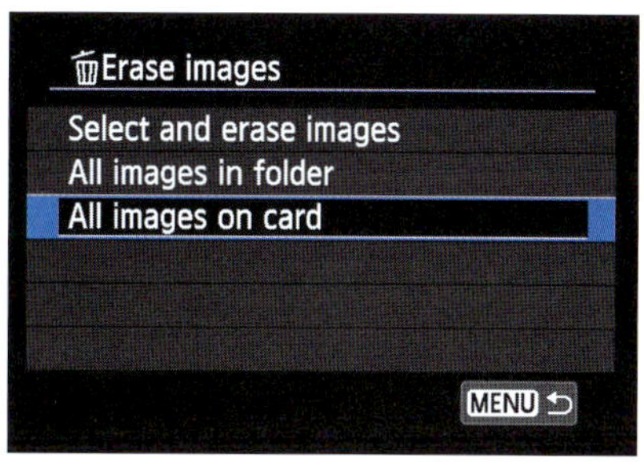

FIGURE 2.2
Erase individual photos or all images on the card.

FORMATTING YOUR MEMORY CARD

1. Insert your memory card into the camera.
2. Press the Menu button and navigate to the first setup menu screen (the sixth from the left).
3. Press the Down cross key on the back of the camera to highlight the Format card option, and press Set (**A**).
4. The default selection for the Format card screen is Cancel, just in case you didn't really want to format the card (**B**). The screen warns that you will lose any data by formatting your card, so make sure you have saved any images that you want onto your computer or elsewhere before formatting. Press the Right cross key to highlight OK.
5. Press the Set button to format the card.

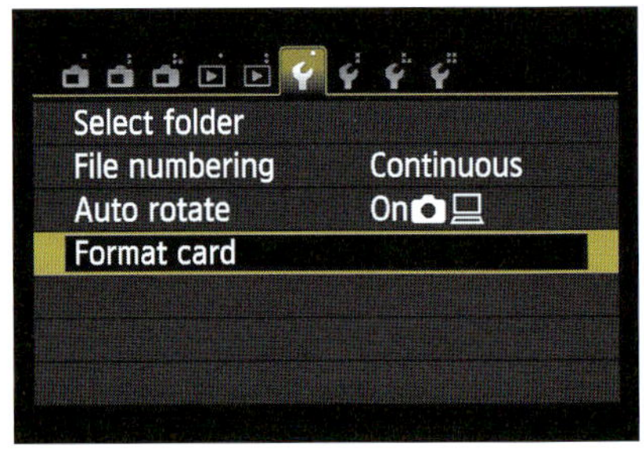

A

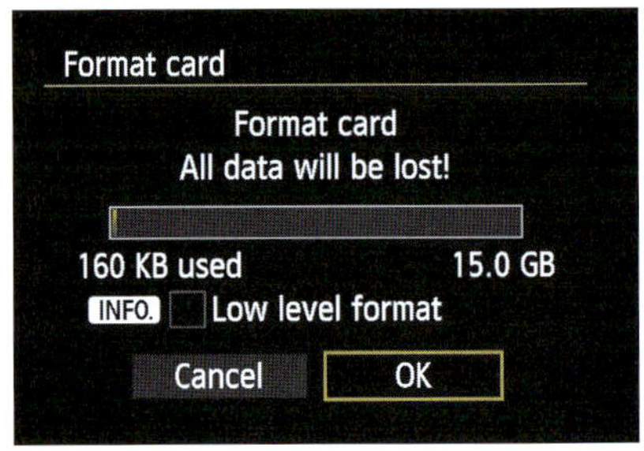

B

If you want to truly erase the contents of a memory card, choose the Low Level Format option when formatting it. During this process, the camera clears all of the recordable sectors on the card (which takes longer than a normal format). You don't need to perform a low level format every time you want to clear your card. You only need to do this if you see a slowdown in card performance or if you want to format a new card or one that was used in another camera. To enable the Low Level Format option, follow the directions above but tap the Low Level Format button (or press the Info button) before starting the formatting process. This will put a check mark next to the Low Level Format option (**Figure 2.3**).

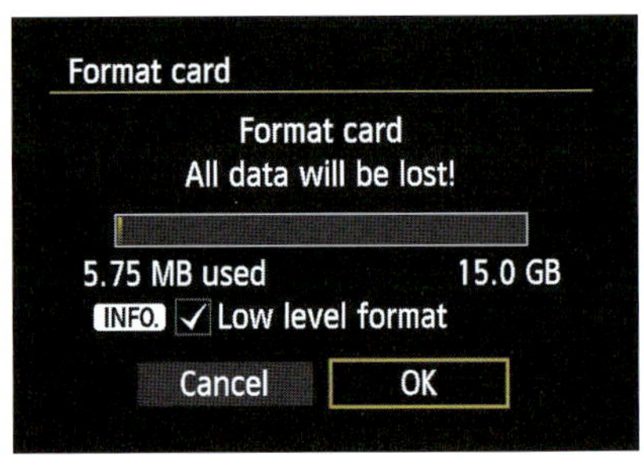

FIGURE 2.3
Press the Info button to enable the Low Level Format option.

UPDATING THE EOS M'S FIRMWARE

Having the proper firmware—the operating instructions that control how your camera functions—can affect the way the camera operates. It can fix problems as well as improve operation, so you should probably take care of it sooner rather than later. Updating this firmware is a great way to not only fix little bugs but also occasionally gain access to new functionality. You will need to check out the information on the Canon firmware update page (www.canon.com/eos-m/) to see if a firmware update is available and review how it will affect your camera, but it is always a good idea to be working with the most up-to-date firmware version available.

CHECKING THE CAMERA'S CURRENT FIRMWARE VERSION NUMBER

1. Tap the Mode button and select P (or any of the other modes in the Creative zone).
2. Press the Menu button to display the menu.
3. Turn the Main dial to get to the fourth camera setup menu (the second one from the right), and press Set (**A**).
4. Check the version numbers for the camera and lens (**B**). If these versions are not the latest ones listed on the Canon website, follow the steps in the next section to load the latest version.

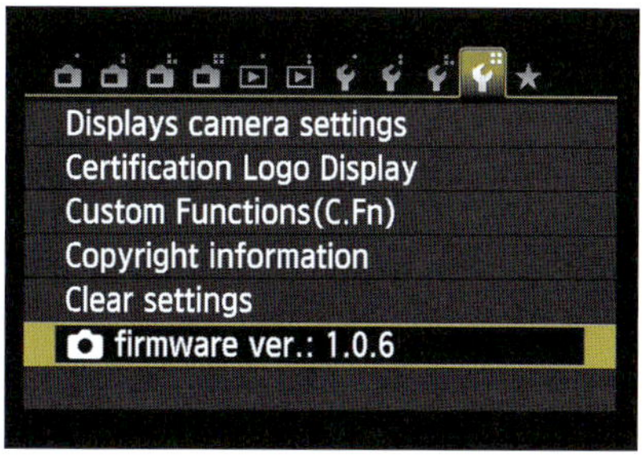

A

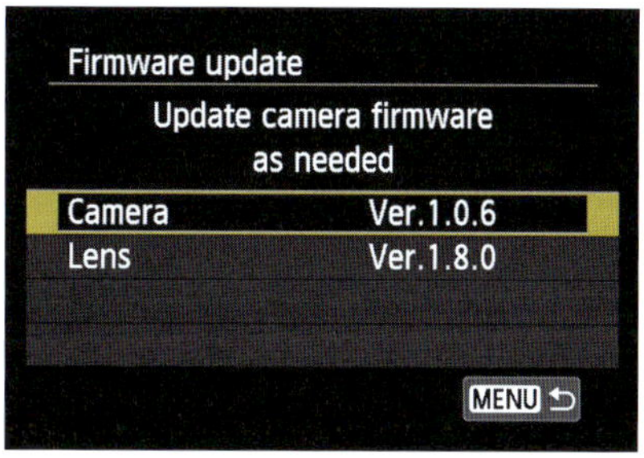

B

At the time of this writing, the firmware versions for the EOS M are 1.0.6 for the camera and 1.8.0 for the lens. Make sure you check the Canon webpage often for any updates, and then follow the directions on the following page for updating your camera.

UPDATING THE FIRMWARE USING THE EOS UTILITY PROGRAM

1. Download the firmware update file from the Canon website, listed in the Firmware Update section (**A**). (You can also find the file by going to the EOS camera site, clicking the Support & Drivers link, and locating your camera model.)

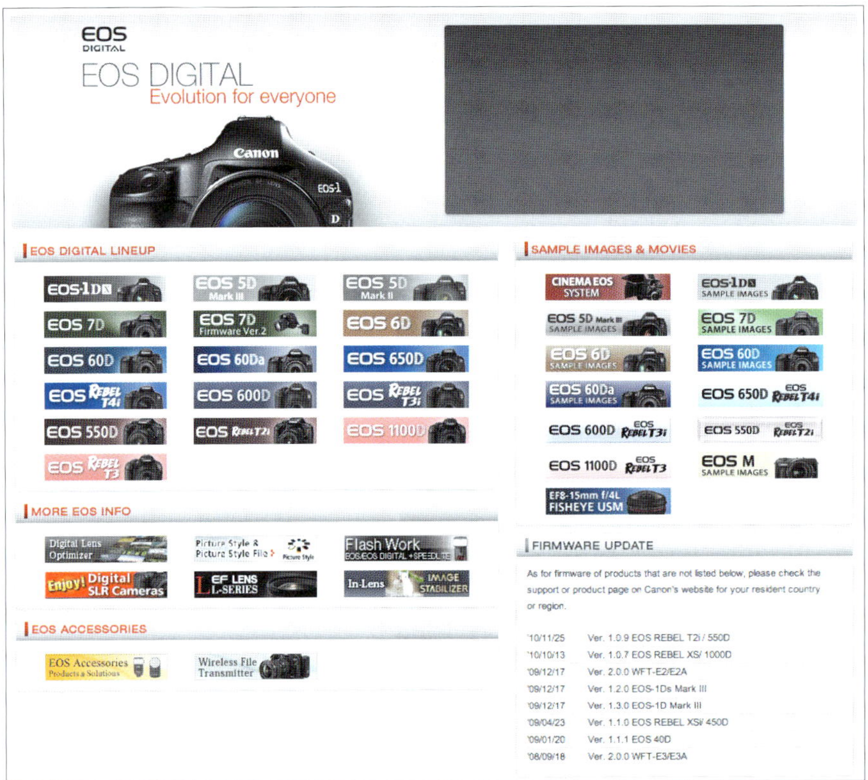

A

2. Download the Firmware Update file that matches your computer operating system (Windows or Mac).
3. Extract the downloaded firmware file as per your operating system.
4. Attach your camera to the computer via USB and turn the camera on (**B**).
5. Open the EOS Utility program and select the Camera Settings option. (This program was included on the CD in your camera box. You will need to

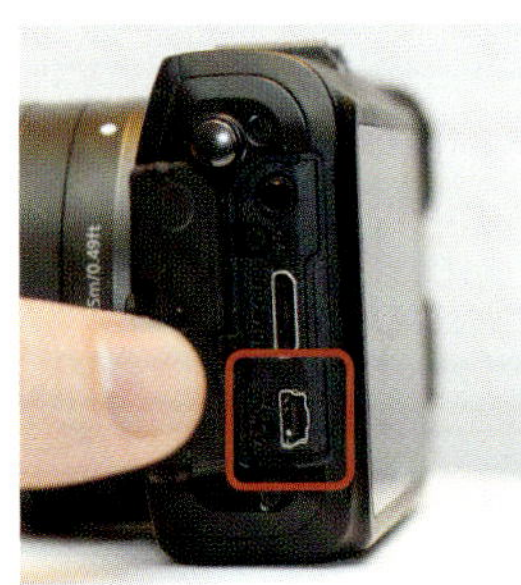

B

install it prior to performing this operation.)

6. When the panel opens, click the Firmware button (**C**).
7. Click OK and then locate the extracted firmware file to begin the update.
8. Click Yes on the confirmation screen to begin the update. Note that the software will not allow you to continue the update unless the camera is plugged into an AC power adapter or the battery is fully charged.

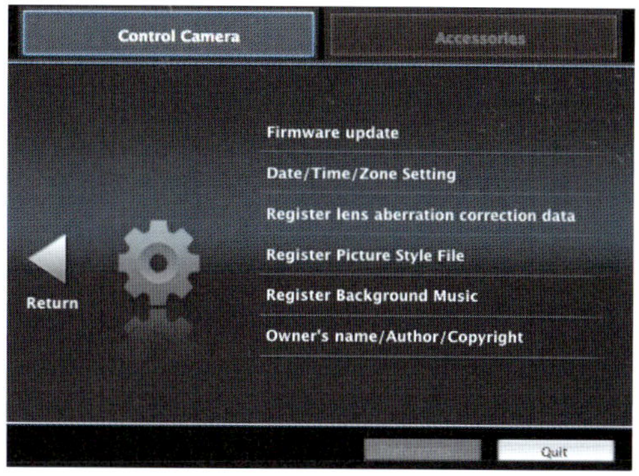

C

UPDATING THE FIRMWARE IN-CAMERA

It is possible to update your camera's firmware by copying the irmware Update file to a formatted SD card and updating in-camera instead of using the EOS Utility program. There is a complete set of instructions for using this method on the firmware download webpage referred to in step 1 on the previous page. You will still need a computer and a card reader to use this method, so make sure you follow the directions to the letter.

CLEANING THE SENSOR

Cleaning camera sensors used to be a nerve-racking process that required leaving the sensor exposed to scratching and even more dust. Now cleaning the sensor is pretty much an automatic function. Every time you turn the camera off, the sensor in the camera vibrates to remove any dust particles that might have landed on it.

There are two choices for cleaning in the camera setup menu: Auto Cleaning and Clean Now. By default, the camera is set to automatically clean the sensor every time you power off. You can disable this function, but it is best to leave it on.

The one cleaning function that you will need to use via this menu is the Clean Now feature. This should be done every time you remove the lens from the camera body. That is because removing or changing a lens will leave the camera body open and susceptible to dust sneaking into the body. It's for this reason that I have added the Clean Now function to the custom My Menu list (see Chapter 10).

The camera sensor is an electrically charged device. This means that when the camera is turned on, there is a current running through the sensor. This electric current can create static electricity, which will attract small dust particles to the sensor area. For this reason, it is always a good idea to turn off the camera prior to removing a lens. You should also consider having the lens mount facing down during lens removal so there is less opportunity for dust to fall into the inner workings of the camera.

USING THE CLEAN NOW FEATURE

1. Press the Menu button and use the Main dial to get to the third camera setup menu.
2. Use the Down cross key to highlight Sensor cleaning, and then press the Set button (**A**).
3. Use the cross keys to select Clean now, and press the Set button again (**B**).
4. Press Set one more time to start the cleaning function.
5. To return to shooting mode, lightly press the shutter release button.

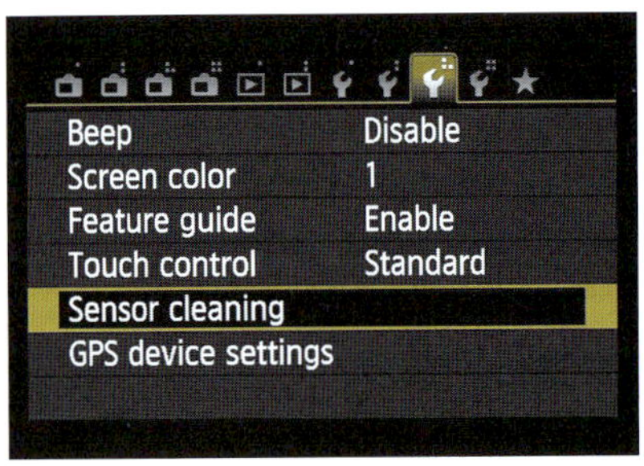

A

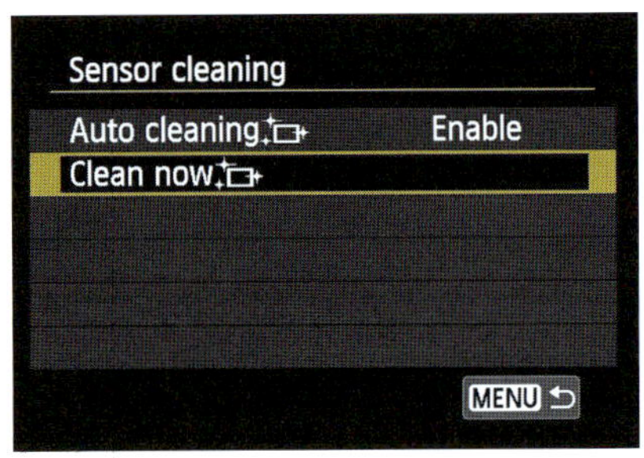

B

USING THE RIGHT FORMAT: RAW VS. JPEG

When shooting with your EOS M, you have a choice of image formats that your camera will use to store the pictures on the memory card. JPEG is probably the most familiar format to anyone who has been using a digital camera. I touched on this topic briefly in Chapter 1, so you already have a little background on what JPEG and RAW files are.

There is nothing wrong with JPEG if you are taking casual shots. JPEG files are ready to use, right out of the camera. Why go through the process of adjusting RAW images of the kids opening presents when you are just going to email them to Grandma? So what is wrong with JPEG? Absolutely nothing—unless you care about having complete creative control over all of your image data (as opposed to what a compression algorithm thinks is important).

As I mentioned in Chapter 1, JPEG is not actually an image format. It is a compression standard, and compression is where things can go bad. When your camera is set to JPEG—whether it is set to High or Low compression—you are telling the camera to process the image however it sees fit and then throw away enough image data to make it shrink into a smaller space. In doing so, you give up subtle image details that you will never get back in post-processing. That is an awfully simplified statement, but it's still fairly accurate.

SO WHAT DOES RAW HAVE TO OFFER?

First and foremost, RAW images are not compressed. (Some cameras offer a compressed RAW format, but it is *lossless* compression, which means there is no loss of actual image data.) Note that RAW image files will require you to perform post-processing on your photographs. This is not only necessary—it is the reason that most photographers use it.

RAW images have a greater dynamic range than JPEG-processed images. This means you can recover image detail in the highlights and shadows that just aren't available in JPEG-processed images.

There is more color information in a RAW image because it is a 14-bit image, which means it contains more color information than a JPEG, which is almost always an 8-bit image. More color information means more to work with and smoother changes between tones—kind of like the difference between performing surgery with a scalpel as opposed to a butcher's knife. They'll both get the job done, but one will do less damage.

Regarding sharpening, a RAW image offers more control because you are the one who is applying the sharpening according to the effect you want to achieve. Once again, JPEG processing applies a standard amount of sharpening that you cannot change after the fact. Once it is done, it's done.

Finally, and most importantly, a RAW file is your negative. No matter what you do to it, you won't change it unless you save your file in a different format. This means you can come back to that RAW file later and try different processing settings to achieve differing results and never harm the original image. By comparison, if you make a change to your JPEG and accidentally save the file, guess what? You have a new original file, and you will never get back to that first image. That alone should make you sit up and take notice.

ADVICE FOR NEW RAW SHOOTERS

Don't give up on shooting RAW just because it means more work. Hey, if it takes up more space on your card, buy bigger cards or more smaller ones. Will it take more time to download your images? Yes, but good things come to those who wait. Don't worry about needing to purchase expensive software to work with your RAW files; you already own a program that will allow you to work with your RAW files. Canon's Digital Photo Professional software comes bundled in the box with your camera and gives you the ability to work directly on the RAW files and then output the enhanced results.

That said, my recommendation is that you shoot in JPEG mode while you are using this book. This will allow you to quickly review your images and study the effects of future lessons. Once you have become comfortable with all of the camera features, switch to shooting in RAW mode so that you can start gaining more creative control over your image processing. After all, you took the photograph—shouldn't you be the one to decide how it looks in the end?

SELECTING RAW + JPEG

Your camera has the added benefit of being able to write two files for each picture you take: one in RAW and one in JPEG. This can be useful if you need a quick version to email but want a higher-quality version for more advanced processing.

Using both formats requires more space on the memory card. I recommend that you use only one format or the other unless you have a specific need to shoot both.

IMAGE RESOLUTION

When discussing digital cameras, image resolution is often used to describe pixel resolution, or the number of pixels used to make an image. This can be displayed as a dimension, such as 5184 x 3456. This is the physical number of pixels in width and height of the image sensor. Resolution can also be referred to in megapixels (MP), such as 18 MP. This number represents the number of total pixels on the sensor and is commonly used to describe the amount of image data that a digital camera can capture.

SELECTING YOUR IMAGE QUALITY SETTING

1. Press the Menu button, and select the first shooting menu tab using the Main dial.
2. Use the cross keys to highlight the Image quality setting (**A**), and press the Set button to enter the settings page.
3. Use the Left/Right cross keys to change the quality setting (**B**).
4. Press the Set button to lock in your changes.

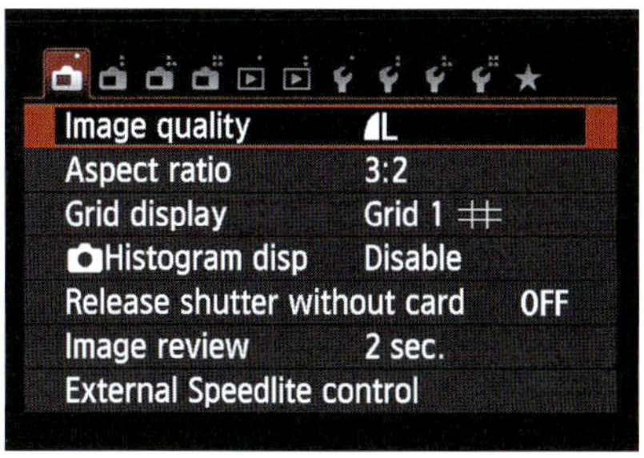

A

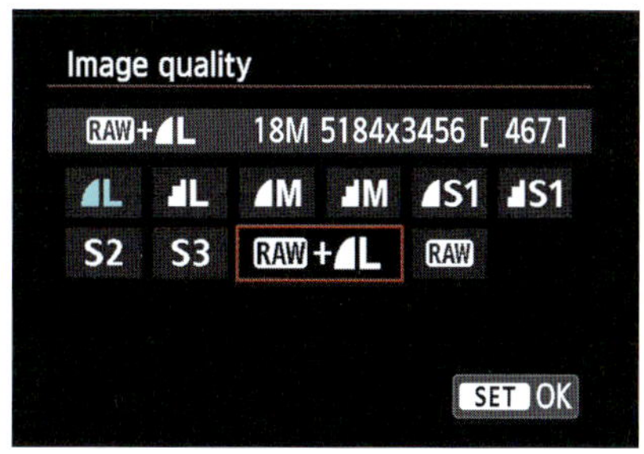

B

LENSES AND FOCAL LENGTHS

If you ask most photographers what they believe to be their most critical piece of photographic equipment, they would undoubtedly tell you it's the lens. The technology and engineering that goes into your camera is a marvel, but it isn't worth a darn if it can't get the light from the outside world onto the sensor. The EOS M uses the lens for a multitude of tasks, from focusing on a subject to metering a scene to delivering and focusing the light onto the camera sensor. The lens is also responsible for the amount of the scene that will be captured (the frame).

Lenses are composed of optical glass that is both concave and convex in shape. The alignment of the glass elements is designed to focus the light coming in from the front of the lens onto the camera sensor. The quality of the glass used in the lens will also have a direct effect on how well the lens can resolve details and the contrast of the scene (the ability to deliver great highlights and shadows). Most lenses now routinely include things like the autofocus motor and, in some cases, an image-stabilization mechanism.

Lenses are identified by focal length, which determines the angle of view delivered through the lens. Canon currently offers two lenses that fit the EOS M, one of which was probably included as the "kit lens" that accompanied the camera body. One has a fixed focal length of 20mm; the other is a moderate zoom with a range of 18mm to 55mm. However, one of the great advantages of the EOS M over other mirrorless cameras is the ability to use *any* Canon EF-model lens using the optional EOS M Mount Adapter, giving you a full range of focal lengths (**Figure 2.4**).

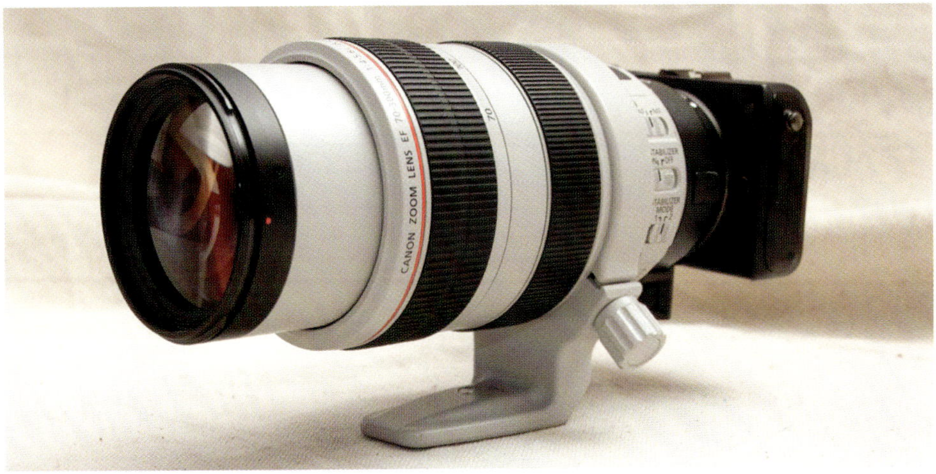

FIGURE 2.4
Mounting a Canon 70–300mm lens on the teeny EOS M looks a bit absurd, but its focal length lets you shoot the action from far away.

Wide-angle lenses cover a field of view from around 110 degrees to about 60 degrees (**Figure 2.5**). They also work well in tight spaces, such as indoors, where there isn't much elbow room available (**Figure 2.6**).

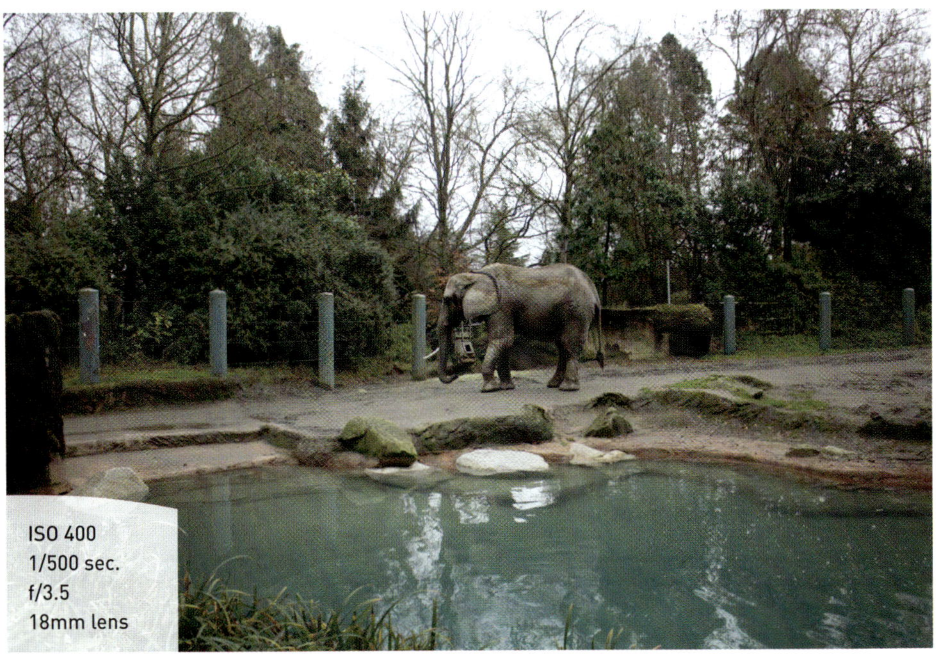

FIGURE 2.5
The 18mm lens setting provides a wide view of the scene but little detail of distant objects.

ISO 400
1/500 sec.
f/3.5
18mm lens

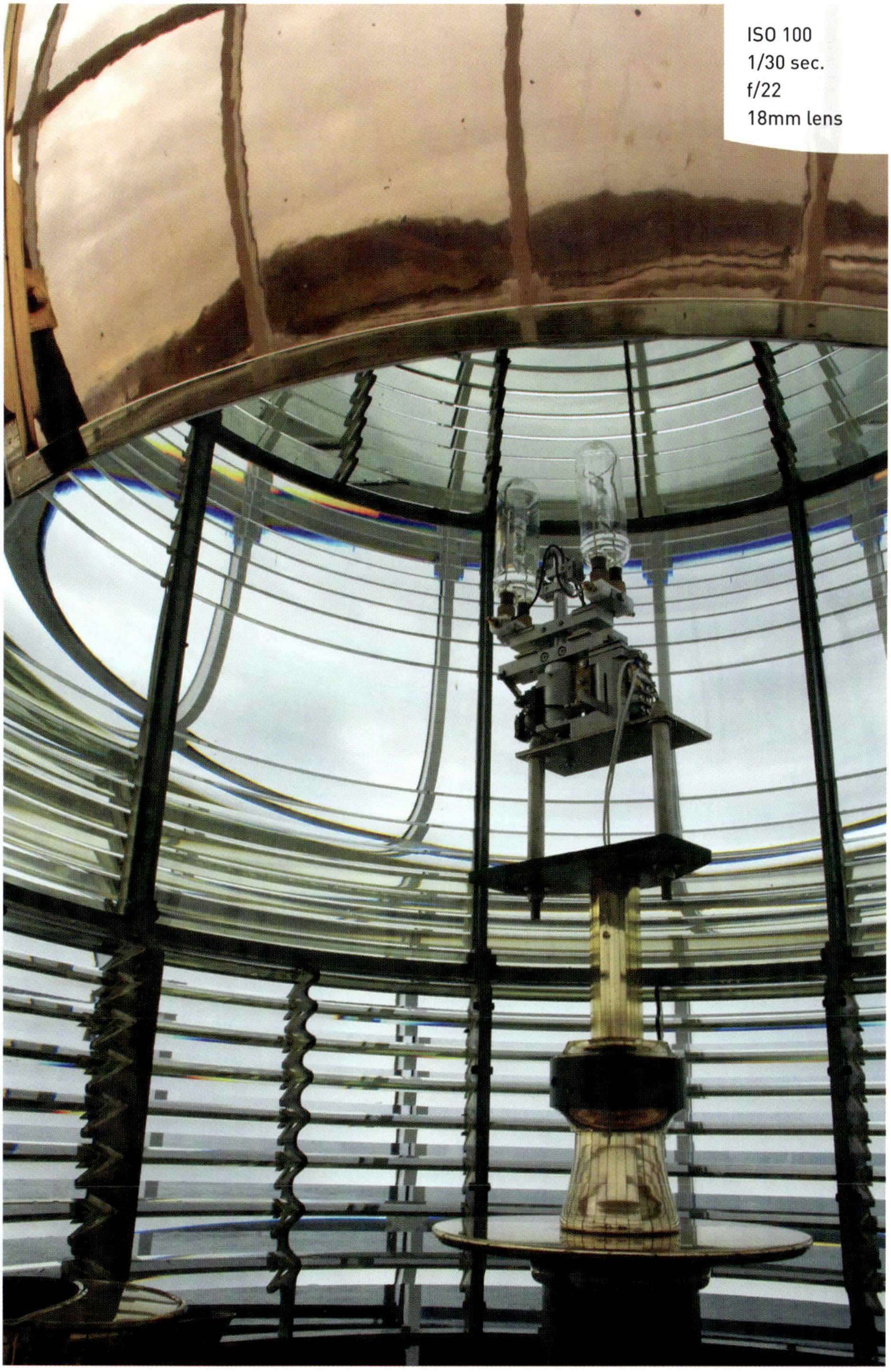

FIGURE 2.6
When shooting in tight spaces where you want to capture a large subject, a nice wide-angle lens helps capture more of the scene.

Wide-angle lenses can display a large depth of field, which allows you to keep the foreground and background in sharp focus. This makes them very useful for landscape photography. There is also a tendency to get some distortion in your image when using extremely wide-angle lenses. This will be apparent toward the outer edges of the frame. They can also be handy for large group shots but, due to the amount of distortion, not so great for close-up portrait work. In general, lenses 30mm or smaller are considered wide angle.

A *normal* lens has a field of view that is about 45 degrees and delivers approximately the same view as the human eye (not in angle of view but in size and perspective of subjects). The perspective is very natural, and there is little distortion in objects (**Figure 2.7**). The normal lens for full-frame cameras is the 50mm lens, but for the lenses attached using the EOS M Mount Adapter it is more in the neighborhood of 35mm. The two lenses designed for the EOS M fall into this category too.

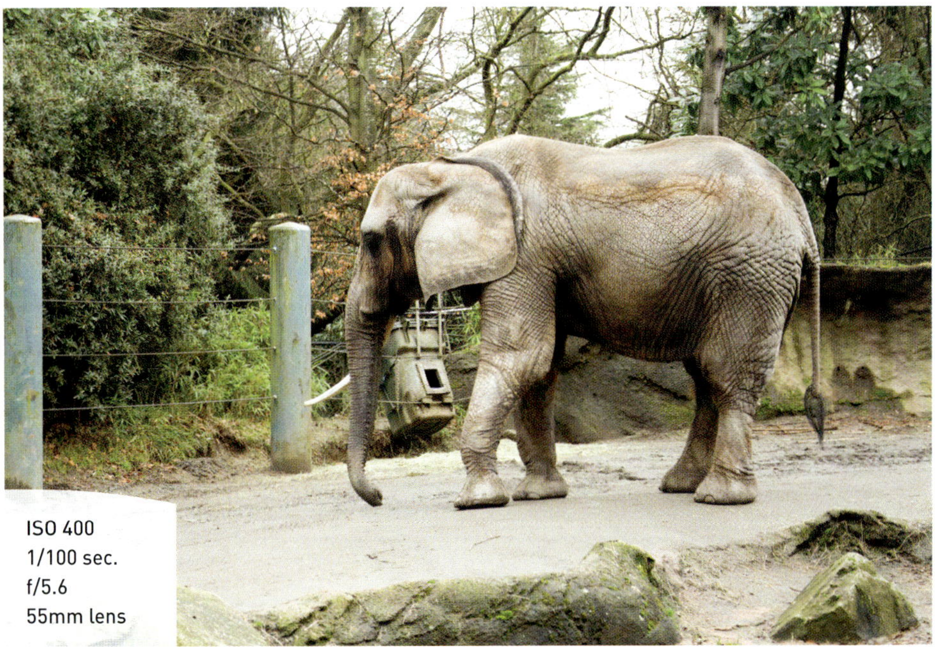

ISO 400
1/100 sec.
f/5.6
55mm lens

FIGURE 2.7
A focal length of around 50mm is "normal," even though on the EOS M that's the maximum range of the 18–55mm lens.

Normal focal length lenses are useful for photographing people, architecture, and most other general photographic subjects. They have very little distortion and offer a moderate range of depth of field (**Figure 2.8**).

Most longer focal length lenses are referred to as *telephoto* lenses. They can range in length from 100mm up to 800mm or longer and have a field of view that is about 35 degrees or smaller. These lenses have the ability to greatly magnify the scene, allowing you to capture details of distant objects, but the angle of view is greatly reduced

(**Figure 2.9**). You will also find that you can achieve a much narrower depth of field. They also demonstrate something called distance compression, which means they make objects at different distances appear to be much closer together than they really are.

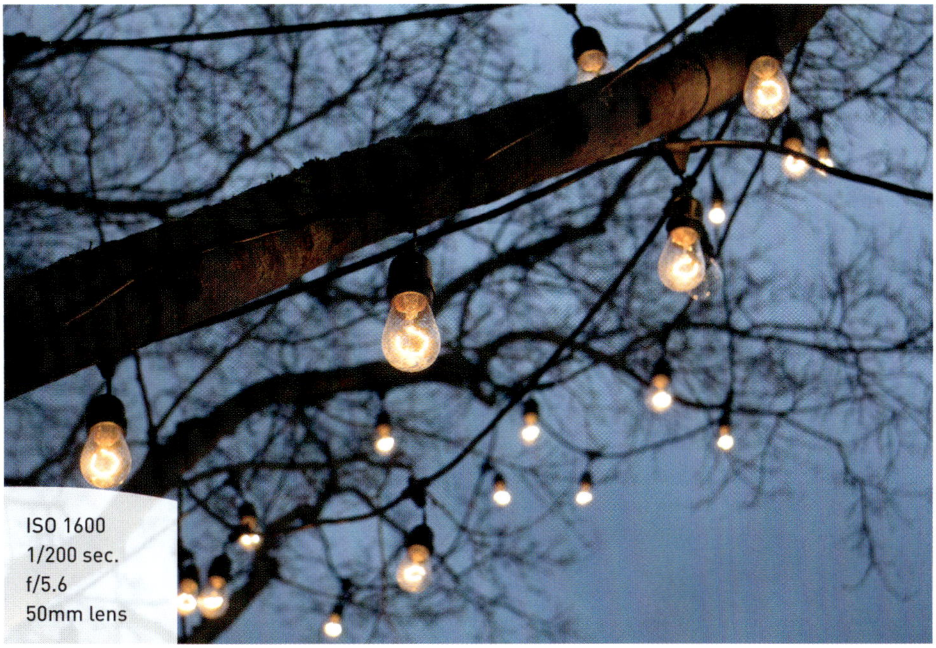

FIGURE 2.8
A normal focal length worked well in this image by providing enough coverage of several branches and strings of lights while focusing on the bulbs in the foreground.

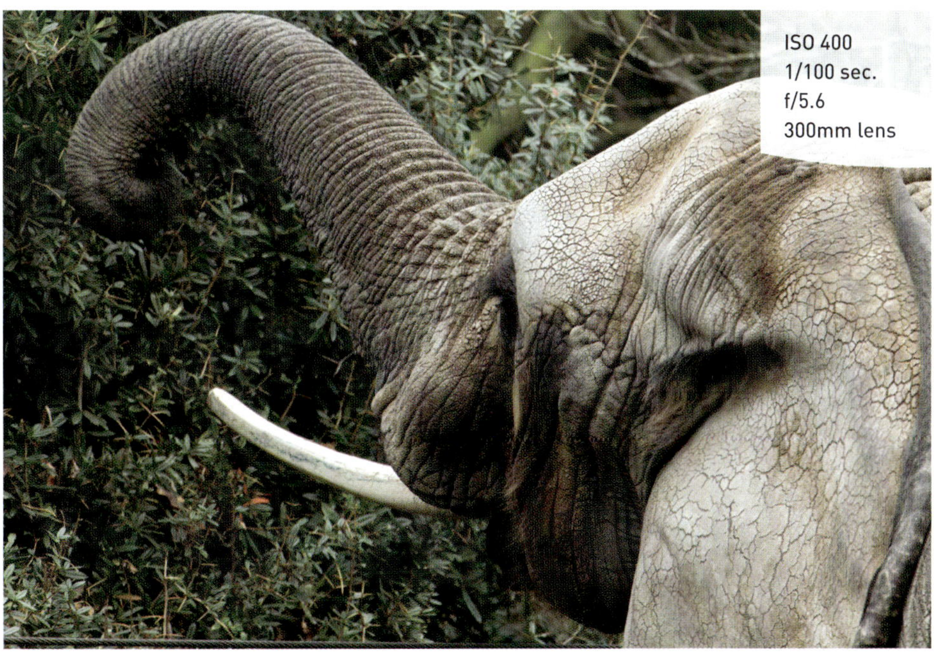

FIGURE 2.9
The telephoto lens allowed me to capture close-up detail of the elephant without having to get physically closer.

Telephoto lenses are most useful for sports photography or any application where you just need to get closer to your subject (**Figure 2.10**). They can have a compressing effect—making objects look closer together than they actually are—and a very narrow depth of field when shot at their widest apertures.

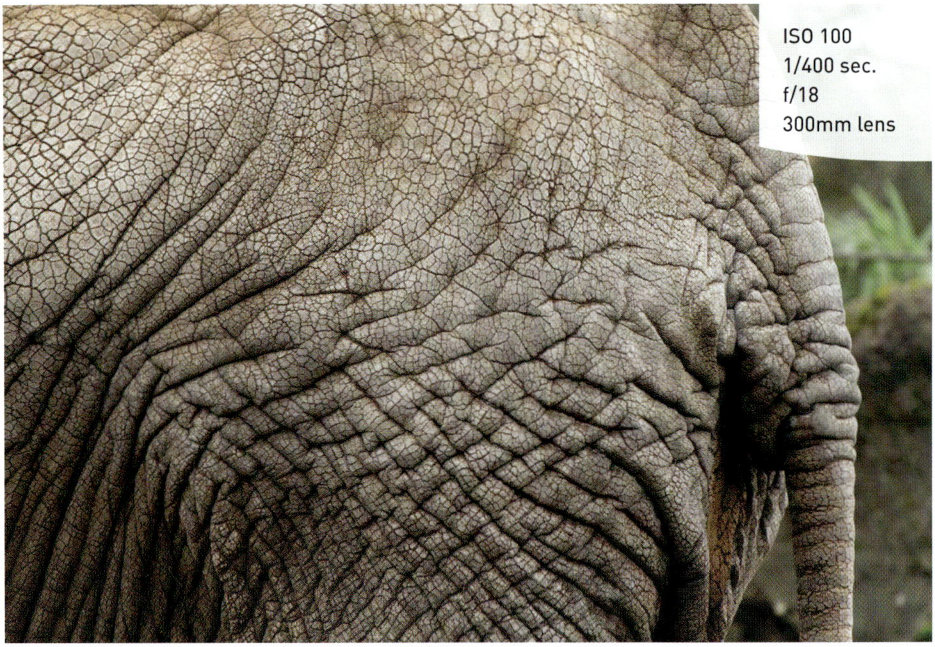

ISO 100
1/400 sec.
f/18
300mm lens

FIGURE 2.10
The long telephoto helped me get a tighter crop, revealing the texture of the elephant's hide.

A *zoom* lens is a great compromise to carrying a bunch of single focal-length lenses (also referred to as "prime" lenses). They can cover a wide range of focal lengths because of the configuration of their optics. However, because it takes more optical elements to capture a scene at different focal lengths, the light must pass through more glass on its way to the image sensor. The more glass, the lower the quality of the image sharpness. The other sacrifice that is made is in aperture. Zoom lenses typically have smaller maximum apertures than prime lenses, which means they cannot achieve a narrow depth of field or work in lower light levels without the assistance of image stabilization, a tripod, or higher ISO settings. (We'll discuss all this in more detail in later chapters.)

WHAT IS EXPOSURE?

In order for you to get the most out of this book, I need to briefly discuss the principles of exposure. Without this basic knowledge, it will be difficult for you to move forward in improving your photography. For our purposes, I will cover just some of the basics of exposure. This will give you the essential tools to make educated decisions in determining how best to photograph a subject.

So what is exposure? It is the process whereby the light reflecting off a subject reflects through an opening in the camera lens for a defined period of time onto the camera sensor. The combination of the lens opening, shutter speed, and sensor sensitivity is used to achieve a proper exposure value (EV) for the scene. The EV is the sum of these components necessary to properly expose a scene. The relationship between these factors is sometimes referred to as the "exposure triangle."

At each point of the triangle lies one of the factors of exposure:

- **ISO:** Determines the sensitivity of the camera sensor. ISO stands for the International Organization for Standardization, but the acronym is used as a term to describe the sensitivity of the camera sensor to light. The higher the sensitivity, the less light is required for a good exposure. These values are a carryover from the days of traditional color and black and white films.
- **Aperture:** Also referred to as f-stop, this determines how much light passes through the lens at once.
- **Shutter Speed:** Controls the length of time that light is allowed to hit the sensor.

So here's how it works. The camera sensor has a level of sensitivity that is determined by the ISO setting. To get a proper exposure—not too much, not too little—the lens needs to adjust the aperture diaphragm (the size of the lens opening) to control the volume of light entering the camera. Then the shutter is opened for a relatively short period of time to allow the light to hit the sensor long enough for it to record on the sensor.

ISO numbers for the EOS M start at 100 and then double in sensitivity as you double the number. So 200 is twice as sensitive as 100. The camera can be set to use 1/2- or 1/3-stop increments, but for ISO just remember that the base numbers double: 100, 200, 400, 800, and so on. There are also a wide variety of shutter speeds that you can use to achieve a proper exposure. The speeds on the EOS M range from as long as 30 seconds to as short as 1/4000 of a second. When using the camera, you will not see the 1 over the number while looking at the LCD, so you will need to remember that anything shorter than a second will be a fraction. (However, the shutter speed is displayed as a fraction when looking at the info display that summarizes all settings.)

Typically, you will be working with a shutter speed range from around 1/30 of a second to about 1/2000, but these numbers will change depending on your circumstances and the effect that you are trying to achieve. The lens apertures will vary slightly depending on which lens you are using. This is because different lenses have different maximum apertures. The typical apertures at your disposal are f/2, f/4, f/5.6, f/8, f/11, f/16, and f/22.

When it comes to exposure, a change to any one of these factors can require adjusting one or more of the other two. This is referred to as a reciprocal change. If you let more light in the lens by choosing a larger aperture opening, you will need to shorten the amount of time the shutter is open. If the shutter is allowed to stay open for a longer period of time, the aperture needs to be smaller to restrict the amount of light coming in to prevent overexposure.

HOW IS EXPOSURE CALCULATED?

We now know about the exposure triangle—ISO, shutter speed, and aperture—so it's time to put all three together to see how they relate to one another and how you can change them as needed.

STOP

You will hear the term *stop* thrown around all the time in photography. It relates back to the f-stop, which is a term used to describe the aperture of your lens. When you need to give some additional exposure, you might say that you are going to "add a stop." This doesn't just equate to the aperture; it could also be used to describe the shutter speed or even the ISO. So when your image is too light or dark or you have too much movement in your subject, you will probably be changing things by a "stop" or two.

When you point your camera at a scene, the light reflecting off your subject enters the lens and is allowed to pass through to the sensor for a period of time dictated by the shutter speed. The amount and duration of the light needed for a proper exposure depends on how much light is being reflected and how sensitive the sensor is. To figure this out, your camera utilizes a built-in light meter that looks through the lens and measures the amount of light. That level is then calculated against the sensitivity of the ISO setting, and an exposure value is rendered. Here is the tricky part: There is more than one way to achieve a perfect exposure, because the f-stop and shutter speed can be combined in different ways to allow the same amount of exposure. See, I told you it was tricky.

Here is a list of reciprocal settings that would all produce the same exposure result. Let's use the "sunny 16" rule, which states that when using f/16 on a sunny day, you can use a shutter speed that is roughly equal to the ISO setting to achieve a proper exposure. For simplification purposes, we will use an ISO of 100.

RECIPROCAL EXPOSURES: ISO 100

F-STOP	2.8	4	5.6	8	11	16	22
SHUTTER SPEED	1/4000	1/2000	1/1000	1/500	1/250	1/125	1/60

If you were to use any one of these combinations, they would each have the same result in terms of the exposure (i.e., how much light hits the camera's sensor). Also take note that every time we cut the f-stop in half, we reciprocated by doubling our shutter speed. For those of you wondering why f/8 is half of f/5.6, it's because those numbers are actually fractions based on the opening of the lens in relation to its focal length. This means that a lot of math goes into figuring out what the total area of a lens opening is, so you just have to take it on faith that f/8 is half of f/5.6 but twice as much as f/11. A good way to remember which opening is larger is to think of your camera lens as a pipe that controls the flow of water. If you have a pipe that is 1/2" in diameter (f/2) and one that is 1/8" (f/8), which would allow more water to flow through? It would be the 1/2" pipe. The same idea works here with the camera f-stops; f/2 is a larger opening than f/4 or f/8 or f/16.

Now that we know this, we can start using this information to make intelligent choices in terms of shutter speed and f-stop. Let's bring the third element into this by changing our ISO by one stop, from 100 to 200.

RECIPROCAL EXPOSURES: ISO 200

F-STOP	2.8	4	5.6	8	11	16	22
SHUTTER SPEED	–	1/4000	1/2000	1/1000	1/500	1/250	1/125

Notice that, since we doubled the sensitivity of the sensor, we now require half as much exposure as before. We have also reduced our maximum aperture from f/2.8 to f/4 because the camera can't use a shutter speed that is faster than 1/4000 of a second.

So why not just use the exposure setting of f/16 at 1/250 of a second? Why bother with all of these reciprocal values when this one setting will give us a properly exposed image? The answer is that the f-stop and shutter speed also control two other important aspects of our image: motion and depth of field.

MOTION AND DEPTH OF FIELD

There are distinct characteristics that are related to changes in aperture and shutter speed. Shutter speed controls the length of time the light has to strike the sensor; consequently, it also controls the blurriness (or lack of blurriness) of the image. The less time light has to hit the sensor, the less time your subjects have to move around and become blurry. This can let you do things like freezing the motion of a fast-moving subject (**Figure 2.11**) or intentionally blurring subjects to give the feel of energy and motion (**Figure 2.12**).

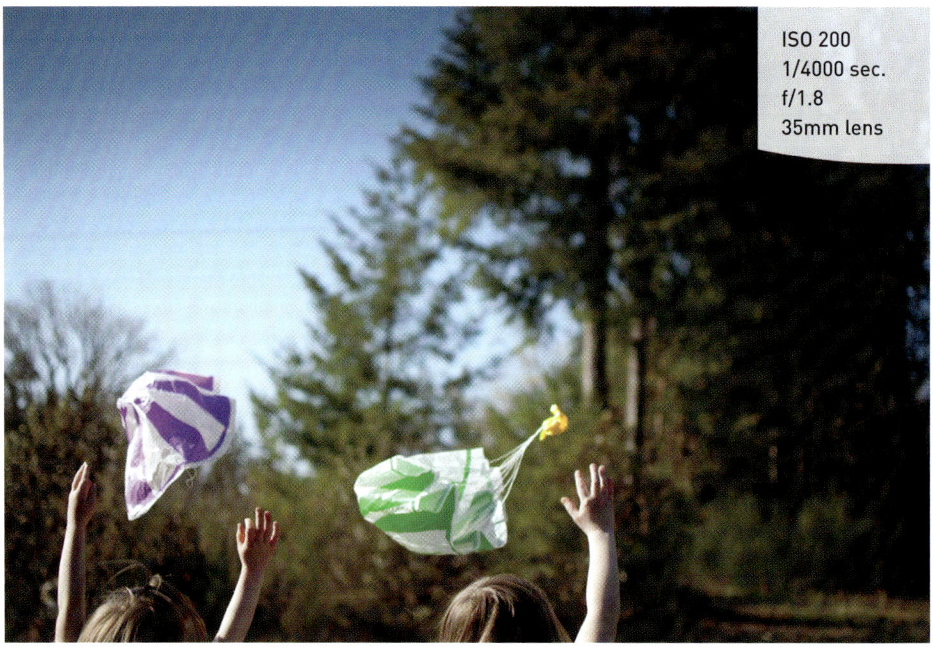

ISO 200
1/4000 sec.
f/1.8
35mm lens

FIGURE 2.11
A fast shutter speed was used to freeze these parachutes in flight.

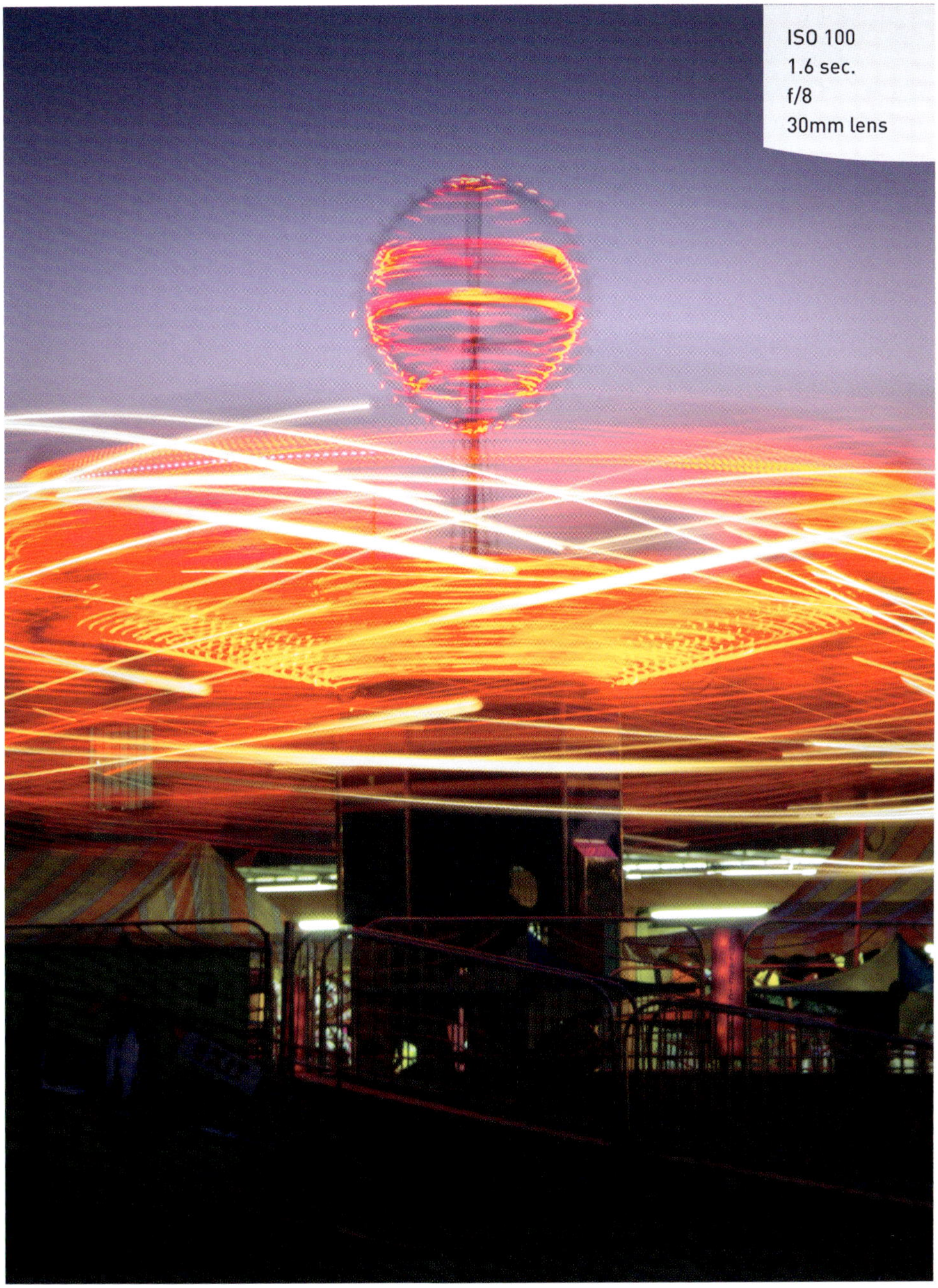

ISO 100
1.6 sec.
f/8
30mm lens

FIGURE 2.12
A slow shutter speed turns this amusement park ride into a moving light sculpture.

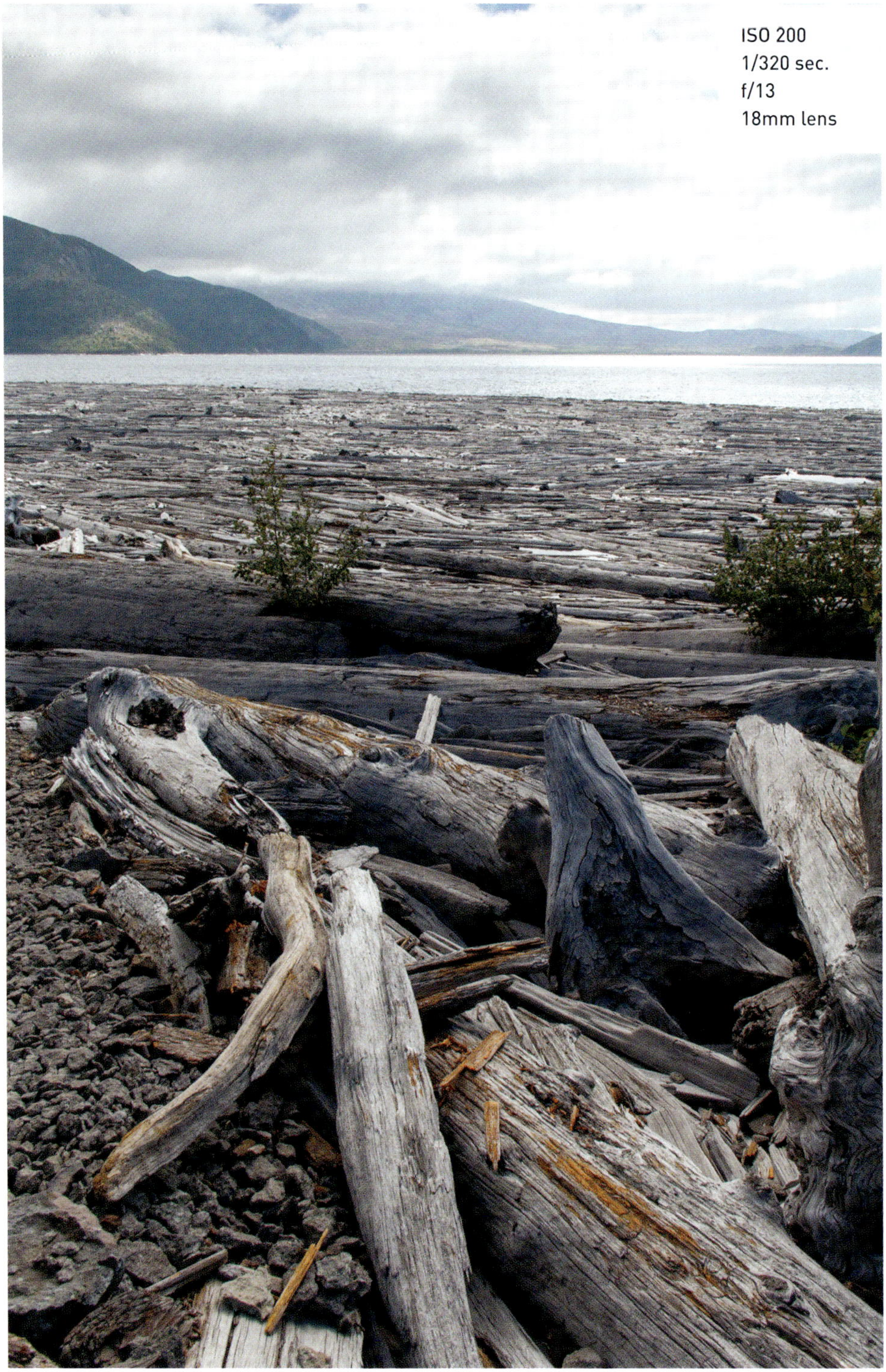

ISO 200
1/320 sec.
f/13
18mm lens

FIGURE 2.13
By using a small aperture, the area of sharp focus extends from a point that is near the camera all the way out to distant objects. In this instance, I wanted to keep the far edge of the lake in focus to define its scope.

The aperture controls the amount of light that comes through the lens, but it also determines what areas of the image will be in focus. This is referred to as depth of field, and it is an extremely valuable creative tool. The smaller the opening (the larger the number, such as f/22), the greater the sharpness of objects from near to far (**Figure 2.13**).

A large opening (or small number, like f/2.8) means more blurring of objects that are not at the same distance from the camera as the subject you are focusing on (**Figure 2.14**).

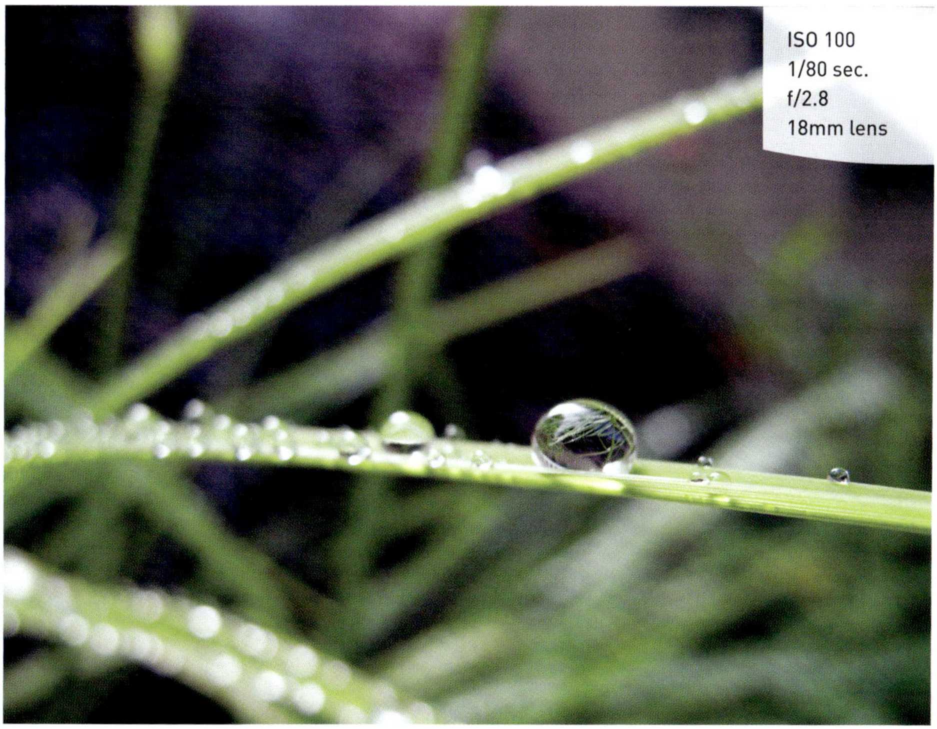

FIGURE 2.14
Isolating a subject is accomplished by using a large aperture, which produces a narrow area of sharp focus.

As we further explore the features of the camera, we will learn not only how to utilize the elements of exposure to capture properly exposed photographs, but also how we can make adjustments to emphasize our subject. It is the manipulation of these elements—motion and focus—that will take your images to the next level.

Chapter 2 Assignments

Formatting your card

Even if you have already begun using your camera, make sure you are familiar with formatting the SD card. If you haven't done so already, follow the directions given earlier in the chapter and format as described (make sure you save any images that you may have already taken). Then perform the Format function every time you have downloaded or saved your images or use a new card.

Checking your firmware version

Using the most up-to-date version of the camera firmware will ensure that your camera is functioning properly. Use the menu to find your current firmware version, and then update as necessary using the steps listed in this chapter.

Cleaning your sensor

You probably noticed the sensor-cleaning message the first time you turned your camera on. Make sure you are familiar with the Clean Now command so you can perform this function every time you change a lens.

Exploring your image formats

I want you to become familiar with all of the camera features before using the RAW format, but take a little time to explore the format menu so you can see what options are available to you.

Exploring your lens

If you are using a zoom lens, spend a little time shooting with all of the different focal lengths, from the widest to the longest. See just how much of an angle you can cover with your widest lens setting. How much magnification will you be able to get from the telephoto setting? Try shooting the same subject with a variety of focal lengths to note the differences in how the subject looks, and also the relationship between the subject and the other elements in the photo.

Share your results with the book's Flickr group!

Join the group here: flickr.com/groups/eosmfromsnapshotstogreatshots

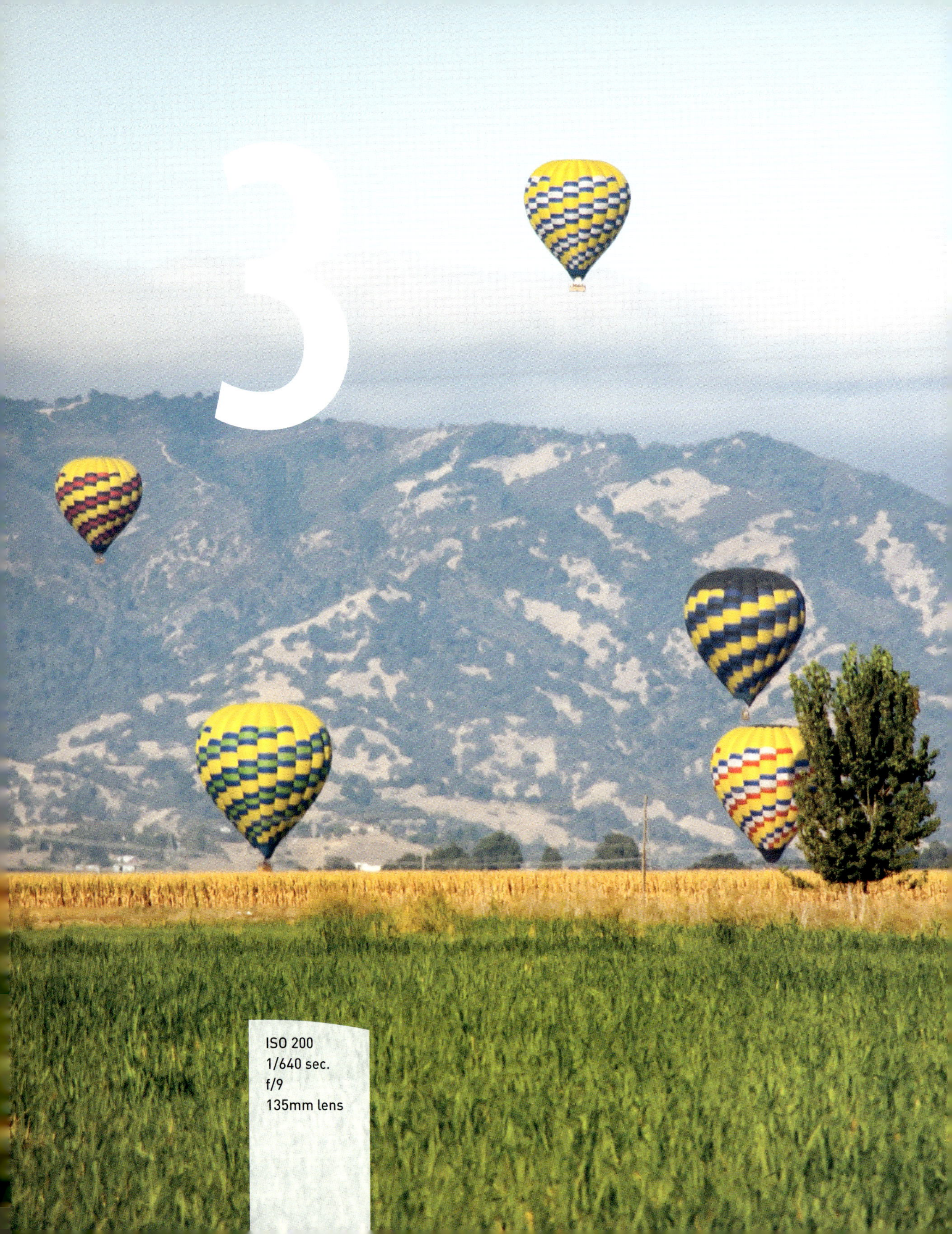

3

ISO 200
1/640 sec.
f/9
135mm lens

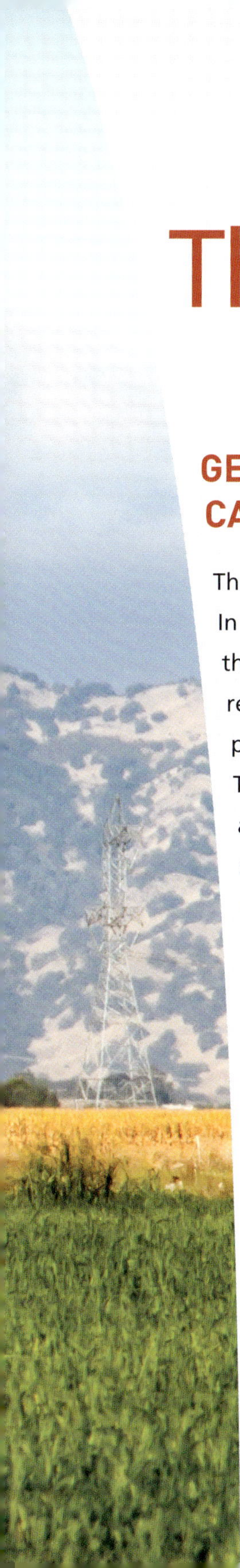

The Basic Zone

GET SHOOTING WITH THE AUTOMATIC CAMERA MODES

The Canon EOS M is an amazing camera that has some incredible features. In fact, all of the technology built into it can be pretty intimidating for the person who is moving up from point-and-shoot photography. For that reason, Canon has made it a little easier for you to get some great-looking photographs without having to do a lot of thinking. Enter the Basic zone. The camera modes in the Basic zone are simple, icon-labeled modes that are set up to use specific features of the camera for various shooting situations. Let's take a look at the different modes and how and when to use them.

PORING OVER THE PICTURE

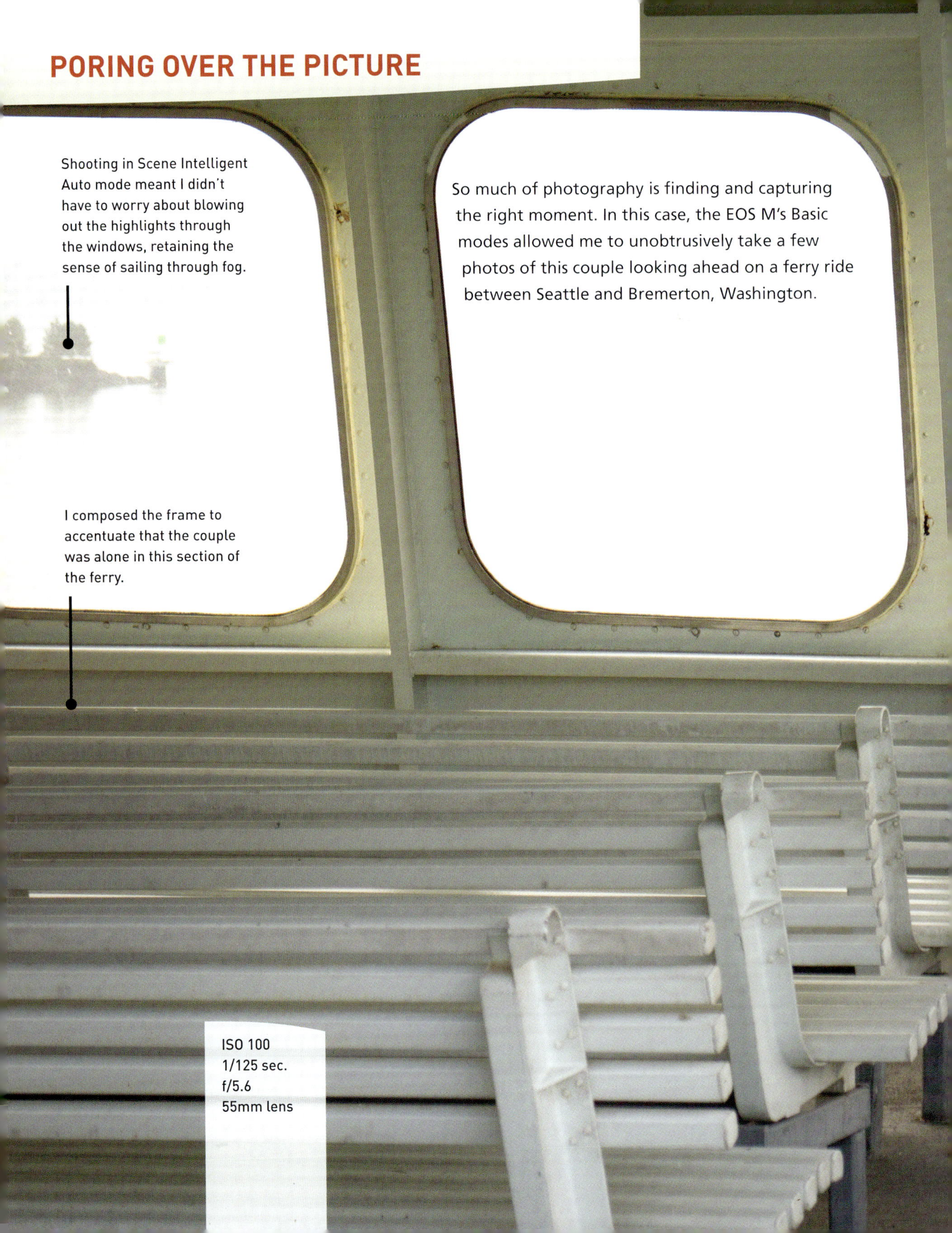

So much of photography is finding and capturing the right moment. In this case, the EOS M's Basic modes allowed me to unobtrusively take a few photos of this couple looking ahead on a ferry ride between Seattle and Bremerton, Washington.

Shooting in Scene Intelligent Auto mode meant I didn't have to worry about blowing out the highlights through the windows, retaining the sense of sailing through fog.

I composed the frame to accentuate that the couple was alone in this section of the ferry.

ISO 100
1/125 sec.
f/5.6
55mm lens

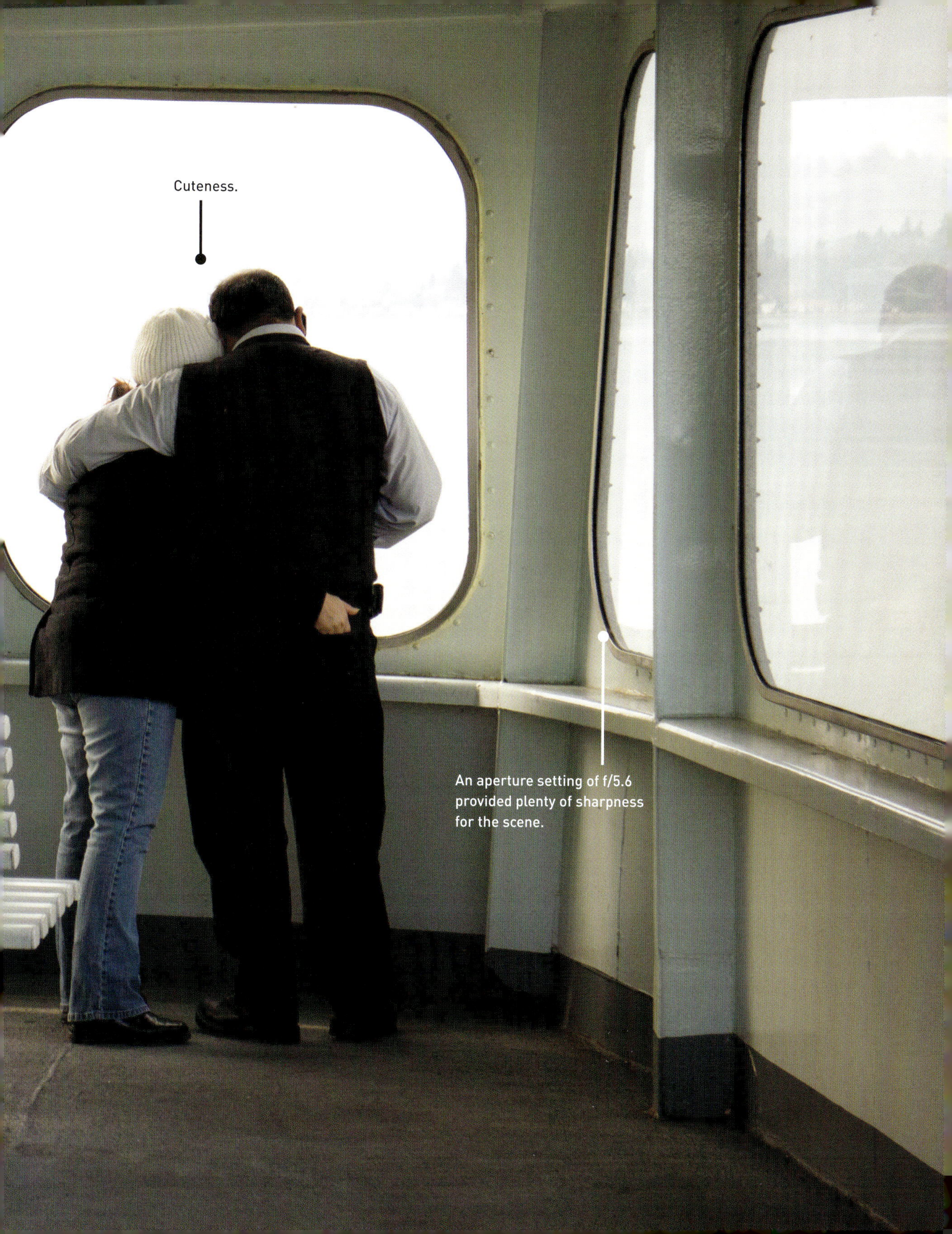
Cuteness.
An aperture setting of f/5.6 provided plenty of sharpness for the scene.

PORING OVER THE PICTURE

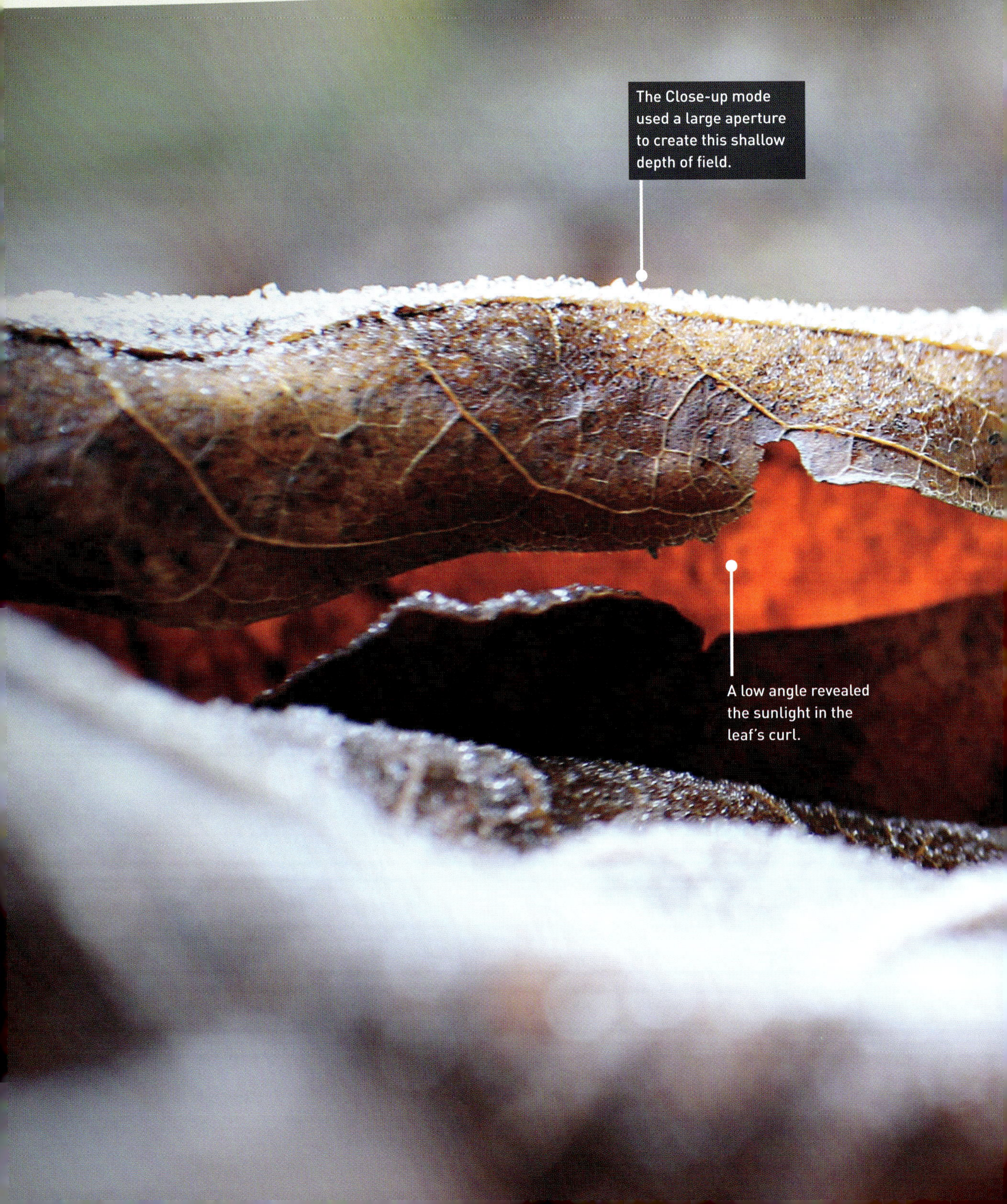

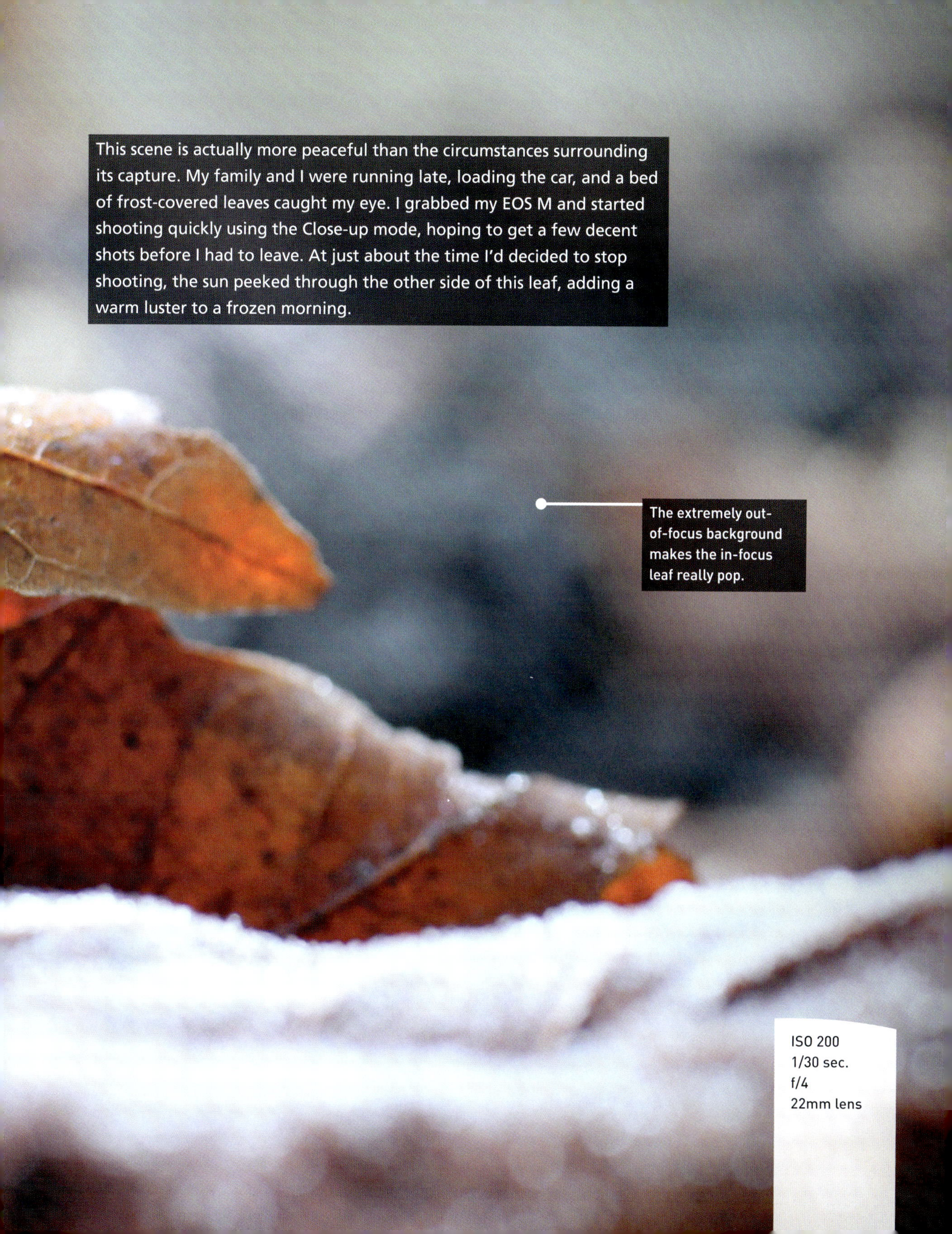

This scene is actually more peaceful than the circumstances surrounding its capture. My family and I were running late, loading the car, and a bed of frost-covered leaves caught my eye. I grabbed my EOS M and started shooting quickly using the Close-up mode, hoping to get a few decent shots before I had to leave. At just about the time I'd decided to stop shooting, the sun peeked through the other side of this leaf, adding a warm luster to a frozen morning.

The extremely out-of-focus background makes the in-focus leaf really pop.

ISO 200
1/30 sec.
f/4
22mm lens

SCENE INTELLIGENT AUTO MODE

Scene Intelligent Auto mode is all about thought-free photography. In fact, it's one of only three modes controlled by the dial on top of the camera (**Figure 3.1**). This is the EOS M's "point and shoot" mode: It evaluates the scene, chooses a shooting mode (such as Landscape), and handles the aperture, shutter speed, and ISO settings for you (**Figure 3.2**).

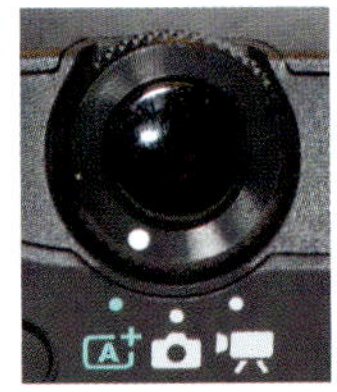

FIGURE 3.1
Scene Intelligent Auto mode

For your part—aside from composing your shot—you can choose the autofocus method and image format by tapping the Quick Control/Set button on the screen or in the middle of the main dial. You can also choose the drive mode by pressing the Drive Mode Selection/Up cross key button, letting you take single, continuous, or time-delayed shots; see the end of this chapter for more information about the drive modes. (Note that switching between Scene Intelligent Auto and the Basic and Creative modes changes the drive mode setting to Single shooting, even if you had previously set it to Continuous or time delayed.)

Let's face it: This is the lazy person's mode. But sometimes it's nice to be lazy and click away without giving thought to anything but preserving a memory. There will be times, though, when you want to use your camera's advanced features, which are tailored to specific shooting environments.

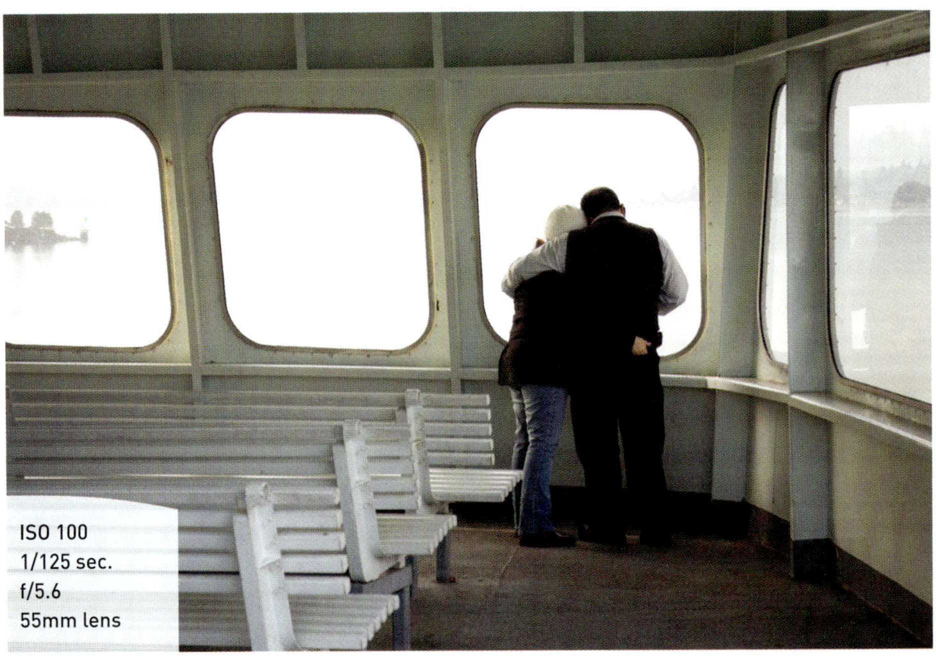

ISO 100
1/125 sec.
f/5.6
55mm lens

FIGURE 3.2
Scene Intelligent Auto mode works great when you just want to snap some shots quickly.

PORTRAIT MODE

One problem with Scene Intelligent Auto mode is that it has little idea what type of subject you are photographing and, therefore, is applying the settings based on its "best guess" for each situation. Shooting portraits is a perfect example. When you are taking a photograph of someone, you typically want the emphasis of the picture to be on them, not necessarily on the stuff going on in the background. This is what Portrait mode is for (**Figure 3.3**).

When you set your camera to this mode, you are telling the camera to select a larger aperture so that the depth of field is much narrower and will give more blur to objects in the background. This blurry background places the attention on your subject. The other feature of this mode is the automatic selection of the EOS M's built-in Portrait picture style (we'll go into more detail about picture styles in later chapters). This style is optimized for skin tones and is also a little softer to improve the look of skin.

There are some options in this mode that are changeable to your liking. These are accessed by pressing the Q button on the back of the camera. They include the Ambience setting, which lets you change the overall look of the image (softer, darker, warmer, cooler, more vivid, etc.); the white balance; and the shooting drive mode (Continuous or Self-timer).

USING THE BEST LENS FOR GREAT PORTRAITS

When using Portrait mode and working with Canon EF lenses (which require the EOS M Lens Adapter), it's usually best to use a lens that is 50mm or longer. The longer lens will give you a natural view of the subject, as well as aid in keeping the depth of field narrow.

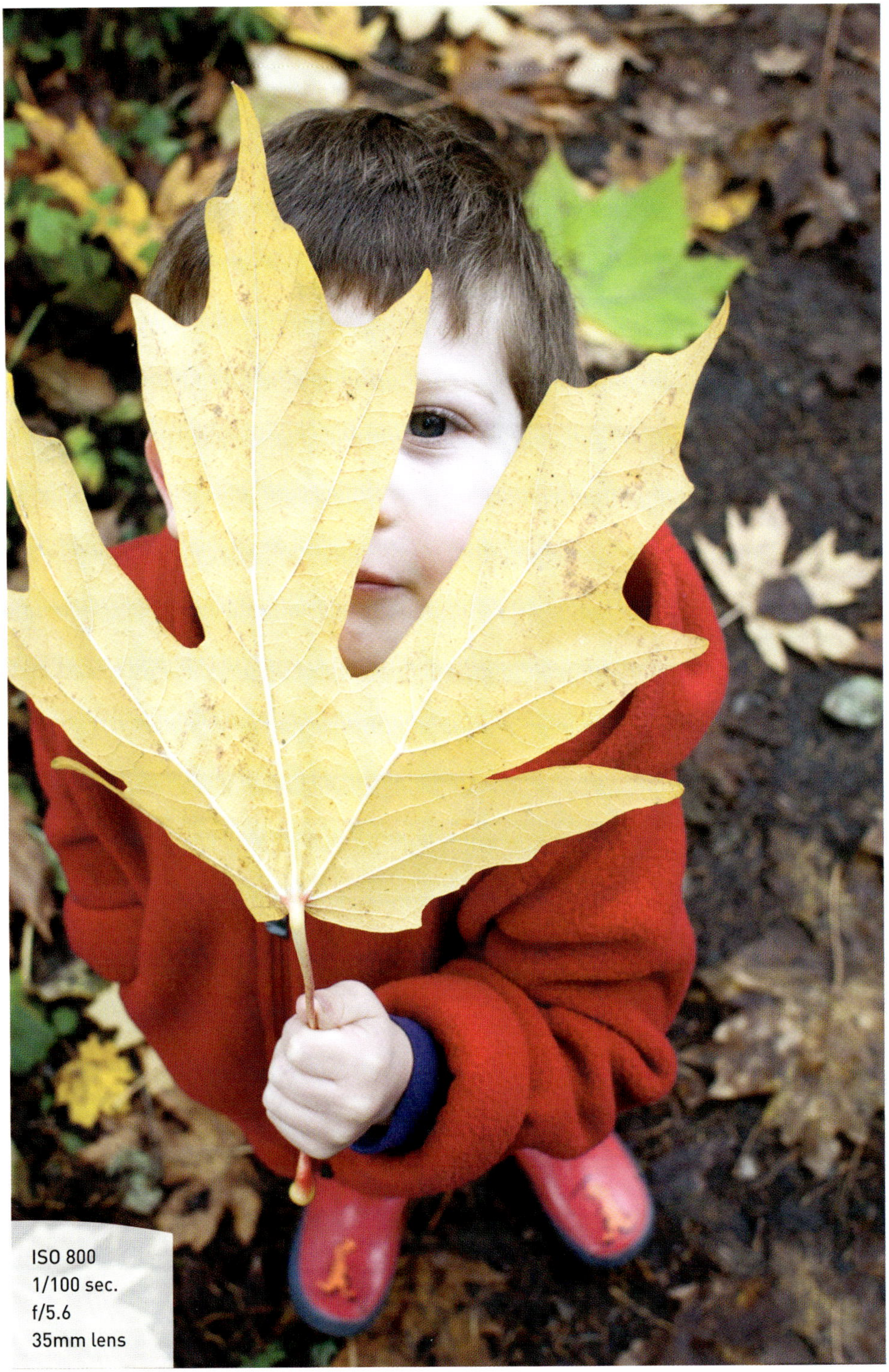

ISO 800
1/100 sec.
f/5.6
35mm lens

FIGURE 3.3
Portrait mode is a great choice for shots like this one.

LANDSCAPE MODE

As you might have guessed, Landscape mode has been optimized for shooting landscape images. Particular emphasis is placed on the picture style, with the camera trying to boost the greens and blues in the image (**Figure 3.4**). This makes sense, since the typical landscape would be outdoors, where grass, trees, and skies should look more colorful. This picture style also boosts the sharpness that is applied during processing. The camera also utilizes the lowest ISO settings possible to keep digital noise to a minimum.

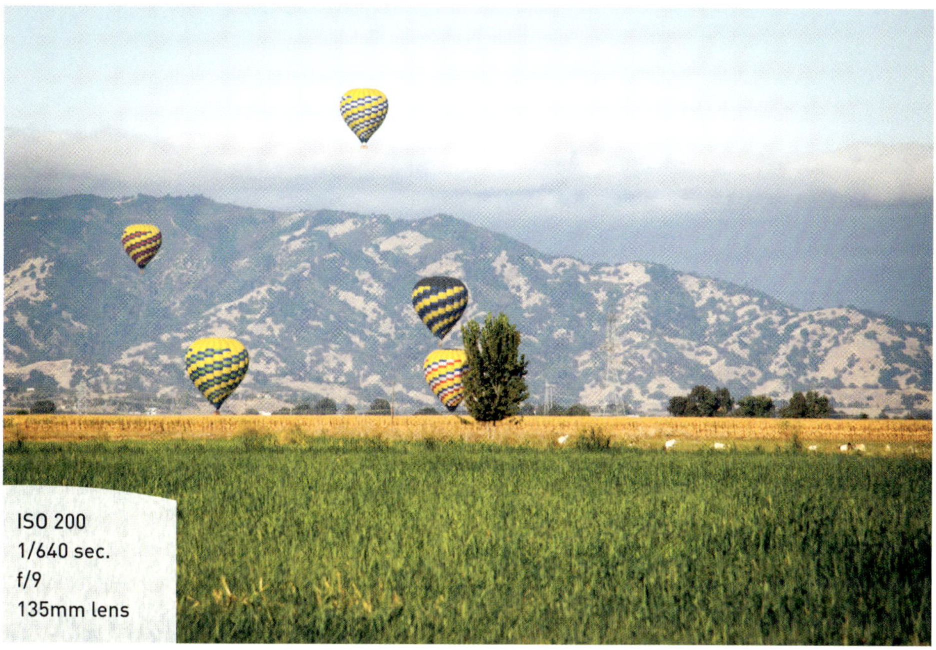

ISO 200
1/640 sec.
f/9
135mm lens

FIGURE 3.4
This type of scene just calls out for Landscape mode. The small aperture helps achieve a greater depth of field.

CLOSE-UP MODE

Although most zoom lenses don't support true "macro" settings, that doesn't mean you can't shoot some great close-up photos. The key here is to use your camera-to-subject distance to fill the frame while still achieving sharp focus. Move yourself as close to your subject as you can while still being able to get a good sharp focus. Often, a lens will be marked with the minimum focusing distance. On the 18–55mm zoom for the EOS M, it is .8 feet; the 22mm EOS M lens is marked at 0.49 feet.

FIGURE 3.5
Close-up mode helped me get this shot down at leaf-level.

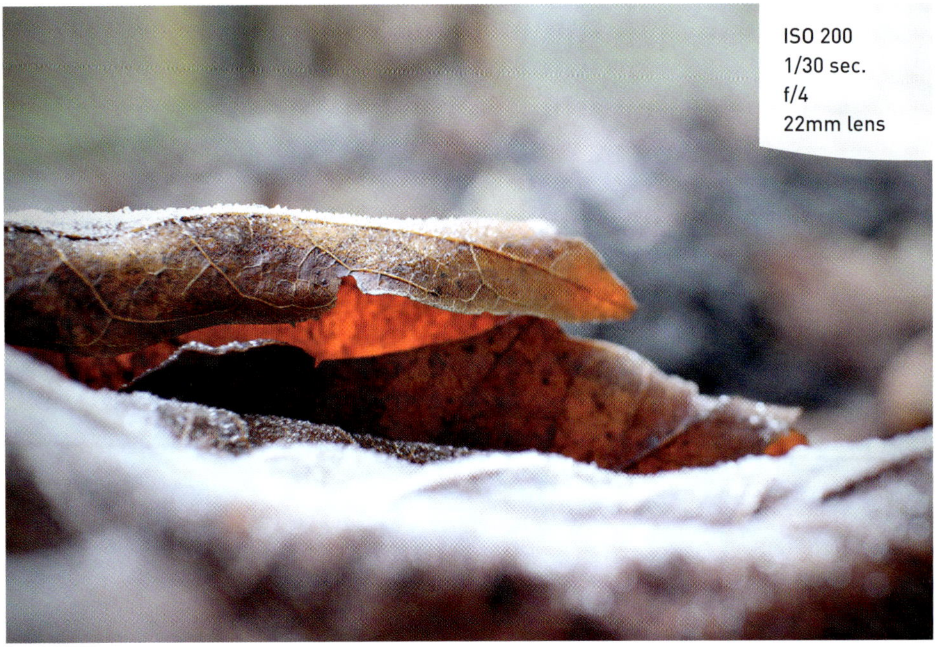

To help get the best focus in the picture, Close-up mode will use the smallest aperture it can while keeping the shutter speed fast enough to get a sharp shot (**Figure 3.5**).

SPORTS MODE

Although this is called Sports mode, you can use it for any moving subject you are photographing. The mode is built on the principles of sports photography: continuous focusing, large apertures, and fast shutter speeds (**Figure 3.6**). To handle these requirements, the camera sets the drive mode to Continuous shooting, the aperture to a very large opening, and the ISO to Auto. Overall, these are sound settings that will capture most moving subjects well. We'll take an in-depth look at all of these features in Chapter 5.

You can, however, run the risk of too much digital noise in your picture if the camera decides that you need a very high ISO (such as 1600 or higher). Also, when using Sports mode, you will need to frame your subject in the middle of the viewfinder so the center focus area is on them. I also recommend setting the image quality to RAW (instead of RAW+JPEG)—or to the highest-quality JPEG option if you want to be able to fire many continuous shots before the image buffer fills up and pauses image capture.

ISO 1600
1/160 sec.
f/5.6
135mm lens

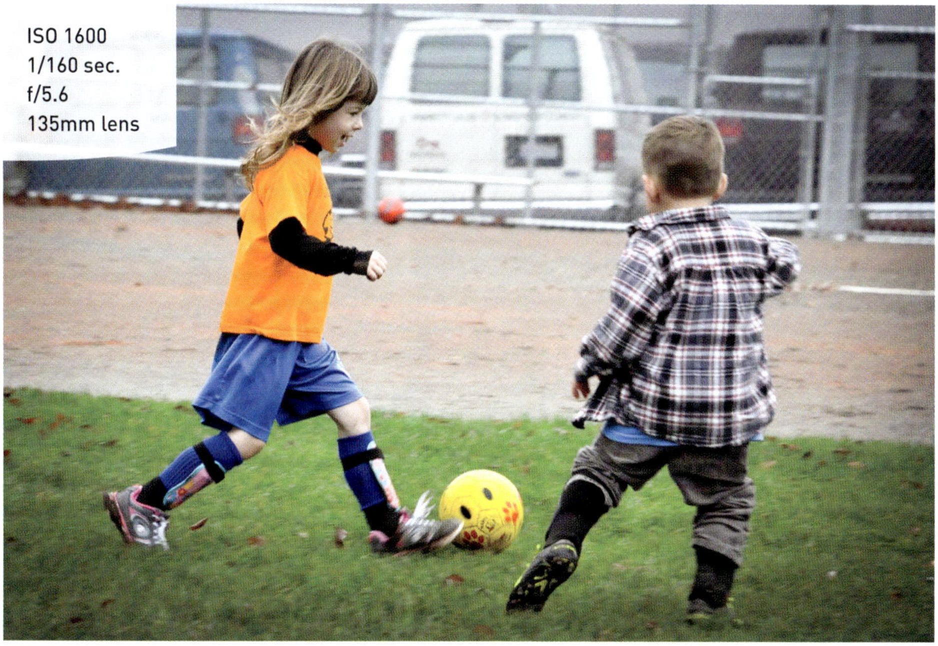

FIGURE 3.6 This is the type of shot that was made for Sports mode, where action-freezing shutter speeds and continuous focusing capture the moment.

NIGHT PORTRAIT MODE

You're out on the town at night and you want to take a nice picture of someone, but you want to show some of the interesting scenery in the background as well. You could use Scene Intelligent Auto mode, which would probably crank up the ISO to take a photo. The problem is that, while it would give you a decent exposure for your subject, you're likely to end up with a lot of noise, and the background might still end up being completely dark. If you have a flash handy, mount it to the hot shoe and use Night Portrait mode. When you switch to this mode, you are telling the camera that you want to use a slower-than-normal shutter speed to give the background more time (and, thus, more light) to achieve a proper exposure.

The typical shutter speed for using flash is about 1/60 of a second or faster (but not faster than 1/200 of a second). By leaving the shutter open for a longer duration, the camera allows more of the background to be exposed so that you get a much more balanced scene (**Figure 3.7**). This is also a great mode for taking portraits during sunset. Once again, the camera sets the ISO automatically, so you will want to keep an eye on it to make sure that value isn't so high that the noise levels ruin your photo.

FIGURE 3.7
Night Portrait mode uses a slower shutter speed and larger aperture to balance the background with the flash exposure. In real life, the sky was much darker.

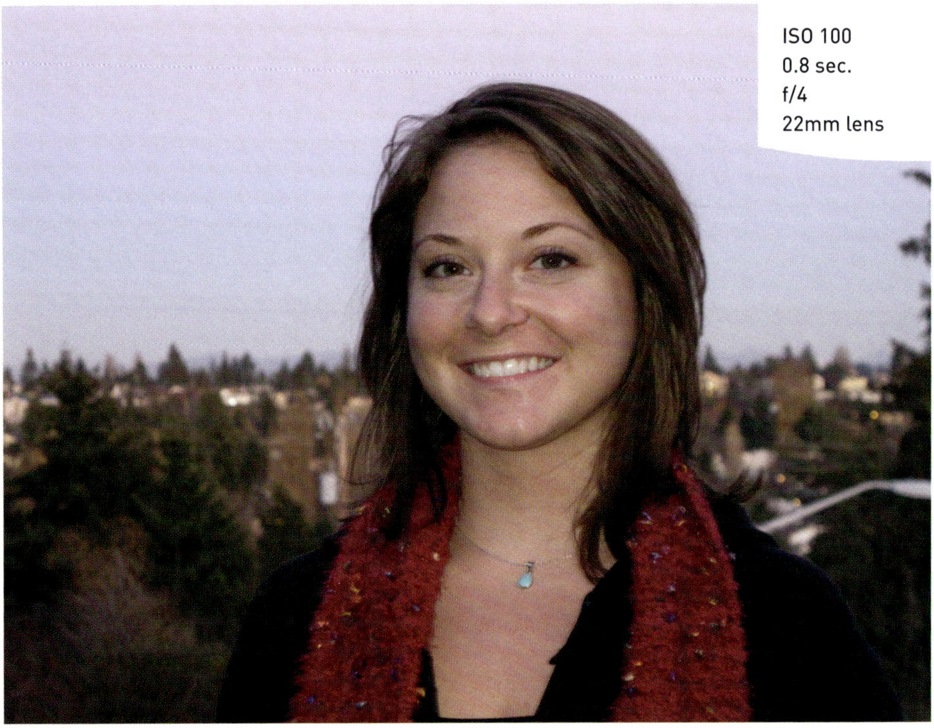

ISO 100
0.8 sec.
f/4
22mm lens

Also, since your shutter speed will be longer, it's a good idea to use a tripod or place your camera on a stable surface so the background elements don't end up looking shaky.

CREATIVE AUTO MODE

Let's face it—these automatic modes in the Basic zone are nice, but there will be times when you want more control over what the camera is doing and how your pictures look. In the Basic zone, this is where the Creative Auto (CA) mode comes in (**Figure 3.8**). You won't have total control over the picture-making process, but you will be able to make some adjustments to gain a little more creative control over things like image brightness and background sharpness.

To allow you to make these adjustments, the camera will display on the LCD a series of settings that can be changed by pressing the Q button and using the cross keys and the Main dial.

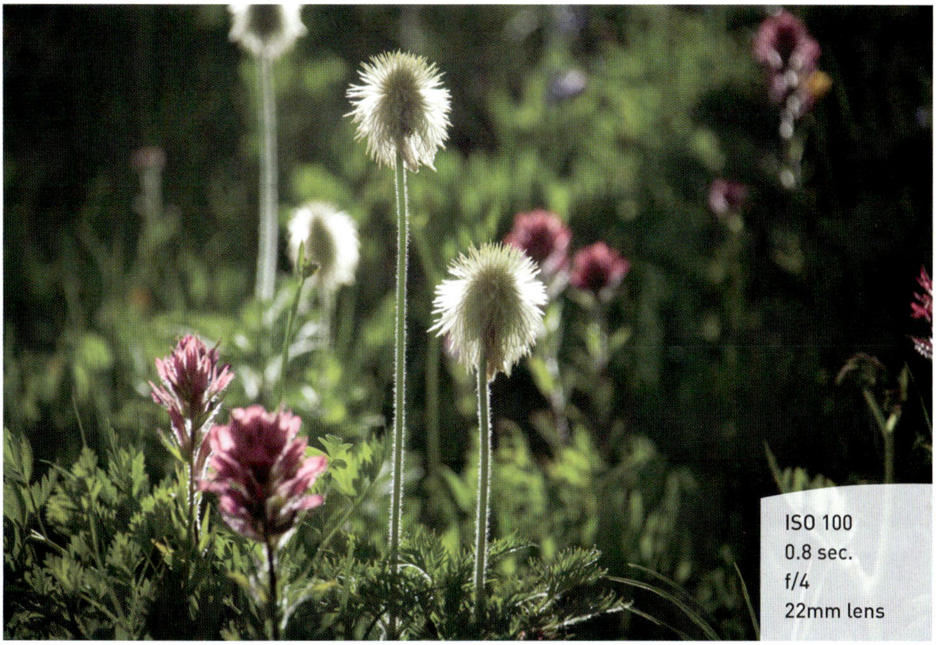

FIGURE 3.8
Creative Auto mode means you can change how your picture looks, such as creating a shallow depth-of-field effect.

AMBIENCE

If you want to change the look of your picture, you can change the Ambience setting and get just the effect you need for your subject. The choices include Standard, Vivid, Soft, Warm, Intense, Cool, Brighter, Darker, and Monochrome. The default setting is Standard, but to change this, press the Q button or tap the Q icon on the touchscreen, highlight the Ambience selection (the second button down on the right), change your selection, and press the Set button. You can also control the intensity of the effect that is applied by choosing the Level button just below the Ambience button (**Figure 3.9**).

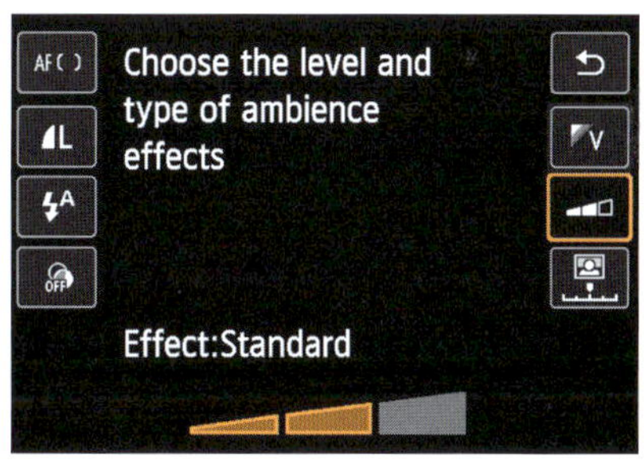

FIGURE 3.9
Change the look of your shot with the Ambience feature.

BACKGROUND SHARPNESS

This setting forces the camera to use either a larger or smaller aperture setting to change the depth of field in your image: The smaller the aperture (which means a larger number, such as f/16 or f/22), the greater the sharpness in your background. To change this setting, tap or highlight the Background scale. Then move the index point to the right for a sharper background or to the left for more blur (**Figure 3.10**). Each step will change the exposure by about one f-stop.

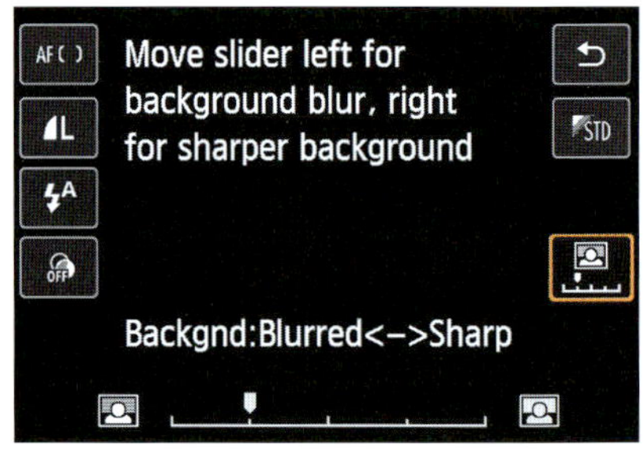

FIGURE 3.10
Moving to the left uses a larger aperture for a shallower depth of field.

CREATIVE FILTERS

The creative filters available in CA mode (and in other modes) apply preset effects to the images you capture. Give the photo a grainy black and white look, for example, or the appearance of a watercolor painting. Select the last button on the left and choose one of the following filters (**Figure 3.11**): Grainy B/W, Soft Focus, Fish-Eye Effect, Art Bold Effect, Water Painting Effect, Toy Camera Effect, or Miniature Effect (**Figure 3.12**).

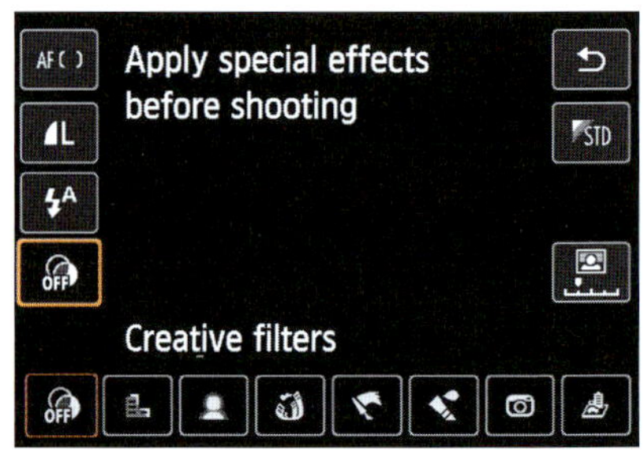

FIGURE 3.11
Choose from a selection of filter effects.

FLASH

When I first spied this option, I had to scratch my head: The EOS M doesn't include a built-in flash. However, if you own Canon's Speedlite 90EX external flash and attach it to the hot shoe, this option allows you to set the flash to one of three positions: Auto, On, or Off. In Auto, the flash will automatically fire whenever the camera determines that there isn't enough light in the scene for a proper exposure. If you want to force the flash to come on no matter what (as when you want to fill in some shadows), set the option to On. The Off setting will keep the flash from firing, just as it does in Flash Off mode. This feature works only with the 90EX; if any other flash is mounted on the camera, the mode remains set to On.

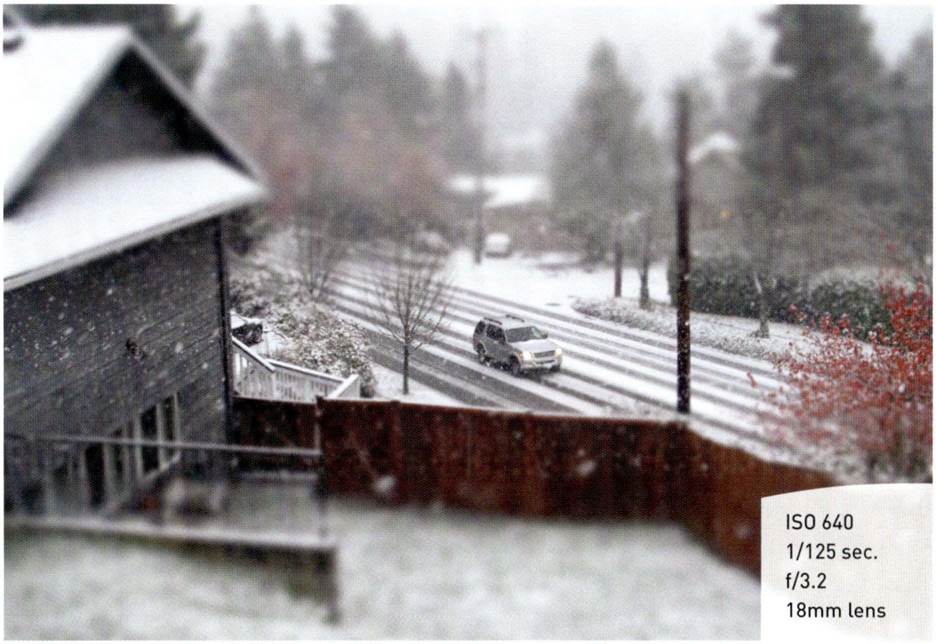

FIGURE 3.12 Miniature Effect concentrates focus on one area and blurs the rest, making otherwise normal scenes appear as if they're miniatures.

SPECIALTY MODES

The Basic zone includes two other modes: Handheld Night Scene and HDR Backlight Control. Since these modes handle specific shooting scenarios, we will cover them later in the book. Look for both modes in Chapter 10.

DRIVE MODES

Five drive modes are available in your camera's shooting modes: Single shooting, Continuous shooting, 10-second Self-timer/Remote, 2-second Self-timer, and Continuous Self-timer (**Figure 3.13**). In Single shooting, the camera takes only one picture when the shutter button is depressed all the way. Taking another picture requires releasing the button and then pressing it again. In Continuous shooting, the camera continually takes photographs at about three frames per second until you release the button. You will probably want to use this setting for capturing action.

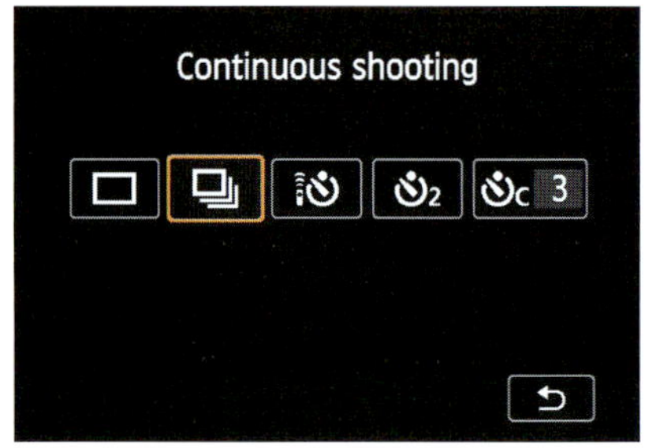

FIGURE 3.13
Decide if you want to take one shot at a time or use a more rapid-fire approach.

The 10-second Self-timer/Remote option allows you to depress the shutter button and have the camera automatically fire 10 seconds later. The obvious use for this setting is to run around and get yourself in the picture. You might also consider using it for macro (close-up) or landscape photography when you can set your camera on a tripod or a stable surface and press the shutter. The self-timer will let you take the picture without having to worry about camera shake from physically having your hands on the camera while activating the shutter. This is also the mode you should select for using a remote release. Of course, if you are using the self-timer instead of a remote but don't need a long time before the shutter fires, then consider the 2-second mode. This option works like the 10-second setting, except you have only 2 seconds between pressing the shutter and taking the picture.

The final mode is Continuous Self-timer, which lets you use the self-timer to take a number of images (from two to ten) with only one press of the shutter release button.

WHY YOU MAY NEVER WANT TO USE THE BASIC ZONE AGAIN

With so many easy-to-use camera modes, why use anything else? Well, the first thing that comes to mind is control. It is the number one reason for using a camera that's more advanced than a point-and-shoot model. The ability to control every aspect of your photography will open up creative avenues that just aren't available in the Basic zone. Let's look at what we are giving up when we work in the Basic zone.

- **ISO.** None of the automatic modes in the Basic zone allow you to change the ISO setting from the default of Auto ISO. This will undoubtedly lead to unwanted digital noise in your images when the ISO begins to reach up into the higher settings.
- **Picture style.** If you are using anything but Creative Auto mode, you cannot change the picture style or any of its attributes to fine-tune your images.
- **White balance.** There is no choice available for white balance in many of the modes. You are simply stuck with the Auto setting. This isn't necessarily a bad thing, but your camera doesn't always get it right. You can make some adjustments to the lighting or scene type in a few of the basic modes—such as Portrait and Landscape—but not in the fully automatic modes.
- **Autofocus.** Each of the modes uses a specific focus type. Sports uses the Servo focus mode, for example. There is no way to change these.
- **Exposure compensation.** None of the modes allows you to adjust the exposure to brighten or darken your image.
- **Color space.** The default is sRGB, and there is no way to change it. If you plan to print any of your pictures, the preferred yet unavailable setting is Adobe RGB.

FOCUS MODES ON THE CANON EOS M

Two focus modes are available on the EOS M. When you're in the Creative zone (discussed in the next chapter), you can easily select the mode that will be most beneficial to the type of photography you're doing. The standard mode is called One Shot, which allows you to focus on one spot and hold the focus until you take the picture or release the shutter button. The Servo mode will constantly refocus the camera on your subject the entire time you are depressing the shutter release button; this is great for sports and action photography.

Chapter 3 Assignments

These assignments will have you shooting in the various Basic modes so you can experience the advantages and disadvantages of using them in your daily photography.

Shooting in Scene Intelligent Auto mode

It's time to give up complete control and just concentrate on what you see in the viewfinder. Set your camera to Scene Intelligent Auto and practice shooting in a variety of conditions, both indoors and outside. Take notice of the camera settings when you are reviewing your pictures. Try picking a focus and then recomposing before taking the picture.

Checking out Portrait mode

Grab your favorite photogenic person and start shooting in Portrait mode. Try switching between Scene Intelligent Auto and Portrait mode while photographing the same person in the same setting. You should see a difference in the sharpness of the background as well as the skin tones. If you are using a zoom lens, set it to about 50mm if available.

Capturing the scenery with Landscape and Close-up modes

Take your camera outside for some landscape and macro work. Find a nice scene, and with your widest available lens, take some pictures using Landscape mode. Then switch back to Scene Intelligent Auto so you can compare the settings used for each image as well as the changes to colors and sharpness. Now, while you are still outside, find something in the foreground—a leaf or a flower–and switch the camera to Close-up mode. See how close you can get, and take note of the f-stop that the mode uses. Then switch to Scene Intelligent Auto and shoot the same subject.

Stopping the action with Sports mode

This assignment will require that you find a subject that is in motion. That could be the traffic in front of your home or a child at play. The only real requirement is that the subject be moving. This will be your opportunity to test out Sports mode. There isn't a lot to worry about here–just point and shoot. Try shooting a few frames one at a time. Then switch the drive mode to Continuous, and hold down the shutter button and shoot a burst of about five or six frames. It will help if your subject is in good available light to start with so that the camera won't be forced to use high ISOs.

Capturing the mood with Night Portrait mode

If you own a flash, wait for it to get dark outside and have a friend sit in a location that has an incandescent lamp in the background (not too bright, though). Switch the camera to Night Portrait, and then, using a wide enough angle to see the subject and some of the room in the background, take a photo. The goal is to get a well-lit picture of your subject and balance that with the light from the lamp in the background. For a comparison, switch the camera back to Scene Intelligent Auto and shoot the same subject. Take notice of the difference in the brightness of the background. Now, take another picture with the camera set to Flash Off, but this time, have your subject sit near the lamp so that it lights up their face. Ask them to sit as still as possible while you hold the camera as still as possible.

Getting a little more creative with Creative Auto mode

Now it's time to have a little fun exploring the options that are available to you using the Creative Auto shooting mode. Get a feel for navigating through the options. Then, working your way down the screen, start making adjustments to each option, taking a picture with each to see how it affects the final photo. The key here is to select one scene and then use it for each change in your settings. This will give you a reference for how each of the images will be affected by changing the options. Try using more than one option to fine-tune your photos.

Share your results with the book's Flickr group!

Join the group here: flickr.com/groups/eosmfromsnapshotstogreatshots

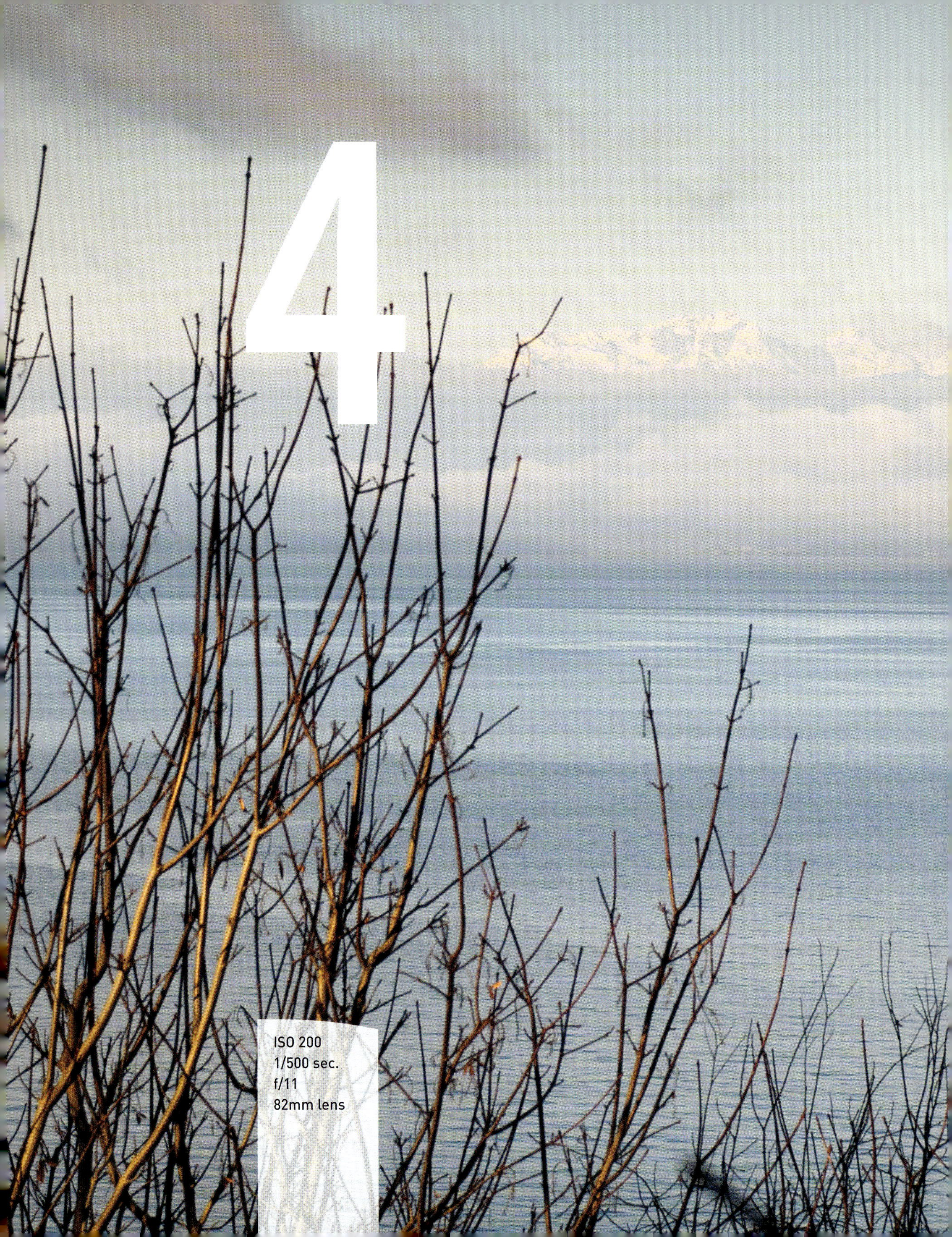

4

ISO 200
1/500 sec.
f/11
82mm lens

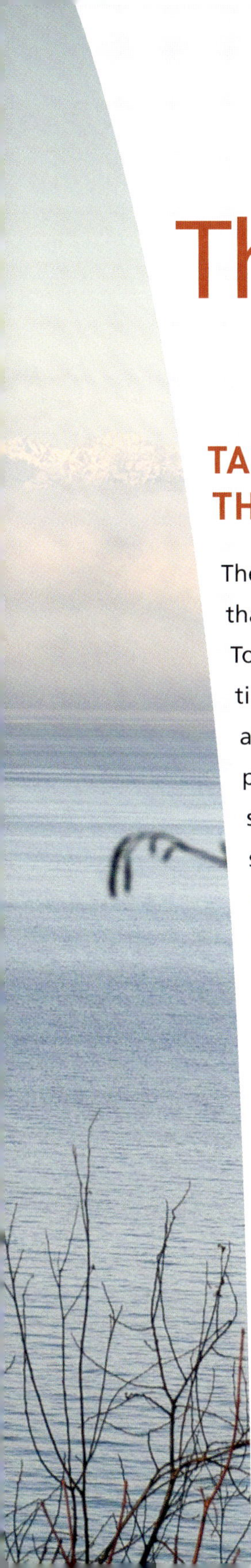

The Creative Zone

TAKING YOUR PHOTOGRAPHY TO THE NEXT LEVEL

The Creative zone is the name given by Canon to the shooting modes that offer you the greatest amount of control over your photography. To anyone who has been involved with photography for any period of time, these modes are known as the backbones of photography. They allow you to influence two of the most important factors for taking great photographs: *aperture* and *shutter speed*. To access these modes, you simply turn the Mode dial to the Creative mode of your choice and begin shooting. But wouldn't it be nice to know exactly what those modes control and how to make them do our bidding? Well, if you really want to take that next step in controlling your photography, it is essential that you understand not only how to control these modes, but why and when to adjust them so that you get the results you want. So let's move that Mode dial to the first of our Creative modes: Program mode.

PORING OVER THE PICTURE

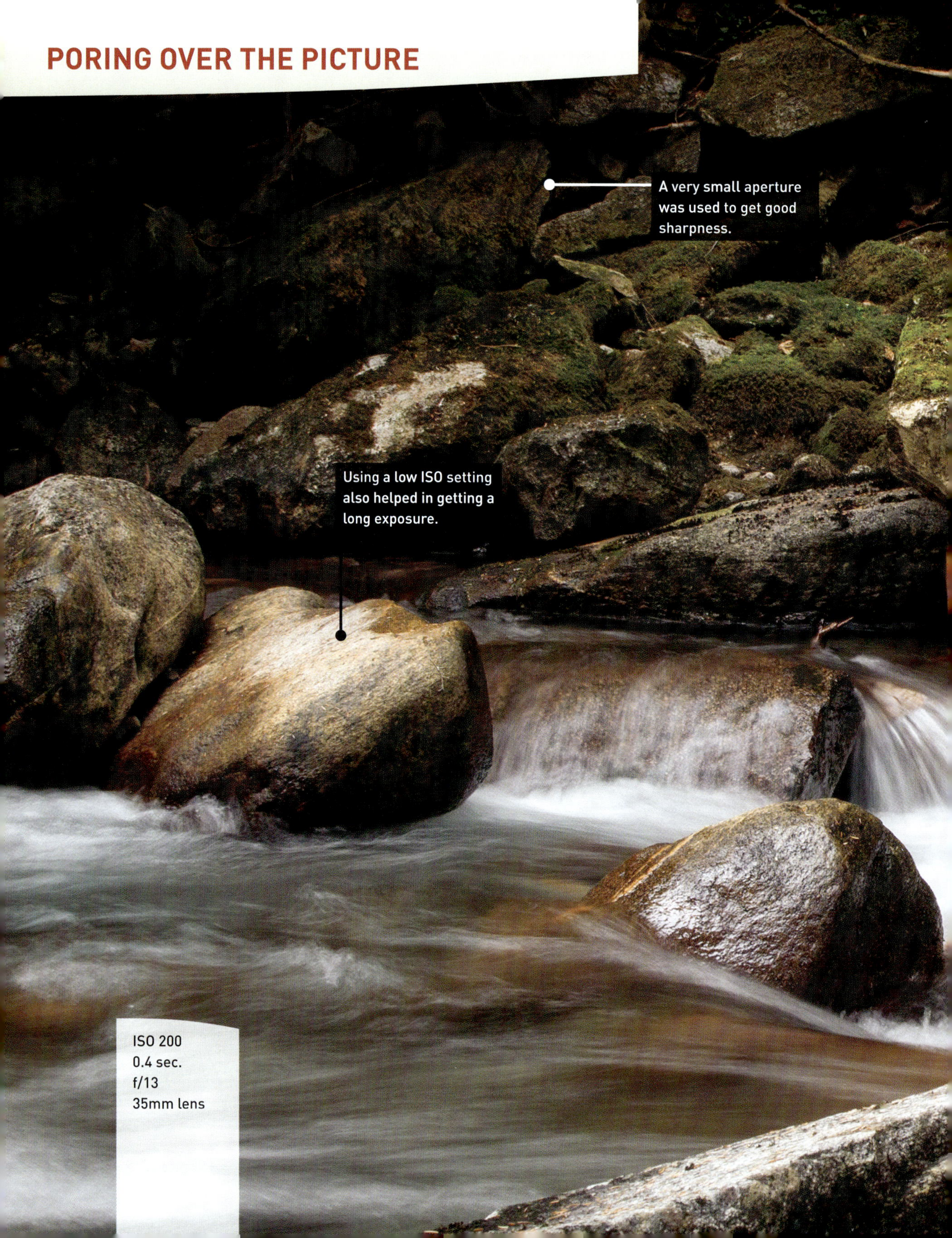

A very small aperture was used to get good sharpness.

Using a low ISO setting also helped in getting a long exposure.

ISO 200
0.4 sec.
f/13
35mm lens

A sure-fire way to boost your photographic confidence is to find a stream and adjust your shutter speed to create silky flowing water. It's easy to do, and you get to spend time next to burbling water (truly one of my favorite things in the world). Look for good compositional elements that work with the water.

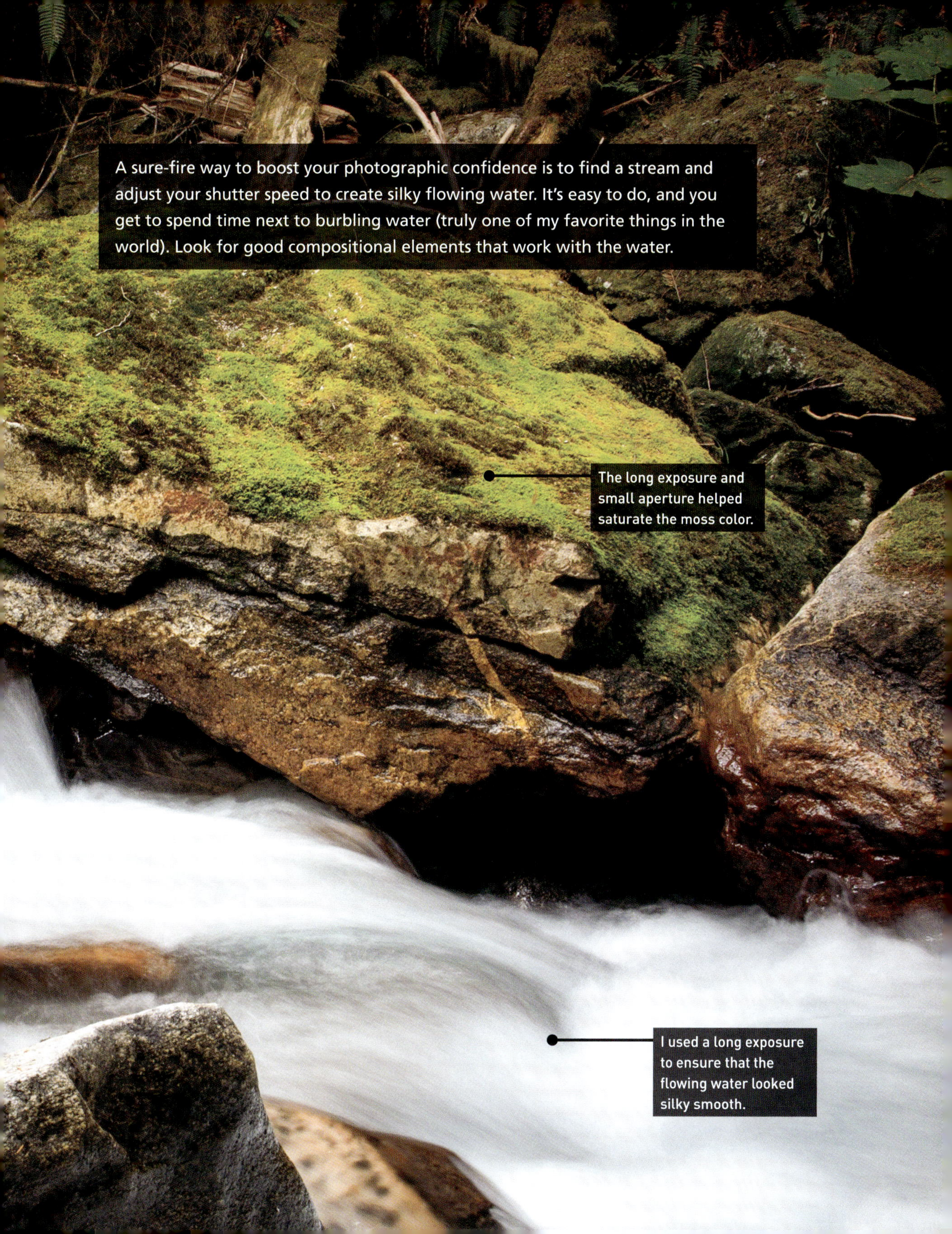

PORING OVER THE PICTURE

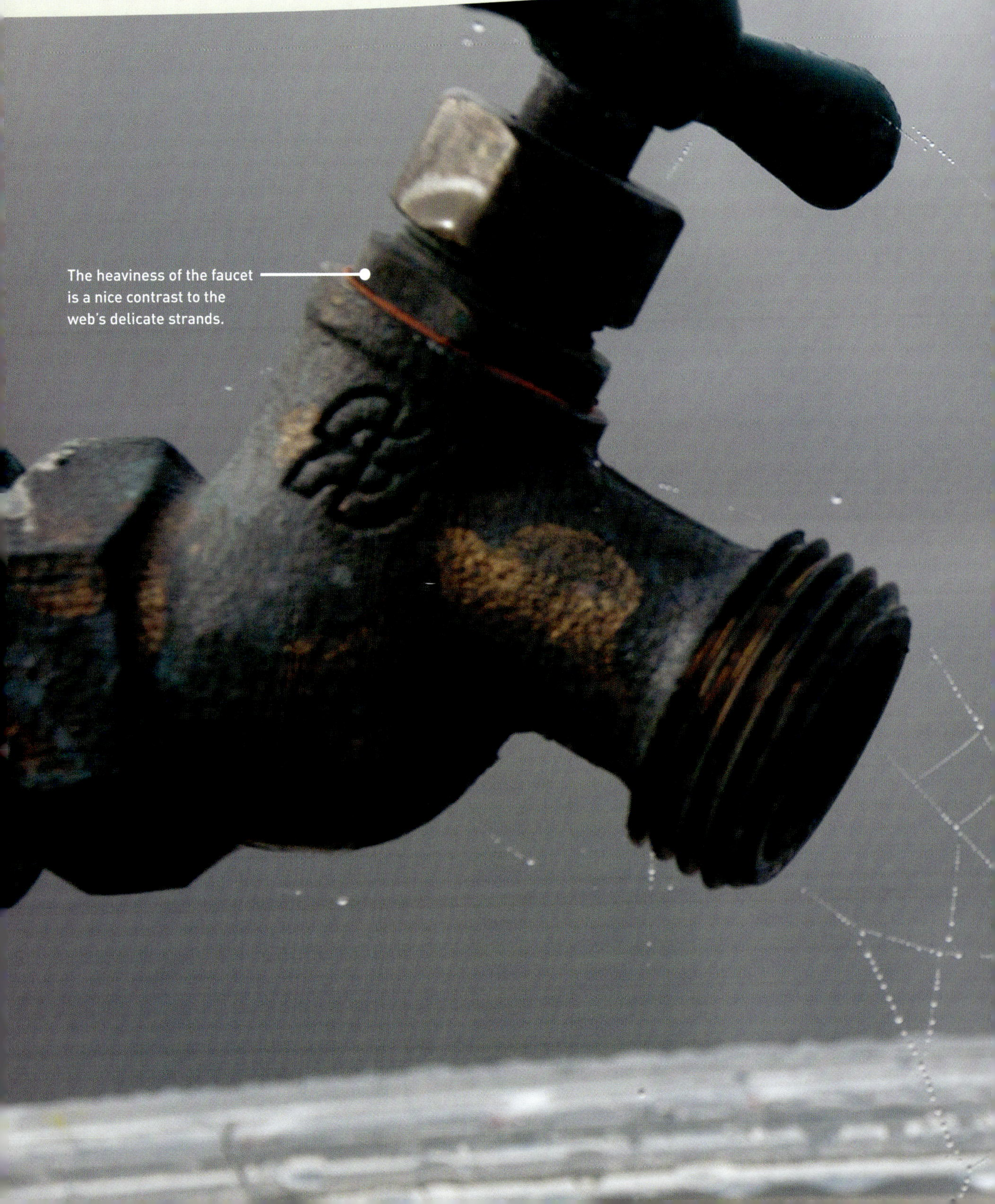

The heaviness of the faucet is a nice contrast to the web's delicate strands.

Walking the docks on a foggy morning around the Puget Sound in Washington, the texture of this faucet caught my eye. But it wasn't until I got closer that I saw this dew-dappled spider web clinging to the ends. Having a tripod helped me set up the shot, careful not to bounce or breathe too hard and risk destroying the threads.

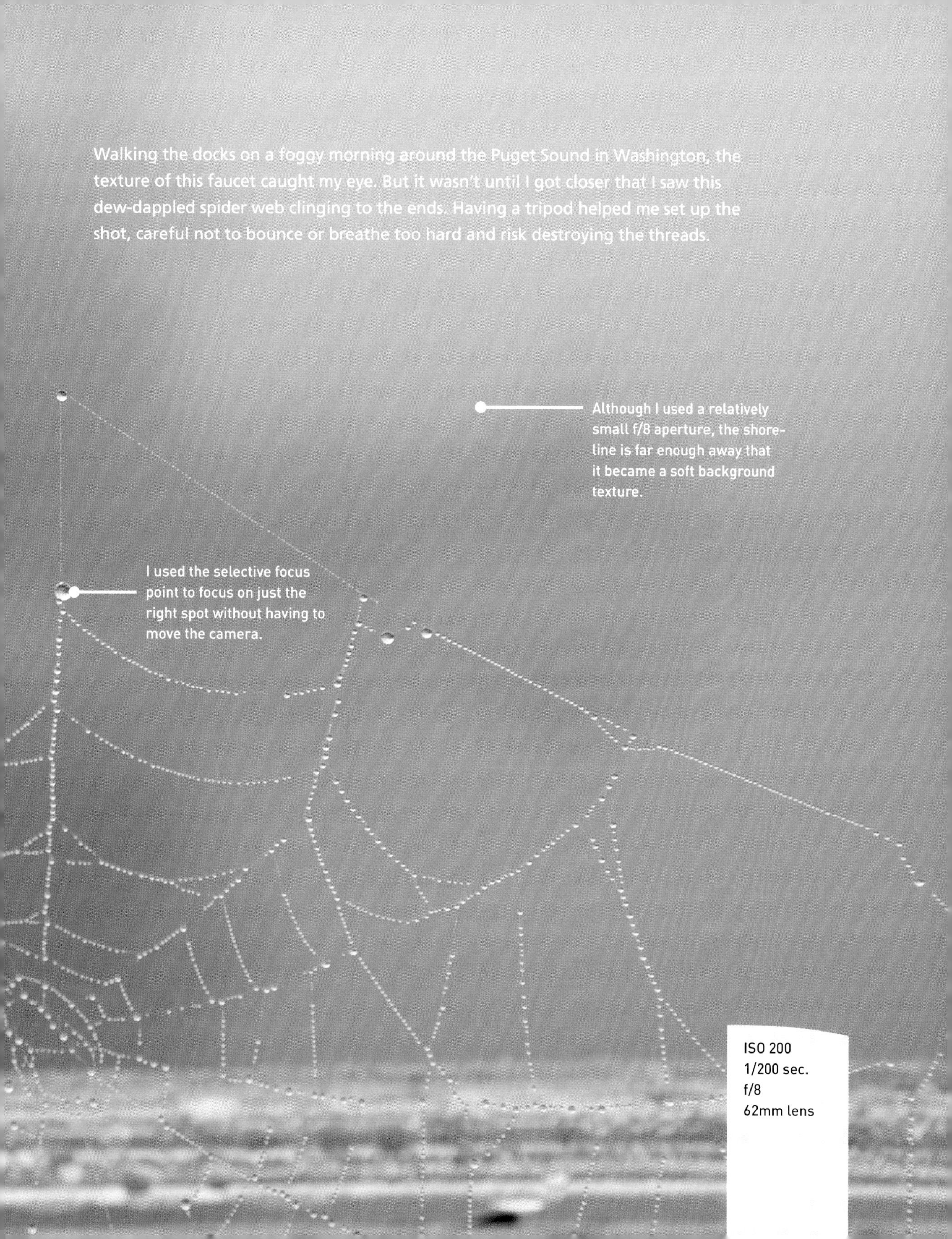

Although I used a relatively small f/8 aperture, the shoreline is far enough away that it became a soft background texture.

I used the selective focus point to focus on just the right spot without having to move the camera.

ISO 200
1/200 sec.
f/8
62mm lens

P: PROGRAM MODE

P There is a reason that Program mode is only one click away from the Basic modes: With respect to apertures and shutter speeds, the camera is doing most of the thinking for you. So, if that is the case, why even bother with Program mode? First, let me say that it is very rare that I will use Program mode, because it just doesn't give as much control over the image-making process as the other Creative modes. There are occasions, however, when it comes in handy, like when I am shooting in widely changing lighting conditions and don't have the time to think through all of my options, or when I'm not very concerned with having ultimate control of the scene. Think of a picnic outdoors in a partial shade/sun environment—I want great-looking pictures, but I'm not looking for anything to hang in a museum. If that's the scenario, why choose Program over one of the Basic modes? Because it gives me choices and control that none of the Basic modes, including Creative Auto, can deliver.

Manual Callout

To see a comparison of all of the different modes in the Basic and Creative zones, check out the tables on pages 296–297 of your owner's manual.

WHEN TO USE PROGRAM (P) MODE INSTEAD OF THE BASIC ZONE MODES

- When shooting in a casual environment where quick adjustments are needed
- When you want control over the ISO
- If you want to make corrections to the white balance
- If you want or need to shoot in the Adobe RGB color space

Let's go back to our picnic scenario. As I said, the light is moving from deep shadow to bright sunlight, which means the camera is trying to balance our three photo factors (ISO, aperture, and shutter speed) to make a good exposure. From Chapter 1, we know that Auto ISO is just not a consideration, so we have already turned that feature off (you did change it, didn't you?). Well, in Program mode, you can choose which ISO you would like the camera to base its exposure on. The lower the ISO number, the better the quality of our photographs, but the less light sensitive the camera becomes. It's a balancing act, with the main goal always being to keep the ISO as low as possible—too low an ISO, and we will get camera shake in our images from a long shutter speed; too high an ISO means we will have an unacceptable amount of digital noise. For our purposes, let's go ahead and select ISO 400 so that we provide enough sensitivity for those shadows while allowing the camera to use shutter speeds that are fast enough to stop motion.

With the ISO selected, we can now make use of the other controls built into Program mode. By rotating the Main dial, we have the ability to shift the program settings. Remember, your camera is using the internal light meter to pick what it believes are suitable exposure values, but sometimes it doesn't know what it's looking at and how you want those values applied (**Figures 4.1** and **4.2**). With the program shift, you can influence what the shot will look like. Do you need faster shutter speeds in order to stop the action? Just turn the Main dial clockwise. Do you want a smaller aperture so that you get a narrow depth of field? Then turn the dial counterclockwise until you get the desired aperture. The camera shifts the shutter speed and aperture accordingly in order to get a proper exposure, and you will get the benefit of your choice as a result.

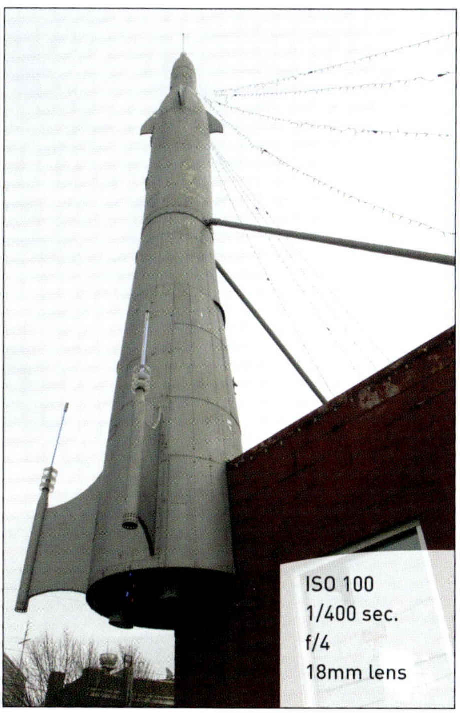

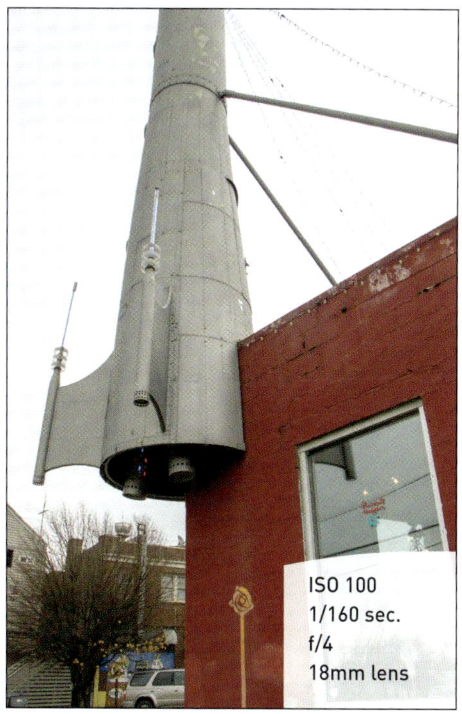

FIGURE 4.1
(left) With a lot of gray sky visible in the shot, the overall exposure is dark.

FIGURE 4.2
(right) With more of the building in the frame, the light meter provides a better exposure.

Let's set the camera for Program mode and see how we can make this come together.

SETTING UP AND SHOOTING IN PROGRAM MODE

1. Tap the Mode button on the LCD, choose P, and tap the Return button (⮌).
2. To select your ISO, tap the ISO button in the lower-right corner of the screen, turn the Main dial or drag to the desired setting, and tap the Return button.
3. Point the camera at your subject and then activate the camera meter by depressing the shutter button halfway.
4. View the exposure information in the bottom of the LCD, to the left of the Exposure Compensation control (**A**).
5. Use your index finger to roll the Main dial left and right to see the changed exposure values.
6. Select the exposure that is right for you and start shooting. (Don't worry if you aren't sure what the right exposure is. We will start working on making the right choices for those great shots beginning with the next chapter.)

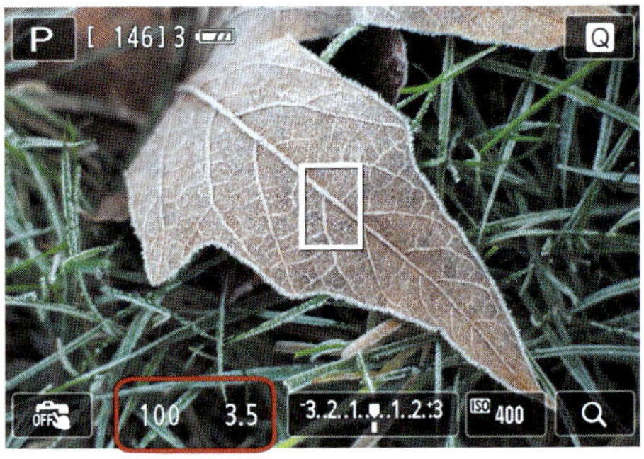

A

STARTING POINTS FOR ISO SELECTION

There is a lot of discussion concerning ISO in this and other chapters, but it might be helpful if you know where your starting points should be for your ISO settings. The first thing you should always try to do is use the lowest possible ISO setting. That being said, here are some good starting points for your ISO settings:

- 100: Bright, sunny day
- 200: Hazy, or outdoor shade on a sunny day
- 400: Indoor lighting at night or cloudy conditions outside
- 800–1600: Late night, low-light conditions or sporting arenas at night

These are just suggestions, and your ISO selection will depend on a number of factors that will be discussed later in the book. You might have to push your ISO even higher as needed, but at least now you know where to start.

TV: SHUTTER PRIORITY MODE

Tv Tv mode is what we photographers commonly refer to as Shutter Priority mode. If you dig deep in your manual, you will see that Tv stands for Time Value. I'm not sure who came up with this term, but I can tell you that it wasn't a photographer. In all my years of shooting, I don't ever recall thinking, "Hey, this would be a great situation to use Time Value mode." But you don't need to know why it is called Tv mode; the important thing is to know why and when to use it.

Like Program mode, Tv mode gives us more freedom to control certain aspects of our photography. In this case, we are talking about shutter speed. The selected shutter speed determines just how long you expose your camera's sensor to light. The longer it remains open, the more time your sensor has to gather light. The shutter speed also, to a large degree, determines how sharp your photographs are. This is different from the image being sharply in focus. Two of the major influences on the sharpness of an image are camera shake and the subject's movement. Because a slower shutter speed means that light from your subject is hitting the sensor for a longer period of time, any movement by you or your subject will show up in your photos as blur.

SHUTTER SPEEDS

A *slow* shutter speed refers to leaving the shutter open for a long period of time—like 1/30 of a second or longer. A *fast* shutter speed means that the shutter is open for a very short period of time—like 1/250 of a second or less.

WHEN TO USE SHUTTER PRIORITY (TV) MODE

- When working with fast-moving subjects where you want to freeze the action (**Figure 4.3**); much more on this in Chapter 5
- When you want to emphasize movement in your subject with motion blur (**Figure 4.4**)
- When you want to use a long exposure to gather light over a long period of time (**Figure 4.5**); more on this in Chapter 8
- When you want to create silky-looking water in a waterfall (**Figure 4.6**)

FIGURE 4.3
A fast shutter speed can freeze action.

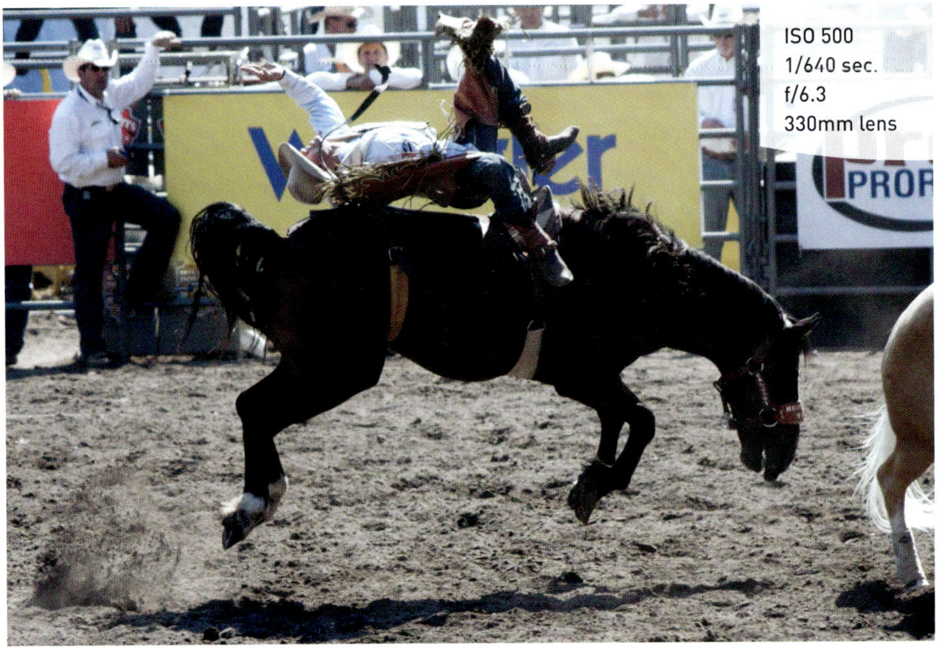

ISO 500
1/640 sec.
f/6.3
330mm lens

FIGURE 4.4
Slowing down the shutter speed allows your photographs to convey a sense of movement.

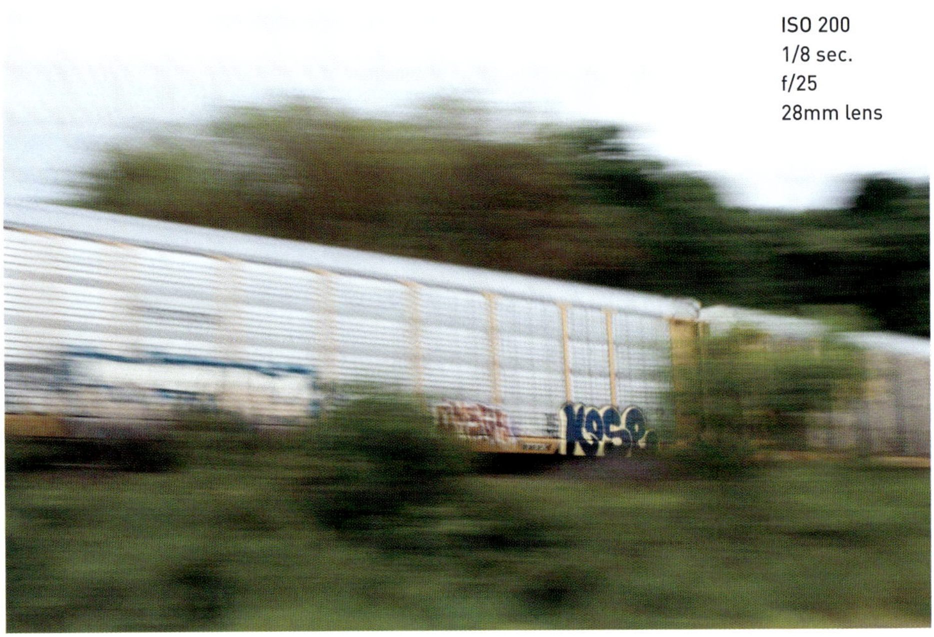

ISO 200
1/8 sec.
f/25
28mm lens

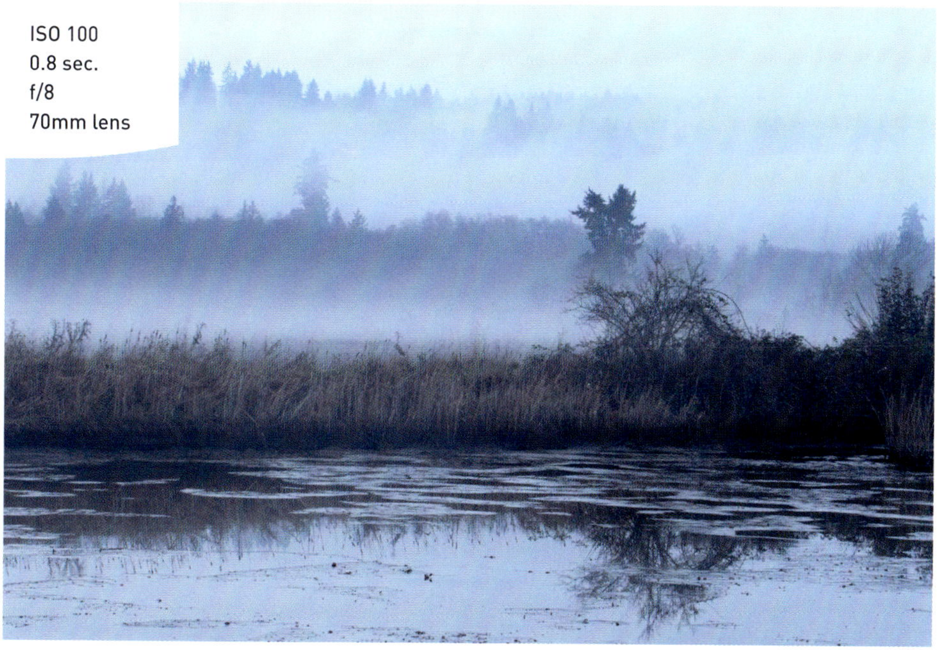

ISO 100
0.8 sec.
f/8
70mm lens

FIGURE 4.5
A long exposure combined with a small aperture and a steady tripod pulled light out of this late-dusk setting.

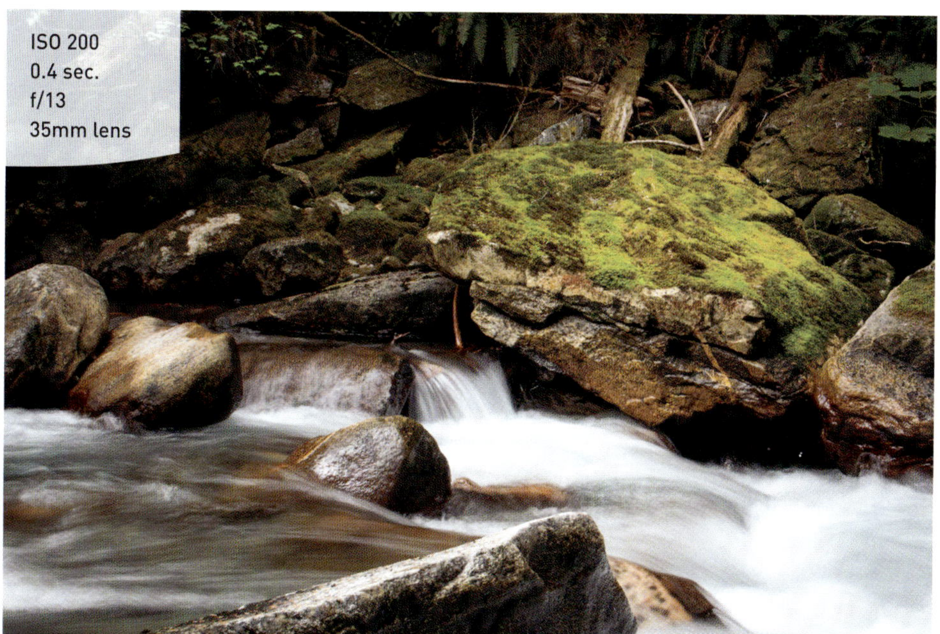

ISO 200
0.4 sec.
f/13
35mm lens

FIGURE 4.6
Increasing the length of the exposure gives flowing water a silky look.

As you can see, the subject of your photo usually determines whether or not you will use Tv mode. It is important that you be able to visualize the result of using a particular shutter speed. The great thing about shooting with digital cameras is that you get instant feedback by checking your shot on the LCD. But what if your subject won't give you a do-over? Such is often the case when shooting sporting events. It's not like you can ask the quarterback to throw that touchdown pass again because your last shot was blurry from a slow shutter speed. This is why it's important to know what those speeds represent in terms of their ability to stop the action.

First, let's examine just how much control you have over the shutter speeds. The EOS M has a shutter speed range from 1/4000 of a second all the way down to 30 seconds. With that much latitude, you should have enough control to capture almost any subject. The other thing to think about is that Tv mode is considered a "semi-automatic" mode. This means that you are taking control over one aspect of the total exposure while the camera handles the other. In this instance, you are controlling the shutter speed and the camera is controlling the aperture. This is important to know because there will be times that you want to use a particular shutter speed but your lens won't be able to accommodate your request.

For example, you might encounter this problem when shooting in low-light situations: If you are shooting a fast-moving subject that will blur at a shutter speed slower than 1/125 of a second but your lens's largest aperture is f/3.5, you might see your aperture value begin to blink. This is your warning that there won't be enough light available for the shot—due to the limitations of the lens—so your picture will be underexposed (too dark).

Another case where you might run into this situation is when you are shooting moving water. To get that look of silky, flowing water, it's usually necessary to use a shutter speed of at least 1/15 of a second, if not longer. If your waterfall is in full sunlight, you may get that blinking aperture display once again because the lens you are using only closes down to f/22 at its smallest opening. In this instance, your camera is warning you that you will be overexposing your image (too light). There are workarounds for these problems, which we will discuss later (see Chapter 7), but it is important to know that there can be limitations when using Tv mode.

SETTING UP AND SHOOTING IN TV MODE

1. Tap the Mode button on the LCD, choose Tv, and tap the Return button (⮌).
2. Select your ISO: Tap the ISO button in the lower-right corner of the screen, turn the Main dial or drag to the desired setting, and tap the Return button.
3. Point the camera at your subject and then activate the camera meter by depressing the shutter button halfway.
4. View the exposure information in the bottom area of the LCD.

5. While the meter is activated, use your index finger to roll the Main dial left and right to see the changed exposure values. Roll the dial to the right for faster shutter speeds and to the left for slower speeds.

AV: APERTURE PRIORITY MODE

You wouldn't know it from its name, but Av mode is one of the most useful and popular modes in the Creative zone. Av stands for Aperture Value, and like Time Value, it's another term that you'll seldom hear a photographer toss around. Av, more commonly referred to as Aperture Priority mode, is also deemed a semiautomatic mode because it allows you to once again control one factor of exposure while the camera adjusts for the other.

WHEN TO USE APERTURE PRIORITY (AV) MODE

- When shooting portraits or wildlife (**Figure 4.7**)
- When shooting most landscape photography (**Figure 4.8**)
- When shooting macro, or close-up, photography (**Figure 4.9**)
- When shooting architectural photography, which often benefits from a large depth of field (**Figure 4.10**)

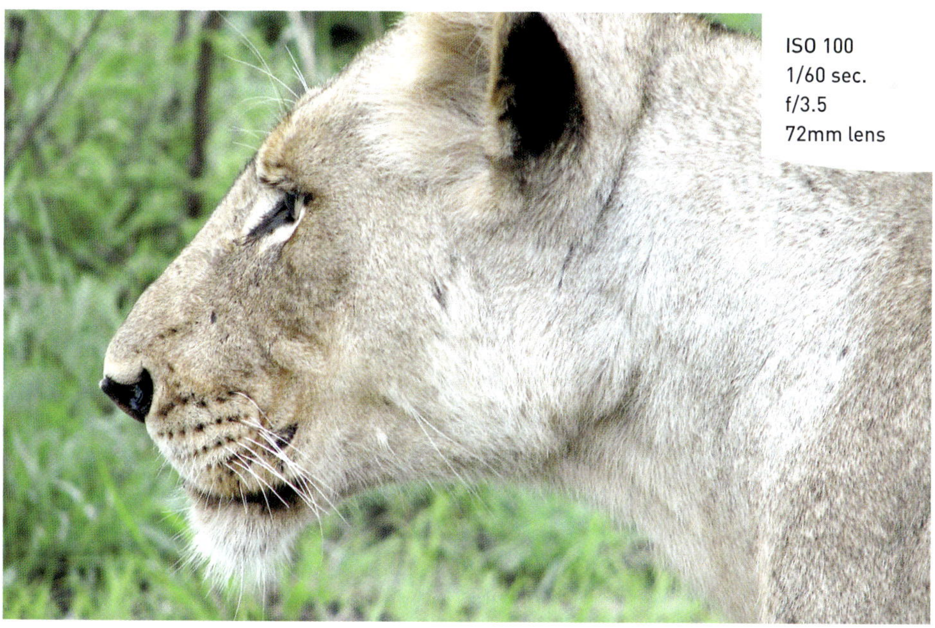

ISO 100
1/60 sec.
f/3.5
72mm lens

FIGURE 4.7
A fairly large aperture coupled with a long focal length created a very blurry background, so all the emphasis was left on the subject.

FIGURE 4.8
The smaller aperture setting brings sharpness to near and far objects.

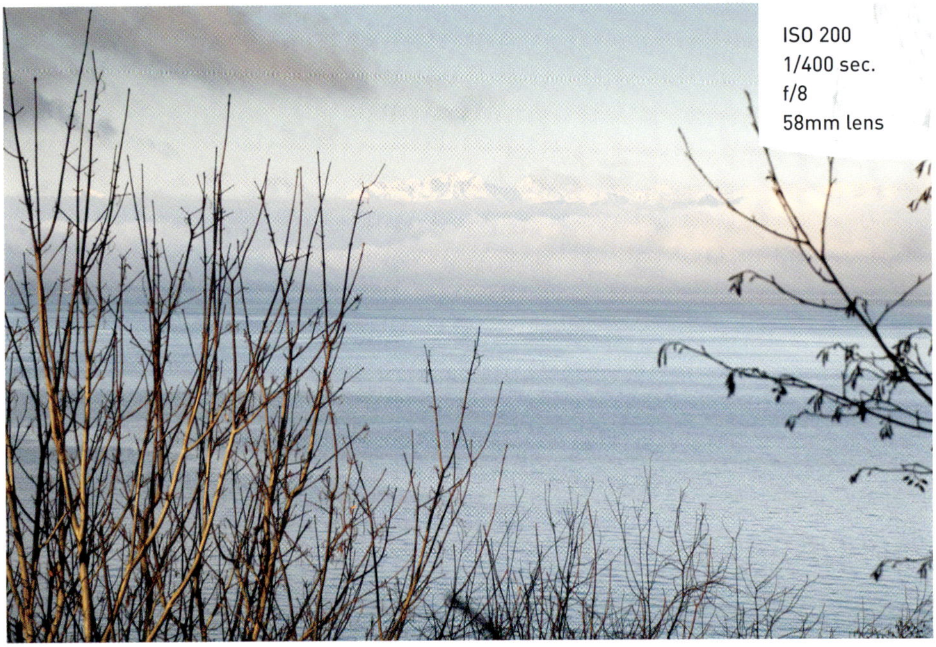

ISO 200
1/400 sec.
f/8
58mm lens

FIGURE 4.9
Small apertures give more sharpness in macro images.

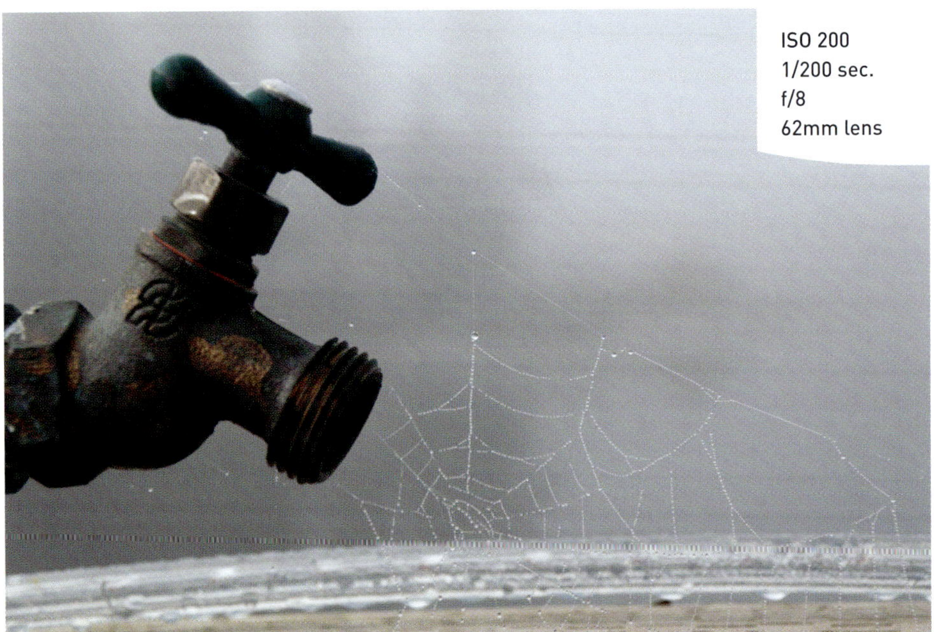

ISO 200
1/200 sec.
f/8
62mm lens

(**Figure 6.13**). The Red and Yellow filters usually lighten skin, while the Green filter can make skin appear a bit darker. Experiment to see which one works best for your subject.

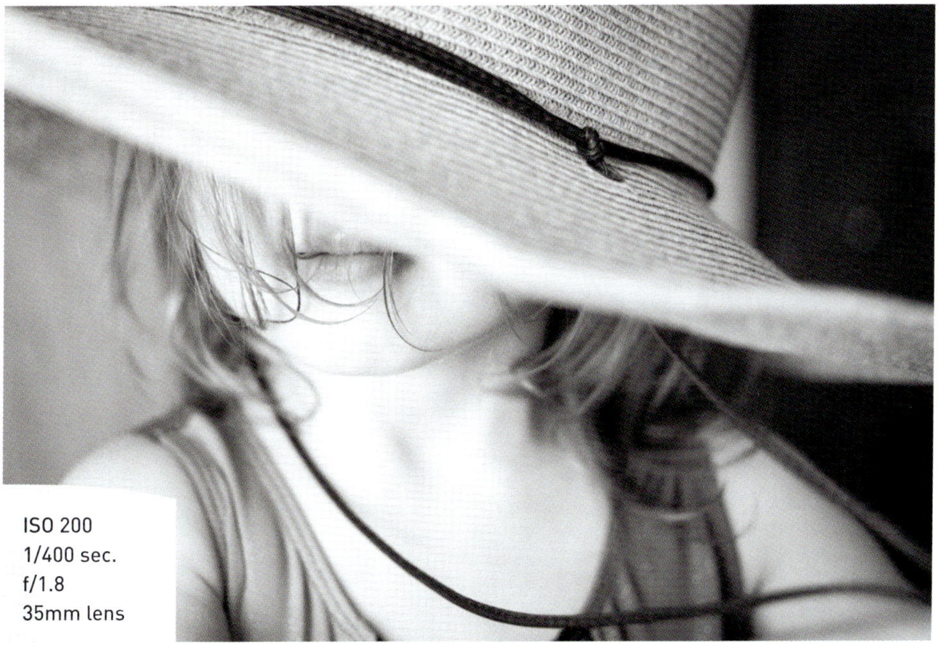

ISO 200
1/400 sec.
f/1.8
35mm lens

FIGURE 6.12
The Monochrome picture style creates high-quality black and white portraits.

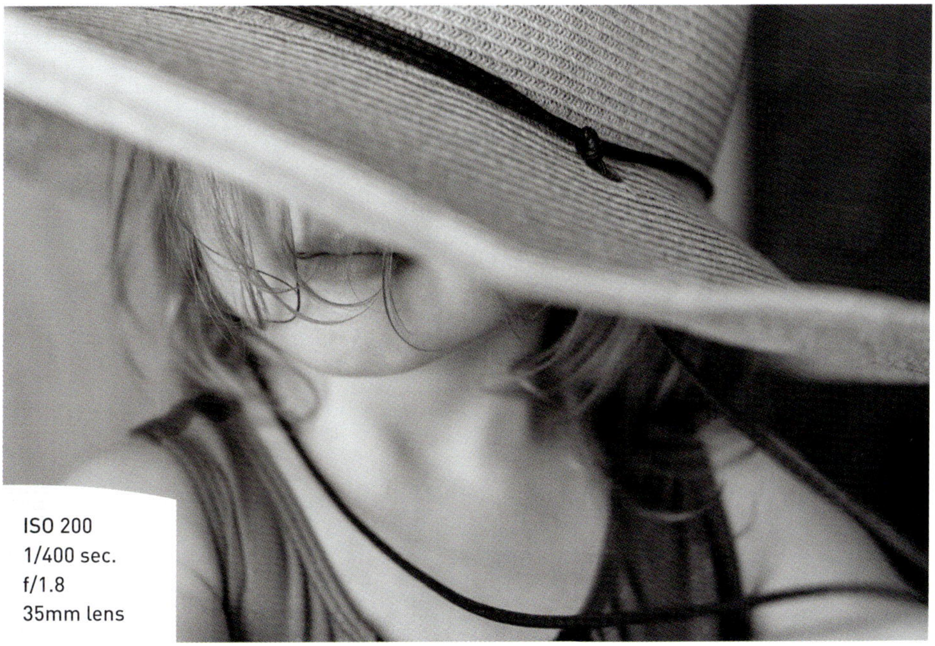

ISO 200
1/400 sec.
f/1.8
35mm lens

FIGURE 6.13
Monochrome filters, such as the Green filter here, create different black and white looks.

But wait, doesn't shooting with the Monochrome style throw out the color information? I've long resisted in-camera effects like this because I don't want to discard image information from the start. If you do it right, however, you can get a nice monochrome *and* a color original. The picture styles are automatically applied when shooting with the JPEG file format. If you are shooting in RAW, the picture that shows up on your rear LCD display will look black and white, but it appears as a color image when you open it in desktop software. Instead, set the EOS M's format to RAW+JPEG; you end up with a monochrome JPEG and a color RAW file for each shot.

SETTING YOUR PICTURE STYLE TO MONOCHROME

1. Start by pressing the Quick Control/Set button.
2. Tap the Picture Style button (third down on the right) (**A**).
3. Tap to highlight the Monochrome setting, and lock it in by pressing the Set button again (**B**). Your camera will continue to shoot with the Monochrome picture style until you change it to another setting.

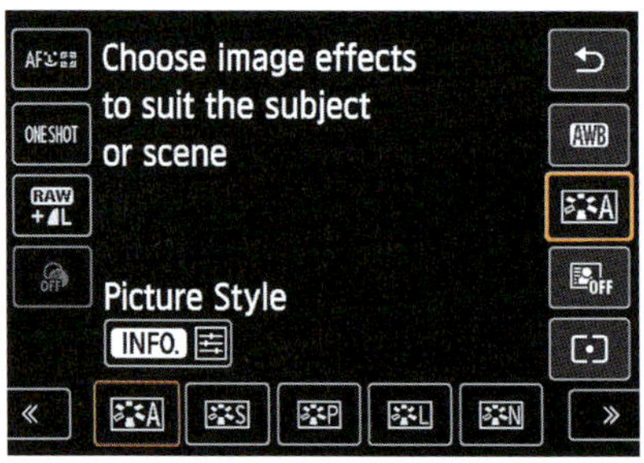

A

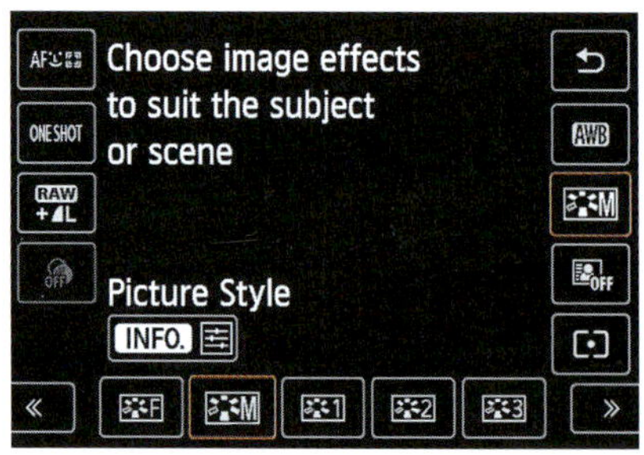

B

CUSTOMIZING THE PICTURE STYLE SETTINGS

1. When you're in the Picture Style section of the menu where you have Monochrome selected, press the Info button.
2. Tap to highlight the setting you would like to change, and press the Set button.
3. Now tap or use the Left/Right cross keys to move the cursor to a new position on the scale (the default setting will remain marked with a gray arrow) or to select a different filter, and press the Set button (**C**).
4. Perform the same process for the other options, then press the Set button to start shooting.

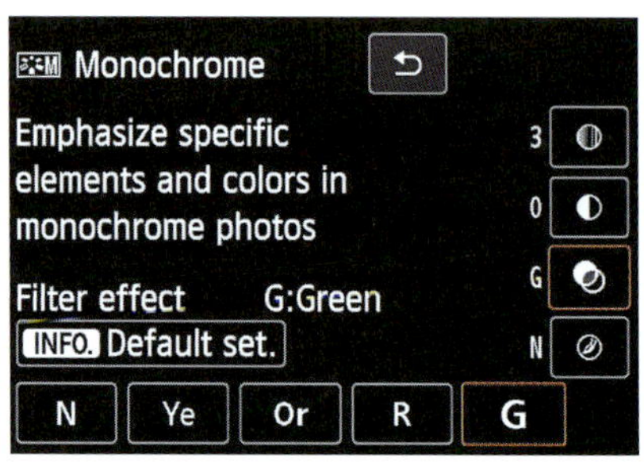

C

USE FILL FLASH FOR REDUCING SHADOWS

A common problem when taking pictures of people outside, especially during the midday hours, is that the overhead sun can create dark shadows under the eyes and chin. You could have your subject turn his or her face to the sun, but that is usually considered cruel and unusual punishment. So how can you have your subject's back to the sun and still get a decent exposure of the face? Try using a flash to fill in the shadows. This also works well when you are photographing someone who's wearing a baseball cap or someone who has a bright scene behind them (**Figure 6.14**). The fill flash helps lighten the subject so they don't appear in shadow, while providing a really nice catchlight in the eyes.

The key to using the flash as a fill is to not use it on full power. If you do, the camera tries to balance the flash with the daylight, resulting in a flat and featureless face.

SETTING UP AND SHOOTING WITH FILL FLASH

1. Attach the 90EX flash to the hotshoe of the EOS M and power it on.
2. Press the Menu button and use the Main dial to access the first screen.
3. Select the External Speedlite Control option and press the Set button.
4. Select Flash function settings and press the Set button.
5. Tap the Flash exposure compensation button (**A**).
6. Use the Left and Right cross keys to select the desired amount of flash compensation (**B**) and then press Set.
7. Lightly press the shutter release button to exit the menus.

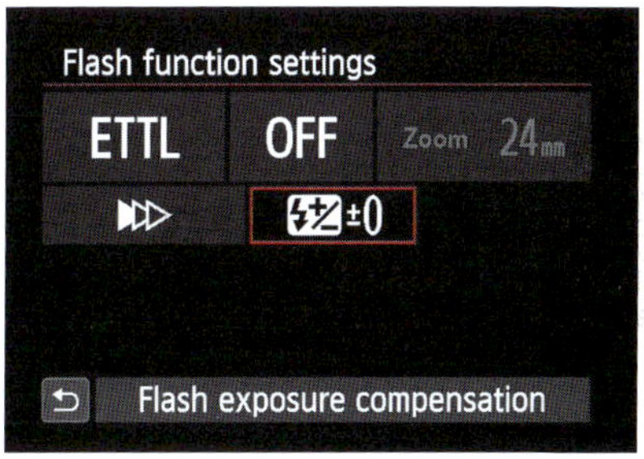

A

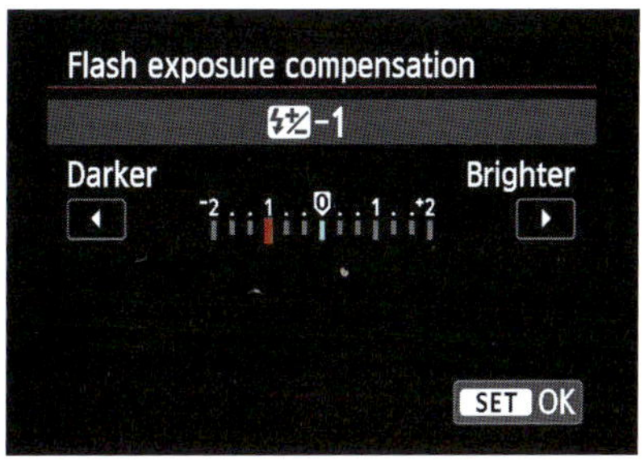

B

FIGURE 6.14
I couldn't resist the sunset in the background, but I added some fill flash to prevent the subject from being a dark silhouette.

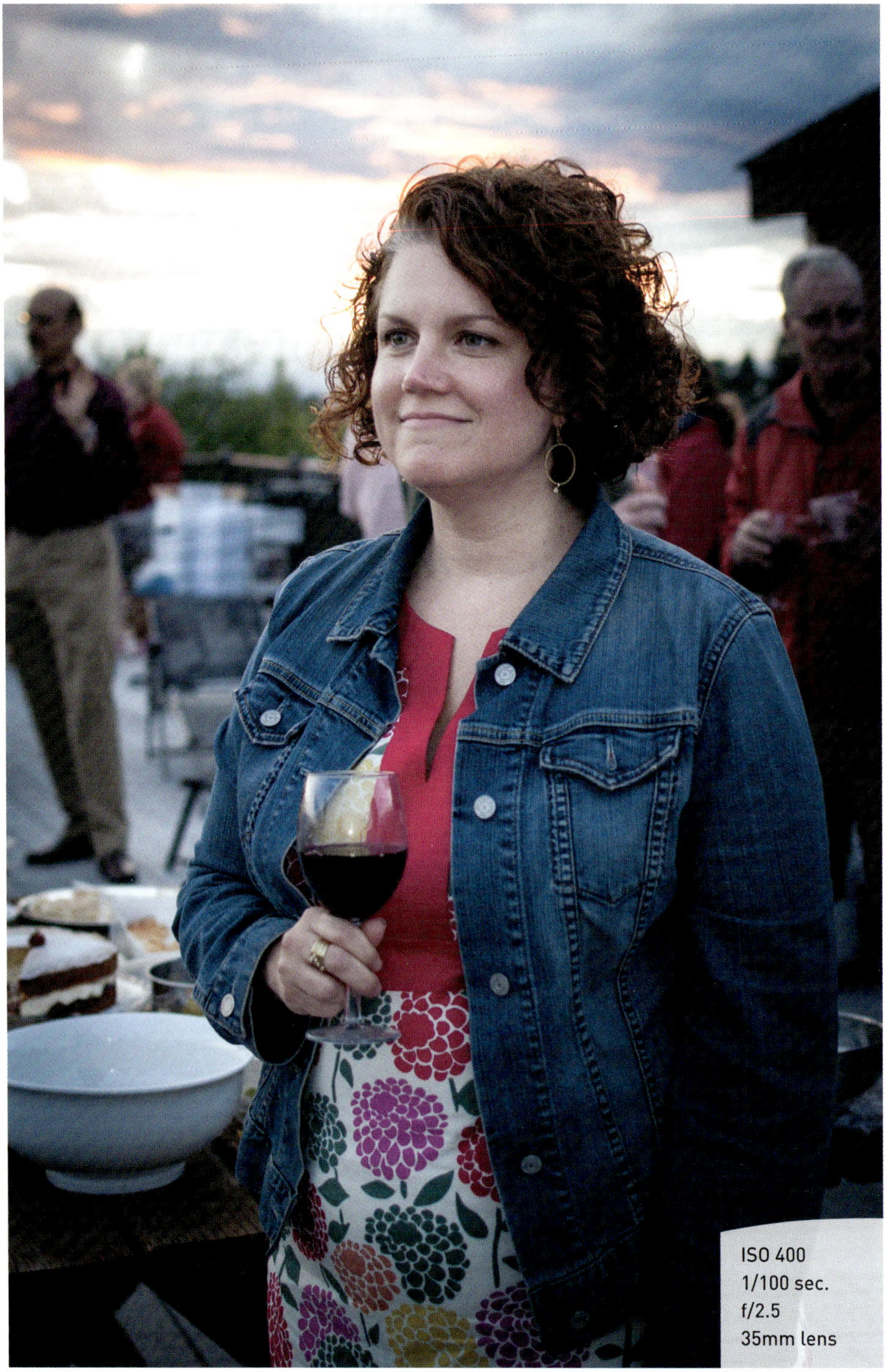

ISO 400
1/100 sec.
f/2.5
35mm lens

PEOPLE ON THE MOVE

Not all portraits are shot with the subject sitting in a chair, posed and ready for the picture. Sometimes you might want to get an action shot that says something about the person, similar to an environmental portrait. Children, especially, just like to move. Why fight it? Capture an action portrait instead.

For the photo in **Figure 6.15**, I wanted to capture the energy of kids playing in Atlanta's Centennial Olympic Park on a hot day. Not only did I want to freeze the kids' movements, I wanted to stop the jets of water, too. With plenty of light available, I set my camera to Shutter Priority mode and a shutter speed of 1/250 of a second. I set the drive mode to Continuous and fired off shots as the children played.

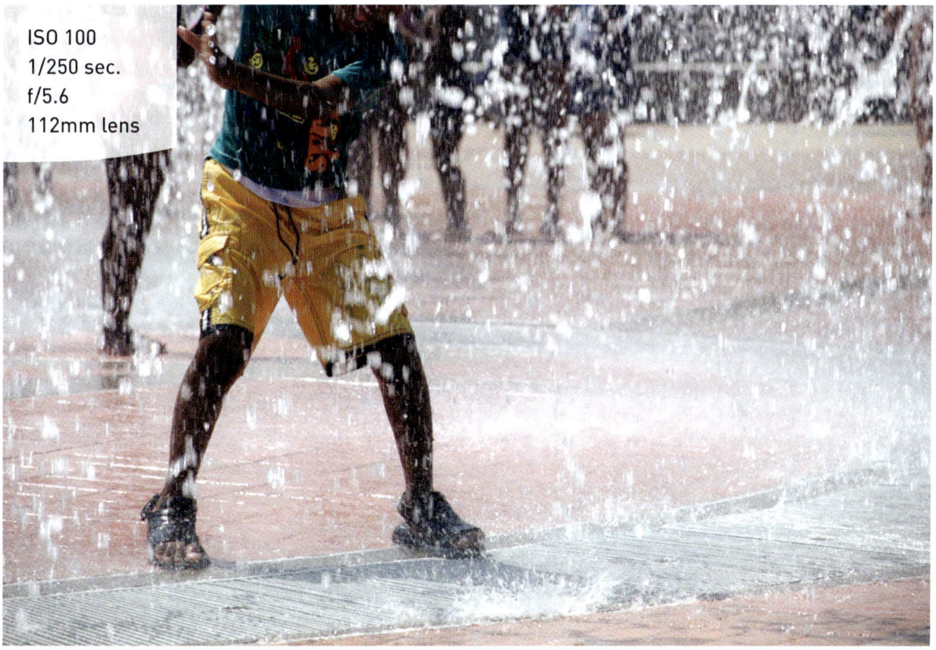

FIGURE 6.15 Although I prefer to shoot my people shots in Aperture Priority mode, the key to this shot was using Shutter Priority mode.

CATCHLIGHT

A *catchlight* is that little sparkle that adds life to the eyes. When you are photographing a person with a light source in front of them, you will usually get a reflection of that light in the eye, be it your flash, the sun, or something else brightly reflecting in the eye. The light is reflected off the surface of the eyes as bright highlights, which brings attention to the eyes.

THE PORTRAIT PICTURE STYLE FOR BETTER SKIN TONES

Your EOS M includes a picture style that has been tuned specifically for portraits—oddly enough, it's called Portrait. To set this style on your camera, simply follow the same directions as described under "Classic Black and White Portraits," except this time select the Portrait style instead of Monochrome. There are also individual options for the Portrait style that, like the Monochrome style, include sharpness and contrast. You can also change the saturation (how intense the colors will be) and the color tone, which lets you change the skin tones from more reddish to more yellowish. I prefer brighter colors, so I like to boost the Saturation setting to +2 and leave everything else at the defaults. You won't be able to use the same adjustments for everyone, especially when it comes to color tone, so do some experimenting to see what works best.

TIPS FOR SHOOTING BETTER PORTRAITS

Before we get to the assignments for this chapter, I thought it might be a good idea to leave you with a few extra portrait pointers that don't necessarily have anything specific to do with your camera. There are entire books that cover things like portrait lighting, posing, and so on, but here are a few pointers that will make your people pics look a lot better.

AVOID THE CENTER OF THE FRAME

This falls under the category of composition. Place your subject to the side of the frame (**Figure 6.16**)—it just looks more interesting than plunking them smack dab in the middle (**Figure 6.17**).

DON'T CUT THEM OFF AT THE KNEES

There is an old rule about photographing people: Never crop the picture at a joint. This means no cropping at the ankles or the knees. If you need to crop at the legs, the proper place to crop is mid-shin or mid-thigh.

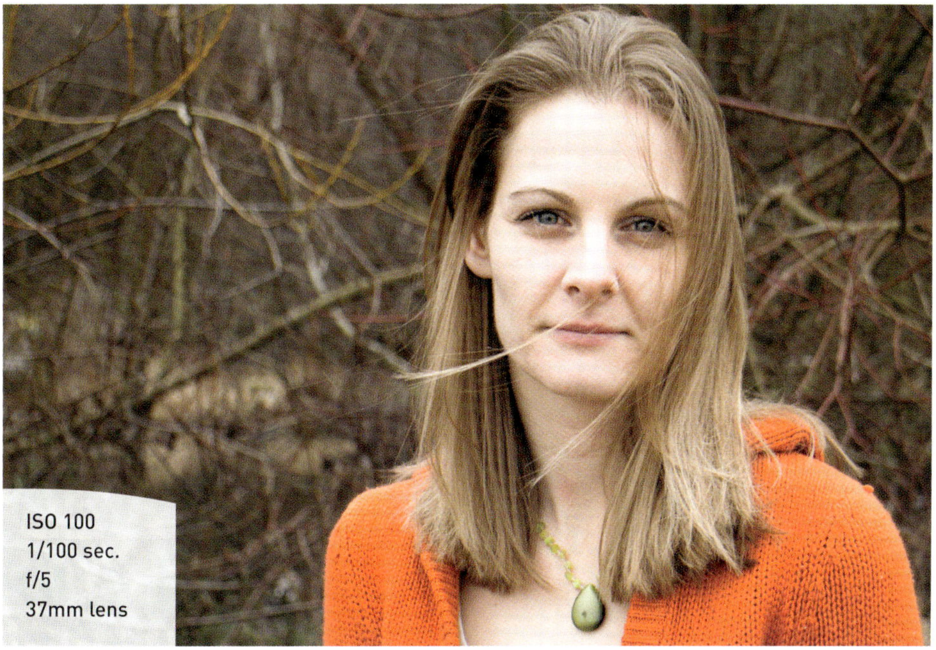

ISO 100
1/100 sec.
f/5
37mm lens

FIGURE 6.16
Try cropping in a bit, and place the subject's face off-center to improve the shot.

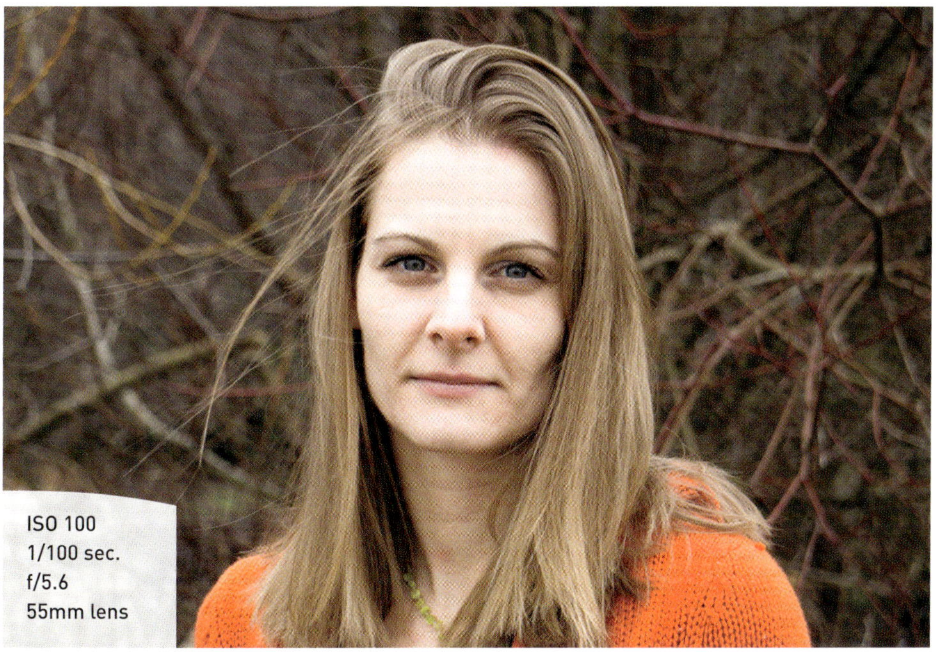

ISO 100
1/100 sec.
f/5.6
55mm lens

FIGURE 6.17
Having the subject in the middle of the frame with empty space on the sides makes for a less-than-interesting portrait.

CHOOSE THE RIGHT LENS

Choosing the correct lens can make a huge impact on your portraits. A wide-angle lens can distort the features of your subject, which can lead to an unflattering portrait (**Figure 6.18**). Select a longer focal length if you will be close to your subject (**Figure 6.19**).

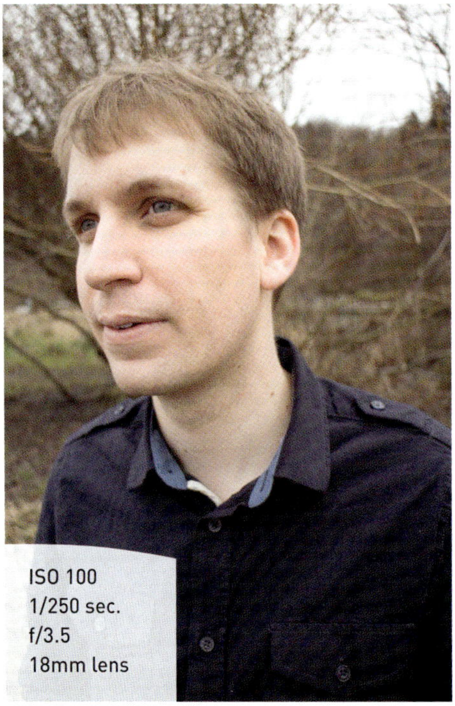

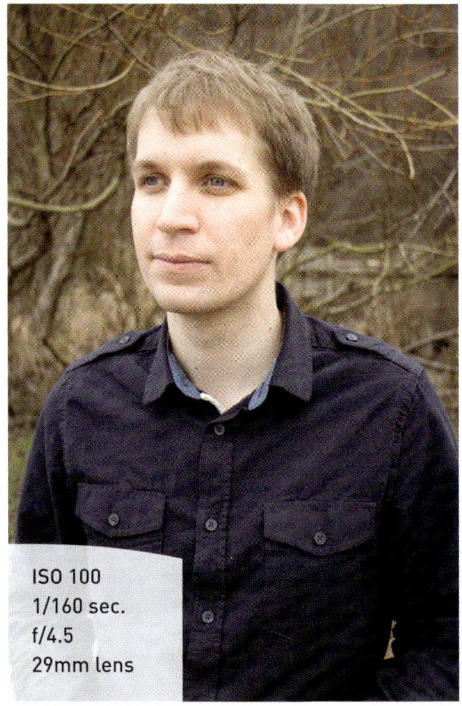

FIGURE 6.18
(left) At this close distance, the 18mm end of the EF-M lens is distorting the subject's face.

FIGURE 6.19
(right) By zooming out to 29mm, I am able to remove the distortion for a much better photo.

USE THE FRAME

Have you ever noticed that most people are taller than they are wide? Turn your camera vertically for a more pleasing composition (**Figure 6.20**).

SUNBLOCK FOR PORTRAITS

The midday sun can be harsh and can do unflattering things to people's faces (**Figure 6.21**). If you can, find a shady spot out of the direct sunlight. You will get softer shadows, smoother skin tones, and better detail (**Figure 6.22**). This holds true for overcast skies as well. Just be sure to adjust your white balance accordingly.

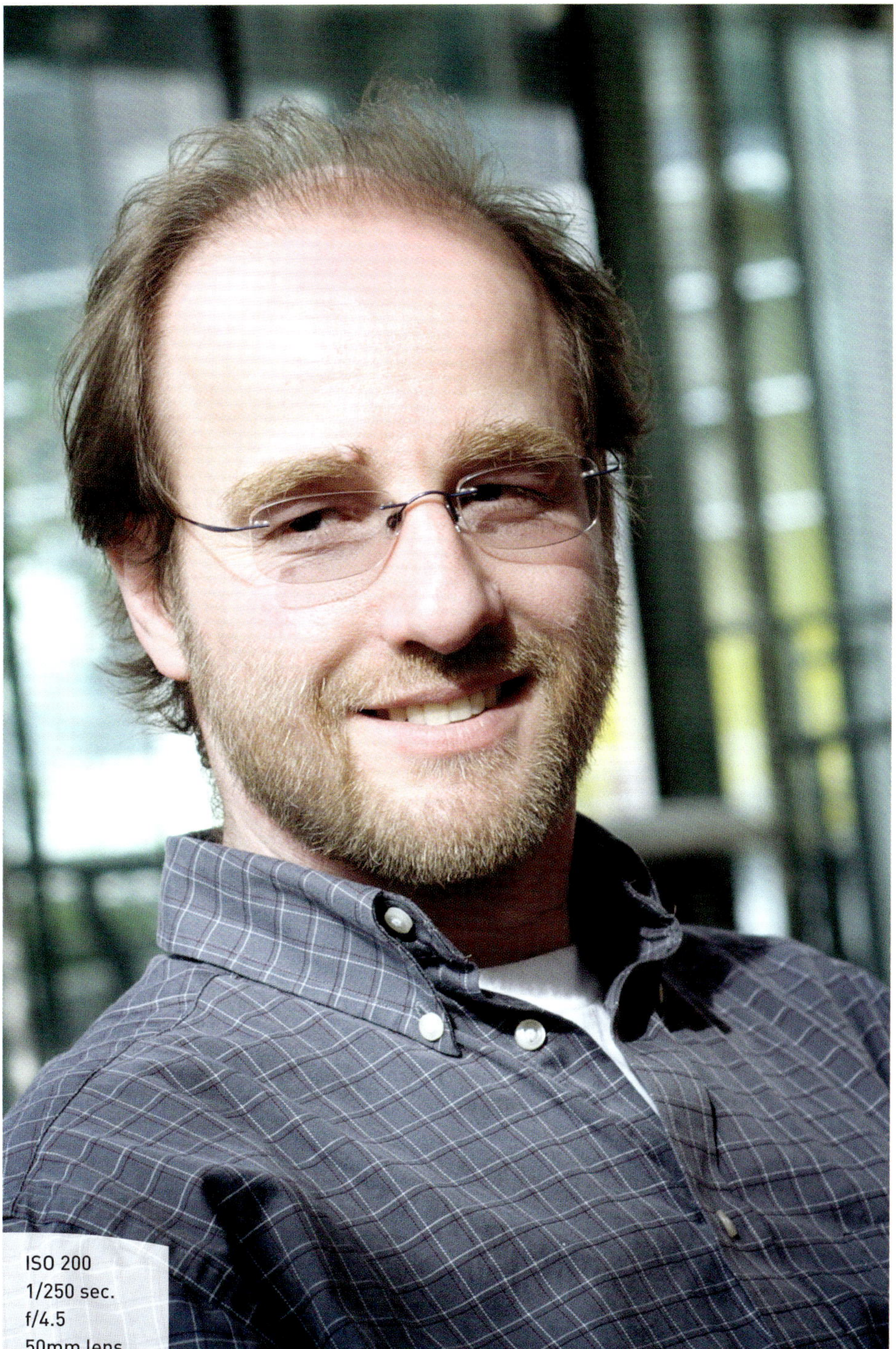

ISO 200
1/250 sec.
f/4.5
50mm lens

FIGURE 6.20
Get in the habit of turning your camera to a vertical position when shooting portraits. This is also referred to as portrait orientation.

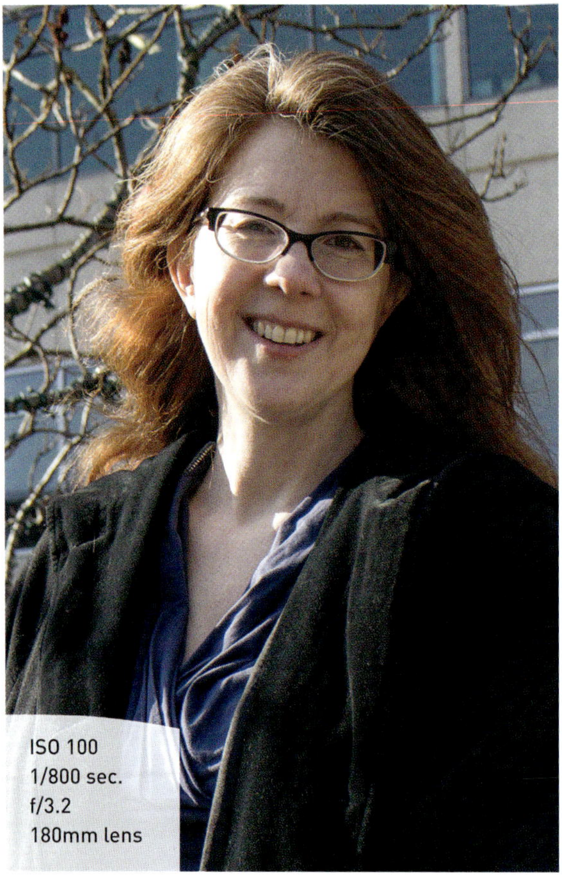

FIGURE 6.21
The bright, direct sunlight looks too harsh on the subject's face.

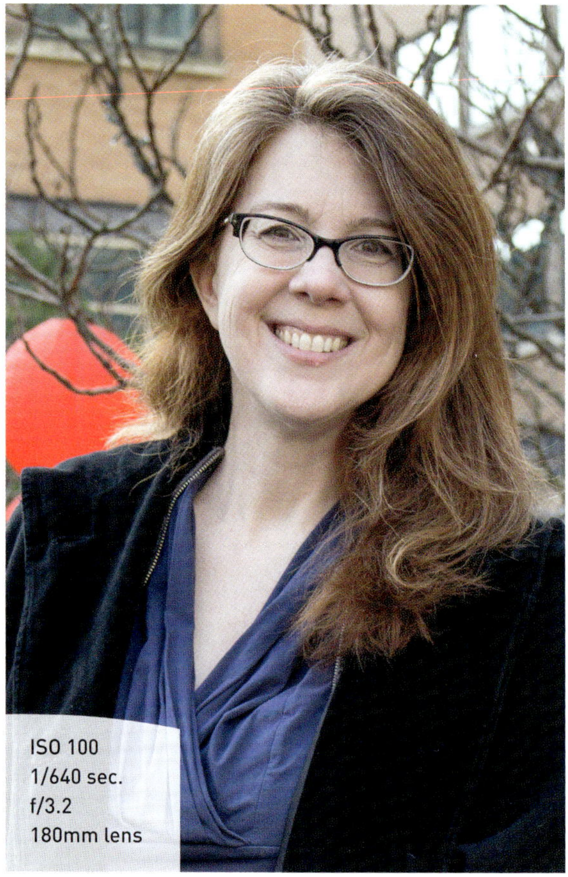

FIGURE 6.22
By moving her over just a couple of feet, I was able to get her out of the direct sun and into a much more flattering situation.

DON'T BE AFRAID TO GET CLOSE

When you are taking someone's picture, don't be afraid of getting close and filling the frame (**Figure 6.23**). This doesn't mean you have to shoot from a foot away—try zooming in to capture the details.

GET DOWN ON THEIR LEVEL

If you want better pictures of children, don't shoot from an adult's eye level. Getting the camera down to the child's level will make your images look more personal (**Figure 6.24**).

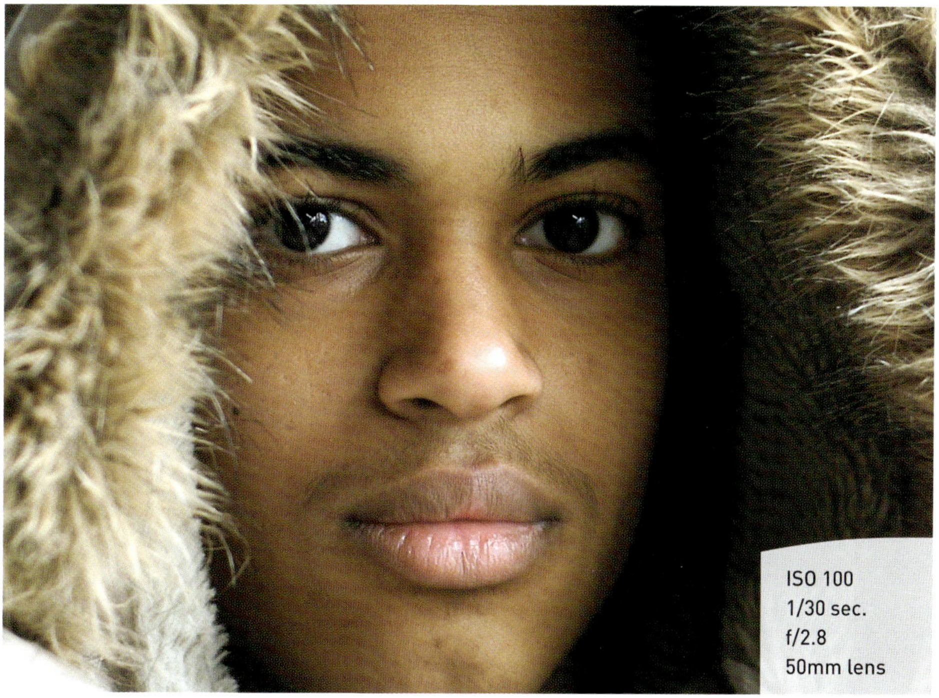

FIGURE 6.23
Filling the frame with the subject's face can lead to a much more intimate portrait.

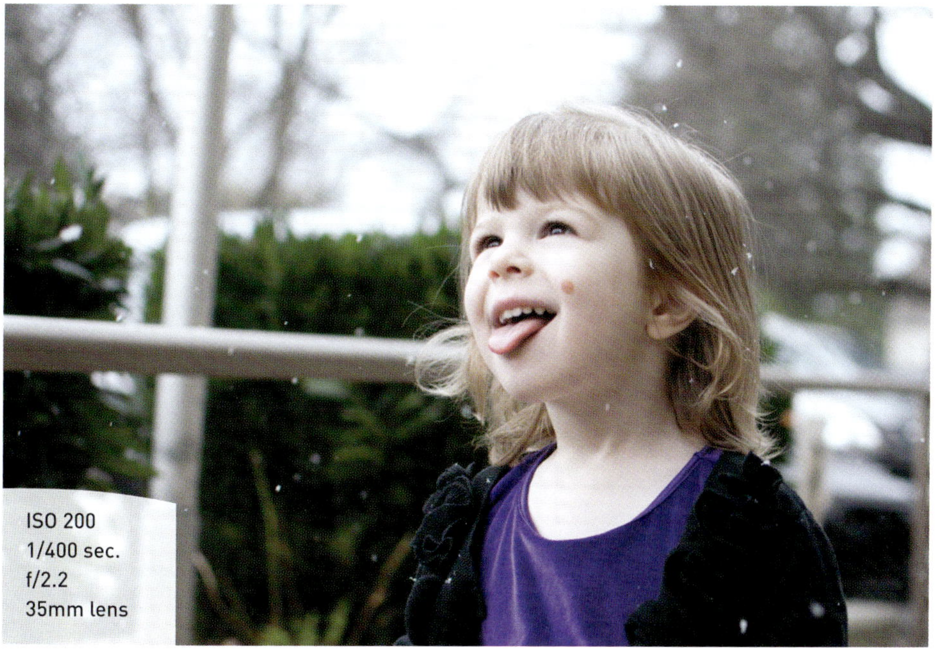

FIGURE 6.24
Whenever you are taking photographs of children, get your camera down on their level for a less imposing view.

FIGURE 6.25
The bridge railing in perspective draws your eye directly to the subjects.

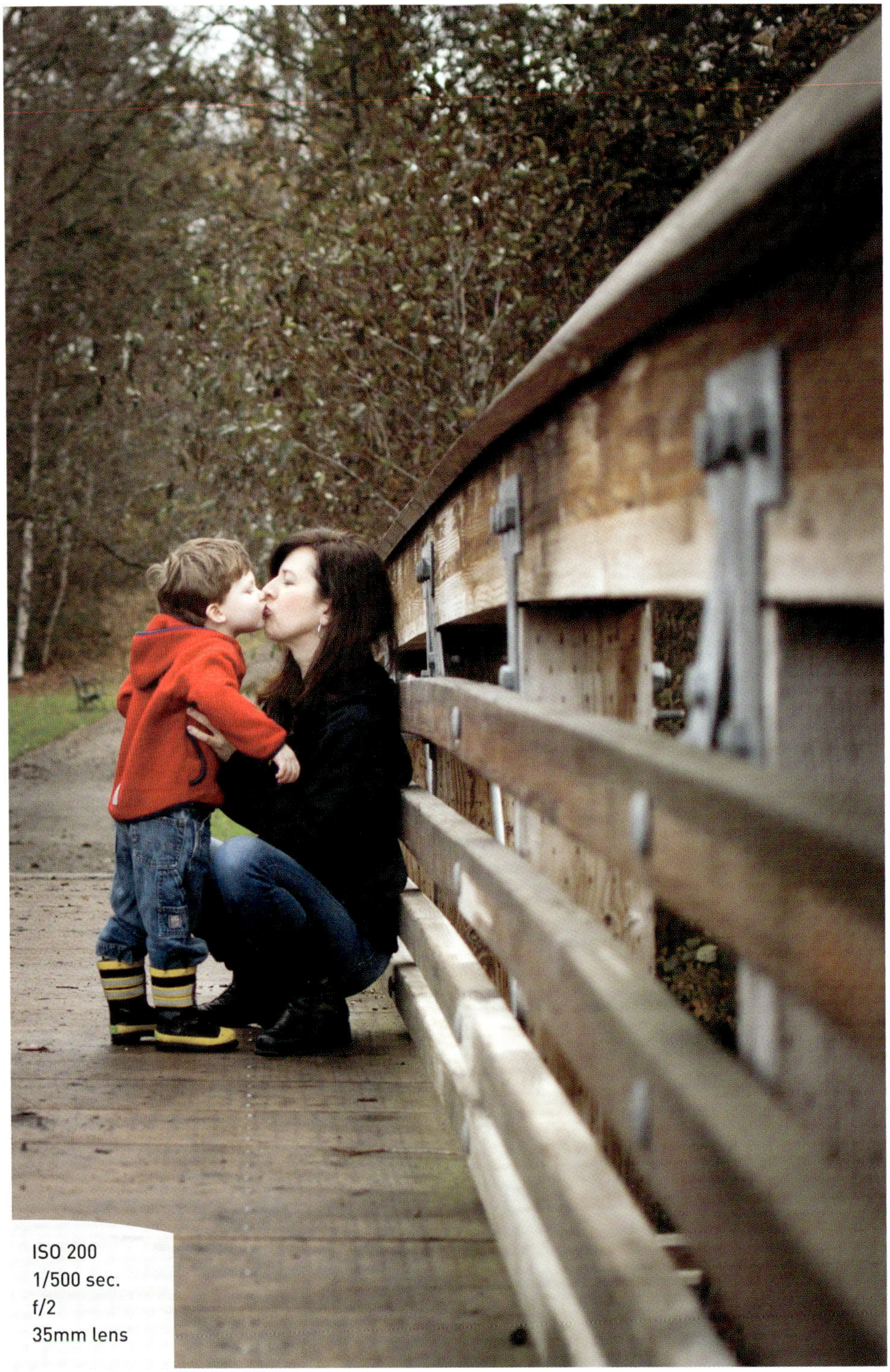

ISO 200
1/500 sec.
f/2
35mm lens

FRAME THE SCENE

Using elements in the scene to create a frame around your subject is a great way to draw the viewer in. You don't have to use a window frame to do this. Just look for elements in the foreground that could be used to force the viewer's eye toward your subject (**Figure 6.25**).

TRY A LONG LENS FOR CANDID SHOTS

Putting a camera in someone's face can elicit some unnatural results. People just feel a need to pose, or they get nervous and stiff. If you really want to capture some nice portraits with a more candid feel, try shooting with a long lens (**Figure 6.26**). The distance will remove you and your camera from the equation, and people will tend to react more normally. If you are looking to be a street photographer, a long lens will be one of your best tools.

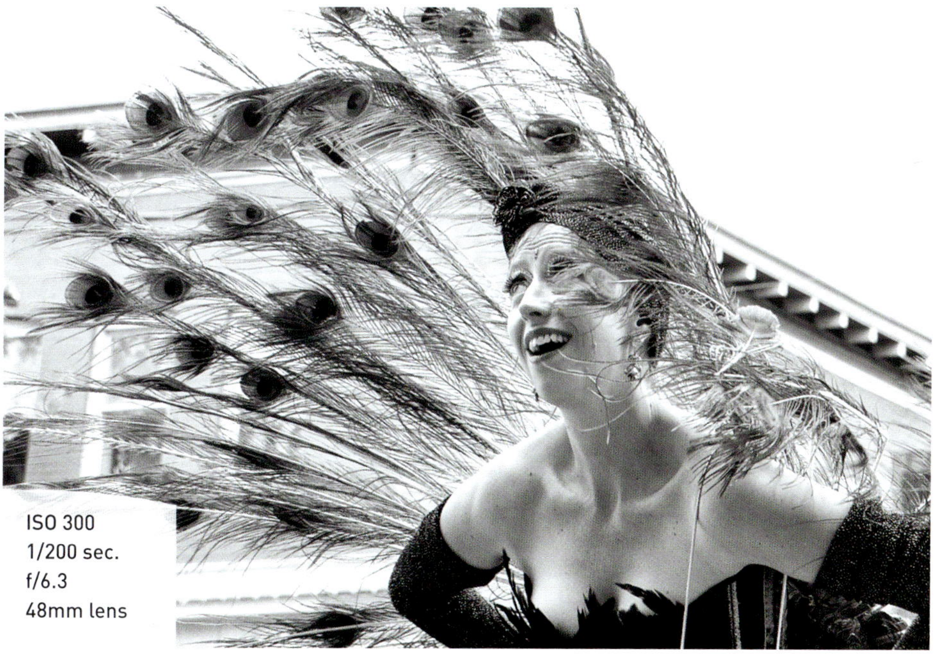

ISO 300
1/200 sec.
f/6.3
48mm lens

FIGURE 6.26
Using a long lens can help you get more candid shots.

Chapter 6 Assignments

Depth of field in portraits

Let's start with something simple. Grab your favorite person and start experimenting with using different aperture settings. Shoot wide open (the widest your lens goes, such as f/2.8 or f/4) and then really stopped down (like f/22). Look at the difference in the depth of field and how it plays an important role in placing the attention on your subject. (Make sure you don't have your subject standing against the background. Give some distance so that there is a good blurring effect of the background at the wide f-stop setting.)

Discovering the qualities of natural light

Pick a nice sunny day and try shooting some portraits in the midday sun. If your subject is willing, have them turn so the sun is in their face. If they are still speaking to you after blinding them, have them turn their back to the sun. Try this with and without the fill flash so you can see the difference. Finally, move them into a completely shaded spot and take a few more.

Picking the right metering method

Find a very dark or light background and place your subject in front of it. Now take a couple of shots, giving a lot of space around your subject for the background to show. Now switch metering modes and use the AE Lock feature to get a more accurate reading of your subject. Notice the differences in exposure between the metering methods.

Picture styles for portraits

Have some fun playing with the different picture styles. Try the Portrait style as compared to the Standard style. Then try out Monochrome and play with the different color filter options to see how they affect skin tones.

Share your results with the book's Flickr group!

Join the group here: flickr.com/groups/eosmfromsnapshotstogreatshots

7

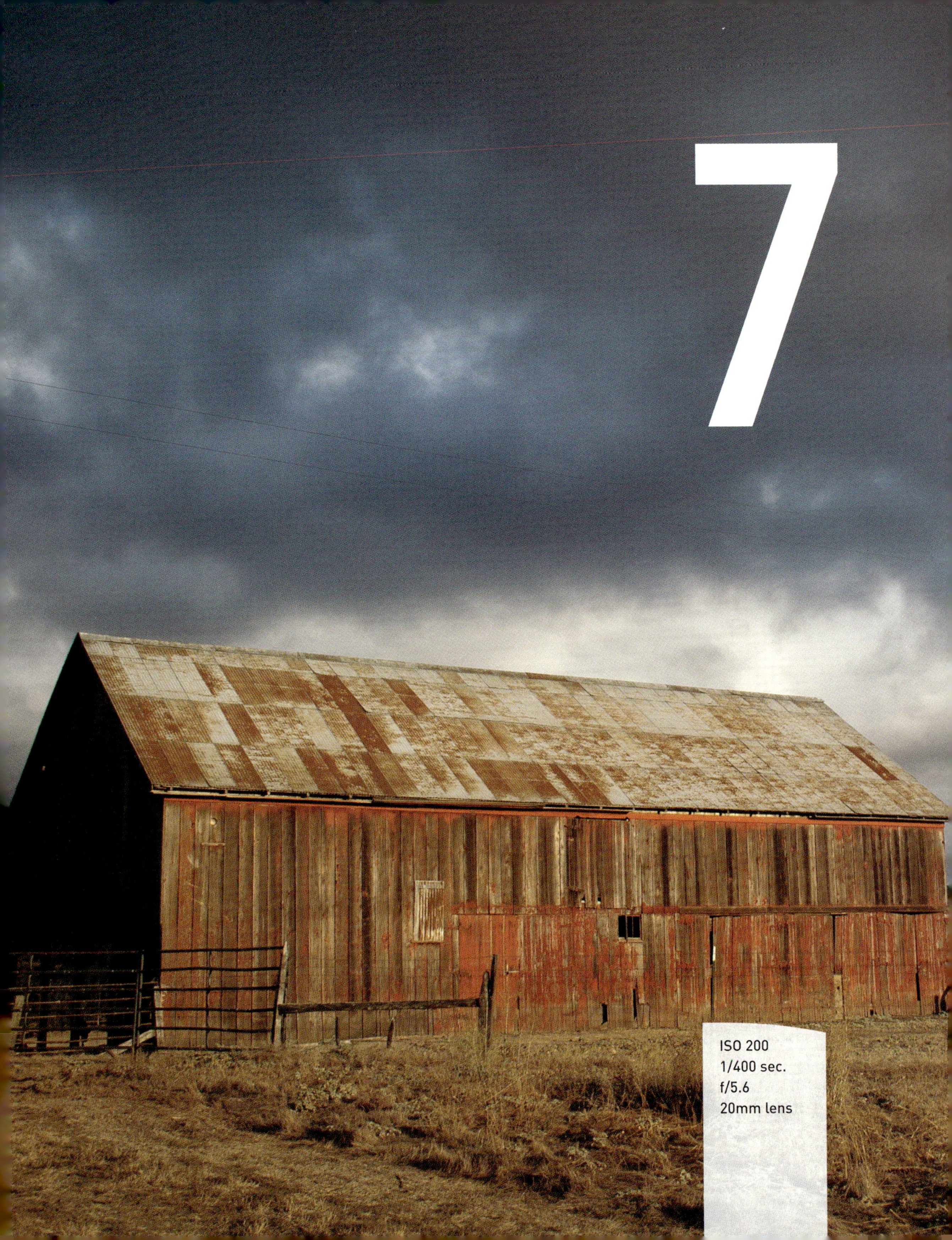

ISO 200
1/400 sec.
f/5.6
20mm lens

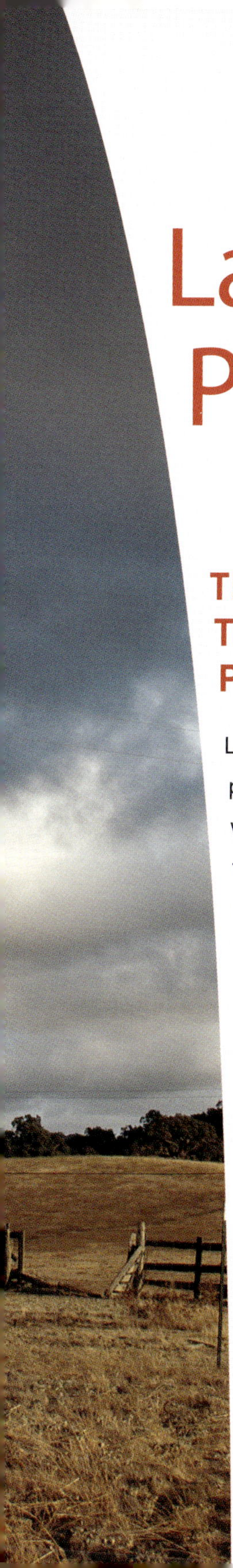

Landscape Photography

TIPS, TOOLS, AND TECHNIQUES TO GET THE MOST OUT OF YOUR LANDSCAPE PHOTOGRAPHY

Landscape photography transports people in ways that other types of photos don't. Viewers long to be where the sun set over the ocean or where the desert sun warms rock and sand. As a photographer, you get to shoot outdoors and work at the mercy of Mother Nature. A landscape shot challenges you to visualize the landscape and try to capture it with the camera. Landscape photography truly is a celebration of light, composition, and the world we live in.

In this chapter, we will explore some of the features of the EOS M that will not only improve the look of your landscape photography but also make it easier to take great shots. We'll also explore typical scenarios and discuss methods to bring out the best in your landscape work.

PORING OVER THE PICTURE

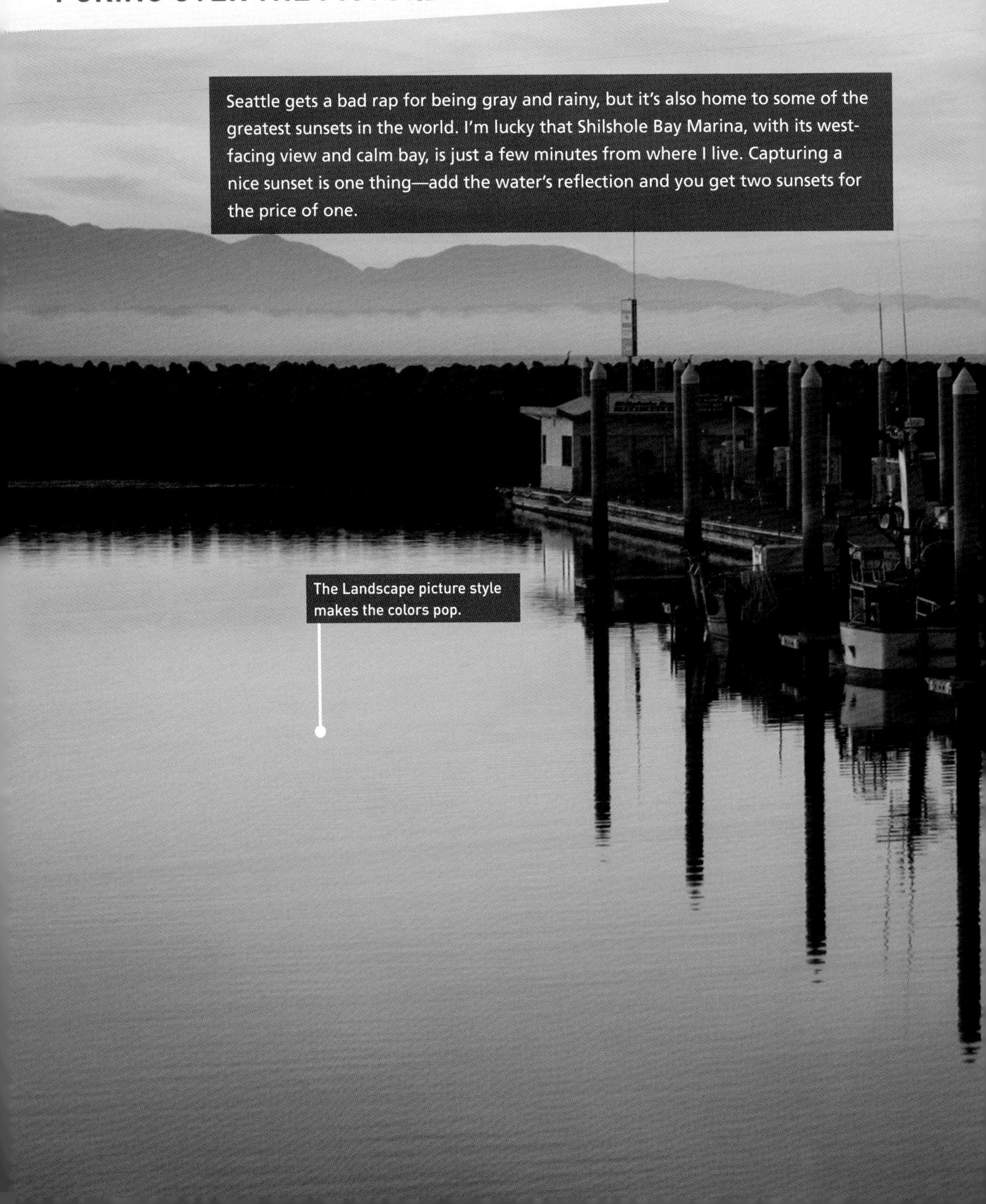

Seattle gets a bad rap for being gray and rainy, but it's also home to some of the greatest sunsets in the world. I'm lucky that Shilshole Bay Marina, with its west-facing view and calm bay, is just a few minutes from where I live. Capturing a nice sunset is one thing—add the water's reflection and you get two sunsets for the price of one.

The Landscape picture style makes the colors pop.

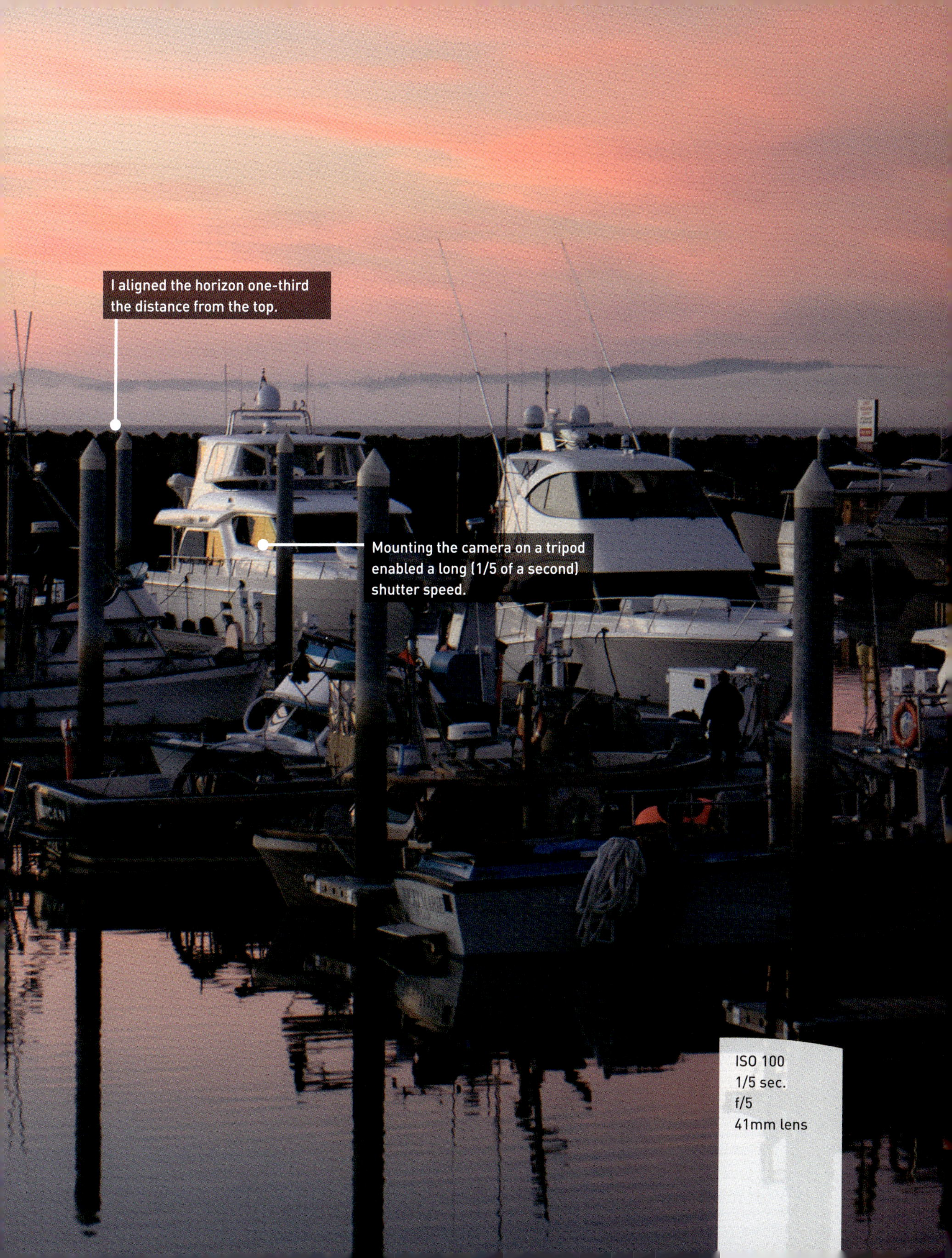
I aligned the horizon one-third the distance from the top.
Mounting the camera on a tripod enabled a long (1/5 of a second) shutter speed.
ISO 100
1/5 sec.
f/5
41mm lens

PORING OVER THE PICTURE

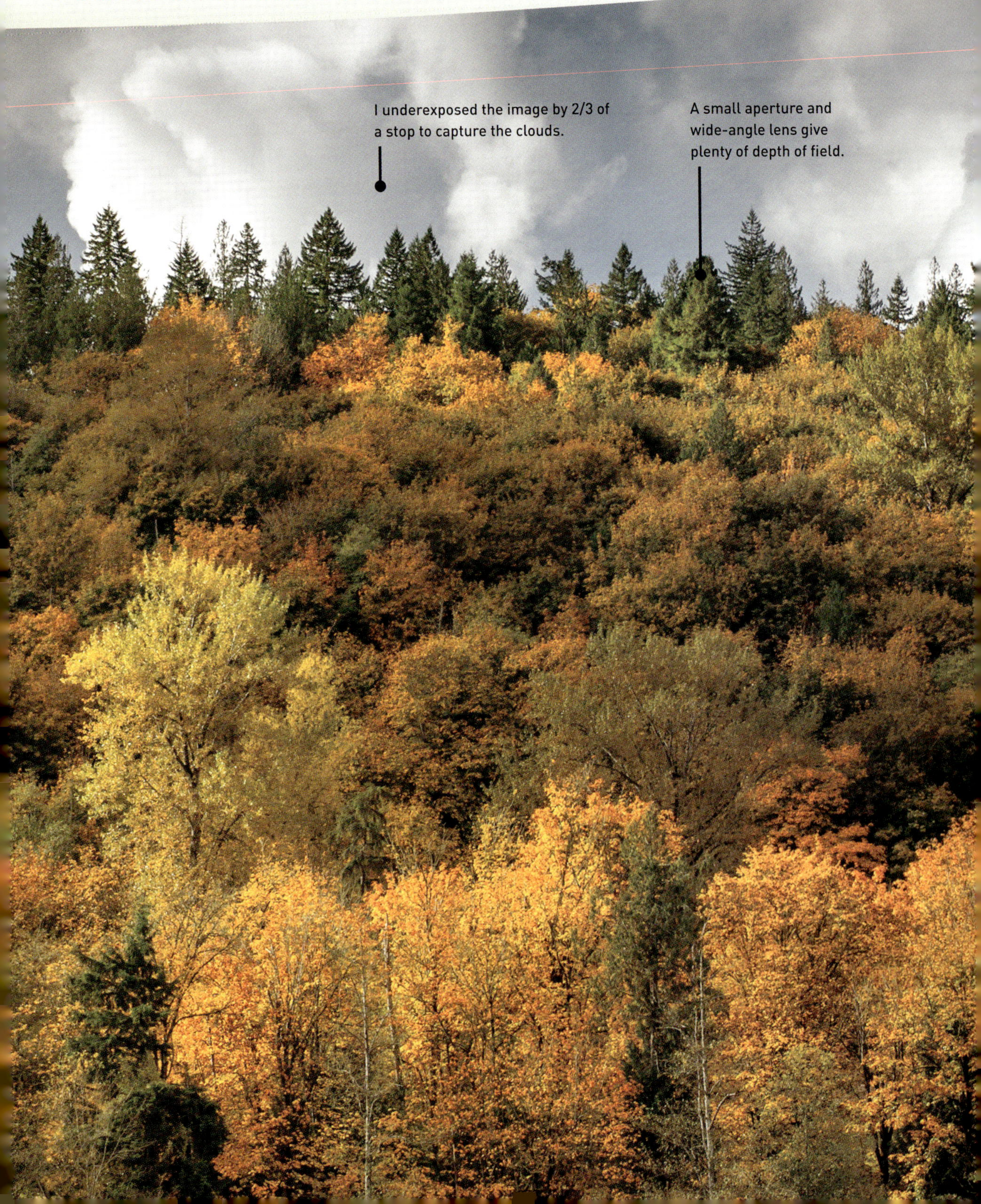

While I was driving through the countryside outside Seattle, my eyes caught sight of this expanse of autumn leaves. The patchy sunlight created wonderful shadows against the hillside, and the clouds were too dramatic to ignore. I pulled over, grabbed my tripod, and shot several exposures (while my family patiently waited for me to indulge my photographic compulsion).

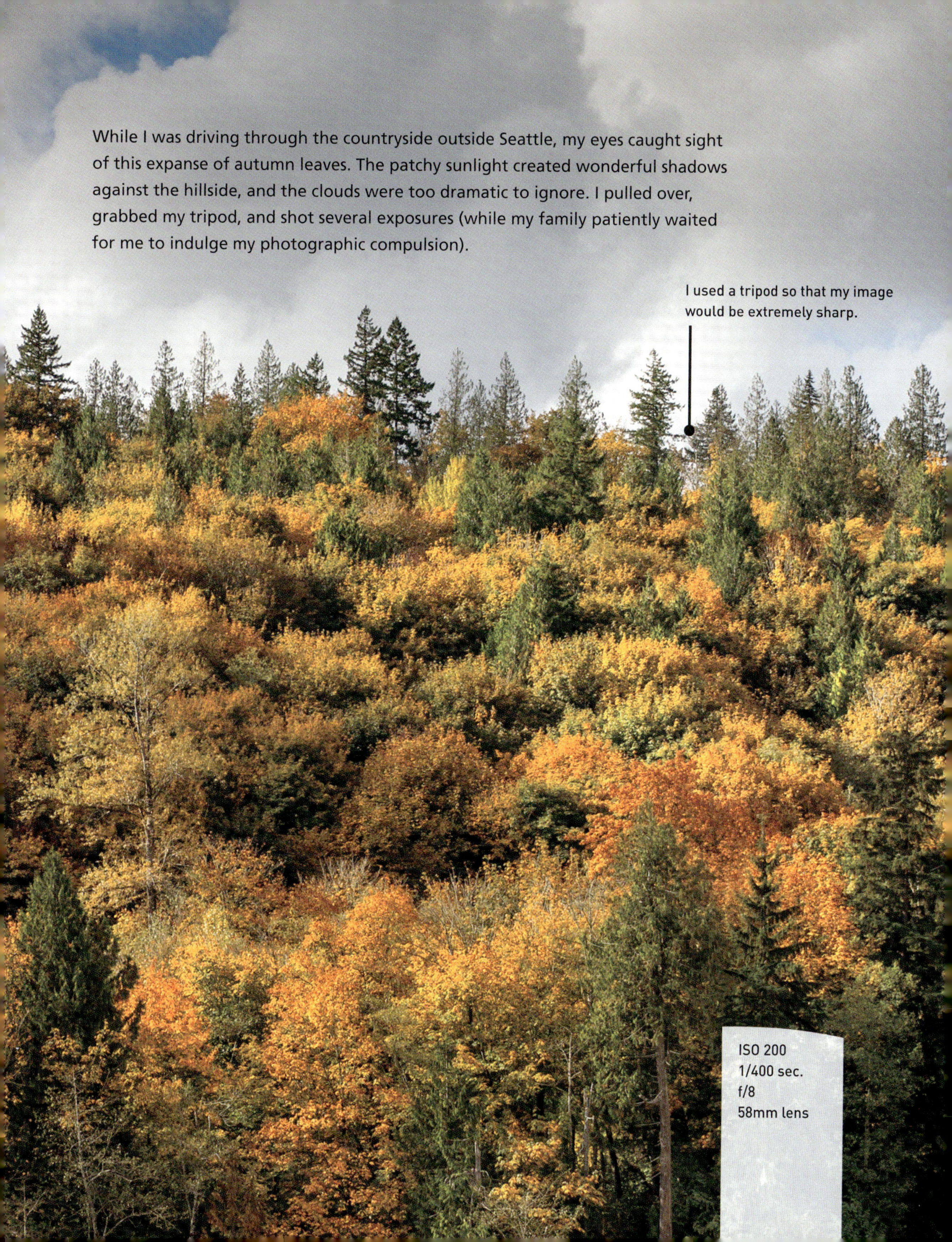

SHARP AND IN FOCUS: USING TRIPODS

Throughout the previous chapters, we have concentrated on using the camera to create great images. We will continue that trend through this chapter, but there is one additional piece of equipment that is crucial in the world of landscape shooting: the tripod. Tripods are critical to your landscape work for a couple of reasons. The first relates to the time of day that you will be working. For reasons that will be explained later, the best light for most landscape work happens at sunrise and just before sunset. While this is the best time to shoot, it's also kind of dark. That means you'll be working with slow shutter speeds. Slow shutter speeds mean camera shake. Camera shake equals bad photos.

The second reason is also related to the amount of light that you're gathering with your camera. When taking landscape photos, you will usually want to be working with very small apertures, as they give you lots of depth of field. This also means that, once again, you will be working with slower-than-normal shutter speeds.

Slow shutter = camera shake = bad photos.

Do you see the pattern here? The one tool in your arsenal to truly defeat the camera shake issue and ensure tack-sharp photos is a good tripod.

So what should you look for in a tripod? Well, first make sure it is sturdy enough to support your camera and any lens that you might want to use. Next, check the height of the tripod. Your day will end much better if you haven't had to bend over all day to look through your viewfinder. Finally, think about getting a tripod that utilizes a quick-release head. This usually employs a plate that screws into the bottom of the camera and then quickly snaps into place on the tripod. This will be especially handy if you are going to move between shooting by hand and using the tripod.

TRIPOD STABILITY

Most tripods have a center column that allows the user to extend the height of the camera above the point where the tripod legs join together. This might seem like a great idea, but the reality is that the higher you raise that column, the less stable your tripod becomes. Think of a tall building that sways near the top. To get the most solid base for your camera, always try to use it with the center column at its lowest point so your camera is right at the apex of the tripod legs.

IMAGE STABILIZATION AND TRIPODS

If you are using Canon EF lenses with image stabilization (IS) along with the EOS M Mount Adapter on your camera, remember to turn this feature off when you use a tripod. This is because the image stabilization can, while trying to minimize camera movement, actually *create* movement when the camera is already stable. To turn off the IS feature, just slide the Stabilizer selector switch on the side of the lens to the Off position.

However, if you're shooting with one of the EF or EF-S lenses designed specifically for the EOS M, you *do not* need to turn off the built-in IS feature.

SELECTING THE PROPER ISO

When you're shooting most landscape scenes, the ISO is the one factor that should only be changed as a last resort. While it is easy to select a higher ISO to get a smaller aperture, the noise that it can introduce into your images can be quite harmful (**Figures 7.1** and **7.2**).

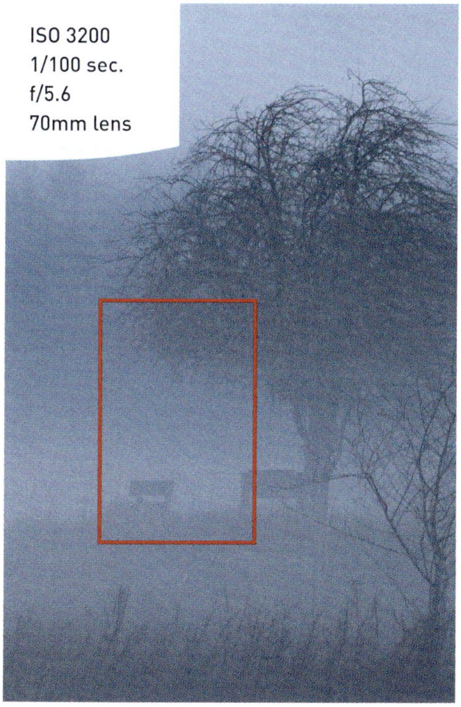

FIGURE 7.1
(left) A high ISO setting created a lot of digital noise.

FIGURE 7.2
(right) When the image is enlarged, the noise is even more apparent.

The noise not only can be visible as large grainy artifacts but can also be multi-colored, which further degrades the image quality. Take a look at the image in Figure 7.2, which was taken with an ISO of 3200. It was already getting dark when I arrived, so I cranked the ISO so I'd pull out detail. Unfortunately, I ended up with a lot of noise.

Now check out another image that was taken in the same light but with a much lower ISO setting (**Figures 7.3** and **7.4**). As you can see, the noise levels are much lower. You'll get blacker blacks and finer details.

When shooting landscapes, set your ISO to the lowest possible setting at all times. Between the use of image stabilization lenses (if you are shooting handheld) and a good tripod (which I used in these examples), there should be few circumstances where you would need to shoot landscapes with anything above an ISO of 400.

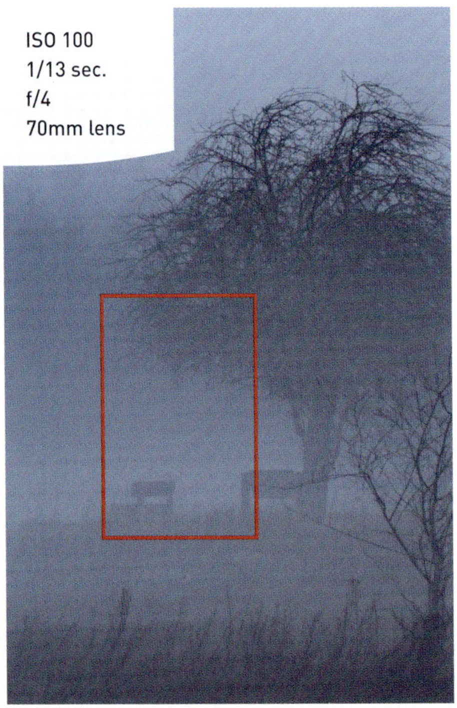

FIGURE 7.3
(left) By lowering the ISO to 100, I was able to avoid the noise and capture a clean image.

FIGURE 7.4
(right) Zooming in shows that the noise levels for this image are almost nonexistent.

USING NOISE REDUCTION

Figures 7.1 and 7.3 were both taken with a tripod, but the image set to an ISO of 100 required a much slower shutter speed (1/14 of a second at ISO 100) than the high-ISO image (1/100 of a second at ISO 3200). There can be an issue when using a low ISO setting: The sometimes-lengthy shutter speeds can also introduce noise. This noise is a result of the heating of the camera sensor as it is being exposed to light. This effect is not visible in short exposures, but as you start shooting with shutter speeds that exceed 1 second, the level of image noise can increase. Your camera has a couple of features that you can turn on to combat noise from long exposures and high ISOs.

SETTING UP NOISE REDUCTION

1. Press the Menu button, use the Main dial to get to the fourth shooting menu, highlight the High ISO speed NR option, and press Set (**A**).
2. The default setting is Standard, but you may require the High setting for really high ISOs (**B**).
3. Press the Set button to apply the change and return to the shooting menu, and then select Long exp. noise reduction. Press the Set button to change the options (**C**).
4. The default setting is Auto, which will handle most scenarios. If you know you are going to be making extremely long exposures, you should probably go ahead and set it to On (**D**).

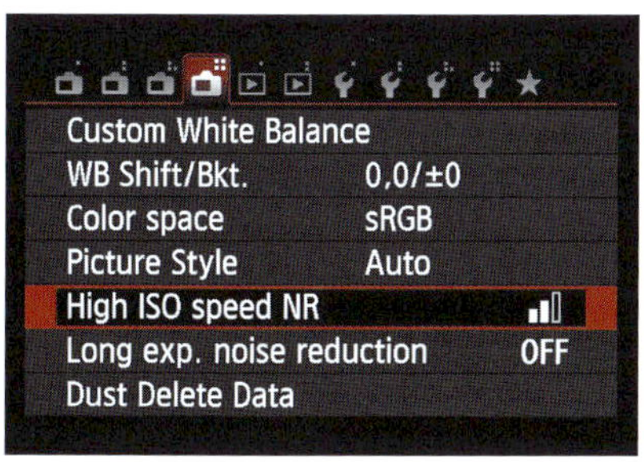

A

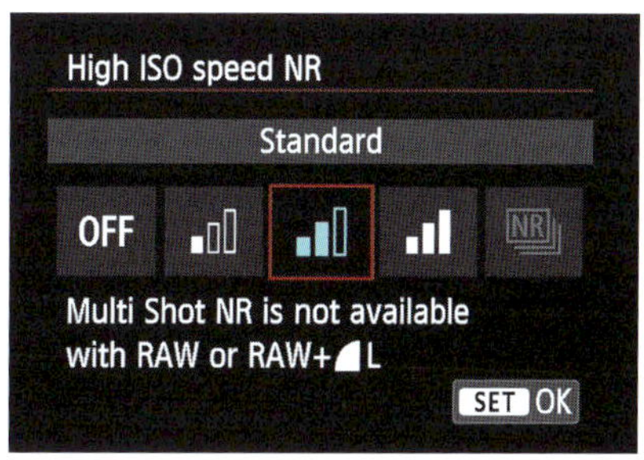

B

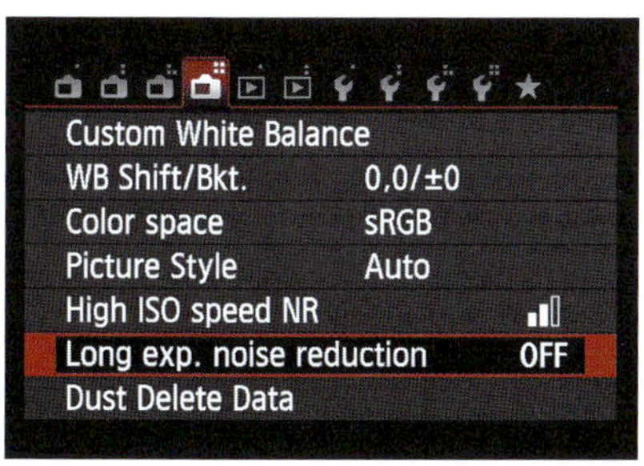

C

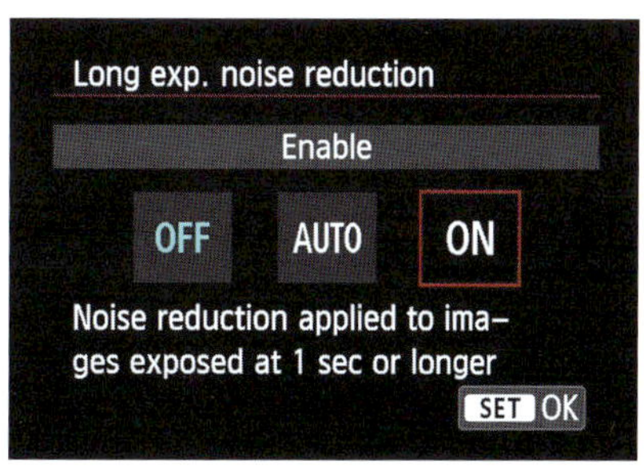

D

SELECTING A WHITE BALANCE

This probably seems like a no-brainer. If it's sunny, select Daylight; if it's overcast, choose the Shade or Cloudy setting. Those choices wouldn't be wrong for those circumstances, but why limit yourself? Sometimes you can change the mood of the photo by selecting a white balance that doesn't quite fit the light for the scene that you are shooting. **Figure 7.5** is an example of a correct white balance. It was late afternoon and the sun was starting to move low in the sky, giving everything that warm afternoon glow. The white balance for this image was set to Daylight. But what if I want to make the scene look like it had been shot in the early morning hours? Simple—I just change the white balance to Fluorescent, which is a much cooler setting (**Figure 7.6**).

When you change the white balance setting on the EOS M, the LCD previews the change, so you can get an immediate idea of how the shot will appear.

CHANGING WHITE BALANCE SETTINGS

1. Press the Q button to bring up the Quick Control screen.
2. Tap the White Balance icon (the second one from the top on the right side of the screen), and then rotate the Main dial, press the Left/Right cross keys, or tap a setting at the bottom of the screen to change the white balance.
3. Select the white balance setting that looks most appropriate for your scene, then press the Q button to lock in your change and resume shooting.

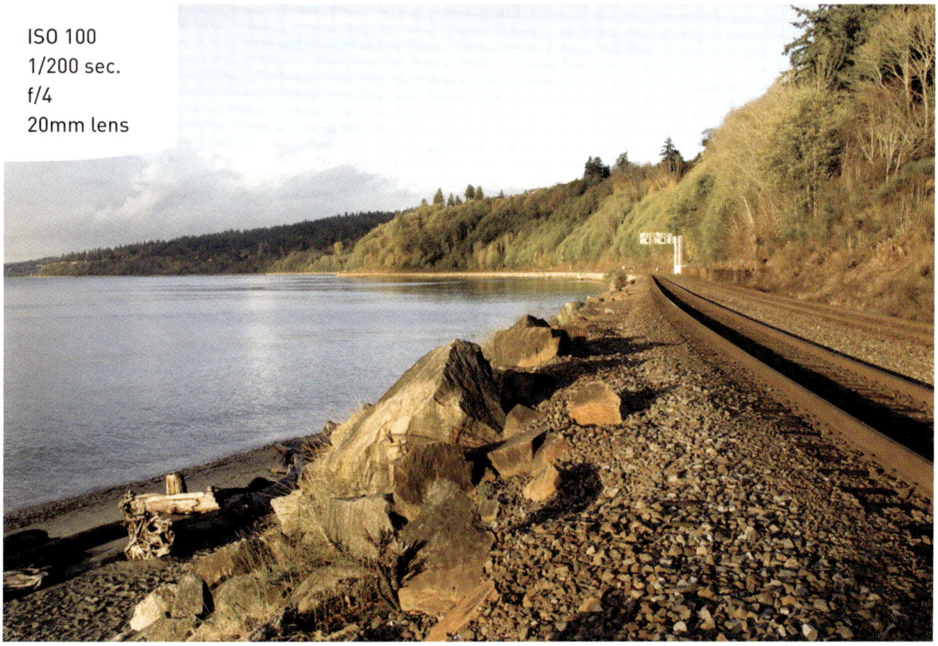

ISO 100
1/200 sec.
f/4
20mm lens

FIGURE 7.5
Using the "proper" white balance yields predictable results.

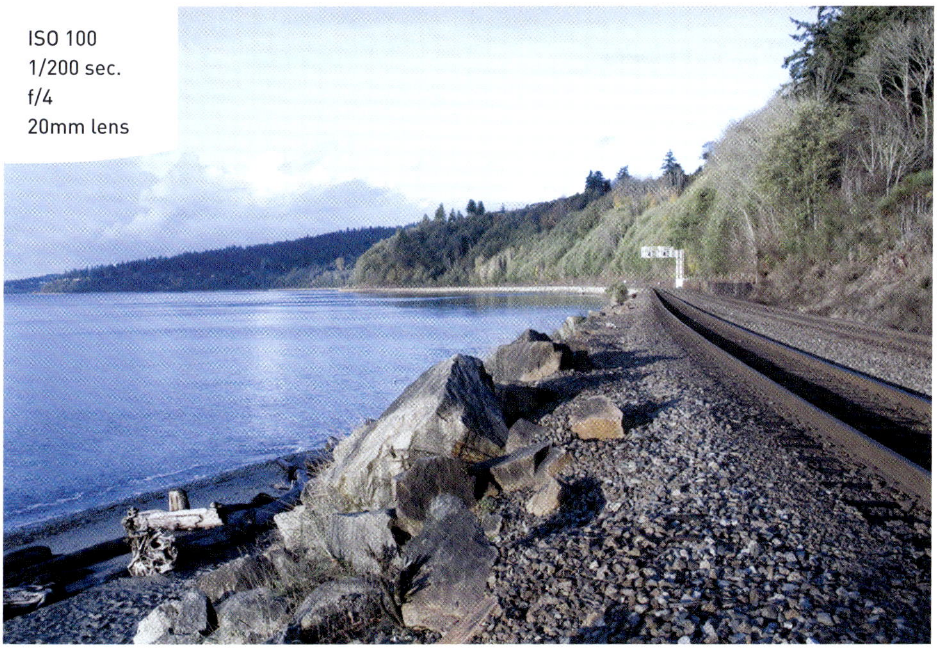

ISO 100
1/200 sec.
f/4
20mm lens

FIGURE 7.6
Changing the white balance to Fluorescent gives the impression that the picture was taken at a different time of day than it really was.

USING THE LANDSCAPE PICTURE STYLE

When shooting landscapes, I always look for great color and contrast. This is one of the reasons that so many landscape shots are taken in the early morning or during sunset. The light is much more vibrant and colorful at these times of day and adds a sense of drama to an image. You can help boost this effect, especially in the less-than-golden hours of the day, by using the Landscape picture style (**Figures 7.7** and **7.8**). Just as in the Landscape mode found in the Basic zone, you can set up your landscape shooting so that you capture images with increased sharpness and a slight boost in blues and greens. This style will add some pop to your landscapes without the need for additional processing in any software.

SETTING UP THE LANDSCAPE PICTURE STYLE

1. Press the Q button to view the Quick Control settings.
2. Tap the Picture Style button (third down on the right side) (**A**).
3. Use the Left/Right cross keys, the Main dial, or tap to highlight the Landscape setting (**B**).
4. To customize the Landscape settings (sharpness, contrast, saturation, and color tone), press the Info button and make adjustments.
5. Press the Set button to lock in your change.

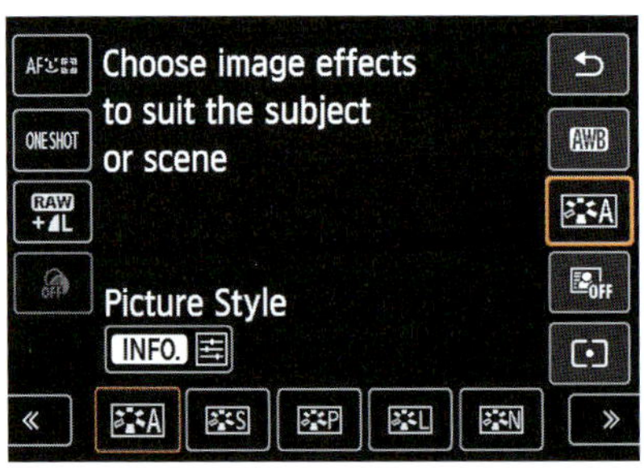

A

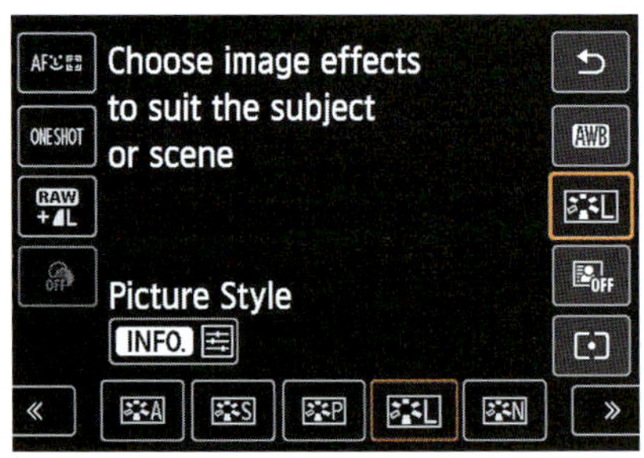

B

If you are shooting RAW, your images will look like they have the picture style applied when you view them on the LCD, but the style will go away once you open the images in post-processing software. You will need to add the picture style back as part of your post-processing. Only JPEGs have the picture style applied as part of the final in-camera image processing. To keep the picture styles, shoot in the JPEG or RAW+JPEG mode.

ISO 100
1/15 sec.
f/8
18mm lens

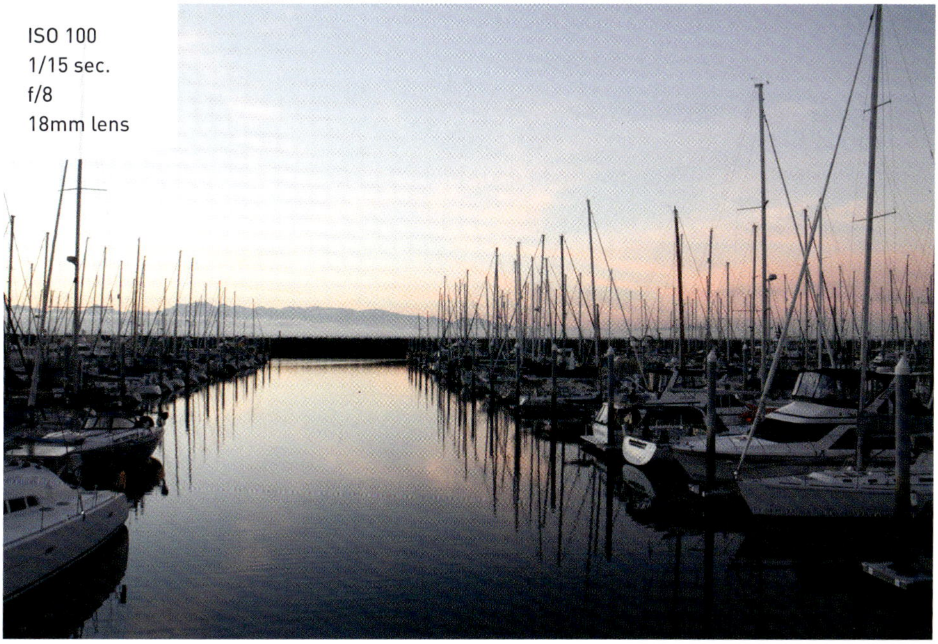

FIGURE 7.7 Using the Standard picture style, the colors are OK but don't really pop.

ISO 100
1/15 sec.
f/8
18mm lens

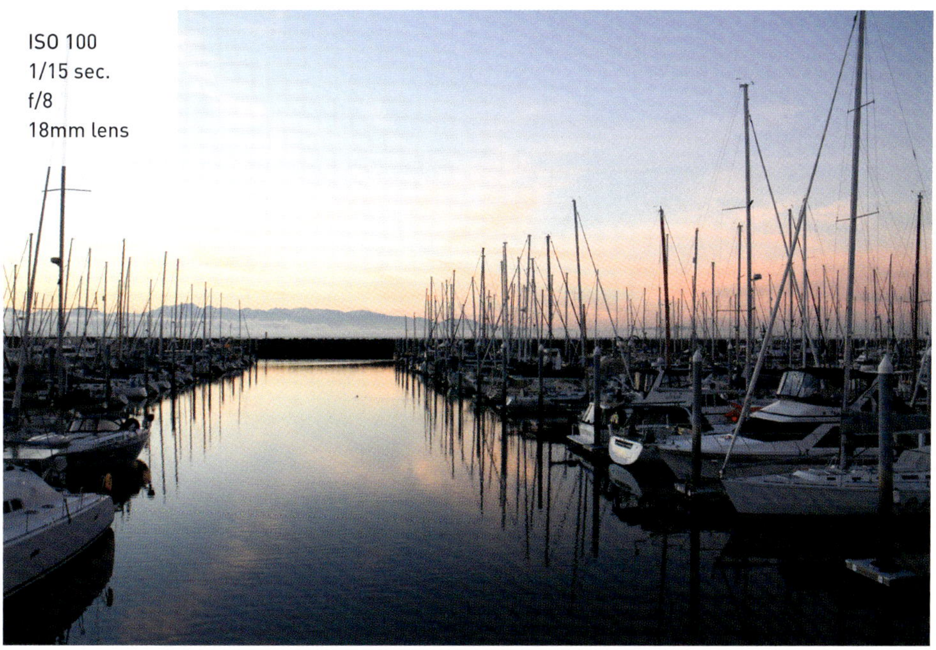

FIGURE 7.8 The Landscape picture style adds sharpness, a little contrast, and more vivid color.

TAMING BRIGHT SKIES WITH EXPOSURE COMPENSATION

Balancing exposure in scenes that have a wide contrast in tonal ranges can be extremely challenging. The one thing you should try not to do is overexpose your skies to the point of blowing out your highlights (unless, of course, that is the look you are going for). It's one thing to have white clouds, but it's a completely different and bad thing to have no detail at all in those clouds. This usually happens when the camera is trying to gain exposure in the darker areas of the image (**Figure 7.9**).

The one way to tell if you have blown out your highlights is to check the Highlight Alert, or "blinkies," feature on your camera (see the "How I Shoot" section in Chapter 4). When you take a shot where the highlights are exposed beyond the point of having any detail, that area will blink on the LCD. Is that particular area important enough to regain detail by altering your exposure? If the answer is yes, then the easiest way to go about it is to use some exposure compensation. With this feature, you can force your camera to choose an exposure that ranges, in 1/3-stop increments, from five stops over to five stops under the metered exposure (**Figure 7.10**).

I generally keep my camera set to –1/3 stop for most of my landscape work unless I am working with a location that is very dark or low key.

USING EXPOSURE COMPENSATION TO REGAIN DETAIL IN HIGHLIGHTS

1. Tap the Exposure Compensation button at the bottom of the screen.
2. Use the Main dial or tap to set the amount of over- or underexposure that you desire.
3. Take another photo.
4. If the blinkies are gone, you are good to go. If not, keep subtracting from your exposure by 1/3 of a stop until you have a good exposure in the highlights.

HIGH-KEY AND LOW-KEY IMAGES

When you hear someone refer to a subject as being *high key*, it usually means that the entire image is composed of a very bright subject with very few shadow areas—think snow or beach. It makes sense, then, that a *low-key* subject has very few highlight areas and a predominance of shadow areas. Think of a cityscape at night as an example of a low-key photo.

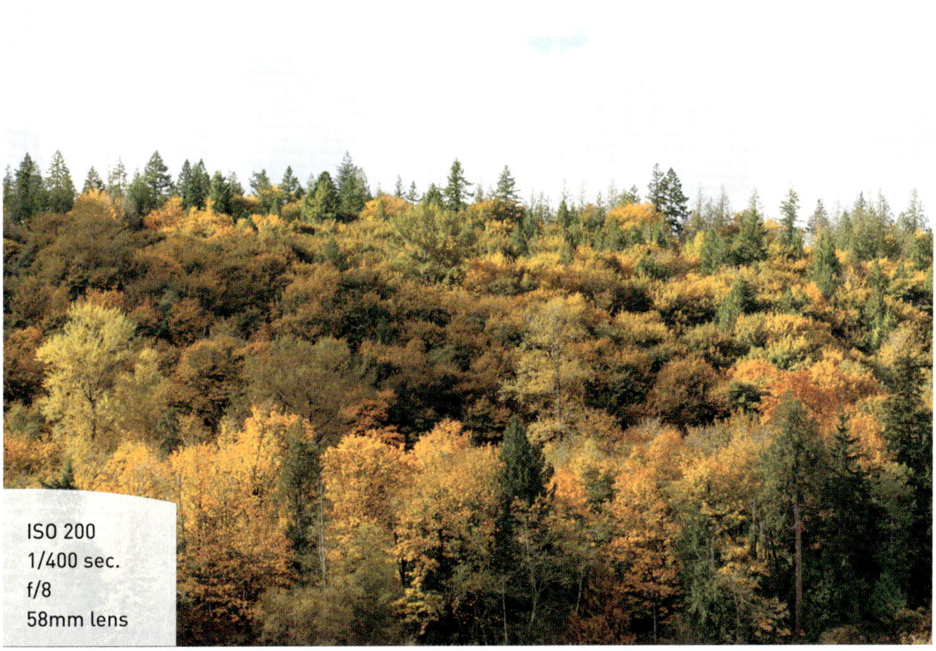

FIGURE 7.9
The camera has done a good job of exposing the foreground, but the sky is too light and lacks detail.

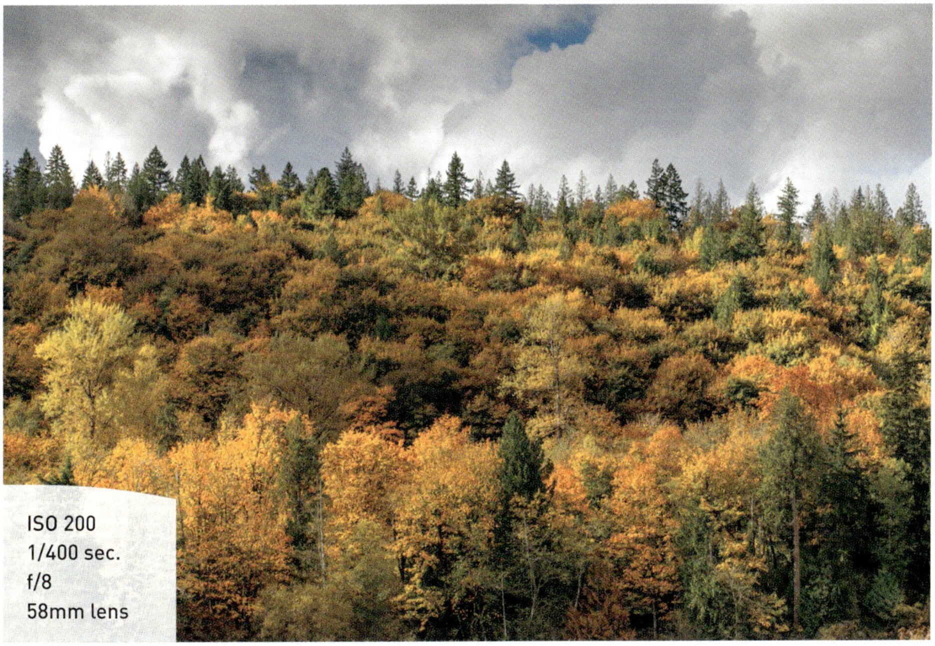

FIGURE 7.10
A compensation of 2/3 stops of under-exposure gave me the darker, more interesting skies that I was after.

SHOOTING BEAUTIFUL BLACK AND WHITE LANDSCAPES

There is nothing as timeless as a beautiful black and white landscape photo. For many, it is the purest form of photography. The genre conjures up thoughts of Ansel Adams out in Yosemite Valley, capturing stunning monoliths with his 8x10 view camera. Well, just because you are shooting with a digital camera doesn't mean you can't create your own stunning photos using the power of the Monochrome picture style. (See the "Classic Black and White Portraits" section of Chapter 6 for instructions on setting up this feature.) Not only can you shoot in black and white, you can also apply built-in filters to lighten or darken different elements within your scene, as well as add contrast and definition.

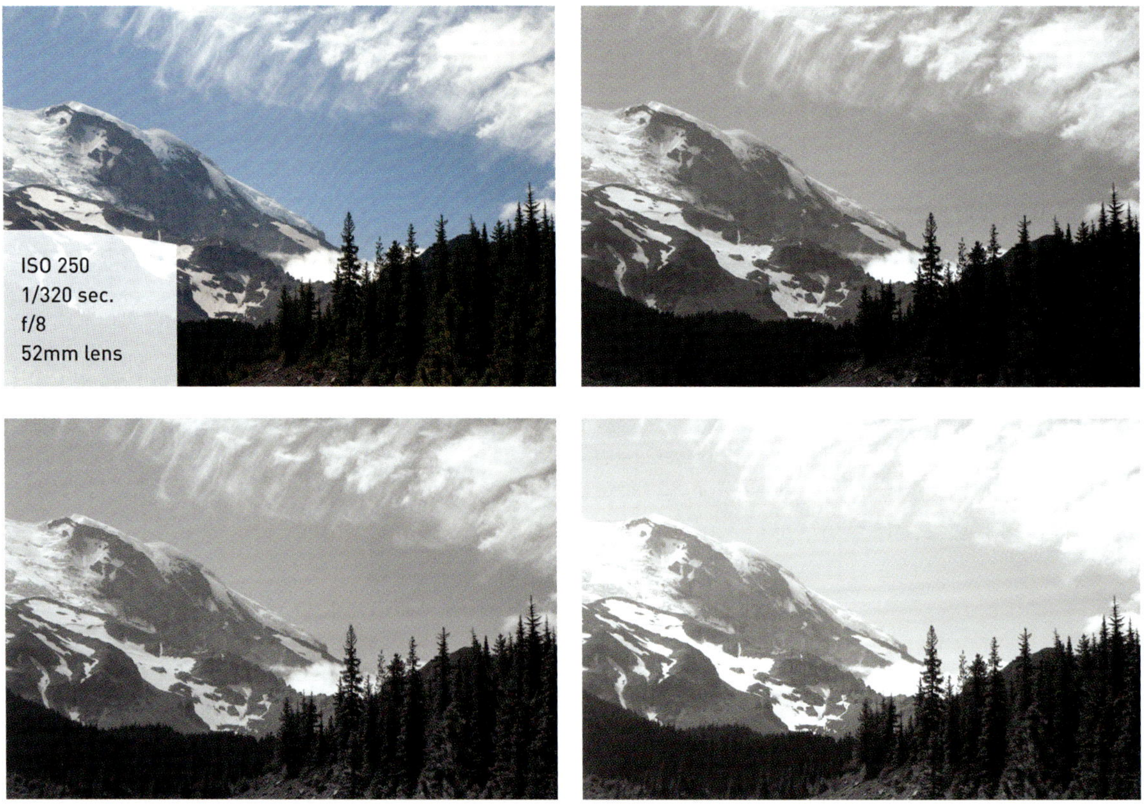

FIGURE 7.11
Adding color filter settings to the Monochrome picture style allows you to brighten or darken elements in your scene. The upper-right image has no filter applied to it. The lower-left has a green filter, and the lower-right has a red filter.

The four filter colors are yellow, orange, red, and green. The most typically used filters in black and white photography are red and yellow. This is because the color of the filter will darken opposite colors and lighten similar colors. So if you want to darken a blue sky, you would use a yellow filter because blue is the opposite of yellow. To darken green foliage, you would use a red filter. Check out the series of shots in **Figure 7.11** with different filters applied.

You can see that there is no real difference in contrast between the color image and the black and white image with no filter. The green filter has the effect of darkening the sky a little and giving a lighter look to the vegetation. Using the red filter makes the sky and the vegetation lighter. For this particular shot, I much prefer the look of the green filter.

Other options in the Monochrome picture style enable you to adjust the sharpness and contrast and even add some color toning to the final image. This information is also in the "Classic Black and White Portraits" section of Chapter 6. Try setting Sharpness to 5 and Contrast to 1 for landscape images. This gives an overall look to the black and white image that is reminiscent of the classic black and white films. Experiment with the various settings to find the combination that is most pleasing to you.

THE GOLDEN LIGHT

If you ask any professional landscape photographer what their favorite time of day to shoot is, chances are they will tell you it's the hours surrounding daybreak and sunset (**Figures 7.12** and **7.13**). The reason for this is that the light is coming from a very low angle to the landscape, which creates shadows and gives depth and character. There is also a quality to the light that seems cleaner and is more colorful than the light you get when shooting at midday. One thing that can dramatically improve any morning or evening shot is the presence of clouds. The sun will fill the underside of the clouds with a palette of colors and add drama to your skies.

WARM AND COOL COLOR TEMPERATURES

These two terms are used to describe the overall color cast of an image. Reds and yellows are said to be *warm*, which is usually the look that you get from the late afternoon sun. Blue is usually the predominant color when talking about a *cool* cast.

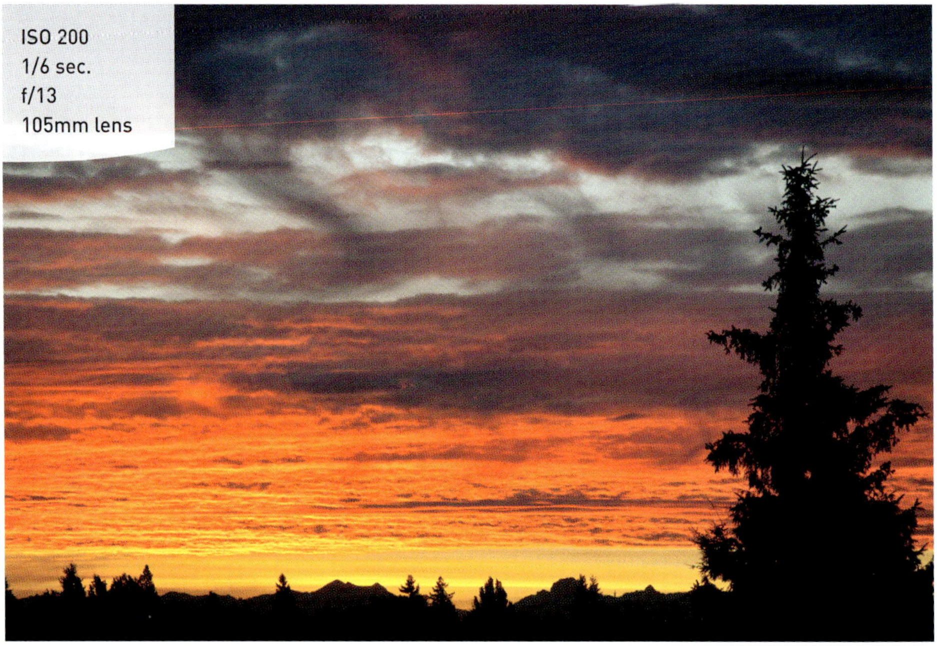

FIGURE 7.12
The right subject can come alive with color during the first few minutes of sunrise.

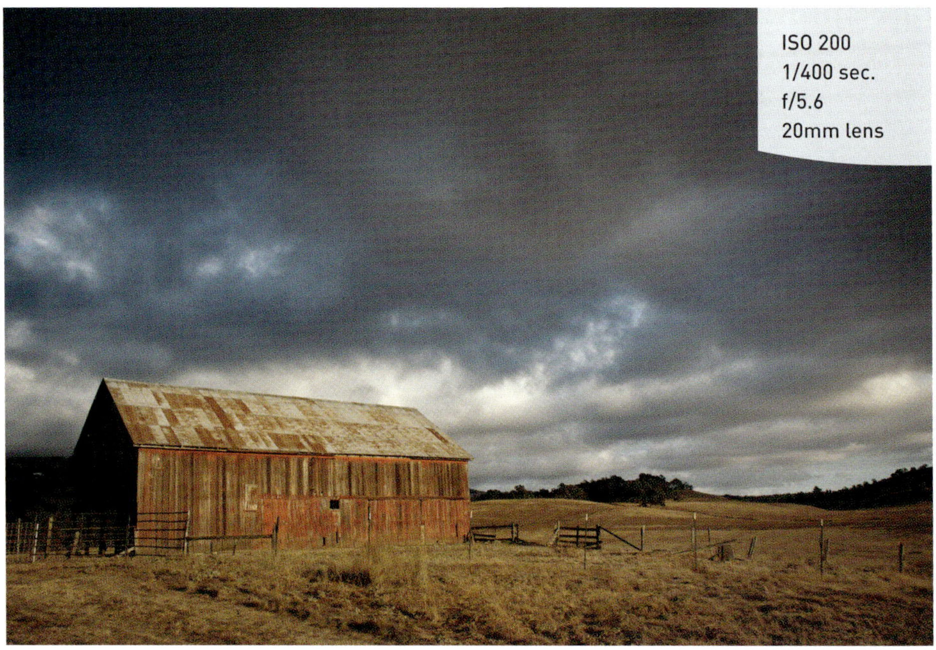

FIGURE 7.13
Late afternoon sun adds drama and warmth to the subject.

WHERE TO FOCUS

Large landscape scenes are fun to photograph, but they can present a problem: Where exactly do you focus when you want everything to be sharp? Since our goal is to create a great landscape photo, we need to concentrate on creating an image that is tack sharp, with a depth of field that renders great focus throughout the scene.

I have already stressed the importance of a good tripod when shooting landscapes. The tripod lets you concentrate on the aperture portion of the exposure without worrying about how long your shutter will be open. This is because the tripod provides the stability to handle any shutter speed you might need when shooting at small apertures. I find that for most of my landscape work I set my camera to Aperture Priority mode and the ISO to 100 (for a clean, noise-free image).

However, shooting with the smallest aperture on your lens doesn't necessarily mean that you will get the proper sharpness throughout your image. The real key is knowing where in the scene to focus your lens to maximize the depth of field for your chosen aperture. To do this, you must utilize something called the "hyper focal distance" of your lens.

Hyper focal distance, also referred to as HFD, is the point of focus that will give you the greatest acceptable sharpness from a point near your camera all the way out to infinity. If you combine good HFD practice with a small aperture, you will get images that are sharp to infinity.

There are a couple of ways to do this, and the one that is probably the easiest is, as you might guess, the one that is most widely used by working pros. When you have your shot all set up and composed, focus on an object that is about one-third of the distance into your frame (**Figure 7.14**). It is usually pretty close to the proper distance and will render favorable results.

TACK SHARP

Here's one of those terms that photographers like to throw around. *Tack sharp* refers not only to the focus of an image but also to the overall sharpness of the image. This usually means that there is excellent depth of field in terms of sharp focus for all elements in the image. It also means that there is no sign of camera shake, which can give soft edges to subjects that should look nice and crisp. To get your images tack sharp, use a small depth of field, don't forget your tripod, use the self-timer to activate the shutter if no cable release is handy, and practice achieving good hyper focal distance when picking your point of focus.

FIGURE 7.14
To get maximum focus from near to far, the focus was set one-third of the way into the image, on the line of trees along the bottom. Using this point of focus with an aperture of f/14 gave me a sharply focused image, from the trees to the distant hills.

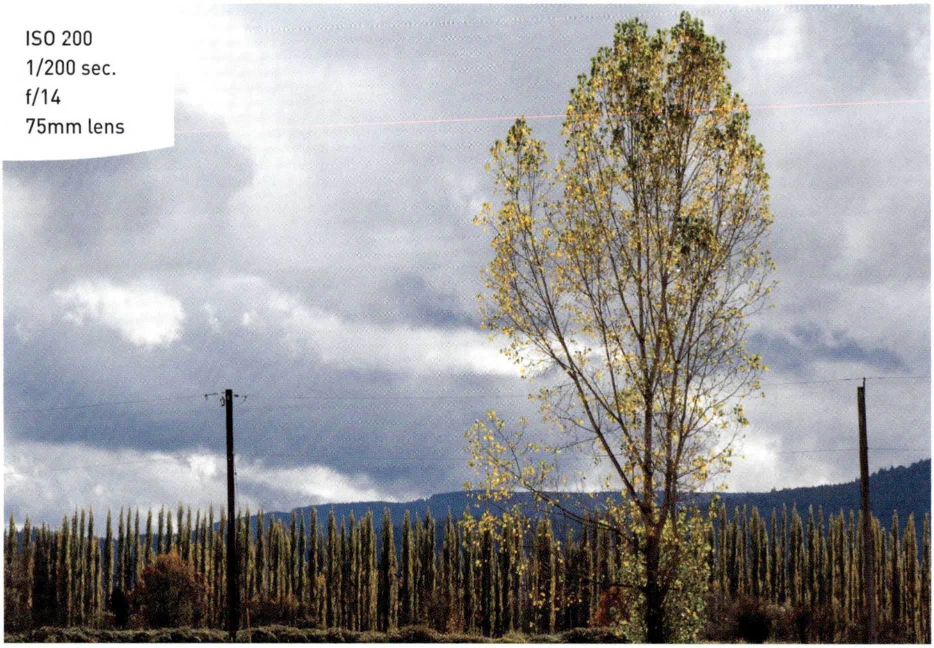
ISO 200
1/200 sec.
f/14
75mm lens

One thing to remember is that as your lens gets wider in focal length, your HFD will be closer to the camera position. This is because the wider the lens, the greater the depth of field you can achieve. This is yet another reason why a good wide-angle lens is indispensable to the landscape shooter.

MAKING WATER FLUID

There's nothing quite as satisfying for the landscape shooter as capturing a silky waterfall shot. Creating the smooth-flowing effect is as simple as adjusting your shutter speed to allow the water to be in motion while the shutter is open. The key is to have your camera on a stable platform (such as a tripod) so that you can use a shutter speed that's long enough to work (**Figure 7.15**). To achieve a great effect, use a shutter speed that is at least 1/15 of a second or longer.

If the water is blinking on the LCD (the highlight alert; see "How I Shoot" in Chapter 4), that indicates a loss of detail in the highlights. Use the Exposure Compensation feature (as discussed earlier in this chapter) to bring details back into the waterfall.

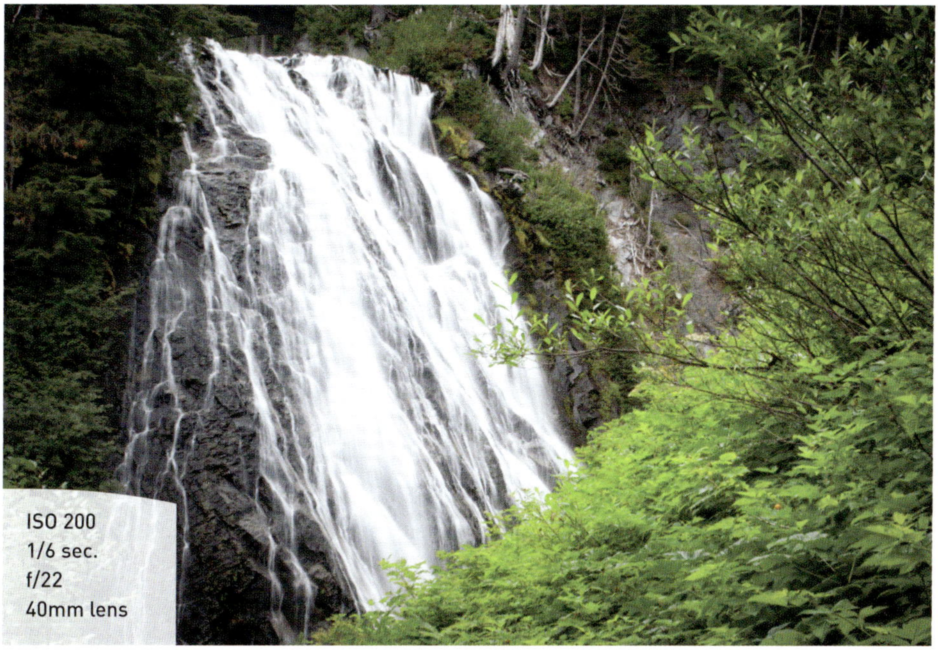

FIGURE 7.15 Using a tripod combined with a small aperture, I was able to get this 1/6-second exposure and make the water look silky smooth.

SETTING UP FOR A WATERFALL SHOT

1. Attach the camera to your tripod, then compose and focus your shot.
2. For the best quality, make sure the ISO is set to 100.
3. Using Av mode, set your aperture to the smallest opening (such as f/22).
4. Press the shutter button halfway so the camera takes a meter reading.
5. Check to see if the shutter speed is 1/15 of a second or slower.
6. Take a photo and then check the image on the LCD.

There is a possibility that you will not be able to have a shutter speed that is long enough to capture a smooth, silky effect, especially if you are shooting in bright daylight conditions. To overcome this obstacle, you need a filter for your lens—either a polarizing filter or a neutral density filter. The polarizing filter redirects wavelengths of light to create more vibrant and accurate colors, reduce reflections, and darken blue skies. It is a handy filter for landscape work. The neutral density filter is typically just a dark piece of glass that serves to darken the scene by one, two, or three stops. This allows you to use slower shutter speeds during bright conditions. Think of it as sunglasses for your camera lens.

DIRECTING THE VIEWER: A WORD ABOUT COMPOSITION

As a photographer, it's your job to lead the viewer through your image. You accomplish this by utilizing the principles of composition, which is the arrangement of elements in the scene that draws the viewer's eye through your image and holds their attention.

There is a general order in which we look at elements in a photograph. The first is brightness. The eye wants to travel to the brightest object within a scene. So if you have a bright sky, it's probably the first place the eye will travel to. The second order of attention is sharpness. Sharp, detailed elements will get more attention than soft, blurry areas. Finally, the eye will move to vivid colors while leaving the dull, flat colors for last. It is important to know these essentials in order to grab—and keep—the viewer's attention and then direct them through the frame.

In **Figure 7.16**, the eye is drawn to the bright white snow and sharp edges of Mount Rainier. From there, it is pulled toward the lightness of the sky and clouds. The eye moves around the green and curved landscape in the foreground, where it is then lifted back up to the mountain, right back to the beginning. The elements within the image all help to keep the eye moving but never leave the frame.

RULE OF THIRDS

There are, in fact, quite a few philosophies concerning composition. The easiest one to begin with is known as the "rule of thirds." Using this principle, you simply divide your viewfinder into thirds by imagining two horizontal and two vertical lines that divide the frame equally.

The key to using this method of composition is to have your main subject located at or near one of the intersecting points (**Figure 7.17**). By placing your subject near these intersecting lines, you are giving the viewer space to move within the frame. The one thing you don't want to do is place your subject smack dab in the middle of the frame. This is sometimes referred to as "bull's eye" composition, and it requires the right subject matter for it to work. It's not always wrong, but it will usually be less appealing and may not hold the viewer's focus.

On the EOS M, the grid overlay can help. This is a feature that actually places a grid over your image, dividing it into thirds, which can be of great benefit in properly composing your image. Press the Menu button, and from the first shooting menu select the Grid display option. Press Set and then choose Grid 1. (The grid doesn't appear on the final photo.)

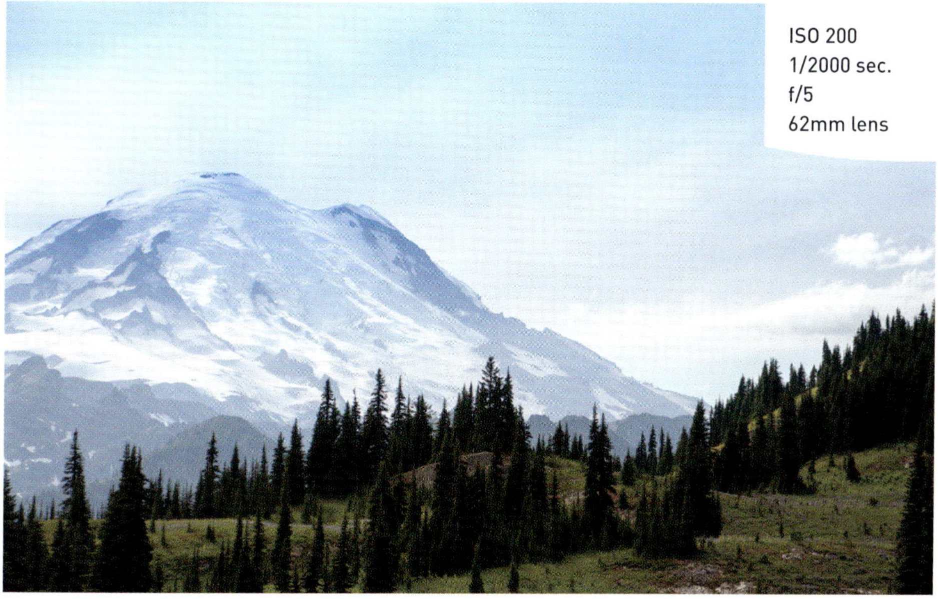

ISO 200
1/2000 sec.
f/5
62mm lens

FIGURE 7.16
The composition of the elements pulls the viewer's eyes around the image, leading from one element to the next in a circular pattern.

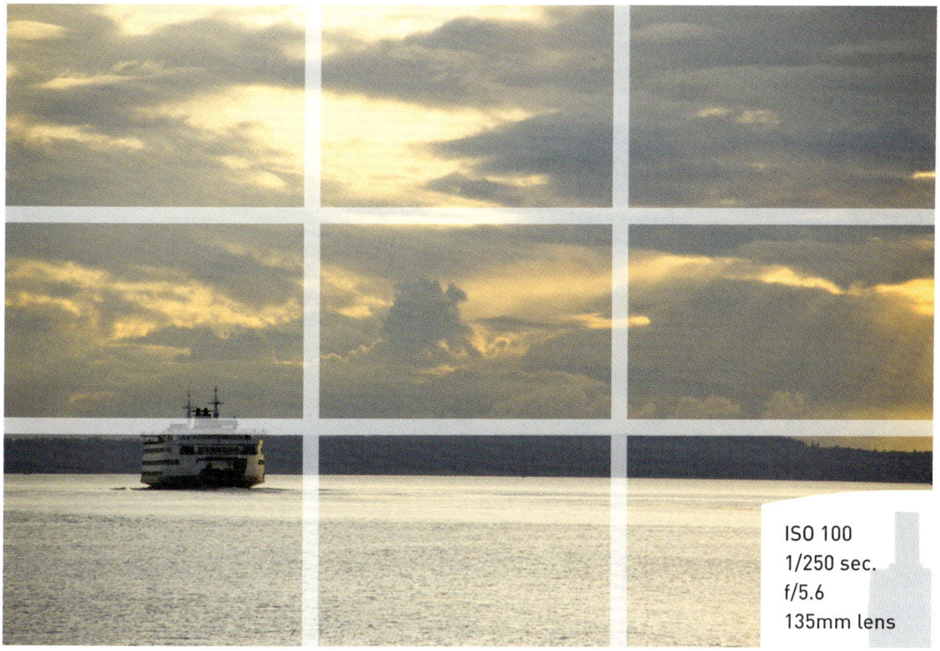

ISO 100
1/250 sec.
f/5.6
135mm lens

FIGURE 7.17
With the rule-of-thirds grid atop this image, you can see that I composed the shot so that the ferry is at the bottom-left intersection and the sky dominates the top two thirds.

The other general rule of thirds deals with horizon lines. Generally speaking, you should position the horizon one third of the way up or down in the frame. Splitting the frame in half by placing your horizon in the middle of the picture is akin to placing the subject in the middle of the frame—it doesn't lend a sense of importance to either the sky or the ground.

In **Figure 7.18**, I incorporated the rule of thirds by aligning the horizon in the top third of the frame, with the boats and water occupying the bottom two-thirds. In doing so, I have created a sense of depth in the image. By selecting the right lens focal length (41mm, in this instance) and the right vantage point, I was able to place my horizon line so that it puts the greatest emphasis on the subject.

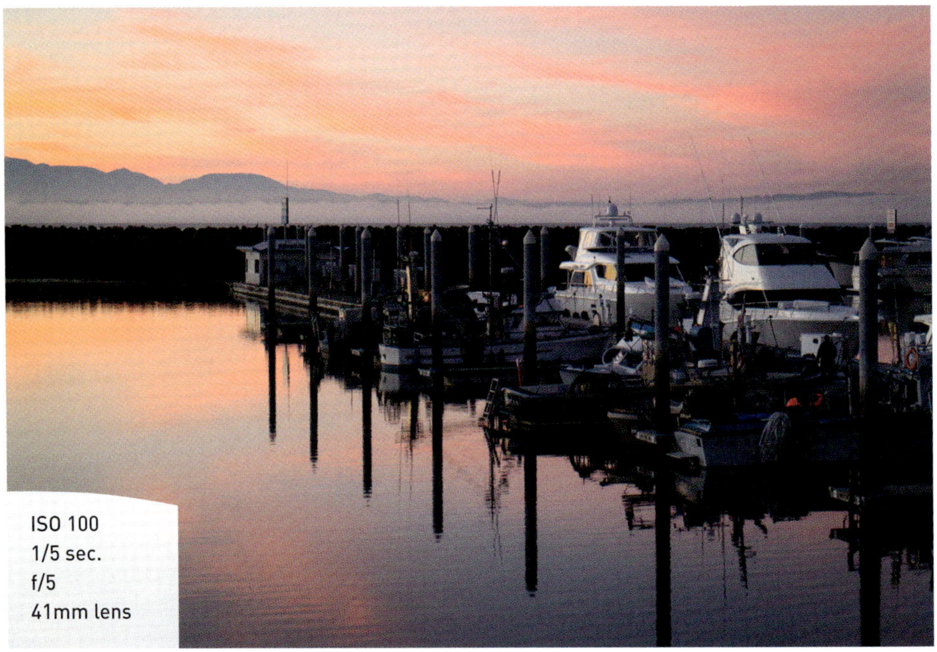

ISO 100
1/5 sec.
f/5
41mm lens

FIGURE 7.18
Placing the horizon of this image in the top third of the frame places emphasis on the marina and water reflection below.

ADVANCED TECHNIQUES TO EXPLORE

This section comes with a warning attached. All of the techniques and topics up to this point have been centered on your camera. The following two sections, covering panoramas and high dynamic range (HDR) images, require you to use image-processing software to complete the photograph. They are, however, important enough that you should know how to correctly shoot for success should you choose to explore these two popular techniques.

SHOOTING PANORAMAS

If you have ever visited the Grand Canyon, you know just how large and wide open it truly is—so much so that it would be difficult to capture its splendor in just one frame. The same can be said for a mountain range or a cityscape or any extremely wide vista. There are two methods that you can use to capture the feeling of this type of scene.

THE "FAKE" PANORAMA

The first method is to shoot as wide as you can and then crop out the top and bottom portion of the frame. Panoramic images are generally two or three times wider than a normal image.

CREATING A FAKE PANORAMA

1. To create the look of a panorama, find your widest lens focal length. If you're using the 18–55mm kit lens that came with the EOS M, it would be the 18mm setting. (If your EOS M's kit lens was the 22mm pancake lens, 22mm is your setting.)
2. Using the guidelines discussed earlier in the chapter, compose and focus your scene, and select the smallest aperture possible.
3. Shoot your image. That's all there is to it from a photography standpoint.
4. Then, open the image in your favorite image-processing software and crop the extraneous foreground and sky from the image, leaving you with a wide panorama of the scene.

Figure 7.19 shows an example using a photo taken near sunset.

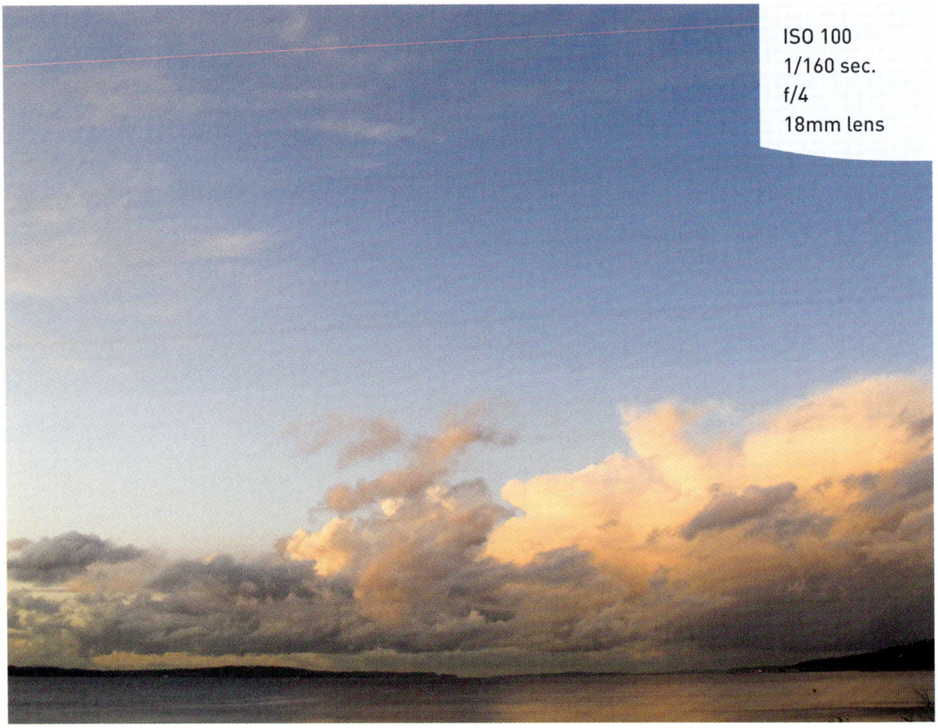

FIGURE 7.19
This is a nice shot, but the clouds are not very interesting and detract from the image.

As you can see, the image was shot with a lot of headroom, which includes a large portion of the sky. It looked like a good crop at the time, but after opening it in my post-processing software I had second thoughts. I opened the Crop tool, took off the top two-thirds of the frame, and came up with a panorama that is much more dynamic and visually interesting (**Figure 7.20**).

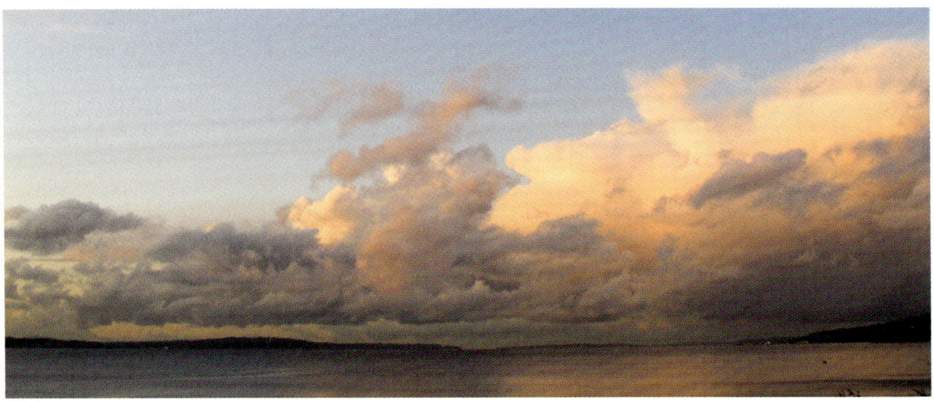

FIGURE 7.20
Cropping adds more impact and makes for a more appealing image.

THE MULTIPLE-IMAGE PANORAMA

The reason the previous method is sometimes referred to as a "fake" panorama is because it is made with a standard-size frame and then cropped down to a narrow perspective. To shoot a true panorama, you need to use either a special panorama camera that shoots a very wide frame, or the following method, which requires the combining of multiple frames.

The multiple-image pano has gained in popularity in the past few years; this is principally because of advances in image-processing software. Many software options are available now that will take multiple images, align them, and then "stitch" them into a single panoramic image. The real key to shooting a multiple-image pano is to overlap your shots by about 30 percent from one frame to the next (**Figures 7.21** and **7.22**).

It is possible to handhold the camera while capturing your images, but the best method for capturing great panoramic images is to use a tripod.

SHOOTING PROPERLY FOR A MULTIPLE-IMAGE PANORAMA

1. Mount your camera on your tripod and make sure it is level.
2. Choose a focal length for your lens that is, ideally, somewhere between 35mm and 50mm. (I used an 18mm here, which worked well, but a wide-angle lens can distort the edges of the images, making it harder to stitch them together.)
3. In Av mode, use a very small aperture for the greatest depth of field. Take a meter reading of a bright part of the scene, and make note of it.
4. Now change your camera to Manual mode (M), and dial in the aperture and shutter speed that you obtained in the previous step.
5. Set your lens to manual focus, and then focus your lens for the area of interest using the HFD method of finding a point one-third of the way into the scene. (If you use the autofocus, you risk getting different points of focus from image to image, which will make the image stitching more difficult for the software.) If you want to use the autofocus, just remember to set the lens to MF before shooting your images.
6. While carefully panning your camera, shoot your images to cover the entire area of the scene from one end to the other, leaving a 30 percent overlap from one frame to the next.

Now that you have your series of overlapping images, you can import them into your image-processing software to stitch them together and create a single panoramic image.

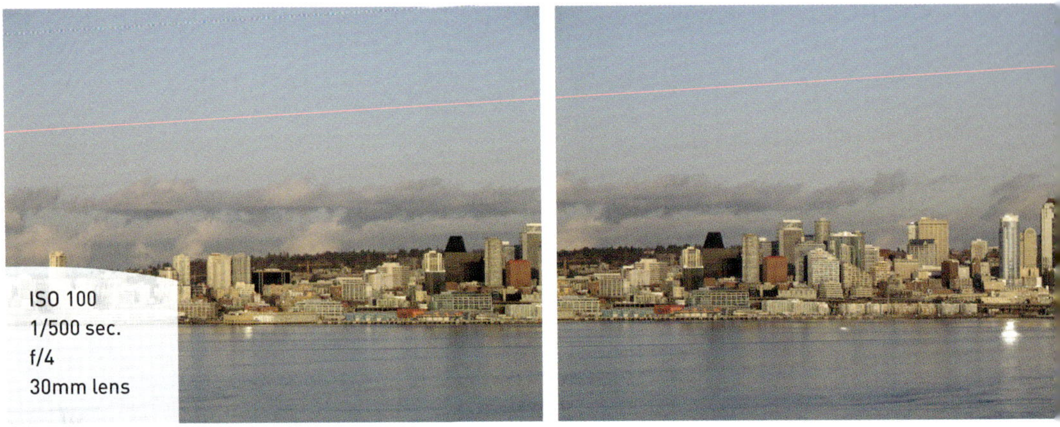

FIGURE 7.21
Here you see the makings of a panorama, with four shots overlapping by about 30 percent from frame to frame.

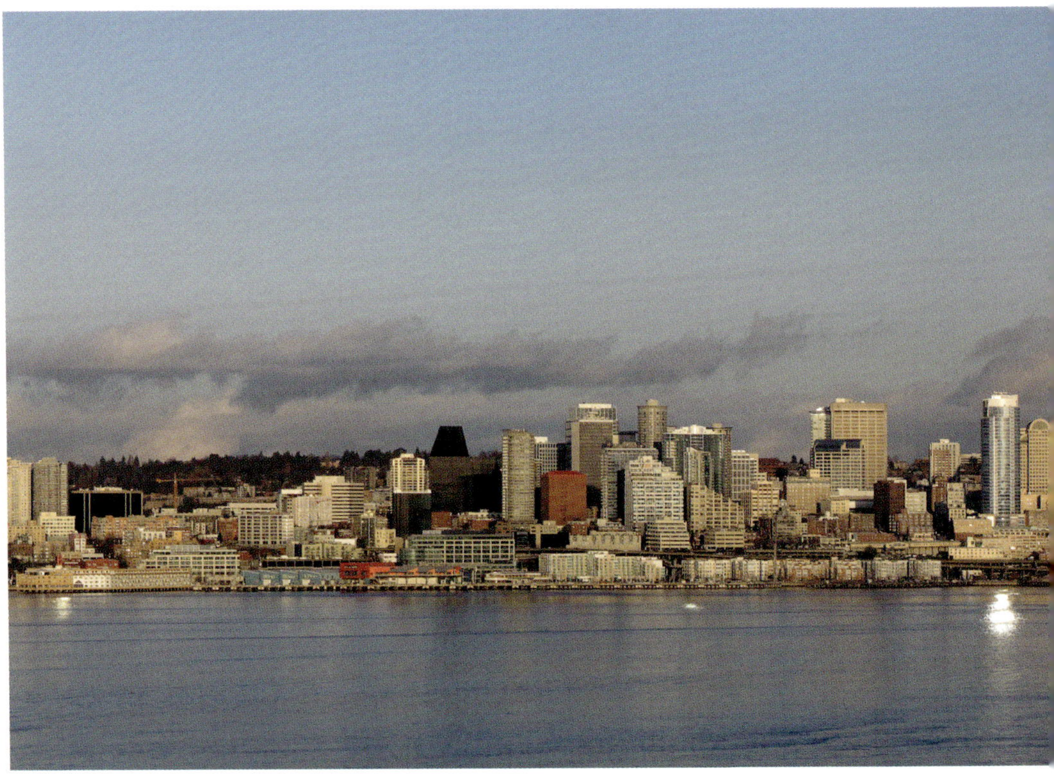

FIGURE 7.22
I used Adobe Photoshop to combine all of the exposures into one large panoramic image.

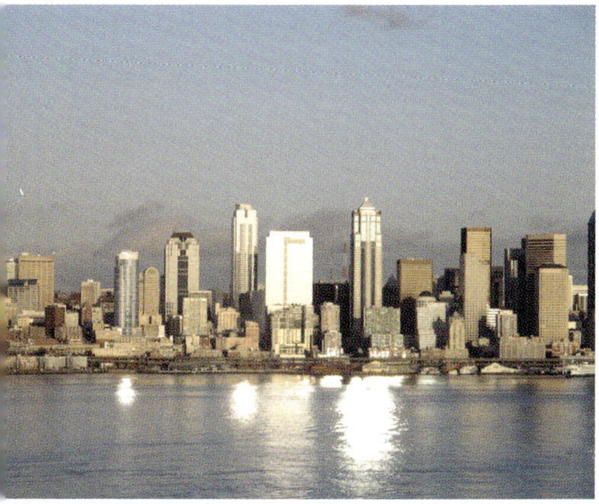

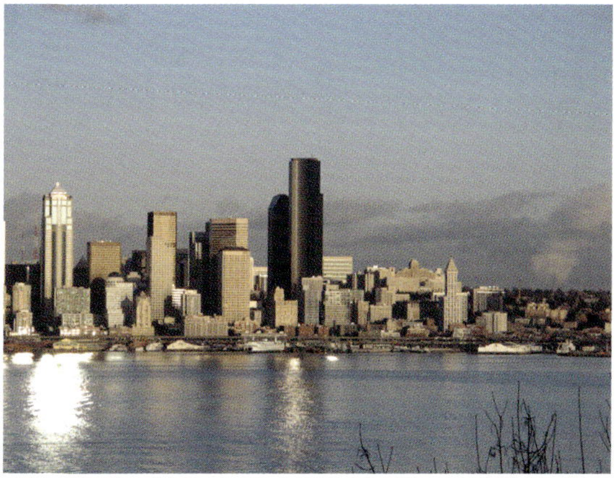

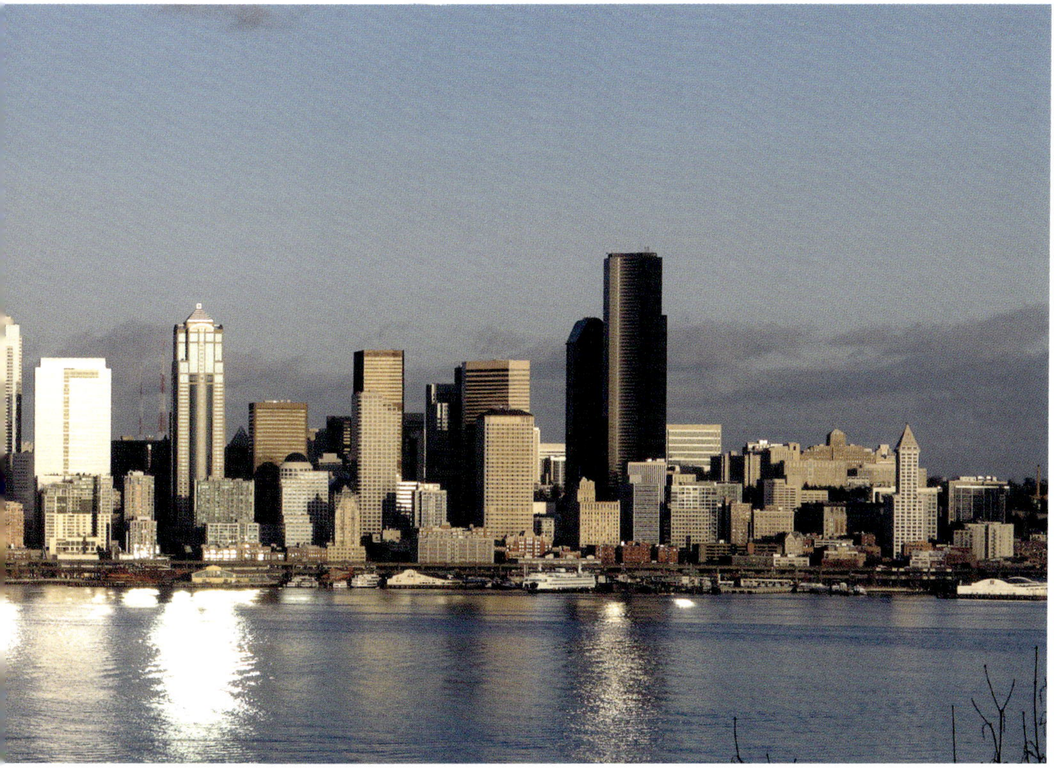

SORTING YOUR SHOTS FOR THE MULTI-IMAGE PANORAMA

If you shoot more than one series of shots for your panoramas, it can sometimes be difficult to know when one series of images ends and the other begins. Here is a quick tip for separating your images.

Set up your camera using the steps listed here. Before you take your first good exposure in the series, hold up one finger in front of the camera and take a shot. Now move your hand away and begin taking your overlapping images. When you have taken your last shot, hold two fingers in front of the camera and take another shot.

Now, when you go to review your images, use the series of shots that fall between the frames with one and two fingers in them. Then just repeat the process for your next panorama series.

SHOOTING HIGH DYNAMIC RANGE (HDR) IMAGES

One of the more recent trends in digital photography is the use of high dynamic range (HDR) to capture the full range of tonal values in your final image. Typically, when you photograph a scene that has a wide range of tones from shadows to highlights, you have to make a decision regarding which tonal values you are going to emphasize, and then adjust your exposure accordingly. This is because your camera has a limited dynamic range, at least as compared to the human eye. HDR photography allows you to capture multiple exposures for the highlights, shadows, and midtones and then combine them into a single image using software (**Figures 7.23** through **7.26**). A number of software applications allow you to combine the images and then perform a process called "tonemapping," whereby the complete range of exposures is represented in a single image. I will not be covering the software applications, but I will explore the process of shooting a scene to help you render properly captured images for the HDR process. Note that using a tripod is absolutely necessary for this technique, since you need to have perfect alignment of each image when they are combined.

(The EOS M features an HDR Backlight Control mode that's similar to this process, but the exposures are all shot and combined into one image within the camera. See Chapter 10 for more information.)

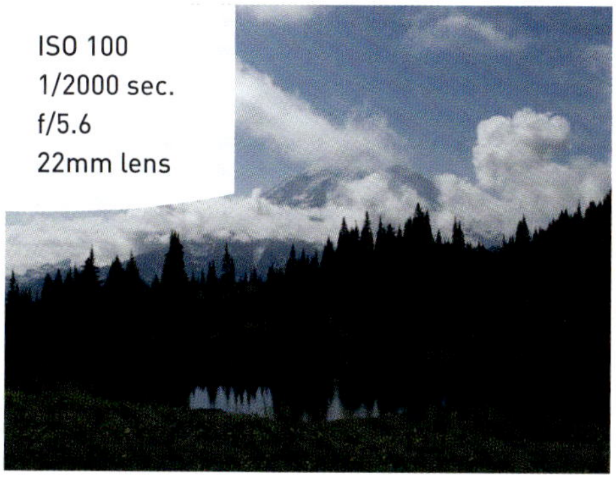

FIGURE 7.23
Underexposing will render more detail in the highlight areas of the clouds and sky.

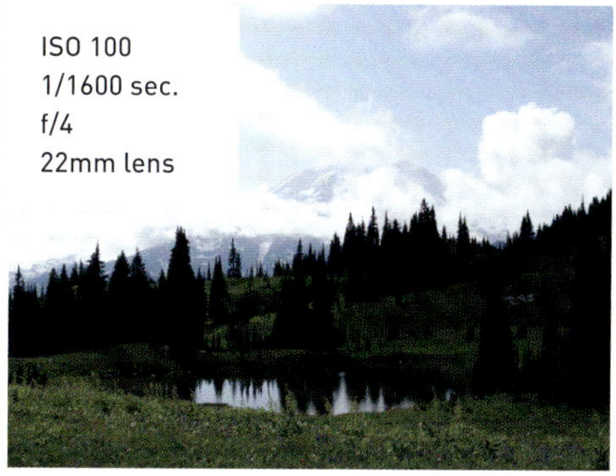

FIGURE 7.24
This is the normal exposure as dictated by the camera meter.

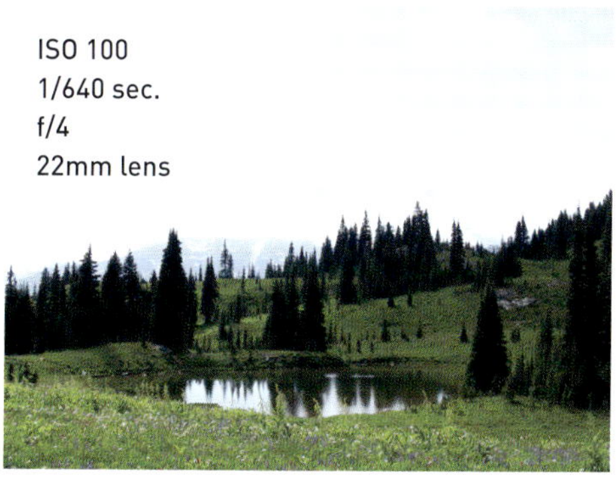

FIGURE 7.25
Overexposing ensures that the darker areas are exposed to get detail in the shadows.

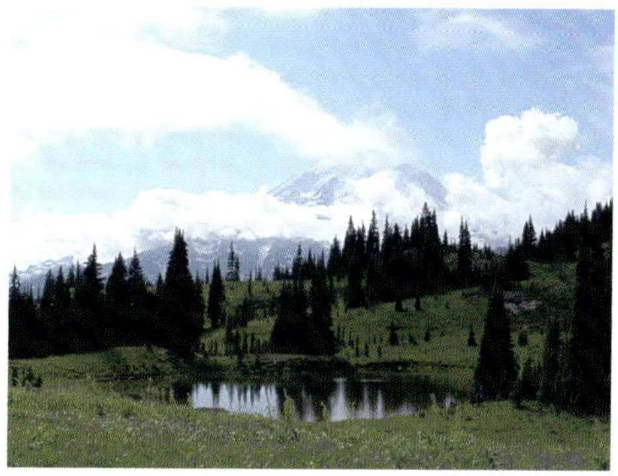

FIGURE 7.26
This is the final HDR image that was rendered from the three other exposures you see here.

SETTING UP FOR SHOOTING AN HDR IMAGE

1. Set your ISO to 100 if possible to ensure clean, noise-free images.
2. Set your program mode to Av. During the shooting process, you will be taking three shots of the same scene, creating an overexposed image, an underexposed image, and a normal exposure. Since the camera is going to be adjusting the exposure, you want it to make changes to the shutter speed, not the aperture, so that your depth of field is consistent.
3. Set your camera file format to RAW. This is extremely important because the RAW format contains a much larger range of exposure values than a JPEG file, and the HDR software will need this information.

4. Change your shooting mode to Continuous. This will allow you to capture your exposures quickly. Even though you will be using a tripod, there is always a chance that something within your scene will be moving (like clouds or leaves). Shooting in the Continuous mode minimizes any subject movement between frames.
5. Adjust the auto exposure bracket (AEB) mode to shoot three exposures in two-stop increments. To do this, first press the Info button until you're viewing just the settings without an image preview (**A**).
6. Tap the Exposure Compensation button, or, if it's not already selected, use the cross keys to highlight it and press the Set button.
7. Turn the Main dial to the right until the AEB indicators move all the way out to –2 and +2 (**B**). Press the Set button to lock in your changes.
8. Press the Info button to return to a preview of the scene on the LCD.
9. Focus the camera using the manual focus method discussed earlier in the chapter, compose your shot, secure the tripod, and hold down the shutter button until the camera has fired three consecutive times.

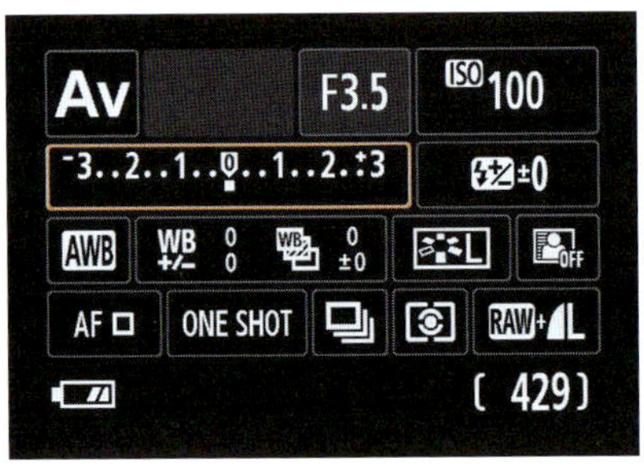

A

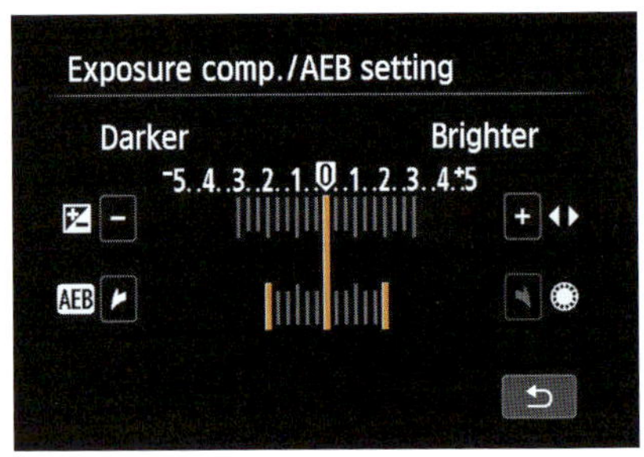

B

A software program—such as Adobe Photoshop, Photomatix Pro, or Nik's HDR Efex Pro—can now process your exposure-bracketed images into a single HDR file.

BRACKETING YOUR EXPOSURES

In HDR, *bracketing* is the process of capturing a series of exposures at different stop intervals. You can bracket your exposures even if you aren't going to be using HDR. Sometimes this is helpful when you have a tricky lighting situation and want to ensure that you have just the right exposure to capture the look you're after. You can bracket in increments as small as a third of a stop. This means that you can capture several images with very subtle exposure variances and then decide later which one is best.

Chapter 7 Assignments

We've covered a lot of ground in this chapter, so it's definitely time to put this knowledge to work in order to get familiar with these new camera settings and techniques.

Comparing depth of field: wide-angle vs. telephoto

You should practice using the hyper focal distance of your lens to maximize the depth of field. You can do this by picking a focal length to work with on your lens. If you have a zoom lens, try using the longest length. Compose your image and find an object to focus on. Set your aperture to f/22 and take a photo.

Now do the same thing with the zoom lens at its widest focal length. Use the same aperture and focus point.

Review the images and compare the depth of field when using a wide-angle focal length as opposed to a telephoto focal length. Try this again with a large aperture as well.

Applying hyper focal distance to your landscapes

Pick a scene that has objects that are near the camera position as well as something that is clearly defined in the background. Try using a wide to medium-wide focal length for this (18–35mm). Use a small aperture and focus on the object in the foreground; then recompose and take a shot. Without moving the camera position, use the object in the background as your point of focus and take another shot. Finally, find a point that is one-third of the way into the frame from near to far and use that as the focus point. Compare all of the images to see which method delivered the greatest range of depth of field.

Using the rule of thirds

With the grid display active, practice shooting while placing your main subject in one of the intersecting line locations. Then take some comparison shots with the same subject in the middle of the frame.

Share your results with the book's Flickr group!

Join the group here: flickr.com/groups/eosmfromsnapshotstogreatshots

8

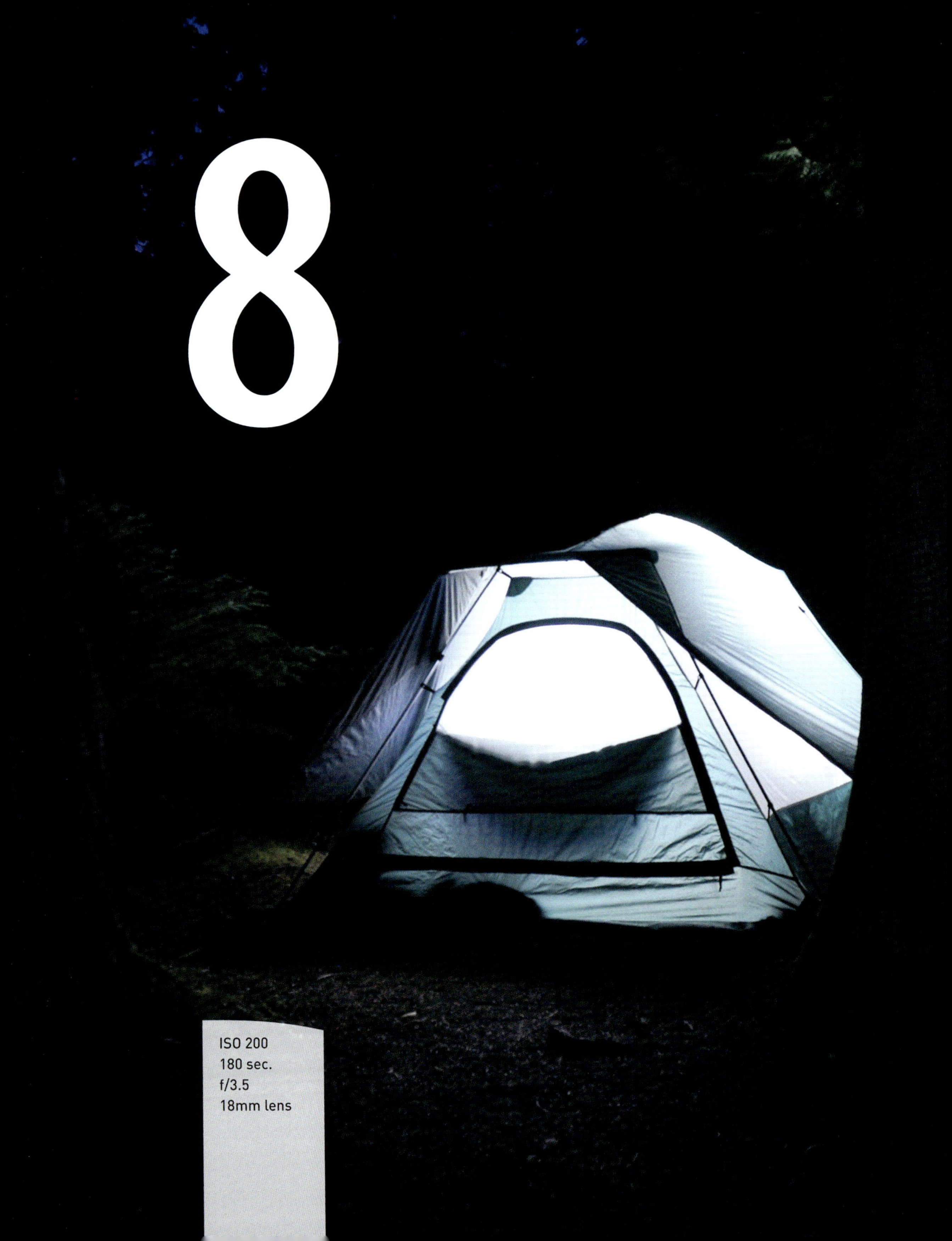

ISO 200
180 sec.
f/3.5
18mm lens

Mood Lighting

SHOOTING WHEN THE LIGHTS GET LOW

There is no reason to put your camera away when the sun goes down. Your EOS M has some great features that let you work with available light or with an optional flash. In this chapter, we will explore ways to push your camera's technology to the limit in order to capture great photos in difficult lighting situations. We will also explore the use of flash and how best to utilize flash features to improve your photography. But let's first look at working with low-level available light.

PORING OVER THE PICTURE

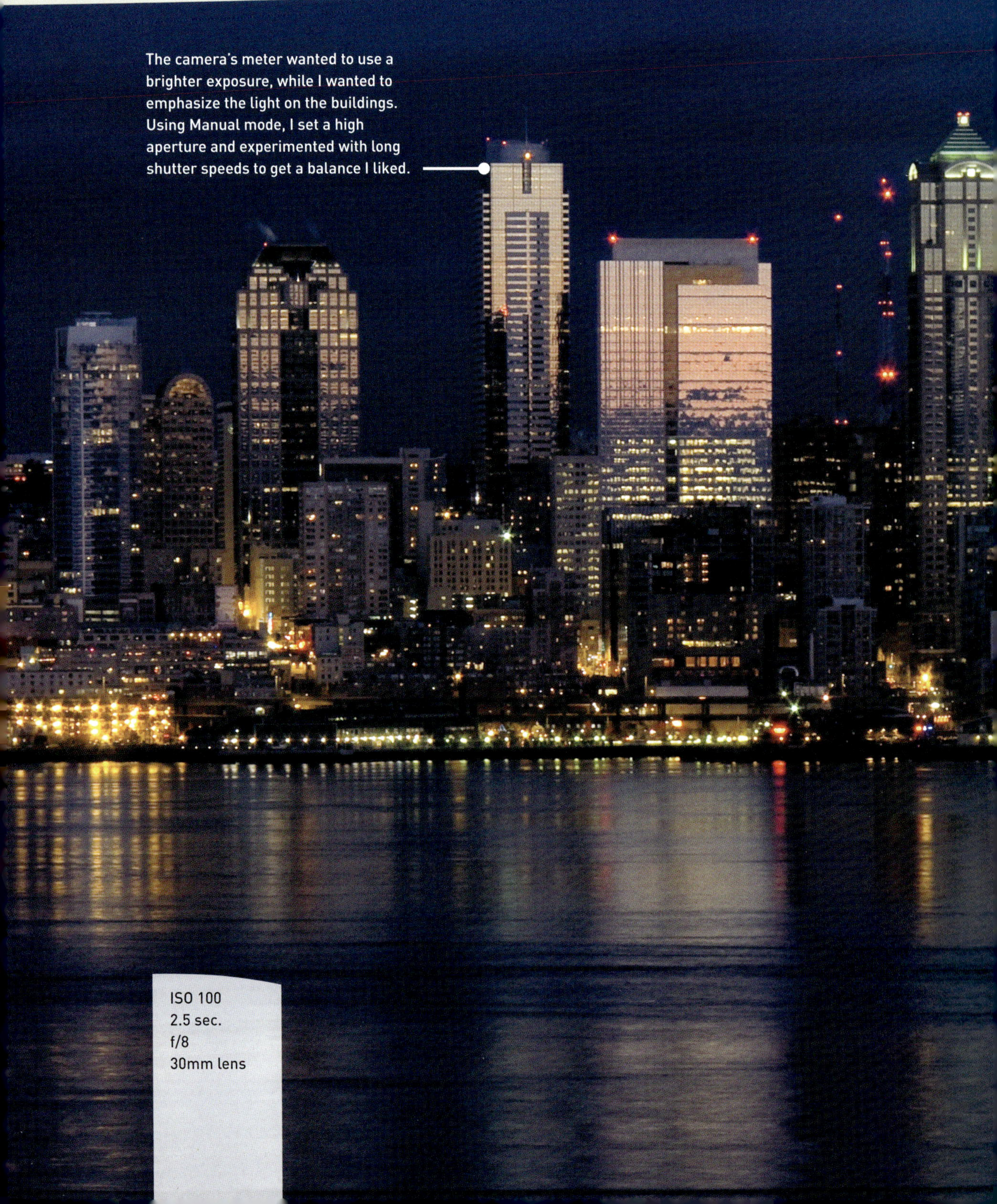

The camera's meter wanted to use a brighter exposure, while I wanted to emphasize the light on the buildings. Using Manual mode, I set a high aperture and experimented with long shutter speeds to get a balance I liked.

ISO 100
2.5 sec.
f/8
30mm lens

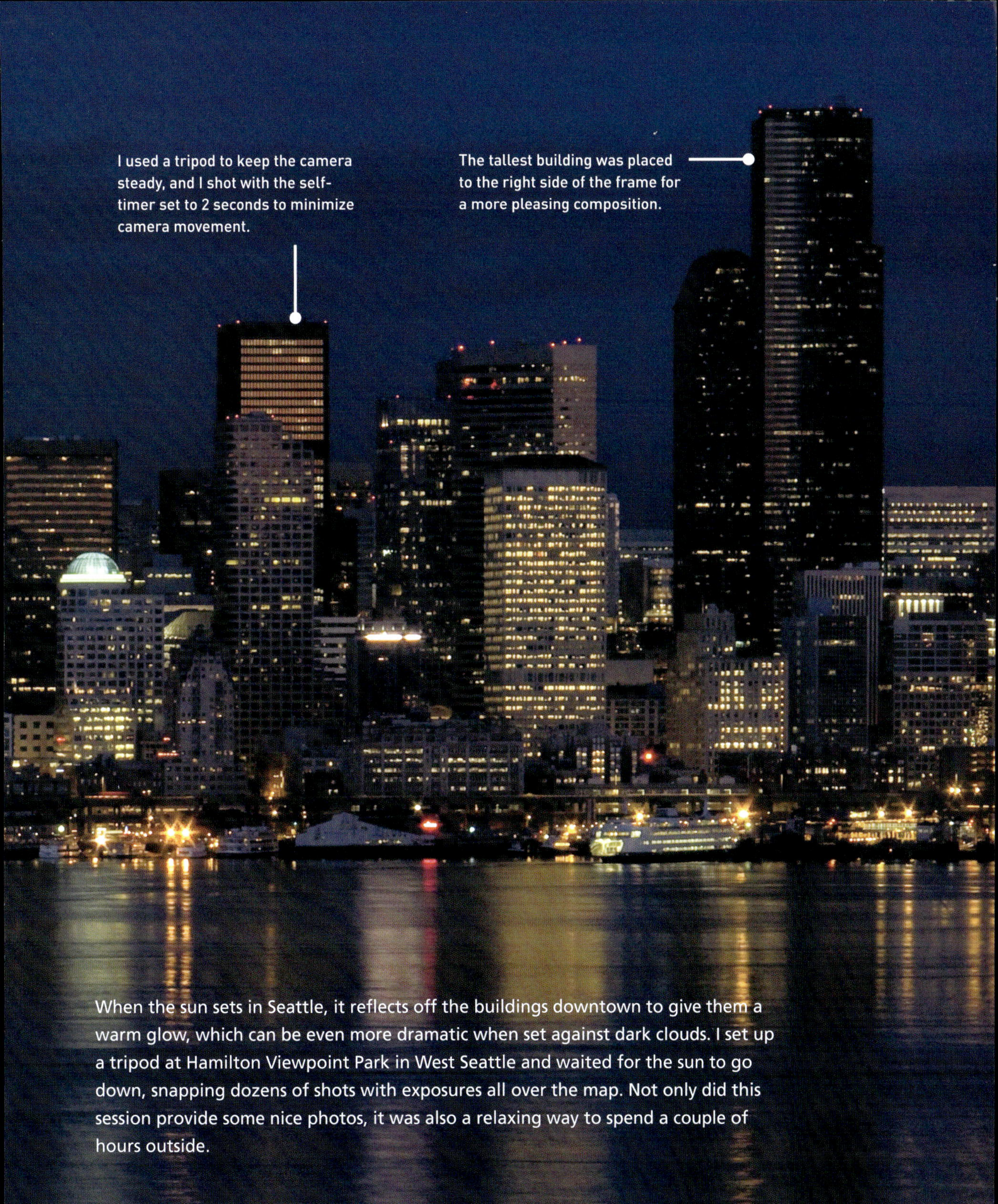

When the sun sets in Seattle, it reflects off the buildings downtown to give them a warm glow, which can be even more dramatic when set against dark clouds. I set up a tripod at Hamilton Viewpoint Park in West Seattle and waited for the sun to go down, snapping dozens of shots with exposures all over the map. Not only did this session provide some nice photos, it was also a relaxing way to spend a couple of hours outside.

PORING OVER THE PICTURE

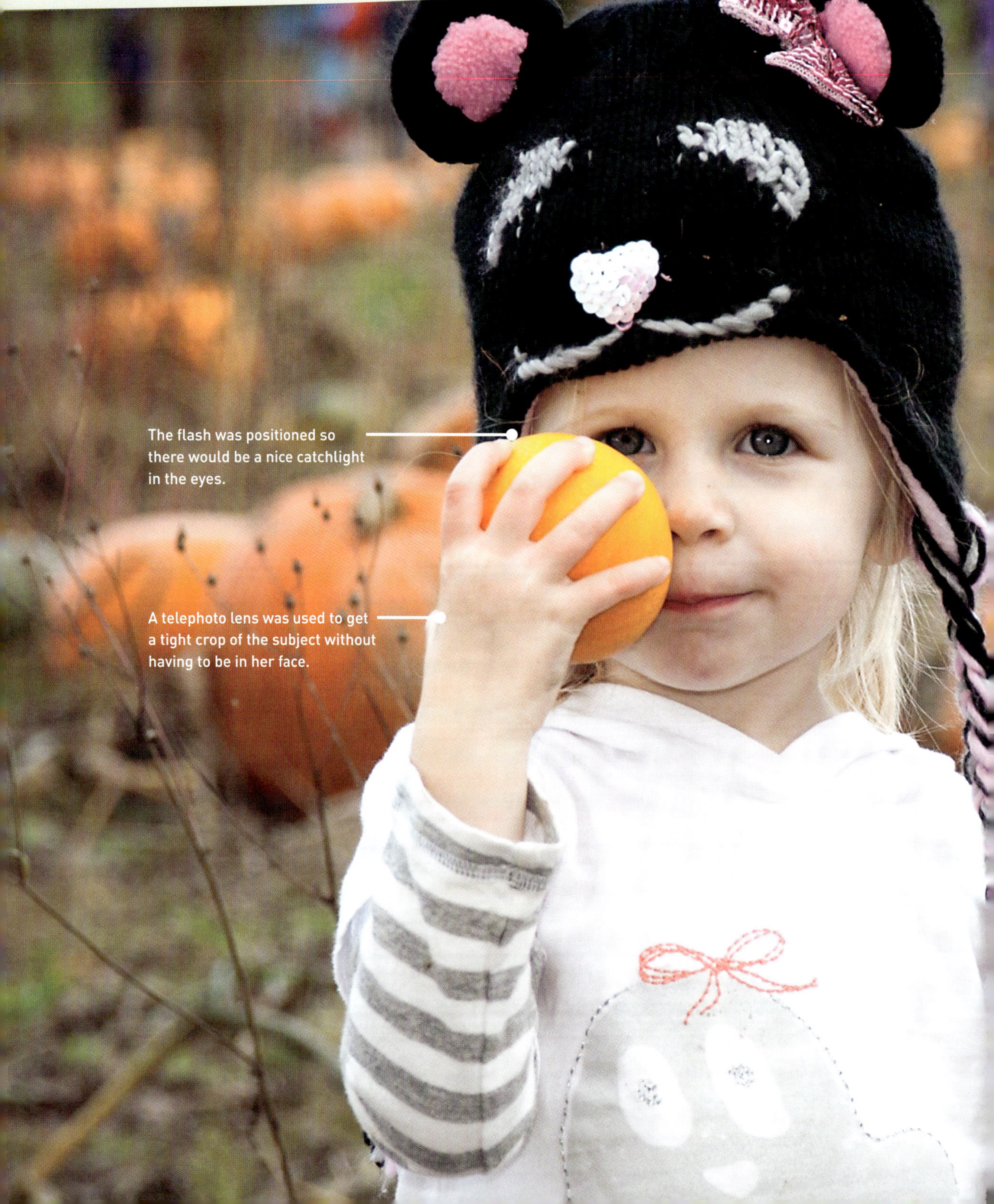

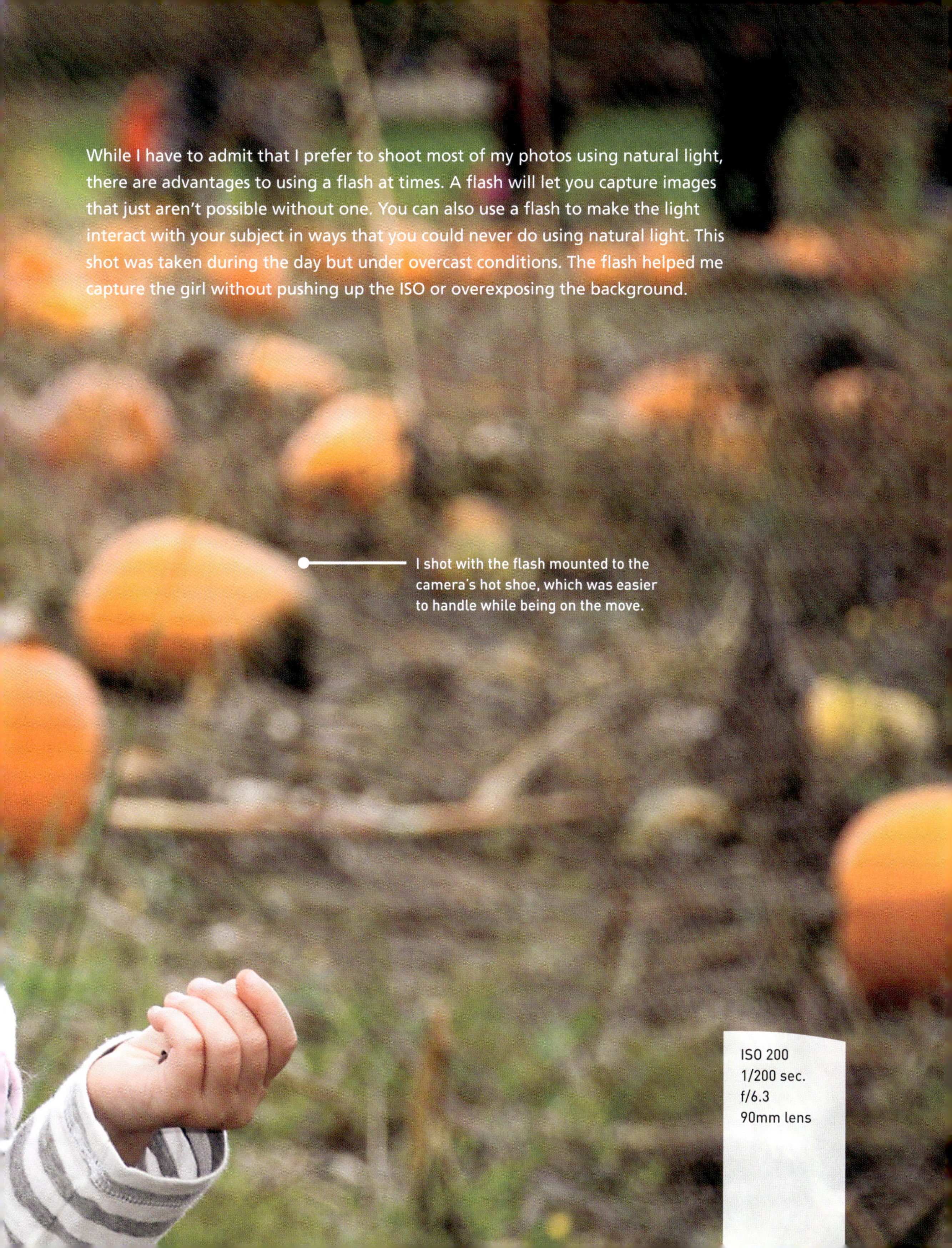

While I have to admit that I prefer to shoot most of my photos using natural light, there are advantages to using a flash at times. A flash will let you capture images that just aren't possible without one. You can also use a flash to make the light interact with your subject in ways that you could never do using natural light. This shot was taken during the day but under overcast conditions. The flash helped me capture the girl without pushing up the ISO or overexposing the background.

I shot with the flash mounted to the camera's hot shoe, which was easier to handle while being on the move.

ISO 200
1/200 sec.
f/6.3
90mm lens

RAISING THE ISO: THE SIMPLE SOLUTION

Let's begin with the obvious way to keep shooting when the lights get low: raising the ISO (**Figure 8.1**). By now you know how to change the ISO: Tap the ISO button on the LCD and turn the Main dial to adjust. In typical shooting situations, you should keep the ISO in the 100–800 range. This will keep your pictures nice and clean by keeping the digital noise to a minimum. But as the available light gets low, you might find yourself working in the higher ranges of the ISO scale, which could lead to more noise in your image.

You could use a flash, but that has a limited range (15–20 feet) that might not work for you. Also, you could be in a situation where flash is prohibited or at least frowned upon, like at a wedding or in a museum.

And what about a tripod in combination with a long shutter speed? That is also an option, and we'll cover it a little further into the chapter. The problem with using a tripod and a slow shutter speed in low-light photography, though, is that it performs best when subjects aren't moving. Besides, try to set up a tripod in a Metro station and see how quickly you grab the attention of the security guards.

So if the only choice to get the shot is to raise the ISO to 800 or higher, make sure that you turn on the High ISO Speed Noise Reduction feature. This menu function is set to Standard by default, but as you start using higher ISO values you should consider changing it to the Strong setting. (See Chapter 7 for setting the noise-reduction features.)

Raising the noise reduction to the Strong setting slightly increases the processing time for your images, so if you are shooting in the Continuous drive mode you might see a little reduction in the speed of your frames per second.

NOISE REDUCTION SAVES SPACE

When shooting at very high ISO settings, running High ISO Speed NR at the Standard or Strong setting can save you space on your memory card. If you are saving your photos as JPEGs, the camera will compress the information in the image to take up less space. When you have excessive noise, you can literally add megabytes to the file size. This is because the camera has to deal with more information: It views the noise in the image as photo information and, therefore, tries not to lose that information during the compression process. That means more noise equals bigger files. So not only will turning on the High ISO Speed NR feature improve the look of your image, it will also save you some space so you can take a few more shots.

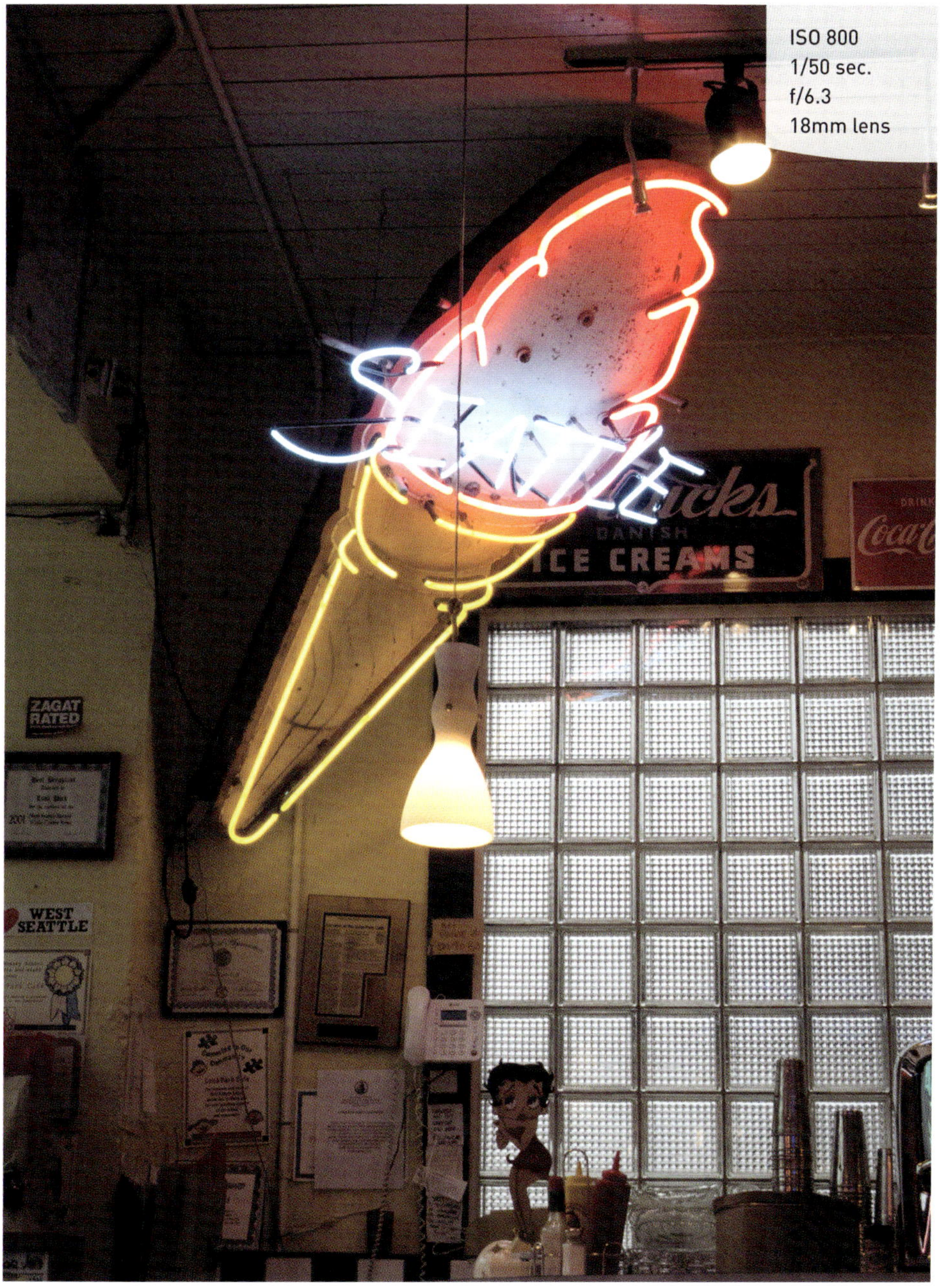

ISO 800
1/50 sec.
f/6.3
18mm lens

FIGURE 8.1
A moderate or high ISO level enables you to shoot in low-light situations without incurring motion blur.

To see the effect of High ISO Speed Noise Reduction, you need to zoom in and take a closer look (**Figures 8.2** and **8.3**).

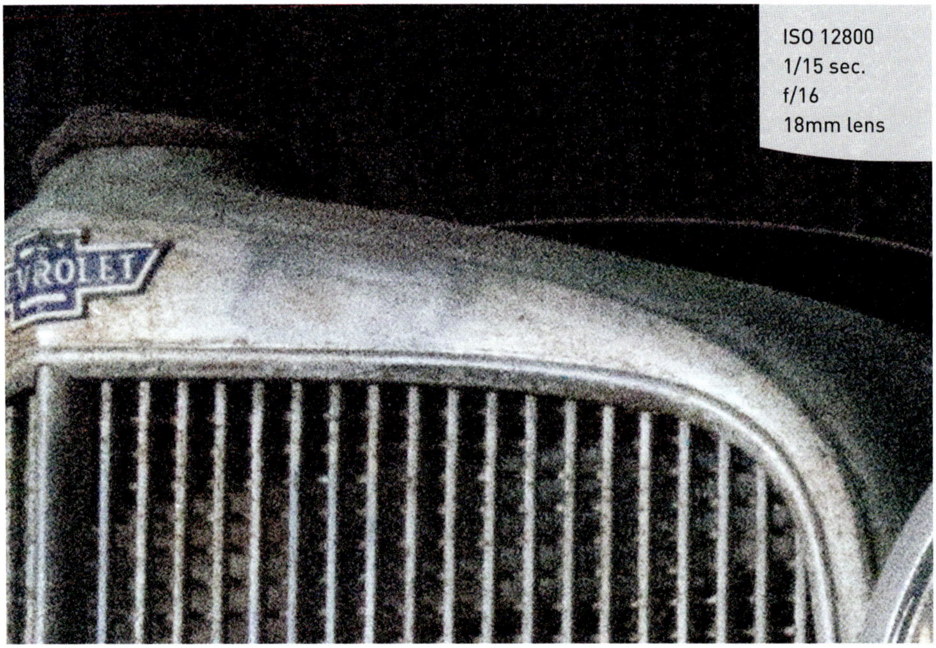

FIGURE 8.2
Here is an enlargement of a car shot without any noise reduction.

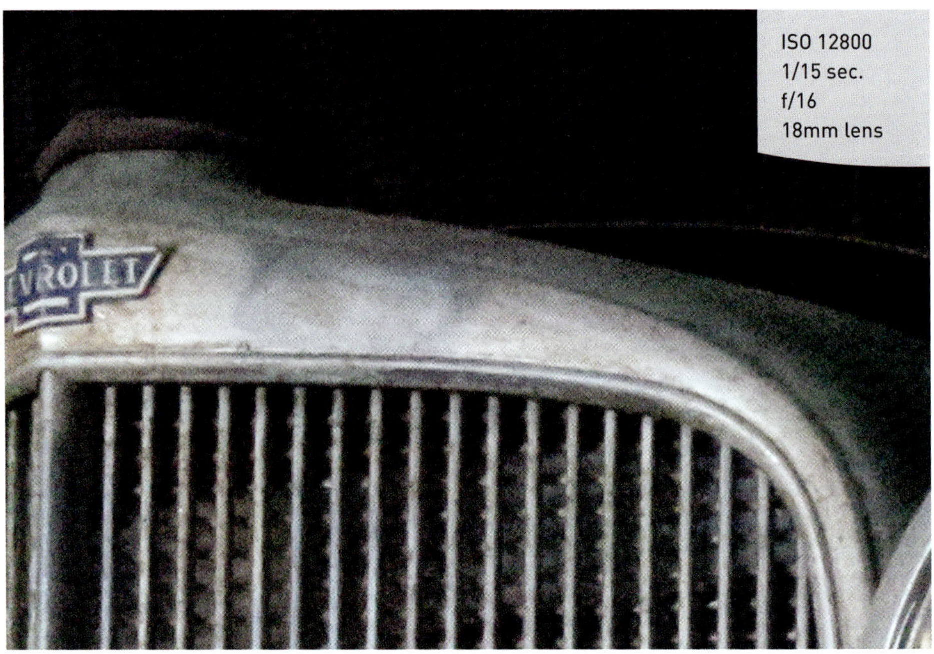

FIGURE 8.3
Here's the same image shot with High ISO NR set to Strong.

USING VERY HIGH ISOS

Is ISO 12800 just not enough for you? Well in that case, you will need to turn on the ISO Expansion setting. This setting opens up another stop of ISO, raising the new limit to an incredible 25600. The highest setting will not appear in your ISO scale as a number, but as H for 25600.

SETTING UP THE ISO EXPANSION FEATURE

1. Press the Menu button and locate the Custom Functions screen (**A**).
2. Press the Left/Right cross keys until you see the C. Fn I: Exposure ISO expansion menu.
3. Press Set and change the setting from Off to On (**B**).
4. Press the Menu button twice to exit, then press the ISO button to find the additional ISO setting of H (25600).

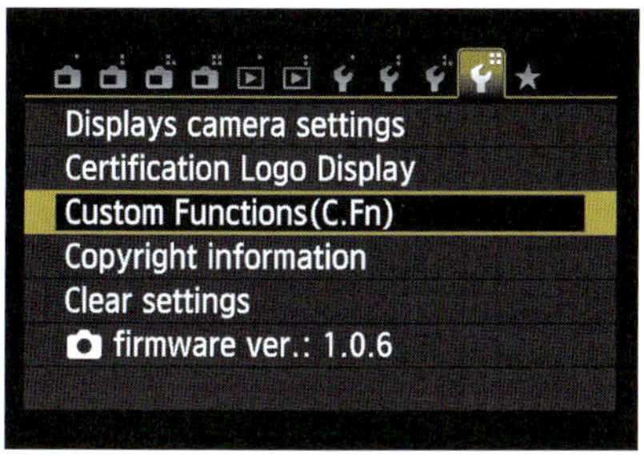

A

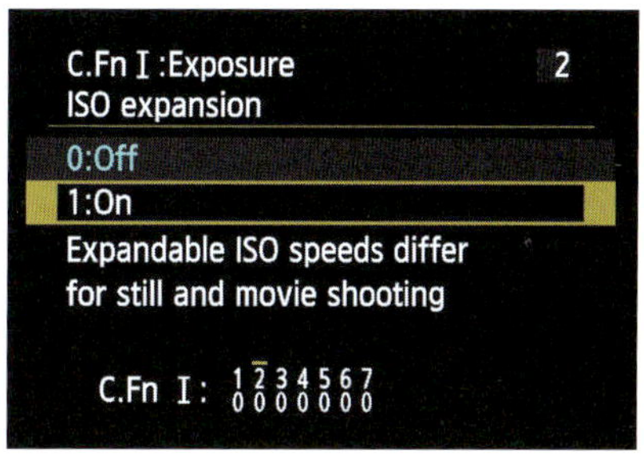

B

A word of warning about the expanded ISO settings: Although it is great to have high ISO settings available during low-light shooting, they should always be your last resort. Even with the High ISO Speed NR setting turned on, the amount of visible noise will be extremely high. I can't think of a situation where I ever needed to use the 25600 (H) setting, but you might find yourself at a nighttime sporting event under the lights, which would require an ISO of 3200 or 6400 to improve your shutter speeds and capture the action.

STABILIZING THE SITUATION

If you own the Canon EF-M 18–55mm or one of Canon's other image stabilizer (IS) lenses (and you also own the EF-EOS M Mount Adapter), the lens can squeeze two stops of exposure out of your camera when you're shooting without a tripod. Typically, the average person can handhold their camera down to about 1/60 of a second before blurriness results due to hand shake. As the length of the lens is increased (or zoomed), the ability to handhold at slow shutter speeds (1/60 and slower) and still get sharp images is further reduced.

The Canon IS lenses contain small gyro sensors and servo-actuated optical elements, which correct for camera shake and stabilize the image. The IS function is so good that it is possible to improve your handheld photography by two or three stops, meaning that if you are pretty solid at a shutter speed of 1/60, the IS feature lets you shoot at 1/15 and possibly even 1/8 of a second (**Figures 8.4** and **8.5**).

SELF-TIMER

Whether you are shooting with a tripod or even resting your camera on a wall, you can increase the sharpness of your pictures by taking your hands out of the equation. Whenever you use your finger to depress the shutter release button, you are increasing the chance that there will be a little bit of shake in your image. To eliminate this possibility, try setting your camera up to use the self-timer. To turn on the self-timer, press the Drive Mode Selection button and then turn the Main dial until the self-timer icon appears. There are three self-timer modes to choose from. I generally use the 2-second mode to cut down on time between exposures.

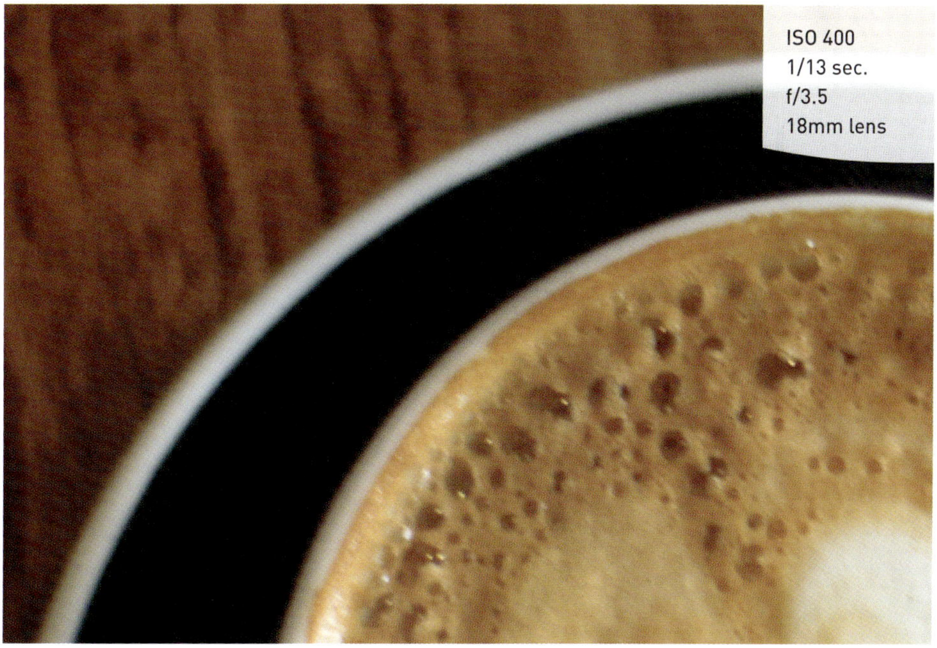

FIGURE 8.4
This image was shot handheld with the IS turned off (zoomed in to show detail).

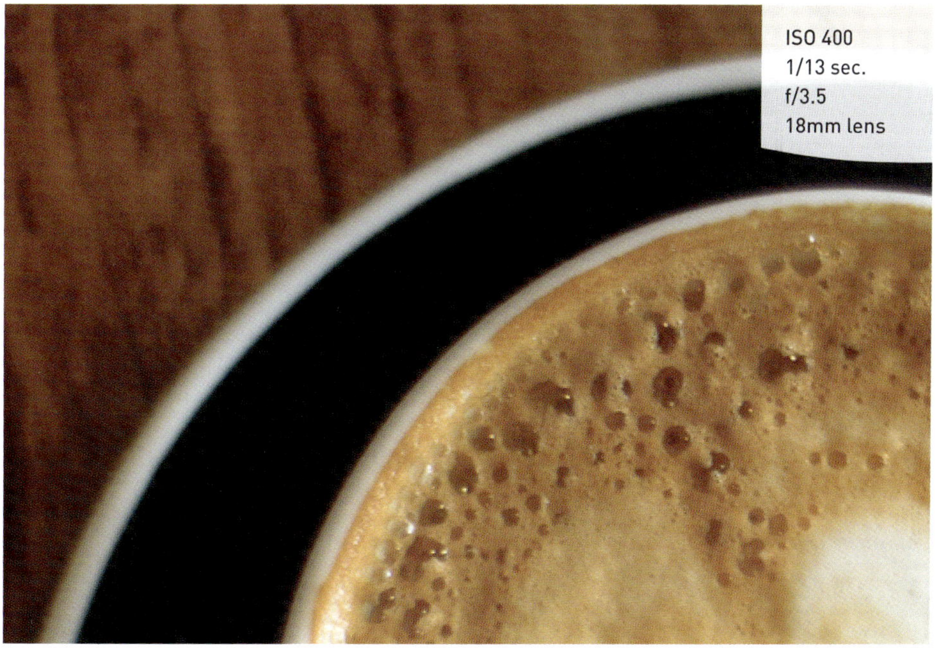

FIGURE 8.5
Here is the same subject shot with the same settings, but this time with IS turned on.

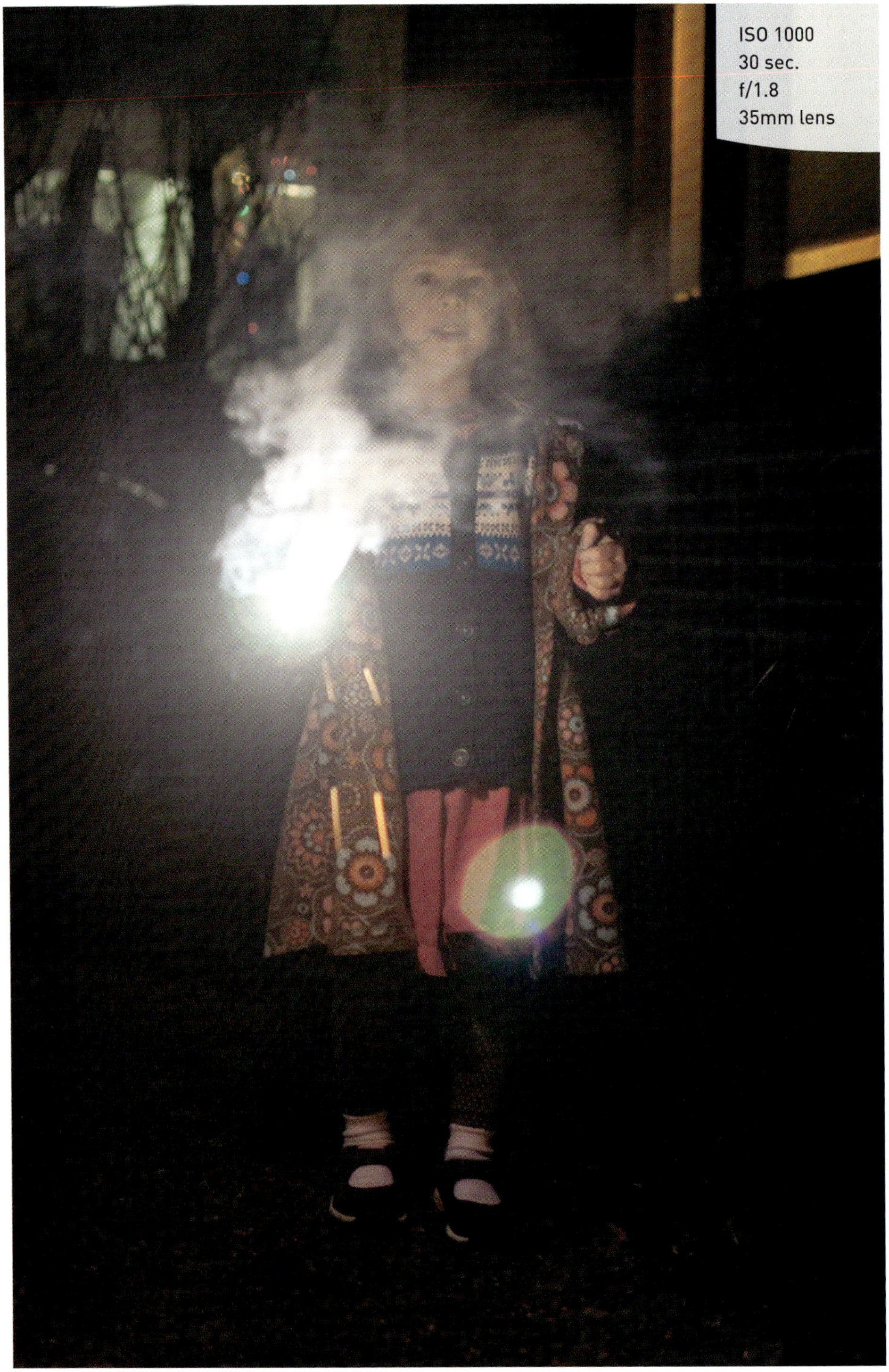

FIGURE 8.6
Sometimes manual focusing is required to get a night shot.

ISO 1000
30 sec.
f/1.8
35mm lens

FOCUSING IN LOW LIGHT

Occasionally the light levels might be too low for the camera to achieve an accurate focus. There are a few things that you can do to overcome this obstacle.

First, you should know that the camera utilizes contrast in the viewfinder to establish a point of focus. This is why your camera will not be able to focus when you point it at a white wall or a cloudless sky; it simply can't find any contrast in the scene to work with. Knowing this, you might be able to use the FlexiZone – Single option in One Shot mode to find an area of contrast that is at the same distance as your subject. You can then hold that focus by holding down the shutter button halfway and recomposing your image.

Then there are those times when there just isn't anything there for you to focus on. On these occasions, take advantage of the AF+MF mode or turn off the autofocus feature and manually focus the lens (**Figure 8.6**). Don't forget to put it back in AF mode at the end of your shoot.

One example of this would be a fireworks display. If you point your lens to the night sky in any automatic focus (AF) mode, it will just keep searching for—and not finding—a focus point.

FOCUS ASSIST

Another way to ensure good focus is to enable the EOS M's Focus Assist mode. Focus Assist uses a small red beam of light to shine some light on the scene, which assists the autofocus system in locating more detail. This feature is automatically activated when shooting in the Basic zone (except in Landscape, Sports, and Flash Off modes for the following reasons: in Landscape mode, the subject is usually too far away; in Sports mode, the subject is probably moving; and in Flash Off mode, you've disabled the flash entirely). Focus Assist should be enabled by default, but you can check the menu just to make sure.

TURNING ON THE FOCUS ASSIST FEATURE

1. Press the Menu button, use the Main dial to get to the Custom Functions menu tab, highlight Custom Functions, and press the Set button (**A**).
2. Use the Left/Right cross keys to get to the C. Fn III: Autofocus/Drive AF-assist beam firing feature and see the current setting for this function (**B**).

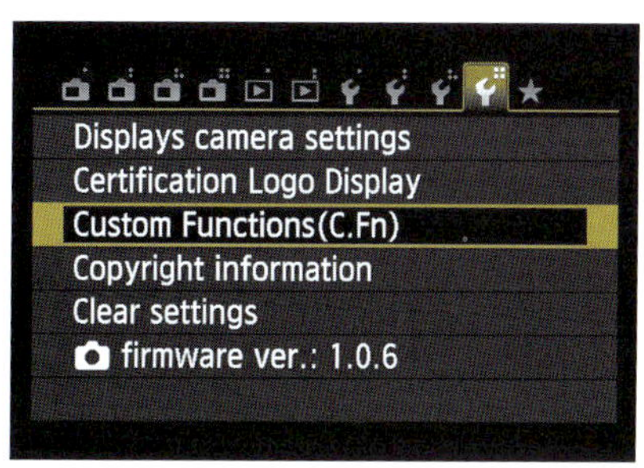

A

3. If it is not enabled, press the Set button, highlight Enable, and press the Set button again.
4. Press the shutter button to focus; Focus Assist will activate if necessary.

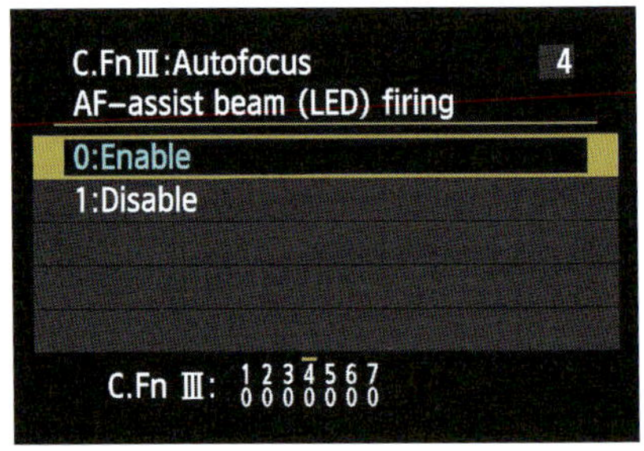

B

DISABLING THE FLASH

1. If a flash is connected but you don't want it to fire, press the Menu button and then scroll the Main dial to highlight the first shooting menu (far left).
2. Scroll down to External Speedlite control, and press the Set button (**A**).
3. Select Flash firing, and press the Set button (**B**).
4. Set the Flash firing option to Disable (**C**).

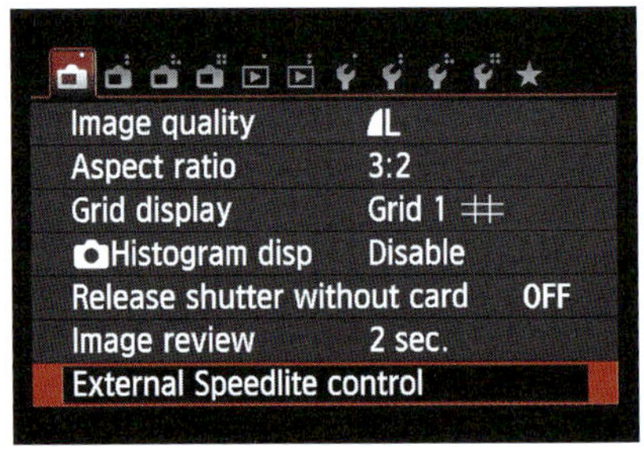

A

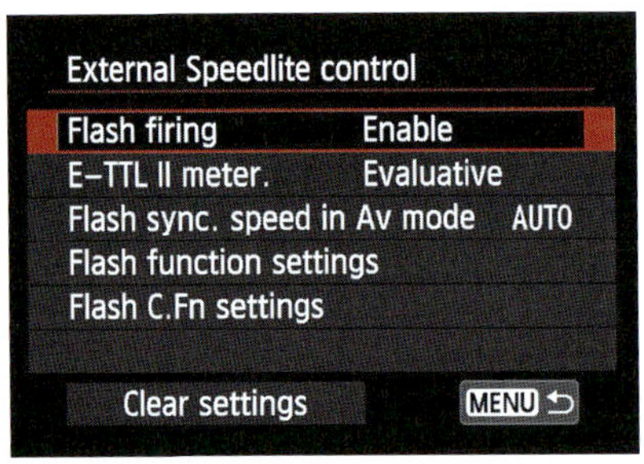

B

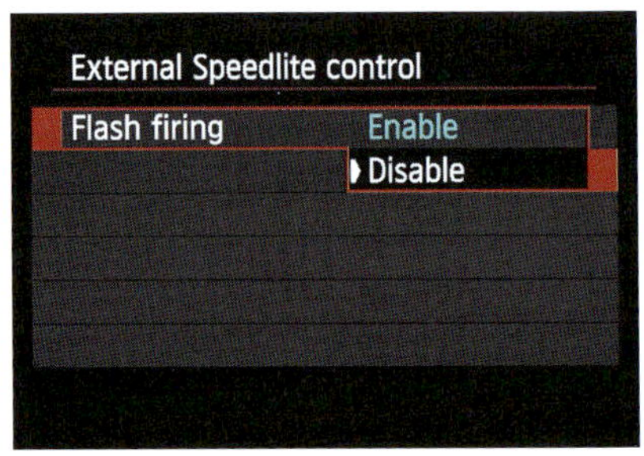

C

SHOOTING LONG EXPOSURES

We have covered some of the techniques for shooting in low light, so let's go through the process of capturing a night or low-light scene for maximum image quality (**Figure 8.7**). The first thing to consider is that in order to shoot in low light with a low ISO, you will need to use shutter speeds that are longer than you could possibly handhold (longer than 1/15 of a second). This will require the use of a tripod or stable surface for you to place your camera on. For maximum quality, the ISO should be low—somewhere at or below 400. The long exposure noise reduction should be turned on to minimize the effects of exposing for longer durations. (To set this up, see Chapter 7.)

Once you have the noise reduction turned on, set your camera to Aperture Priority (Av) mode. That way, you can concentrate on the aperture that you believe is most appropriate and let the camera determine the best shutter speed. If it is too dark for the autofocus to function properly, try manually focusing. Finally, consider using a cable release to activate the shutter. If you don't have one, check out the sidebar on using the self-timer (page 194). Once you shoot the image, you may notice some lag time before it is displayed on the rear LCD. This is due to the noise-reduction process, which can take anywhere from a fraction of a second up to 30 seconds, depending on the length of the exposure.

ISO 100
2.5 sec.
f/8
30mm lens

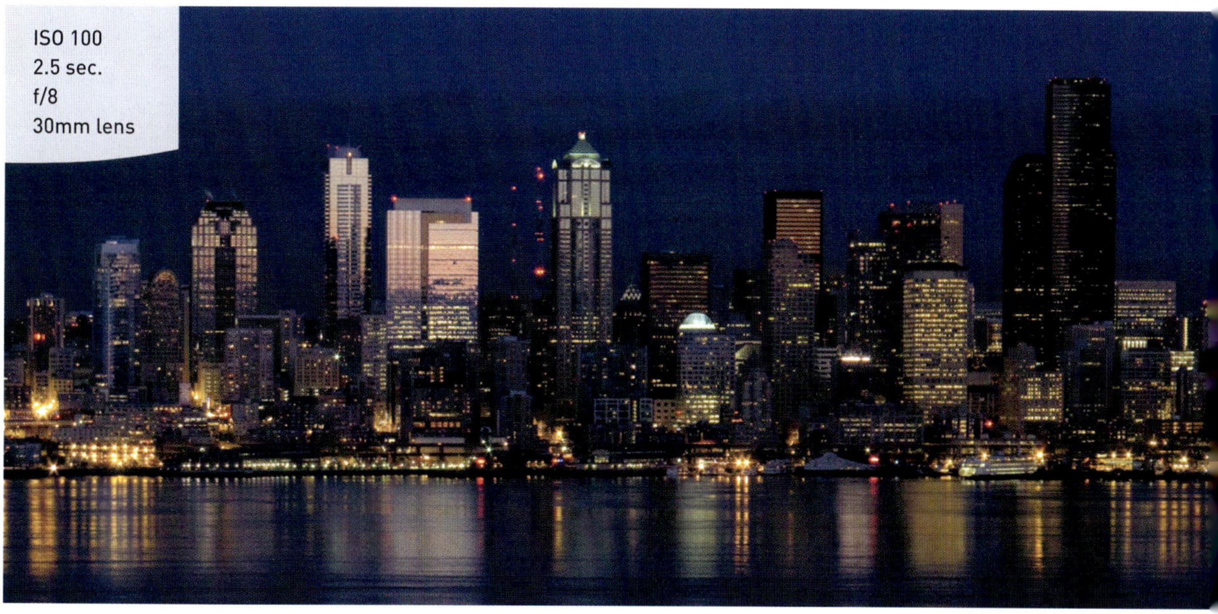

FIGURE 8.7
A long exposure and a tripod were necessary to capture this twilight photo of the Seattle skyline.

USING A FLASH

Sometimes available light is so scarce that you need to turn to a flash to illuminate the scene. The EOS M doesn't offer a built-in flash, so you'll need an external unit like the compact Canon Speedlite 90EX, which is built specifically for the EOS M and is (of course) a separate purchase (**Figure 8.8**). If you own another Canon Speedlite, you don't need the 90EX, but I use it as the example in this chapter. A flash will pour light onto a scene, fill in shadows, or act as the trigger for other flashes (as described later in this chapter).

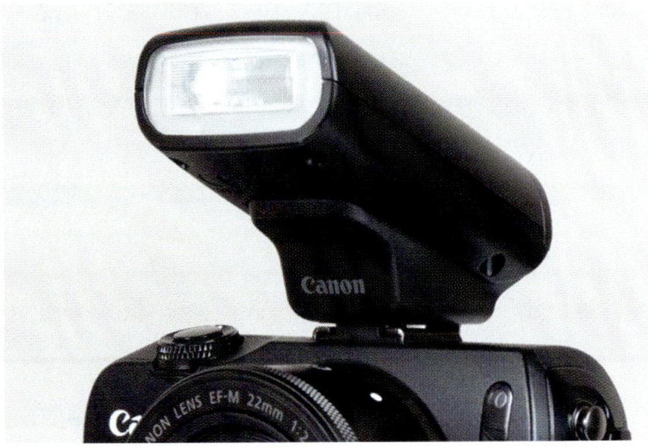

FIGURE 8.8
The Speedlite 90EX attached to the camera's hot shoe

SHUTTER SPEEDS

The standard flash synchronization speed for your camera is between 1/60 and 1/200 of a second. When you are working with the built-in flash in the Basic zone, the camera will typically use a shutter speed of 1/60 of a second. The exception to this is when you use Night Portrait mode, which will fire the flash with a slower shutter speed so that some of the ambient light has time to record in the image.

FLASH SYNC

The basic idea behind the term *flash synchronization* (*flash sync* for short) is that when you take a photograph using the flash, the camera needs to ensure that the shutter is fully open at the time that the flash goes off. This is not an issue if you are using a long shutter speed such as 1/15 of a second but does become more critical for fast shutter speeds. To ensure that the flash and shutter are synchronized so that the flash is going off while the shutter is open, the EOS M implements a top sync speed of 1/200 of a second. This means that when you are using the flash, you will not be able to have your shutter speed set any faster than 1/200. If you did use a faster shutter speed, the shutter would actually start closing before the flash fired, which would cause a black, underexposed area to appear in the frame where the light from the flash was blocked.

The real key to using the flash to get great pictures is to control the shutter speed. The goal is to balance the light from the flash with the existing light so that everything in the picture has an even illumination. Let's take a look at the shutter speeds for the modes in the Creative zone.

Program (P): The shutter speed stays at 1/60 of a second.

Shutter Priority (Tv): You can adjust the shutter speed from as fast as 1/200 of a second all the way down to 30 seconds. The lens aperture will adjust accordingly, but at long exposures the lens will typically be set to its largest aperture.

Manual (M): Manual mode works the same as Tv mode, with a range of 1/200 of a second down to 30 seconds. The difference is that you must manually set the f-stop.

Aperture Priority (Av): This mode has three custom settings for adjusting the shutter speed when using the flash, so you can use the aperture of your choice while still getting good flash exposures.

The default value is Auto, which adjusts from 1/200 of a second all the way down to 30 seconds, depending on the available light. As the aperture gets smaller, the shutter speeds will get longer. There are also two speed-limiting settings to choose from. The first is "1/200–1/60 sec. auto." This limits the shutter speed to a maximum duration of 1/60 of a second. For all other exposures, the camera will moderate the shutter speed to a selection that is within the 1/60–1/200 range. The other setting is "1/200 sec. (fixed)," which maintains a shutter speed of 1/200 of a second no matter what the f-stop is set to. Your flash will try to vary its power output to meet the needs of the setting that you have selected.

SETTING THE SYNC SPEED WHEN USING FLASH IN AV MODE

1. Press the Menu button and go to the first shooting menu. Highlight External Speedlite control, and then press the Set button.
2. Use the cross keys to select Flash sync. speed in Av mode, and press the Set button (**A**).
3. Select the Av sync speed that you desire using the cross keys, and press Set once more (**B**).

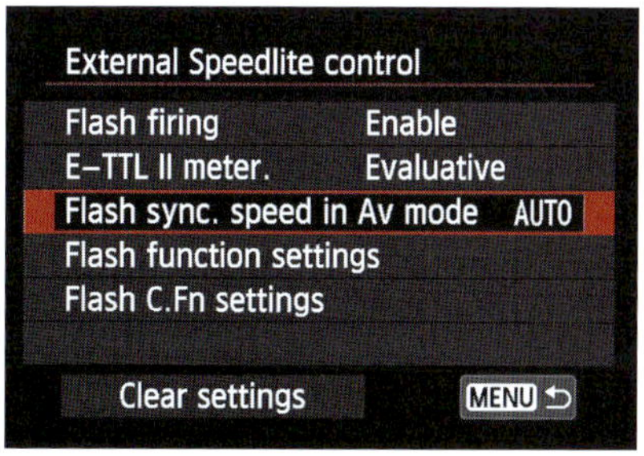

A

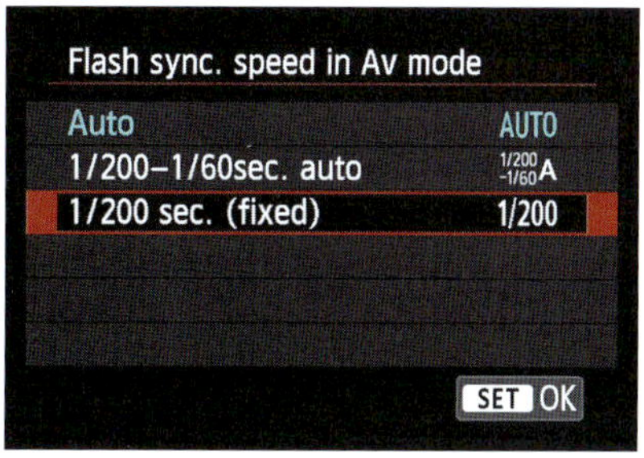

B

METERING MODES

The built-in flash uses a technology called E-TTL II (Evaluative Through The Lens) metering to determine the appropriate amount of flash power to output for a good exposure. When you depress the shutter button, the camera quickly adjusts focus while gathering information from the entire scene to measure the amount of ambient light. As you press the shutter button down completely, a pre-flash occurs to meter the light off the subject from the flash, and a determination is made as to how much power is needed to balance the subject with the ambient light. This applies to all of the modes in the Creative zone, with the exception of Manual mode.

The default setting for the flash meter mode is Evaluative. The meter can also be set to Average mode, but that should probably be avoided. Your best results will come from the E-TTL mode.

But if you have special metering needs, such as a background that is very light or dark, you might consider using the Flash Exposure (FE) Lock to meter off your subject and then recompose your image in the viewfinder.

This feature works much like the Automatic Exposure (AE) Lock function that was discussed in Chapter 6.

USING THE FE LOCK FEATURE

1. Point the camera at the area that you want to base the flash exposure on. This is normally your subject.
2. Press the AE/FE Lock button (∗) (also the Left cross button) to obtain the exposure setting. The flash will fire a small burst to evaluate the exposure, and you will see a red metering circle appear on the screen. The AE/FE Lock symbol (∗) will also appear next to the flash symbol.
3. Recompose the scene as you like, and press the shutter button completely.

The FE Lock will cancel after each exposure, so you have to repeat these steps each time you need to lock the flash exposure.

Using the Average metering mode might also require that you tweak the flash output by using Flash Exposure Compensation. This is because the camera will be metering the entire scene to set the exposure, so you might have to add or subtract flash power to balance out the scene.

COMPENSATING FOR THE FLASH EXPOSURE

The E-TTL system will usually do an excellent job of balancing the flash and ambient light for your exposure, but it does have the limitation of not knowing what effect you want in your image. You may want more or less flash in a particular shot. You can achieve this by using the Flash Exposure Compensation feature.

Just as with exposure compensation, flash compensation allows you to dial in a change in the flash output in increments of 1/3 of a stop. You will probably use this most often to tone down the effects of your flash, especially when you are using the flash as a subtle fill light (**Figures 8.9** and **8.10**).

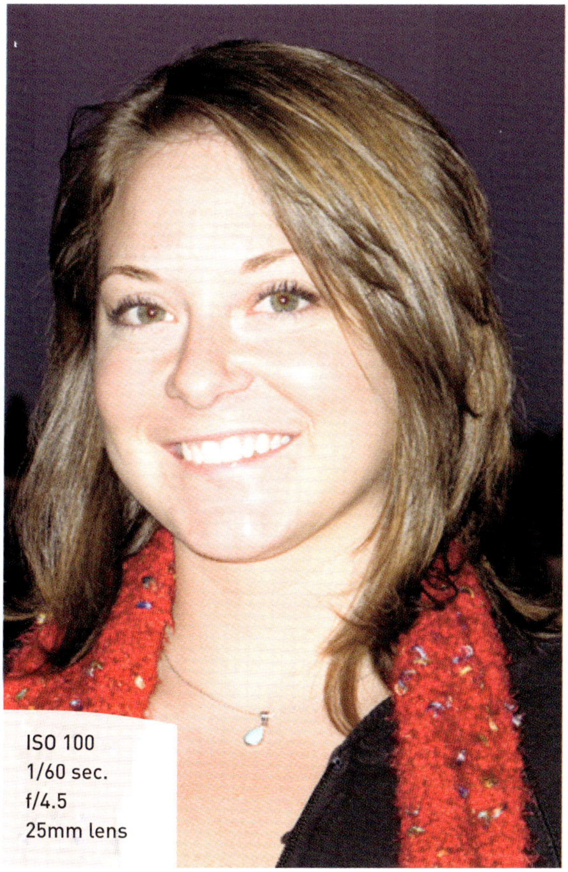

FIGURE 8.9
This shot was taken with the flash set to normal power. As you can see, it was trying too hard to illuminate my subject.

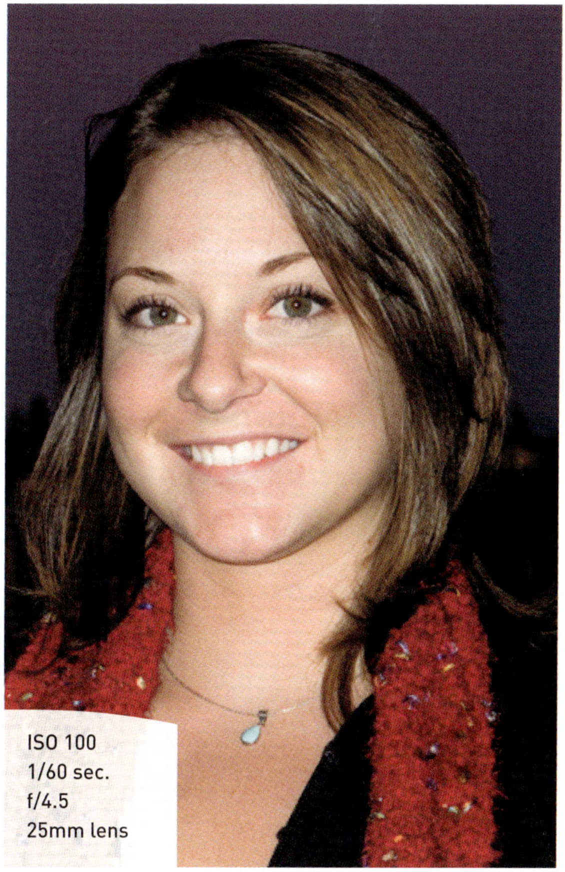

FIGURE 8.10
This image was made with the same camera settings. The difference is that the flash compensation was set to –1 stop.

USING THE FLASH EXPOSURE COMPENSATION FEATURE TO CHANGE THE FLASH OUTPUT

1. Press the Menu button and navigate to the first shooting menu.
2. Select the External Speedlite control option and press the Set button.
3. Select the Flash function settings option and press Set.
4. Highlight the Flash Exposure Compensation icon and press Set (**A**).
5. Use the Left/Right cross keys to adjust the flash compensation in 1/3-stop increments (left to subtract and right to add) (**B**).
6. Press the shutter button halfway to return to shooting mode, and then take the picture.
7. Review your image to see if more or less flash compensation is required, and repeat these steps as necessary.

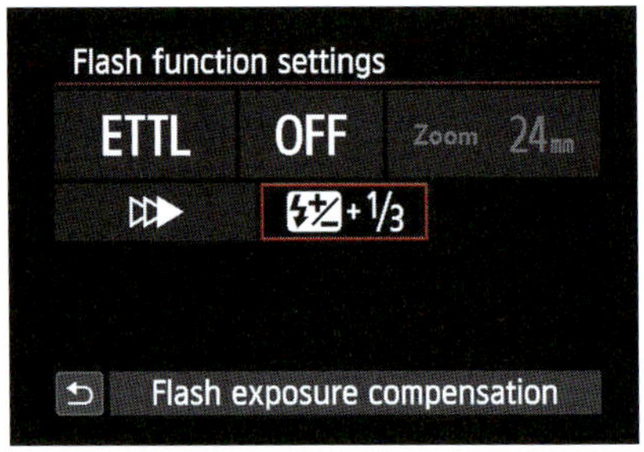

A

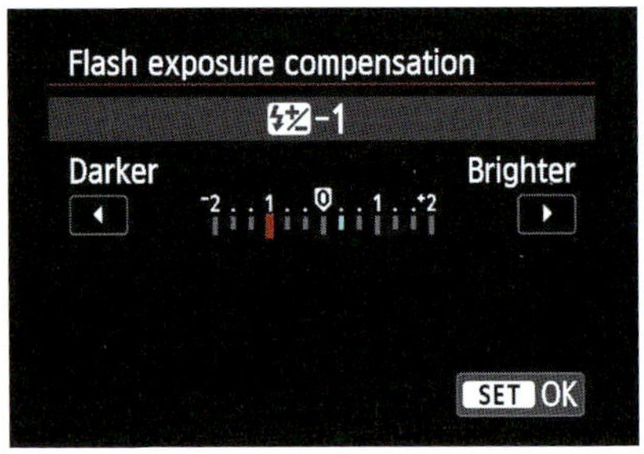

B

The Flash Exposure Compensation feature does not reset itself when the camera is turned off, so the last compensation setting sticks until you change it.

2ND CURTAIN SYNC

There are two flash synchronization modes in the EOS M: 1st Curtain and 2nd Curtain. You may be asking, "What in the world does synchronization do, and what are these 'curtains'?" Good question.

When your camera fires, there are two curtains that open and close to make up the shutter. The first curtain moves out of the way, exposing the camera sensor to the light. At the end of the exposure, the second curtain moves in front of the sensor, ending that picture cycle. In flash photography, timing is extremely important because the flash fires in milliseconds and the shutter is usually opening in tenths or hundredths of a second. To make sure these two functions happen in order, the camera usually fires the flash just as the first curtain moves out of the way (see the sidebar "Flash Sync" earlier in this chapter).

In 2nd Curtain Sync mode, the flash will not fire until just before the second shutter curtain ends the exposure. So, why have this mode at all? Well, there might be times when you want to have a longer exposure to balance out the light from the background to go with the subject needing the flash. Imagine taking a photograph of a friend standing in Times Square at night with all the traffic moving about and the bright lights of the buildings and signs overhead. If the flash fires at the beginning of the exposure and then the objects around the subject move, those objects will often blur the subject a bit. If the camera is set to 2nd Curtain Sync, though, all of the movement of the existing light is recorded first, and then the subject is "frozen" by the flash at the end by the exposure (**Figure 8.11**).

There is no right or wrong to it. It's just a decision on what type of effect you would like to create. Many times, 2nd Curtain Sync is used for artistic purposes or to record movement in the scene without it overlapping the flash-exposed subject. To make sure that the main subject is always getting the final pop of the flash, I leave my camera set to 2nd Curtain Sync.

ISO 200
1/125 sec.
f/2.5
35mm lens

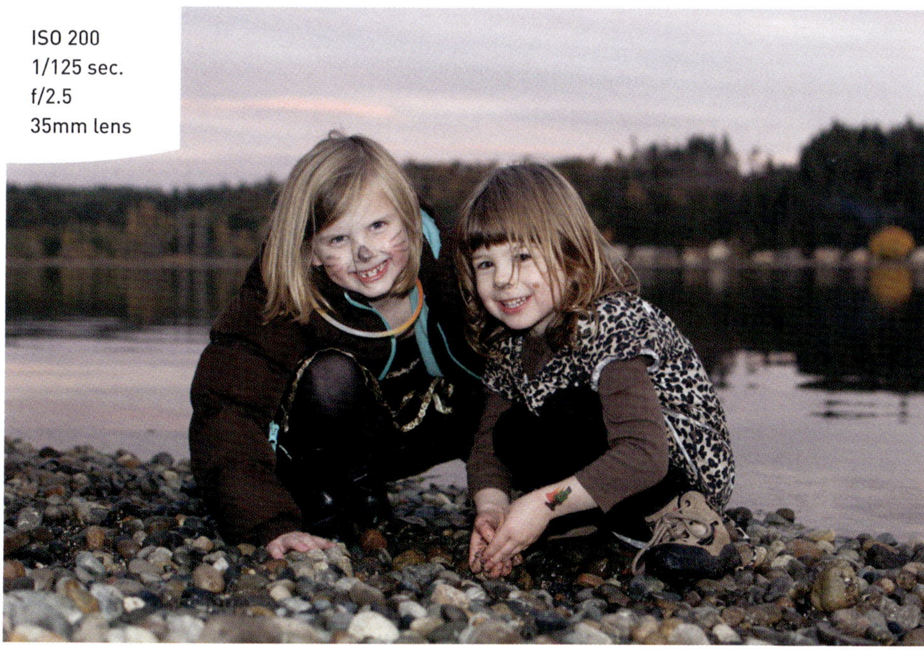

FIGURE 8.11
2nd Curtain Sync allows a lot of background light to hit the sensor before firing the flash and freezing the foreground subjects.

Using 1st Curtain Sync mode will give a similar effect, but the flash will fire at the beginning of the sequence (**Figure 8.12**). If you do intend to use a long exposure with 1st Curtain synchronization, you need to have your subject remain fairly still so that any movement that occurs after the flash goes off will be minimized in the image.

FIGURE 8.12
1st Curtain Sync is the default setting for flash photography and can be used for most of your needs.

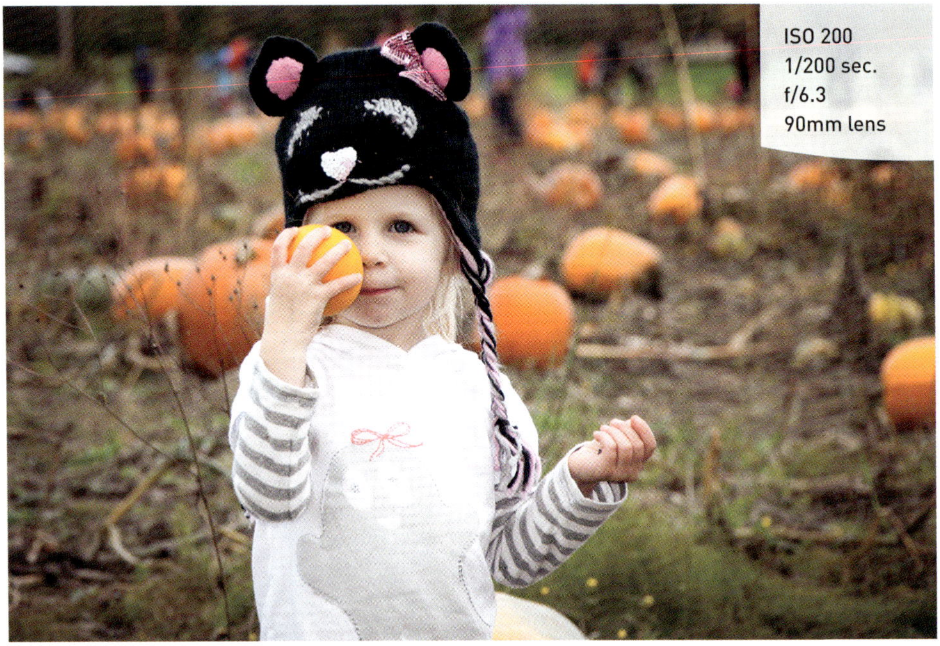

ISO 200
1/200 sec.
f/6.3
90mm lens

SETTING YOUR FLASH SYNC MODE

1. Press the Menu button, navigate to the first shooting menu, select External Speedlite control, and press the Set button.
2. Select Flash function settings, and then press Set.
3. Use the cross keys to select the Shutter sync option (**A**).
4. Select either the First- or Second-curtain option (**B**).

A

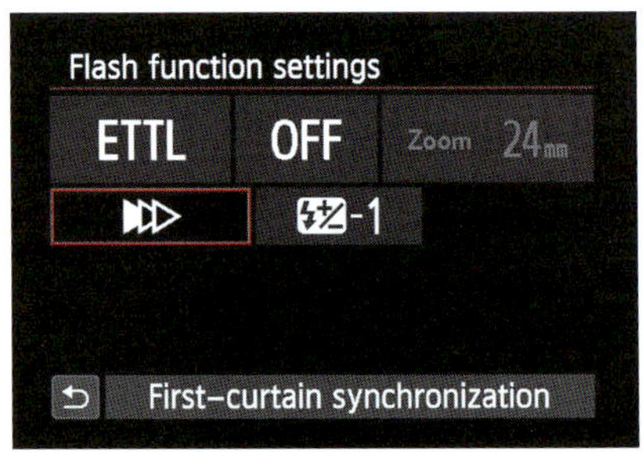

B

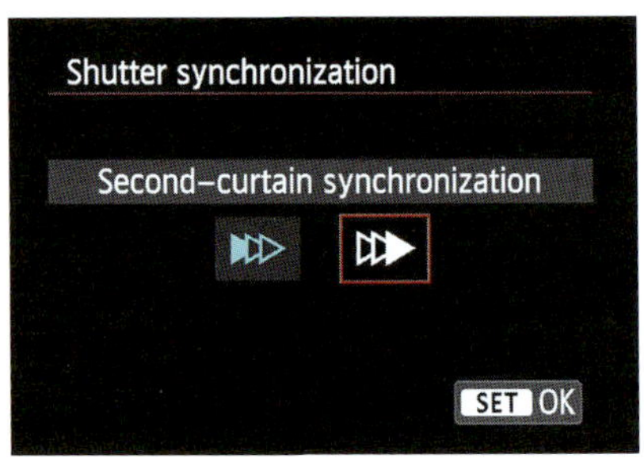

USING AN EXTERNAL SPEEDLITE

One of the problems with having a flash sit directly on top of the camera is the lack of direction you're afforded when shooting. The 90EX points forward only, which can sometimes result in photos that look as if the subject has been blasted by light. This problem also vexes owners of cameras with built-in pop-up flashes. If you own the 90EX (or a controller flash unit such as the ST-E2 transmitter), you can trigger a wireless off-camera flash and give yourself more options for shaping the light in the scene.

The biggest benefit to doing this is that you can get more natural-looking light by moving the flash to the side of the camera or bouncing the light off the ceiling. This gives you better and more natural shadows. You can also do things like fire the external flash through umbrellas, softboxes, or simple diffusion panels to make the quality of light much softer and more complimentary to your subject (**Figure 8.13**).

ISO 200
1/100 sec.
f/1.8
35mm lens

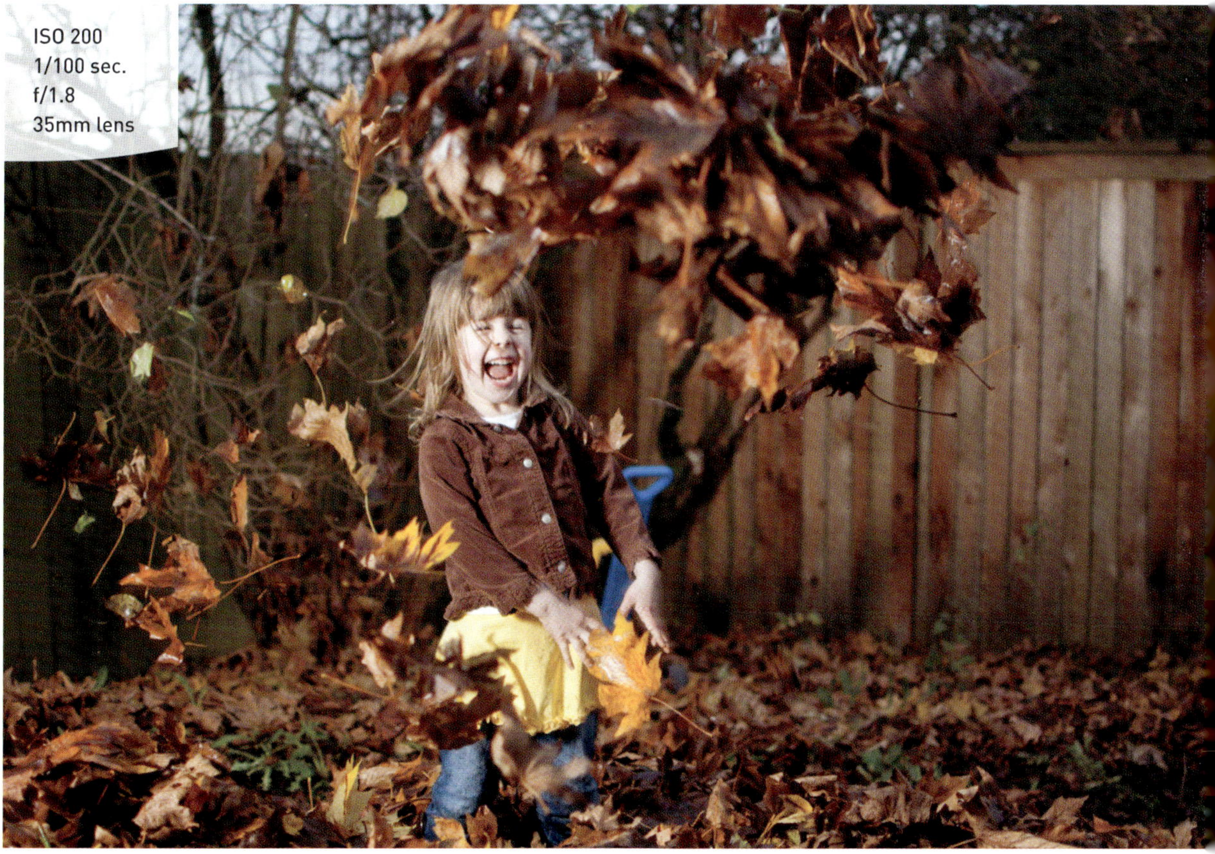

FIGURE 8.13
By moving the flash away from the camera, you can achieve light that is often more interesting than that of a flash fired from the camera's hot shoe.

USING OFF-CAMERA FLASH

In order to use an off-camera Speedlite, you need to do two things. First, purchase the Speedlite. Several models allow you to use the wireless feature, and they range in price from around $225 for the 320EX all the way up to $600 for the top-of-the-line model, the 600EX-RT. The 320EX is notable because it has the added benefit of having a built-in LED light that can be used as both a focus-assist lamp and a video-recording light. It also has a pivoting head that allows the light to be bounced off the ceiling to create softer, more flattering light.

Second, set up the flash using the following steps.

SETTING UP OFF-CAMERA FLASH

1. Press the Menu button and then select the External Speedlite control option in the first shooting menu (**A**).
2. Select the Flash function settings option, and press Set (**B**).
3. Select the Wireless option and then press Set (**C**).
4. Choose the Optical transmission option and press Set (**D**).

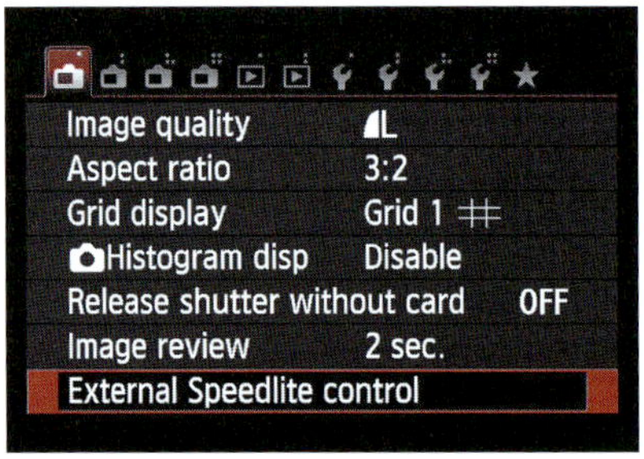

A

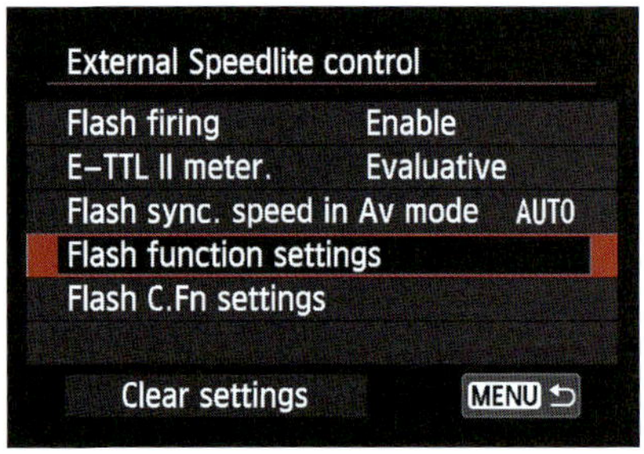

B

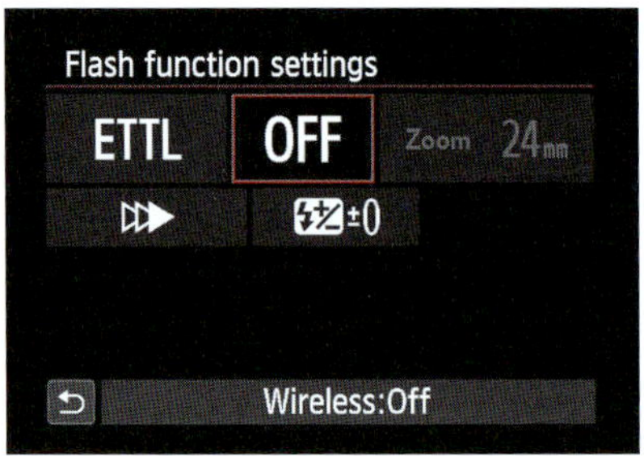

C

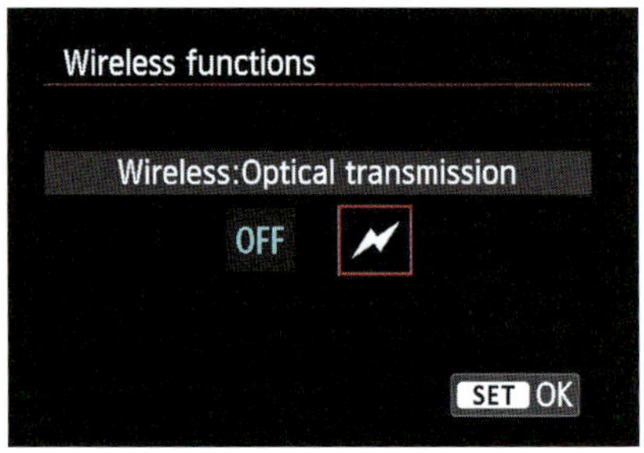

D

5. Select the Optical channel option that appears (**E**) and press Set.
6. Choose the channel number of the slave unit that you want to control (**F**), and you are ready to start shooting. Simply turn on the Speedlite, set it to wireless mode, and start shooting.
7. If you're controlling multiple external flashes in groups, select the Flash group option (**G**) and choose whether to fire all groups, two separate groups (A:B), or three groups (A:B C) (**H**). (Consult the 90EX manual for more specific details.)

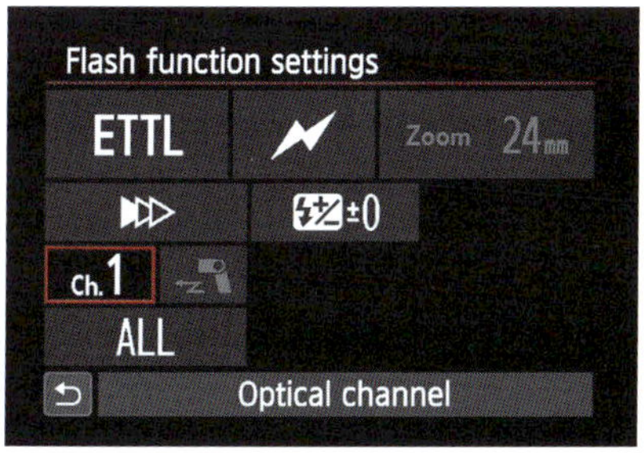

E

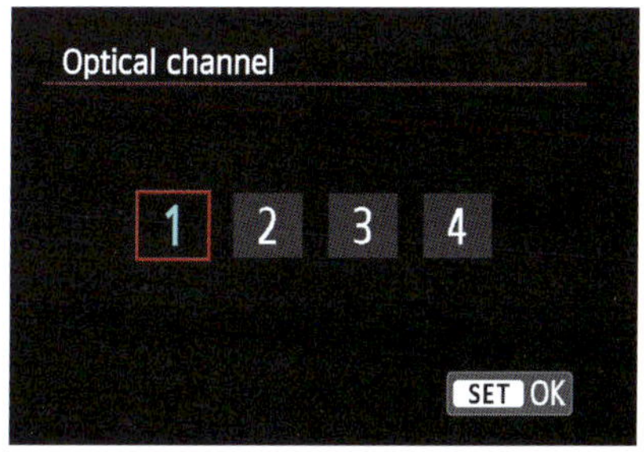

F

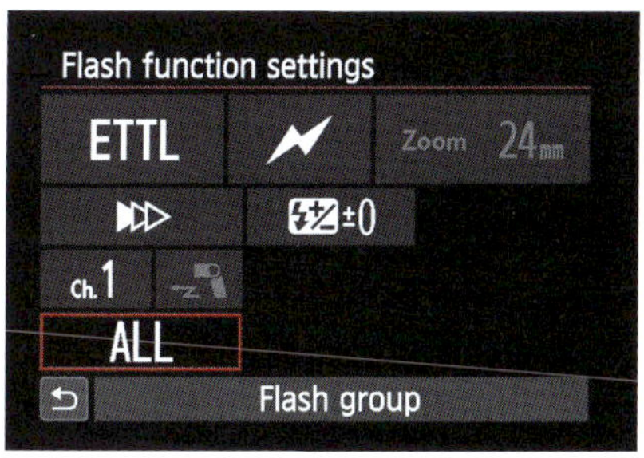

G

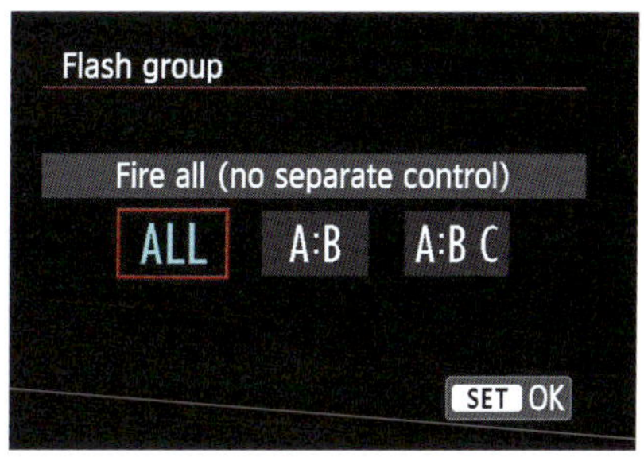

H

FLASH AND GLASS

If you find yourself in a situation where you want to use your flash to shoot through a window or display case, try placing your lens right against the glass so that the reflection of the flash won't be visible in your image. This is extremely useful in museums and aquariums.

Chapter 8 Assignments

Now that we have looked at the possibilities of shooting after dark, it's time to put it all to the test. These assignments cover the full range of shooting possibilities, both with flash and without. Let's get started.

How steady are your hands?

It's important to know just what your limits are in terms of handholding your camera and still getting sharp pictures. This will change depending on the focal length of the lens you are working with. Wider-angle lenses are more forgiving than telephoto lenses, so check this out for your longest and shortest lenses. Using an 18–55mm zoom as an example, set your lens to 55mm and then, with the camera set to ISO 100 and the mode set to Tv, start taking pictures with lower and lower shutter speeds. Review each image on the LCD at a zoomed-in magnification to take note of when you start seeing visible camera shake in your images.

Now do the same for the wide-angle setting on the lens. My limit is about 1/30 of a second. These shutter speeds are with the image stabilizer feature turned off. If you have an IS lens, try it with and without the IS feature enabled to see just how slow you can set your shutter while getting sharp results.

Pushing your ISO to the extreme

Turn on the ISO Expansion feature. Now find a place to shoot where the ambient light level is low. This could be at night or indoors in a darkened room. Using the mode of your choice, start increasing the ISO from 100 until you get to 25600. Make sure you evaluate the level of noise in your image, especially in the shadow areas. Only you can decide how much noise is acceptable in your pictures. I can tell you from personal experience that I never like to stray above the ISO 800 mark.

Getting rid of the noise

Turn on the High ISO Speed Noise Reduction and repeat the previous assignment. Find your acceptable limits with the noise reduction turned on. Also pay attention to how much detail is lost in your shadows with this function enabled.

Long exposures in the dark

If you don't have a tripod, find a stable place to set your camera outside and try some long exposures. Set your camera to Av mode and then use the self-timer to activate the camera (this will keep you from shaking the camera while pressing the shutter button).

Shoot in an area that has some level of ambient light, be it a streetlight, traffic lights, or even a full moon. The idea is to get some late-night, low-light exposures.

Reducing the noise in your long exposures

Now repeat the last assignment with the Long Exposure Noise Reduction set to On. Look at the difference in the images that were taken before and after the noise reduction was enabled. For best results, perform this assignment and the previous assignment in the same shooting session using the same subject.

Testing the limits of a flash

Wait for the lights to get low and then attach a flash (if you own one). Try using the different shooting modes to see how they affect your exposures. Use the Flash Exposure Compensation feature to take a series of pictures while adjusting from -2 stops all the way to +2 stops so that you become familiar with how much latitude you will get from this feature.

Getting creative with 2nd Curtain Sync

Now it's time for a little creative fun. Set your camera up for 2nd Curtain Sync and start shooting. Moving targets are best. Experiment with Tv and Av modes to lower the shutter speeds and exaggerate the effect. Try using a low ISO so the camera is forced to use longer shutter speeds. Be creative and have some fun!

Share your results with the book's Flickr group!

Join the group here: flickr.com/groups/eosmfromsnapshotstogreatshots

9

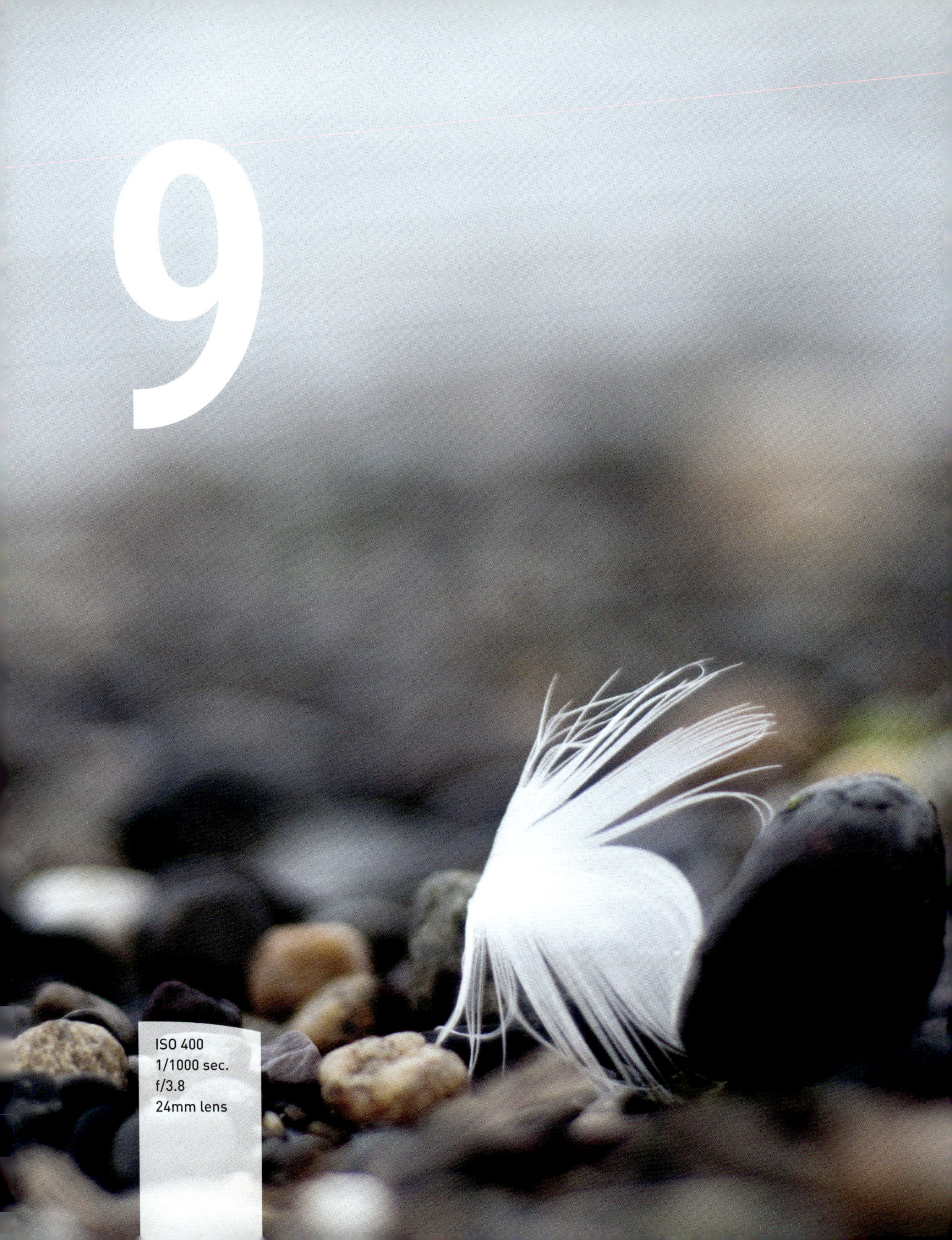

ISO 400
1/1000 sec.
f/3.8
24mm lens

Creative Compositions

IMPROVE YOUR PICTURES WITH SOUND COMPOSITIONAL ELEMENTS

Creating a great photograph takes more than just using the right settings on your camera. To take your photography to the next level, you need to gain an understanding of how the elements within the frame come together to create a compositionally pleasing image. Composition is the culmination of light, shape, and, to borrow a word from the iconic photographer Jay Maisel, gesture. Composition is a way for you to pull your viewing audience into your image and guide them through the scene. Let's examine some common compositional elements you can use to add interest to your photos.

PORING OVER THE PICTURE

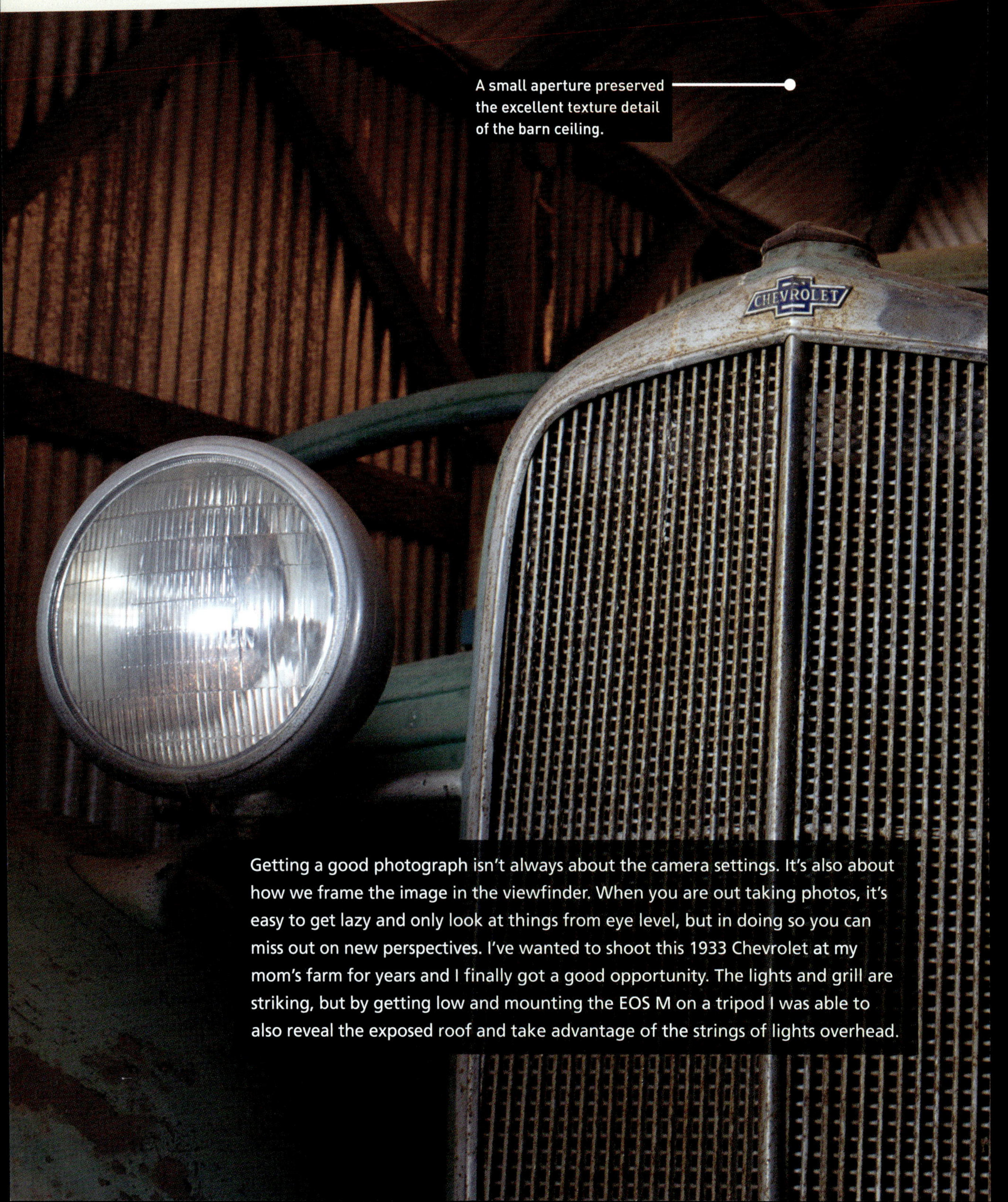

A small aperture preserved the excellent texture detail of the barn ceiling.

Getting a good photograph isn't always about the camera settings. It's also about how we frame the image in the viewfinder. When you are out taking photos, it's easy to get lazy and only look at things from eye level, but in doing so you can miss out on new perspectives. I've wanted to shoot this 1933 Chevrolet at my mom's farm for years and I finally got a good opportunity. The lights and grill are striking, but by getting low and mounting the EOS M on a tripod I was able to also reveal the exposed roof and take advantage of the strings of lights overhead.

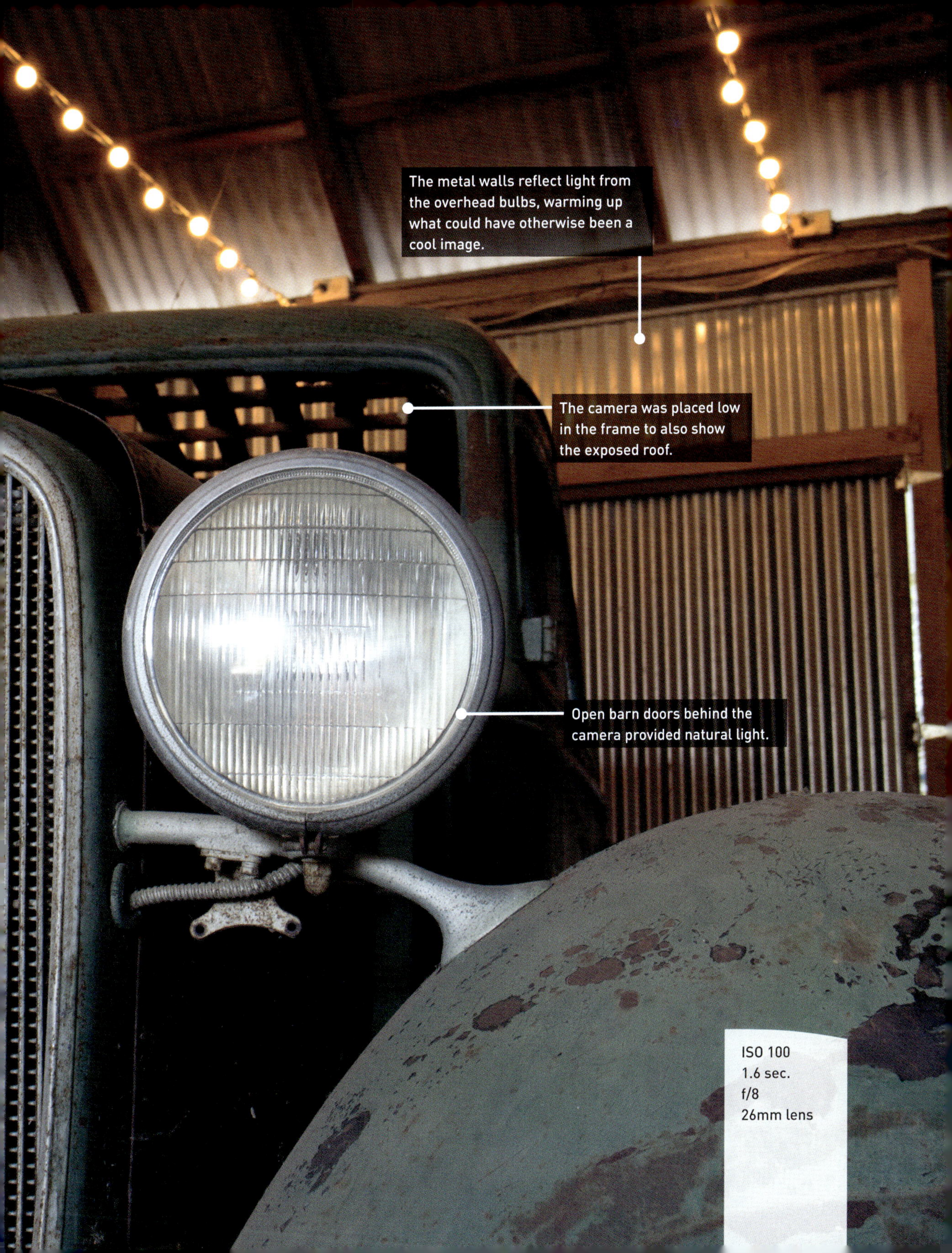
The metal walls reflect light from the overhead bulbs, warming up what could have otherwise been a cool image.
The camera was placed low in the frame to also show the exposed roof.
Open barn doors behind the camera provided natural light.
ISO 100
1.6 sec.
f/8
26mm lens

PORING OVER THE PICTURE

I can't overemphasize how important it is to have a camera on hand even when you're not expecting to do any shooting. I arrived at work one wonderfully foggy morning and spent an hour capturing photos of the sun burning through the fog layer.

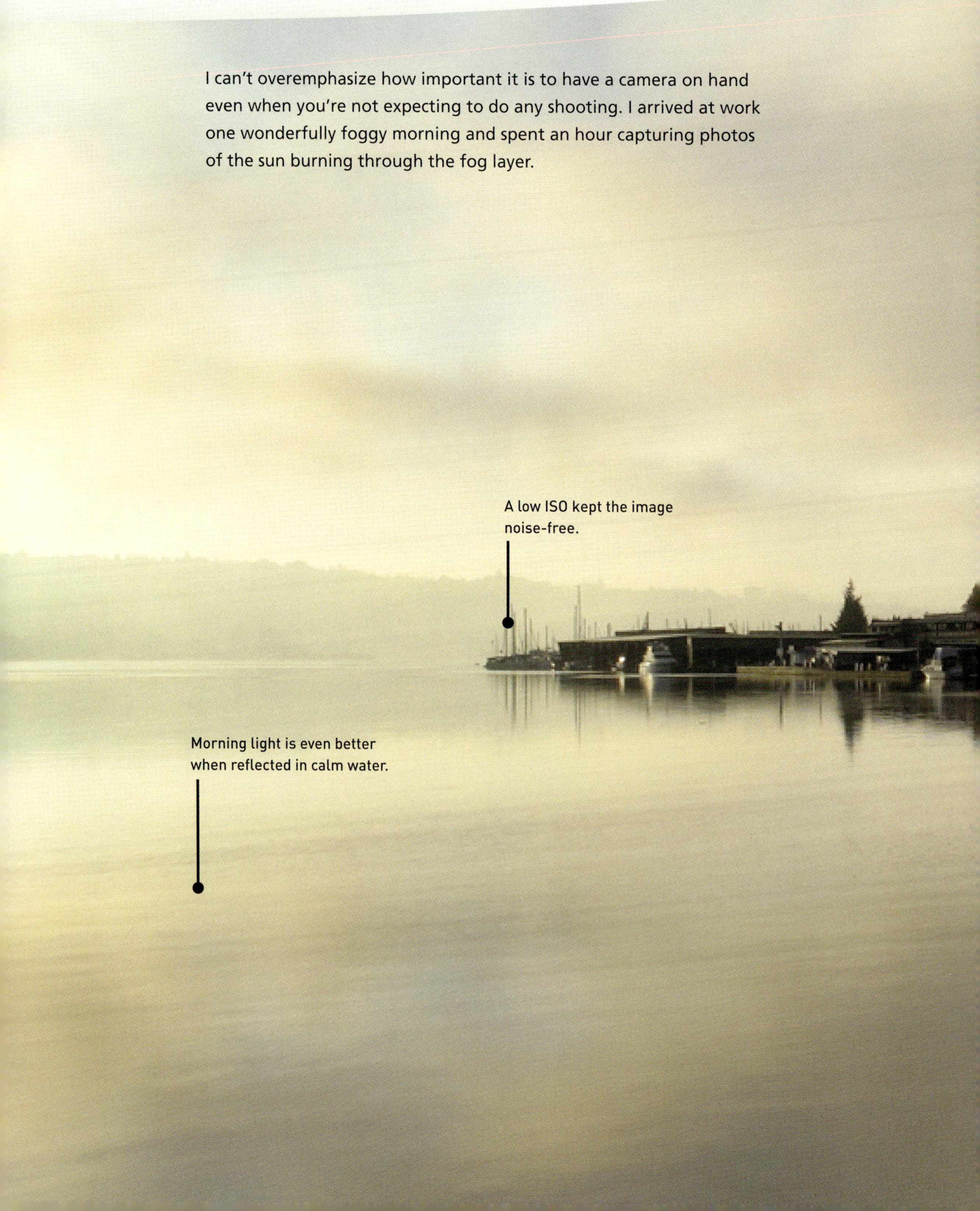

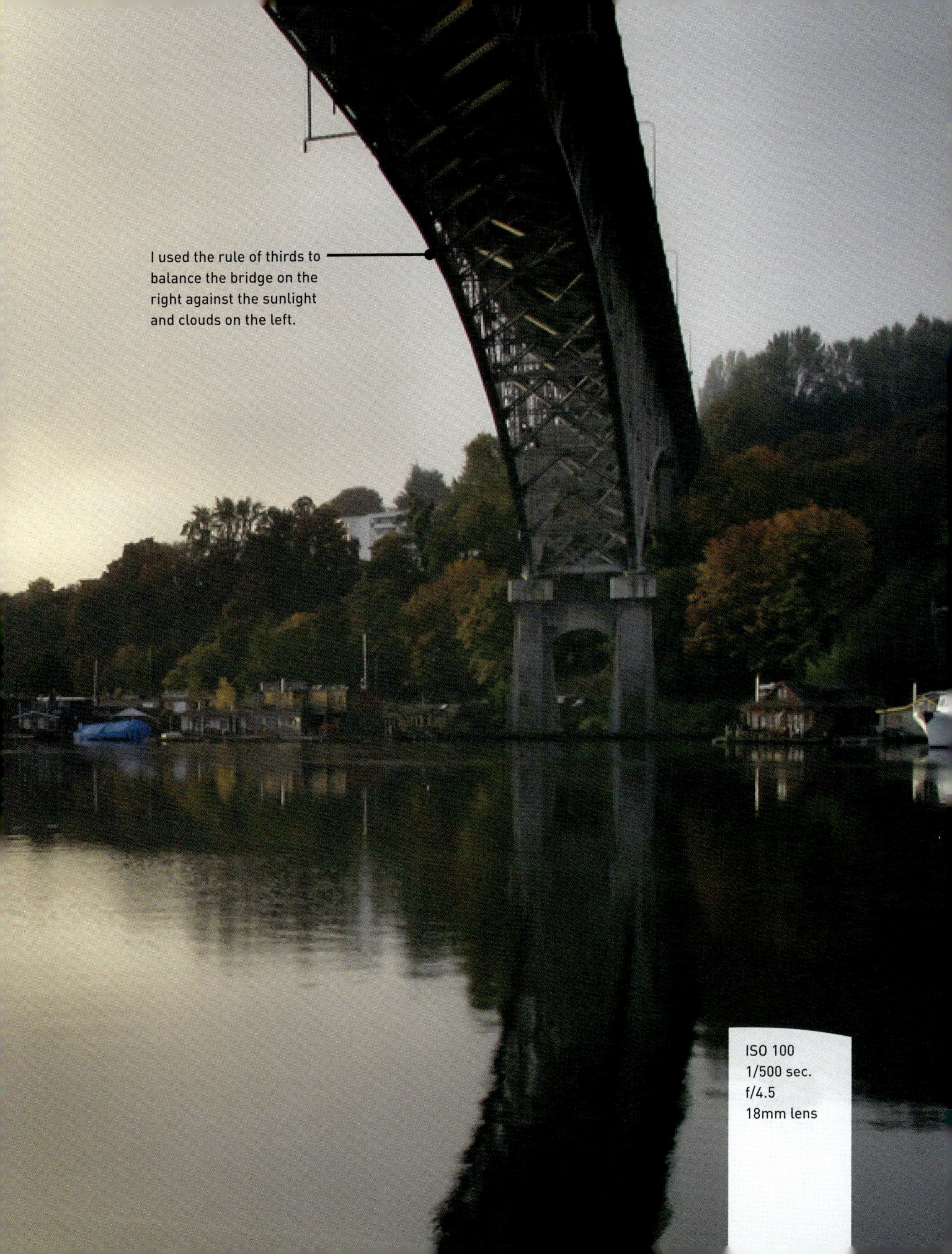
I used the rule of thirds to
balance the bridge on the
right against the sunlight
and clouds on the left.
ISO 100
1/500 sec.
f/4.5
18mm lens

DEPTH OF FIELD

Long focal lengths and large apertures allow you to isolate your subject from the chaos that surrounds it. I utilize the Av mode for the majority of my shooting. I also like to use a longer focal length lens to shrink the depth of field to a very narrow area (**Figure 9.1**).

FIGURE 9.1
A large aperture setting can create a shallow depth of field to isolate the subject.

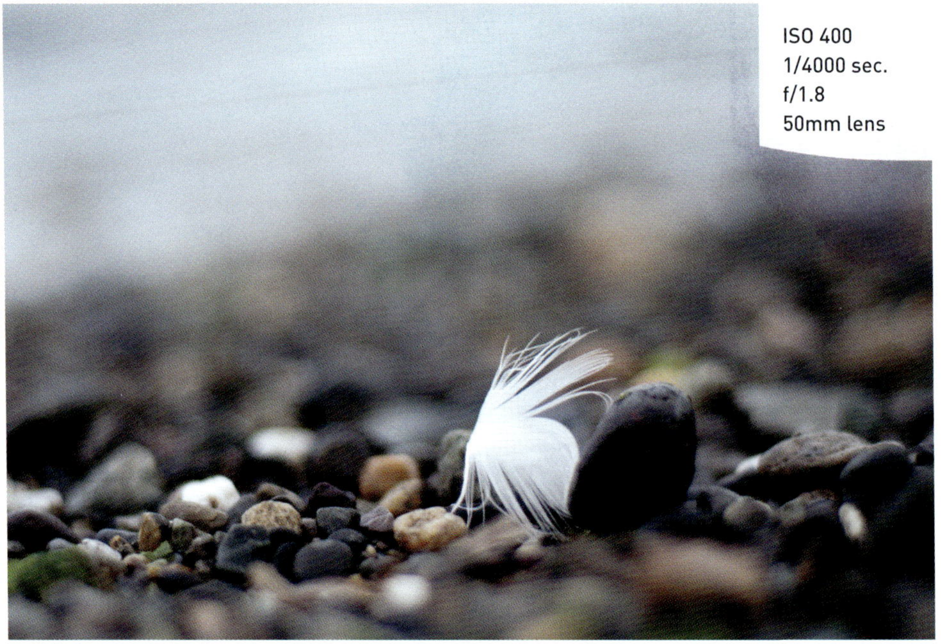

ISO 400
1/4000 sec.
f/1.8
50mm lens

The blurred background and foreground force the viewer's eye toward the sharper, in-focus areas, which gives greater emphasis to the subject.

Occasionally, a greater depth of field is required to maintain sharp focus across a greater distance. This might be due to the sheer depth of your subject, where you have objects that are near the camera but sharpness is desired at a greater distance as well (**Figure 9.2**).

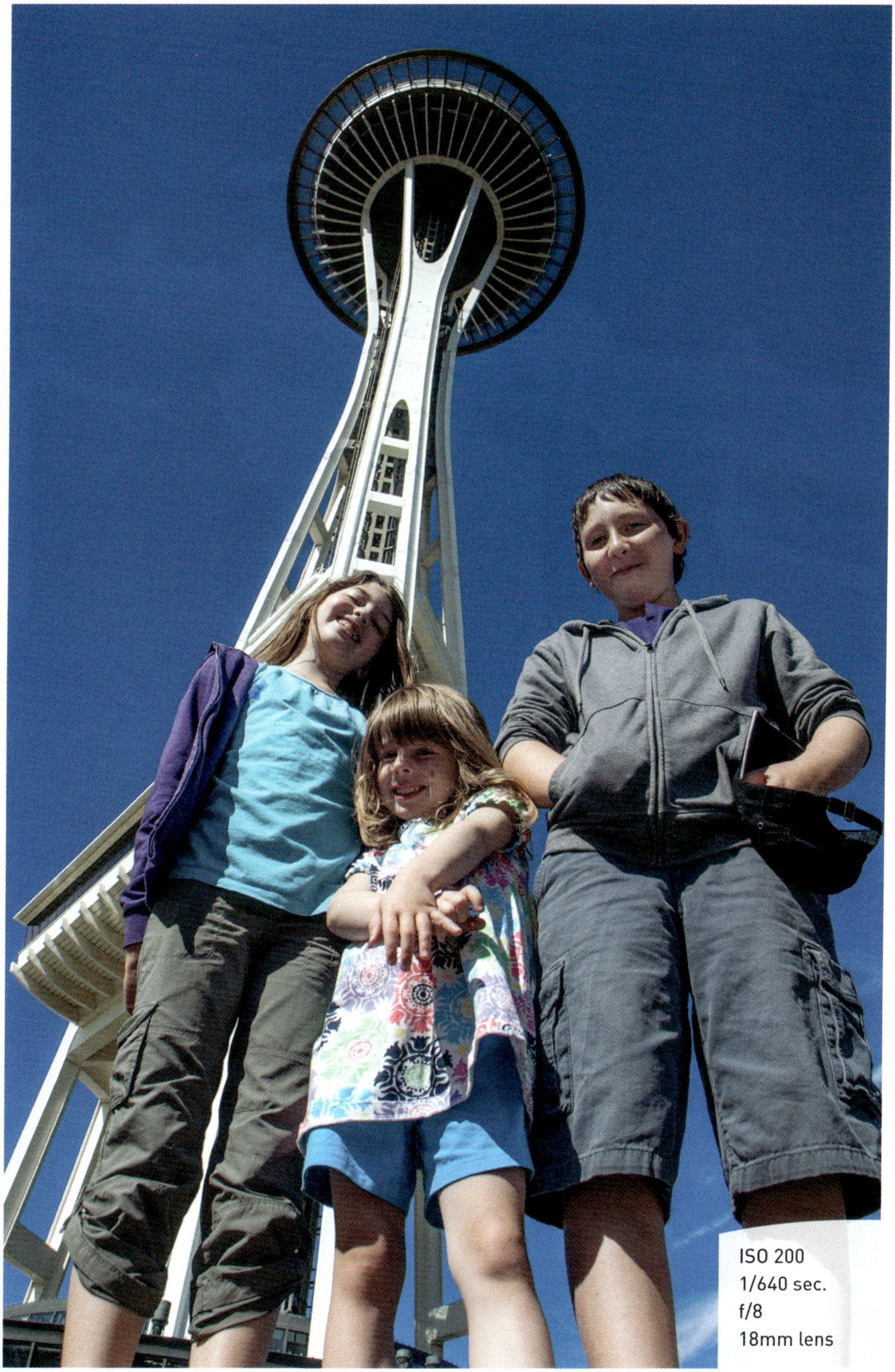

FIGURE 9.2
Getting sharp focus from near to far requires a small aperture setting. A wide-angle lens doesn't hurt either.

ISO 200
1/640 sec.
f/8
18mm lens

Or perhaps you are photographing a reflection in a puddle. With a narrow depth of field, you would only be able to get either the reflected object or the puddle in focus. By making the aperture smaller, you will be able to maintain acceptable sharpness in both areas (**Figure 9.3**).

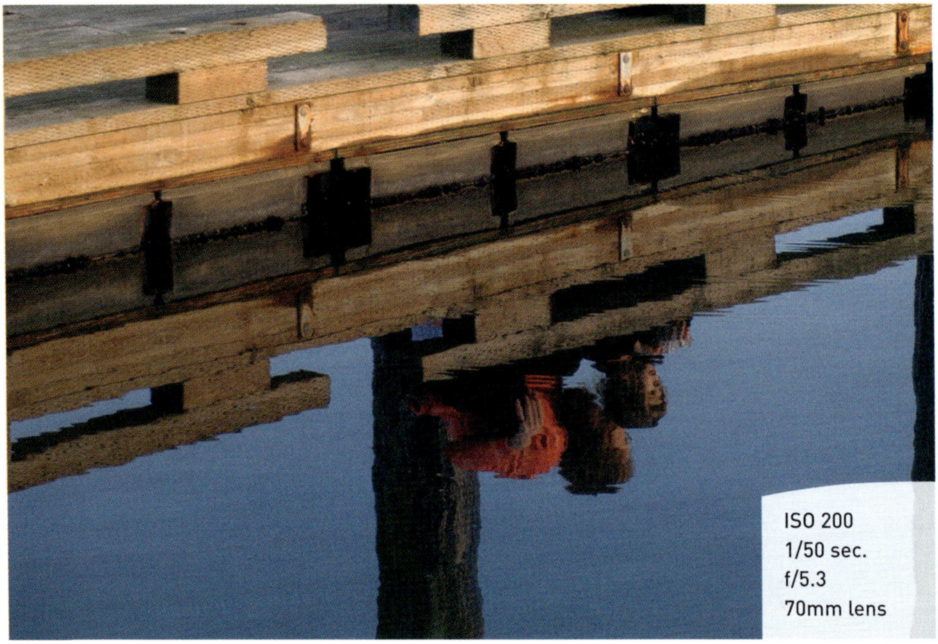

ISO 200
1/50 sec.
f/5.3
70mm lens

FIGURE 9.3 Getting a distant subject in focus in a reflection, along with the reflective surface, requires a small aperture.

PHOTOGRAPHING REFLECTIONS

A mirror is a two-dimensional surface, so why do I have to focus at a different distance for the image in the mirror? This was one of those questions that drove me crazy when I began to learn about photography. The answer is pretty simple, and it has to do with light. When you focus your lens, you are focusing the light being reflected off a surface onto your camera sensor. So if you wanted to focus on the mirror itself, it would be at one distance, but if you wanted to focus on the subject being reflected, you would have to take into account the distance that the object is from the mirror and then to you. Remember that the light from the subject has to travel all the way to the mirror and then to your lens. This is why a smaller aperture can be required when shooting reflected subjects. Sit in your car and take a few shots of objects in the side view mirrors to see what I mean.

ANGLES

Having strong angular lines in your image can add to the composition, especially when they are juxtaposed to each other (**Figure 9.4**). This can create a tension that is different from the standard horizontal and vertical lines that we are so accustomed to seeing in photos.

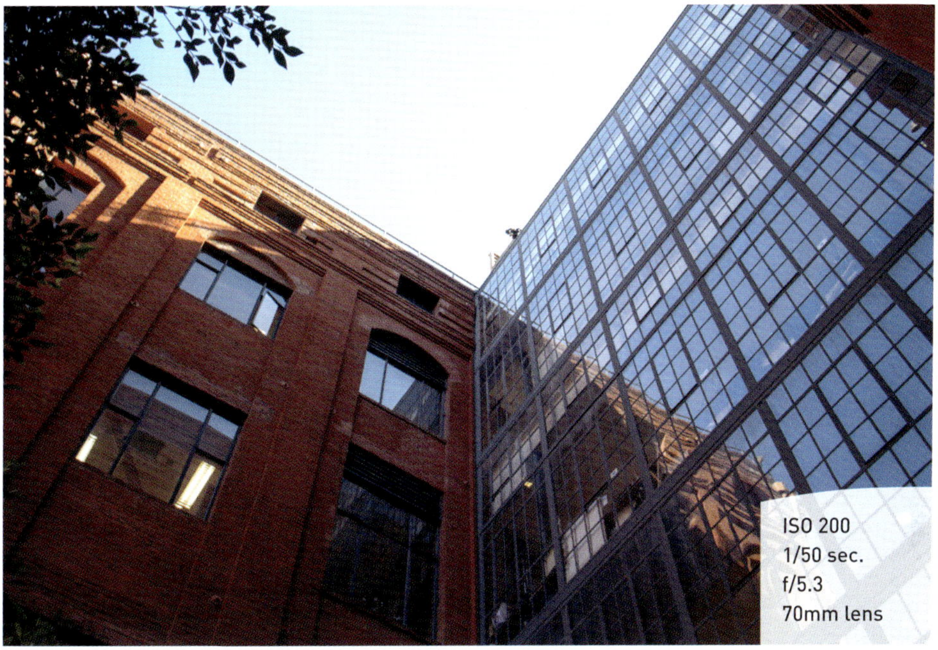

FIGURE 9.4 The strong angular lines of the buildings create a dynamic composition.

POINT OF VIEW

Sometimes the easiest way to influence your photographs is to simply change your perspective. Instead of always shooting from a standing position, try moving your camera to a place where you normally would not see your subject. Try getting down on your knees or even lying on the ground. This low angle can completely change how you view your subject and can create a new interest in common subjects (**Figure 9.5**).

PATTERNS

Rhythm and balance can be added to your images by finding the patterns in everyday life and concentrating on the elements that rely on geometric influences. Try to find the balance and patterns that often go unnoticed (**Figure 9.6**).

FIGURE 9.5
Put your camera into a position that presents an unfamiliar view of your subject.

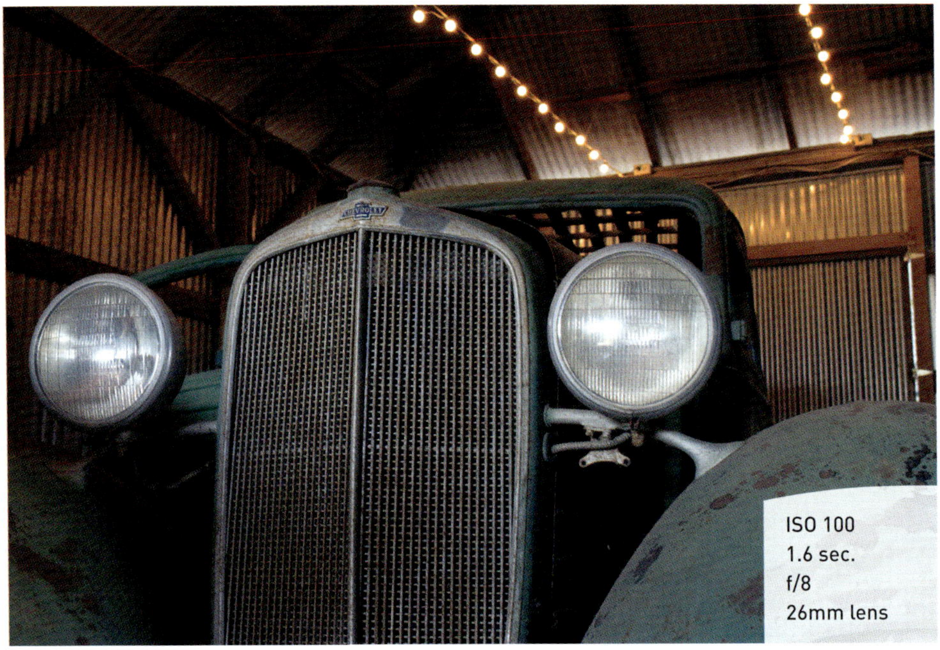

FIGURE 9.6
Stairs make great patterns in photos, with endless variations all around you.

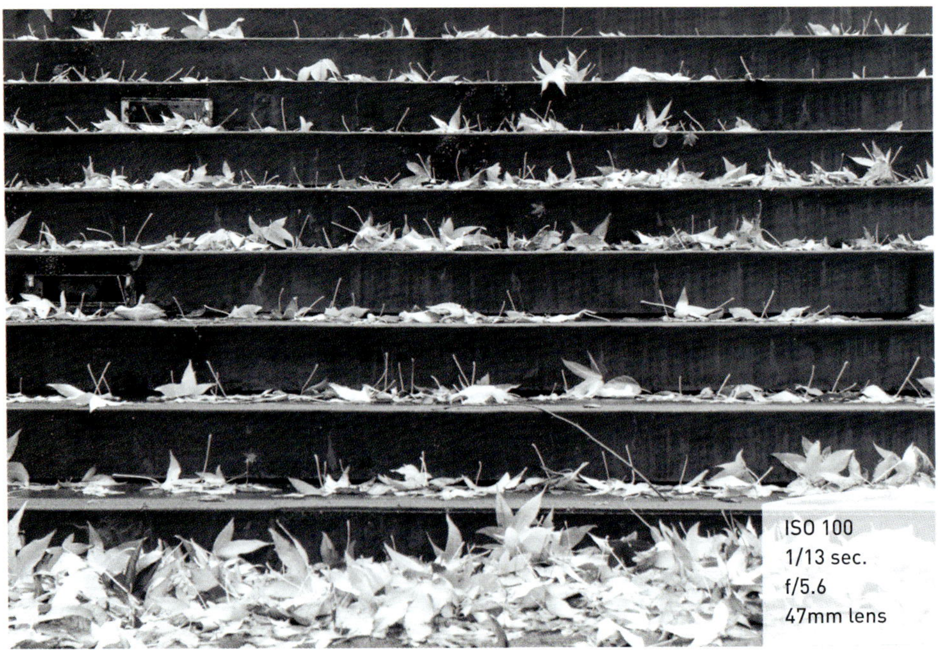

COLOR

Color works well as a tool for composition when you have very saturated colors to work with. Some of the best colors are those within the primary palette. Reds, greens, and blues, along with their complementary colors (cyan, magenta, and yellow), can all be used to create visual tension (**Figure 9.7**). This tension between bright colors will add visual excitement, drama, and complexity to your images when combined with other compositional elements.

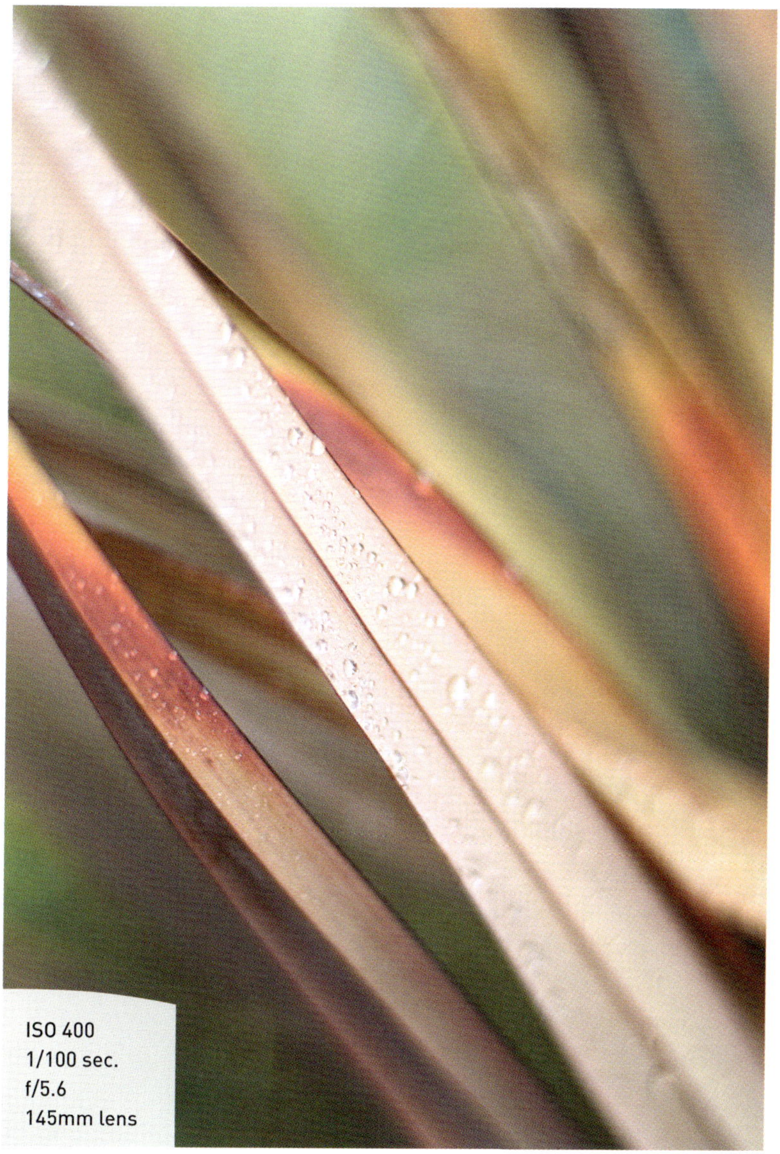

FIGURE 9.7
These leaves were just on the cusp of changing, the warm strokes contrasting with the green in the background.

You can also use a color as a theme for your photography. That can be shooting a blue sky that acts as a pleasing color contrast or picking up a color that's prevalent in a scene (**Figure 9.8**).

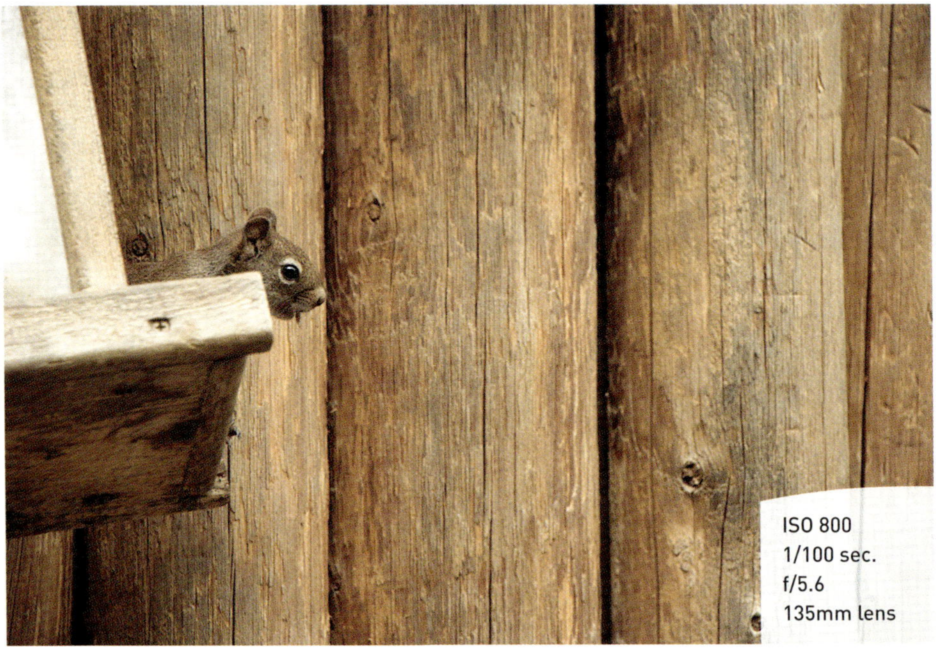

FIGURE 9.8
This squirrel stealing bird food was almost invisible from far away.

CONTRAST

We just saw that you can use color as a strong compositional tool. One of the most effective uses of color is to combine two contrasting colors that make the eye move back and forth across the image (**Figure 9.9**). There is no exact combination that will work best, but consider using dark and light colors, like red and yellow or blue and yellow, to provide the strongest contrasts.

You can also introduce contrast through different geometric shapes that battle (in a good way) for the attention of the viewer. You can combine circles and triangles, ovals and rectangles, curvy and straight, hard and soft, dark and light, and so many more (**Figure 9.10**). You aren't limited to just one contrasting element either. Combining more than one element of contrast will add even more interest. Look for these contrasting combinations whenever you are out shooting, and then use them to shake up your compositions.

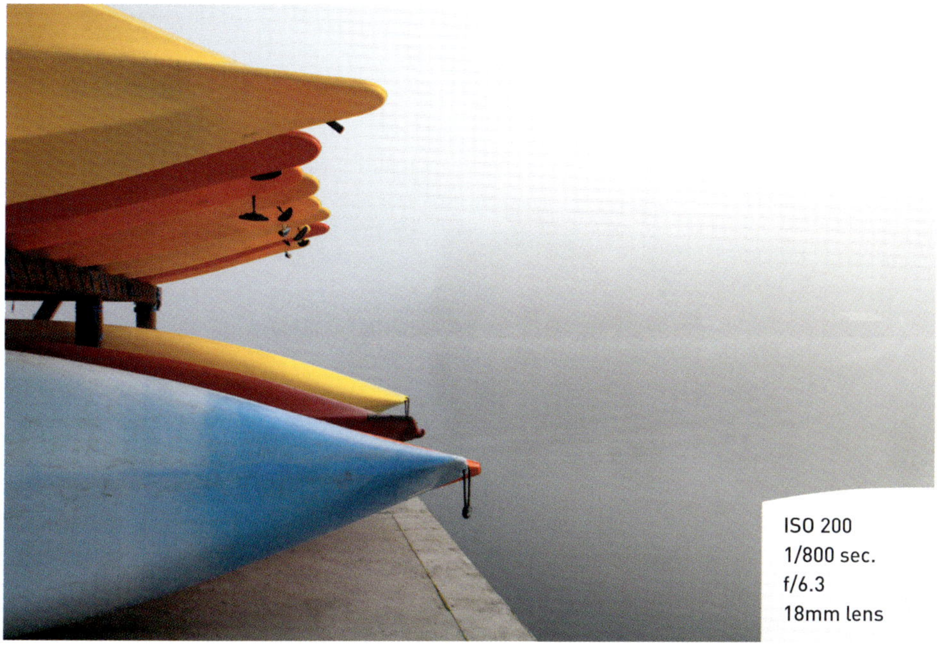

ISO 200
1/800 sec.
f/6.3
18mm lens

FIGURE 9.9
The bright colors of the kayaks really pop on this foggy morning.

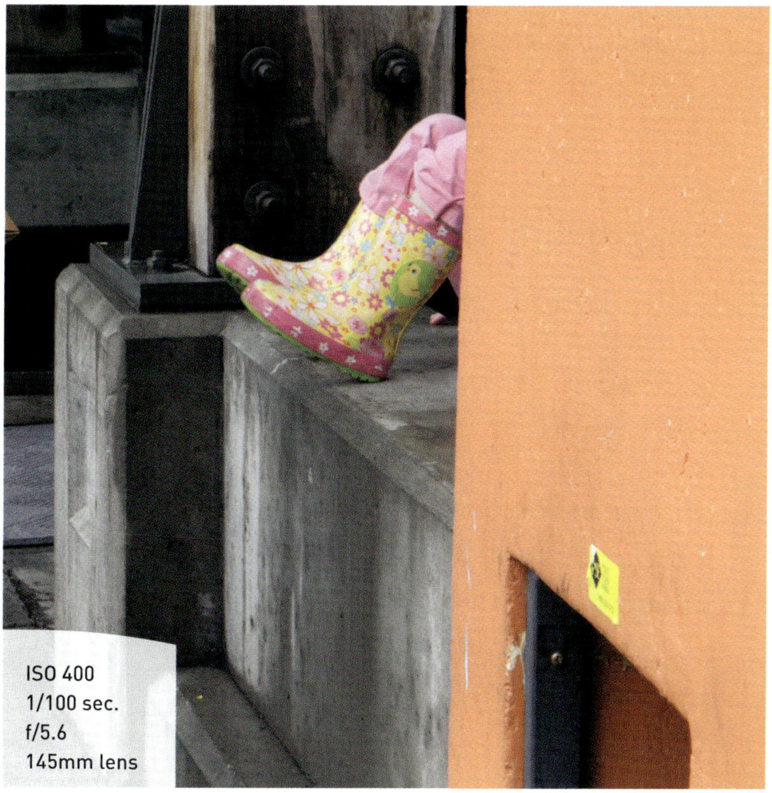

ISO 400
1/100 sec.
f/5.6
145mm lens

FIGURE 9.10
The orange wall contrasts with the gray cement, but the angled boots also break from the vertical and horizontal lines throughout the image.

LEADING LINES

One way to pull a viewer into your image is to incorporate leading lines. These are elements that come from the edge of the frame and then lead into the image toward the main subject (**Figure 9.11**). This can be the result of vanishing perspective lines, an element such as a river, or some other feature used to move from the outer edge in to the heart of the image.

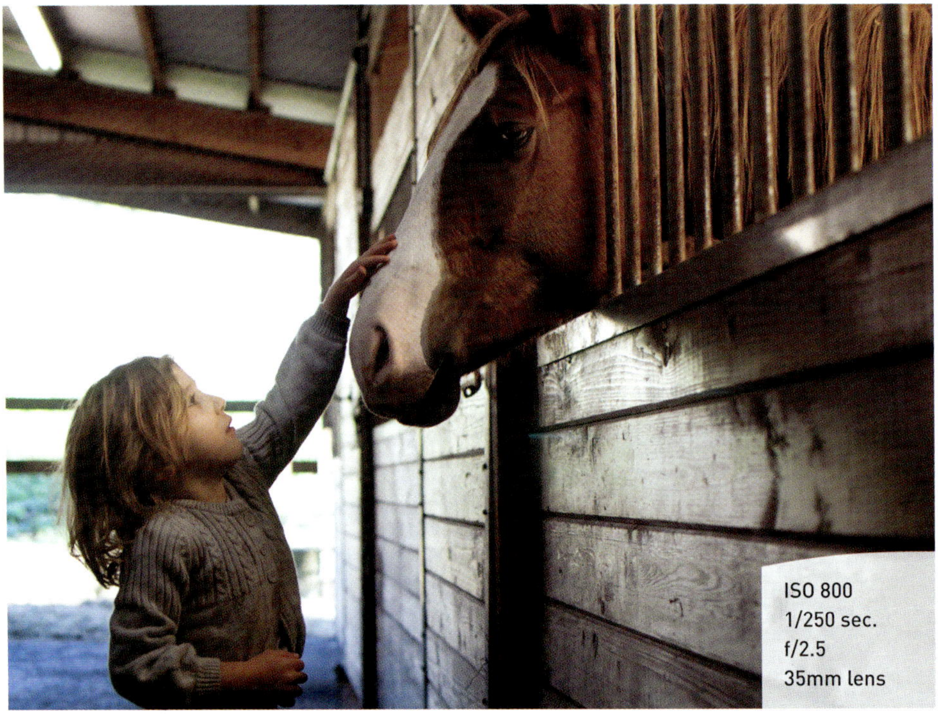

FIGURE 9.11
The perspective of the stall, and how the end of the wall splits the area between the girl and the horse, helps focus the eye on the subjects.

SPLITTING THE FRAME

With horizons, a low horizon will give a sense of stability to the image. Typically, this is done when the sky is more appealing than the landscape below (**Figure 9.12**). When the emphasis is to be placed on the landscape, the horizon line should be moved upward in the frame, leaving the bottom two-thirds to the subject.

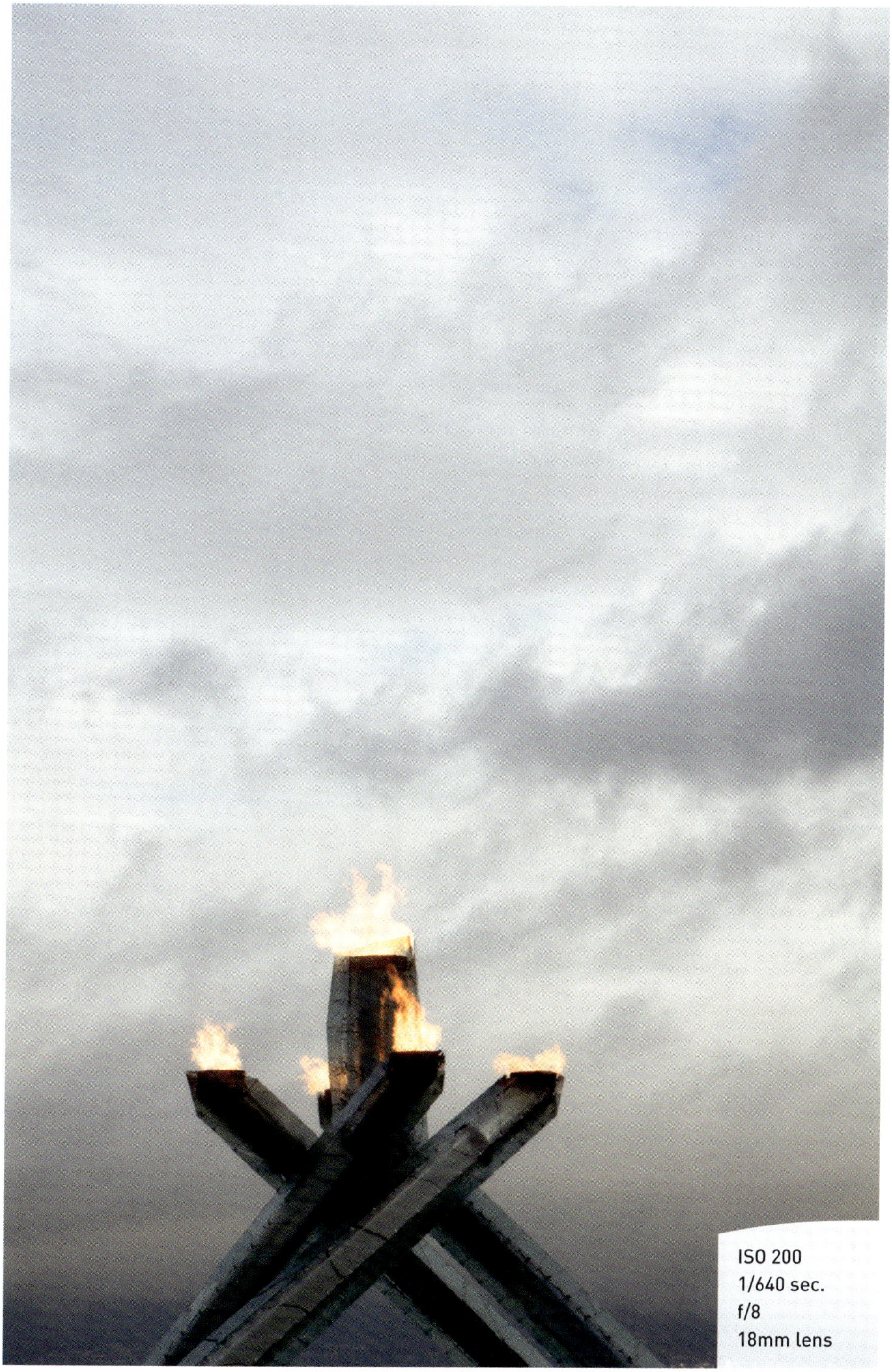

FIGURE 9.12
The spectacular Olympic flame is more dramatic when viewed against a turbulent Vancouver sky.

ISO 200
1/640 sec.
f/8
18mm lens

Generally speaking, splitting the frame right down the middle is not necessarily your best option. While it may seem more balanced, it can actually be pretty boring. You should utilize the rule of thirds when deciding how to divide your frame (**Figure 9.13**).

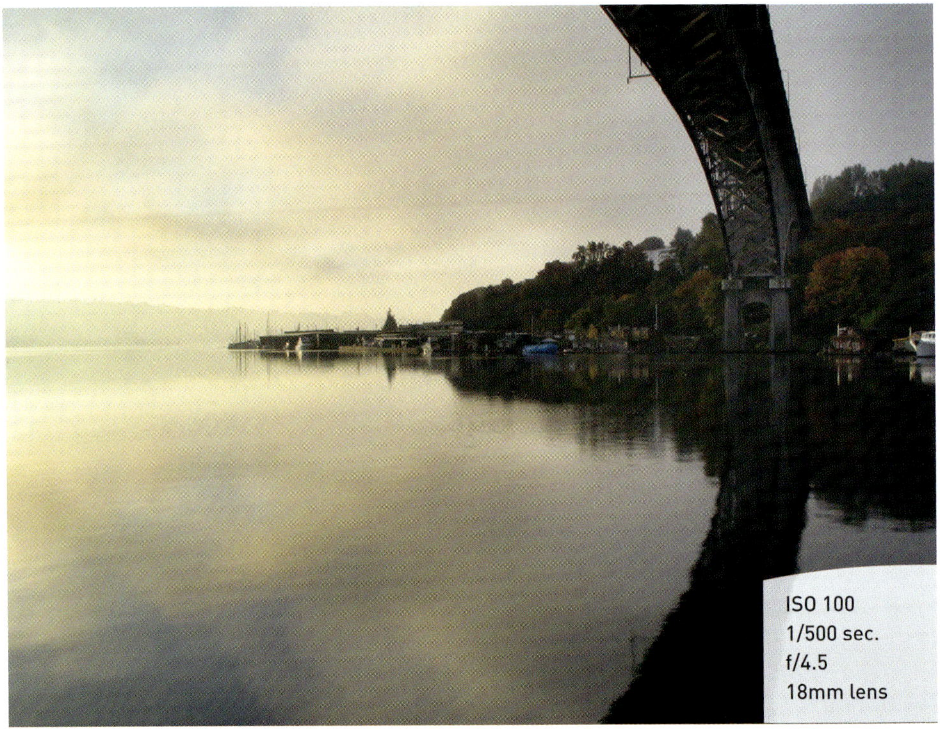

FIGURE 9.13
The rule of thirds works on the left and right sides of the frame. Here, the bridge and reflection counter-balance the light source and clouds.

Chapter 9 Assignments

If you apply the shooting techniques and tools that you have learned in the previous chapters to these assignments, you'll improve your ability to incorporate good composition into your photos. Make sure you experiment with all the different elements of composition and see how you can combine them to add interest to your images.

Learning to see lines and patterns

Take your camera for a walk around your neighborhood and look for patterns and angles. Don't worry as much about getting great shots as about developing an eye for details.

The ABCs of composition

Here's a great exercise: Shoot the alphabet. This will be a little more difficult, but with practice you will start to see beyond the obvious. Don't just find letters in street signs and the like—instead, find objects that aren't really letters but that have the shape of letters.

Finding the square peg and the round hole

Circles, squares, and triangles. Spend a few sessions concentrating on shooting simple geometric shapes.

Using the aperture to focus attention

Depth of field plays an important role in defining your images and establishing depth and dimension. Practice shooting wide open, using your largest aperture for the narrowest depth of field. Then find a scene that would benefit from extended depth of field, using very small apertures to give sharpness throughout the scene.

Leading them into a frame

Look for scenes where you can use elements as leading lines, and then look for framing elements that you can use to isolate your subject and add both depth and dimension to your images.

Share your results with the book's Flickr group!

Join the group here: flickr.com/groups/eosmfromsnapshotstogreatshots

10

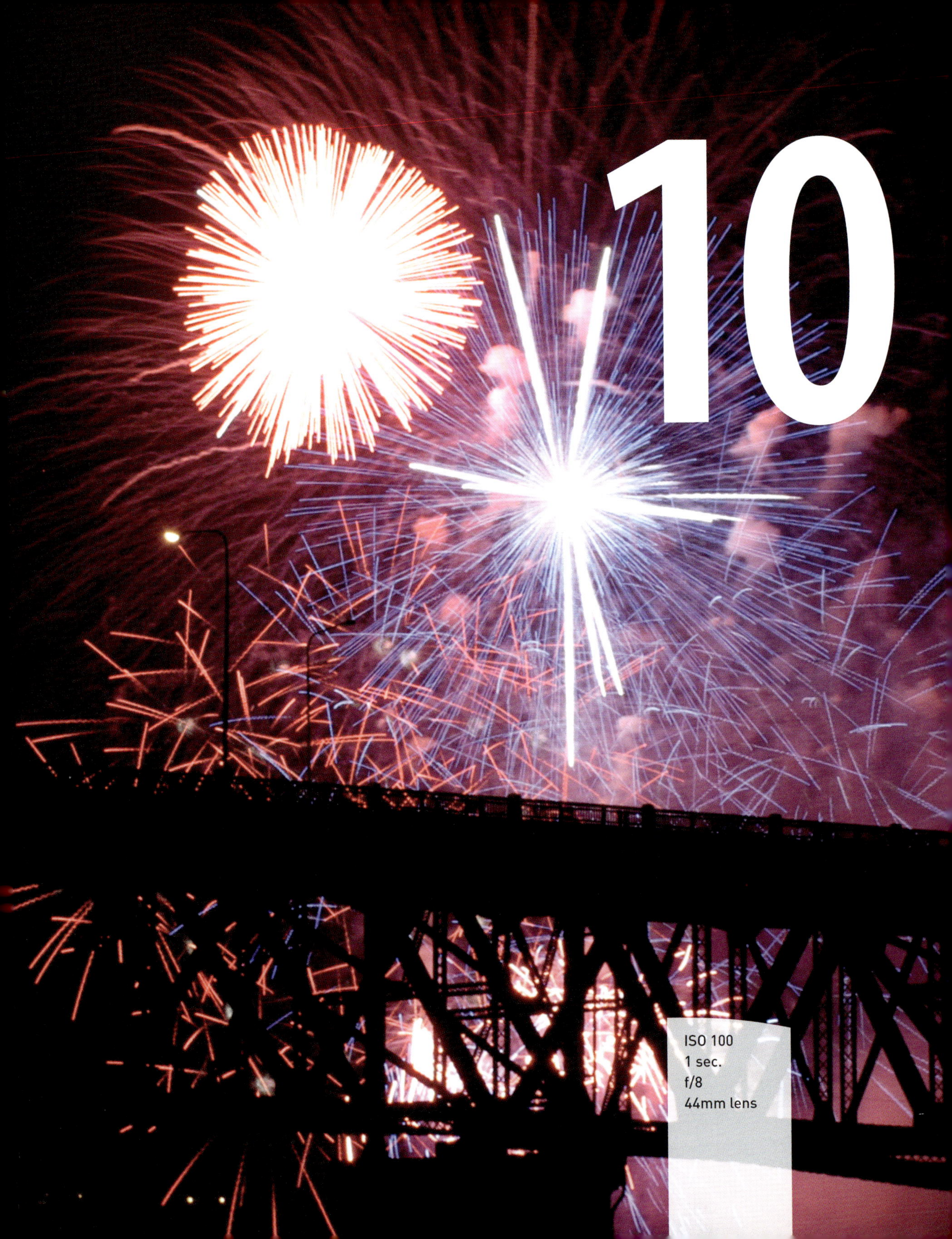

ISO 100
1 sec.
f/8
44mm lens

Advanced Techniques

IMPRESS YOUR FAMILY AND FRIENDS

We covered a lot of ground in the previous chapters, especially on the general photographic concepts that apply to most, if not all, shooting situations. There are, however, some specific tools and techniques that will give you an added advantage in obtaining a great shot. Additionally, we will look at how to customize certain controls on your camera to reflect your personal shooting preferences and always have them at the ready.

PORING OVER THE PICTURE

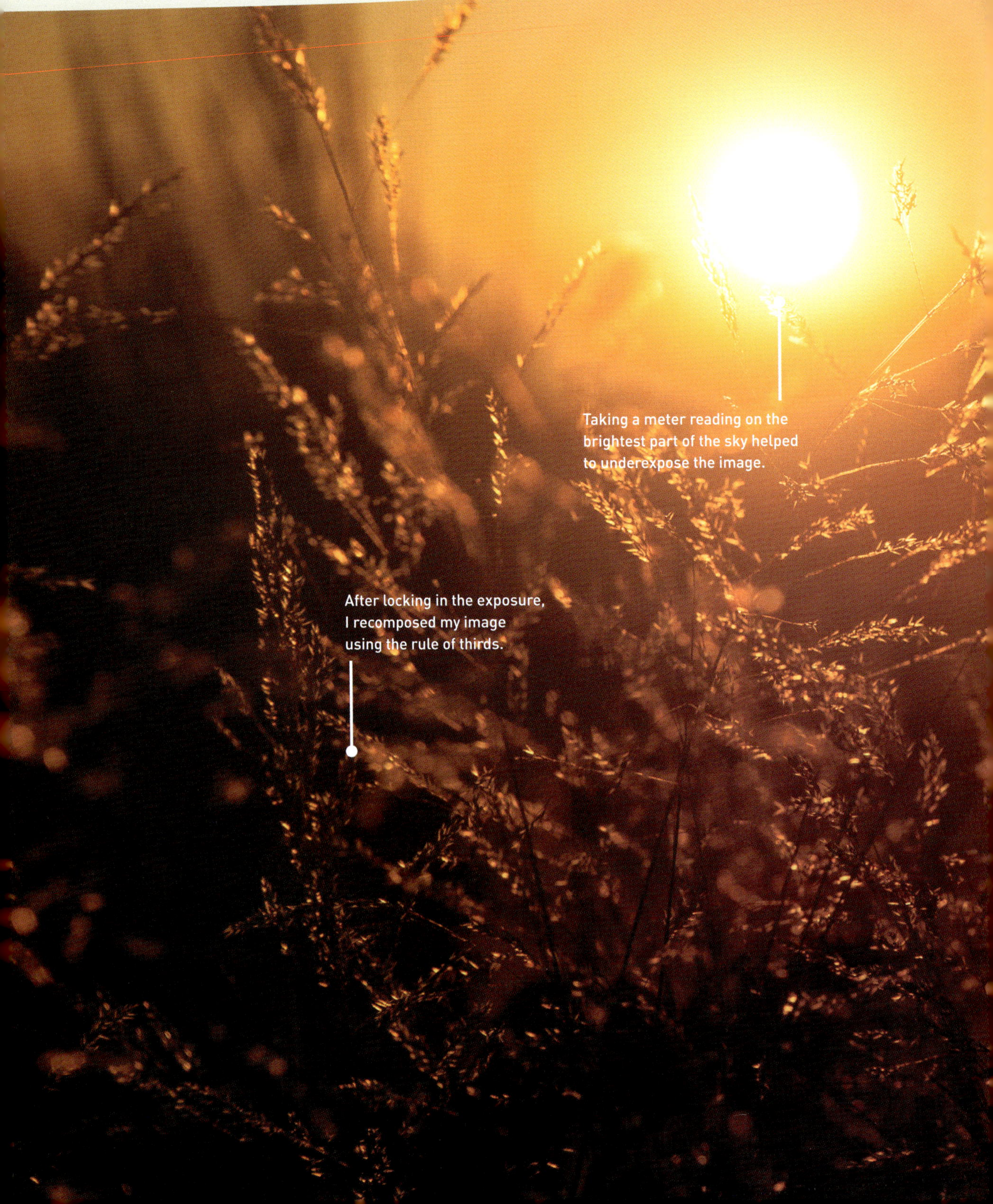

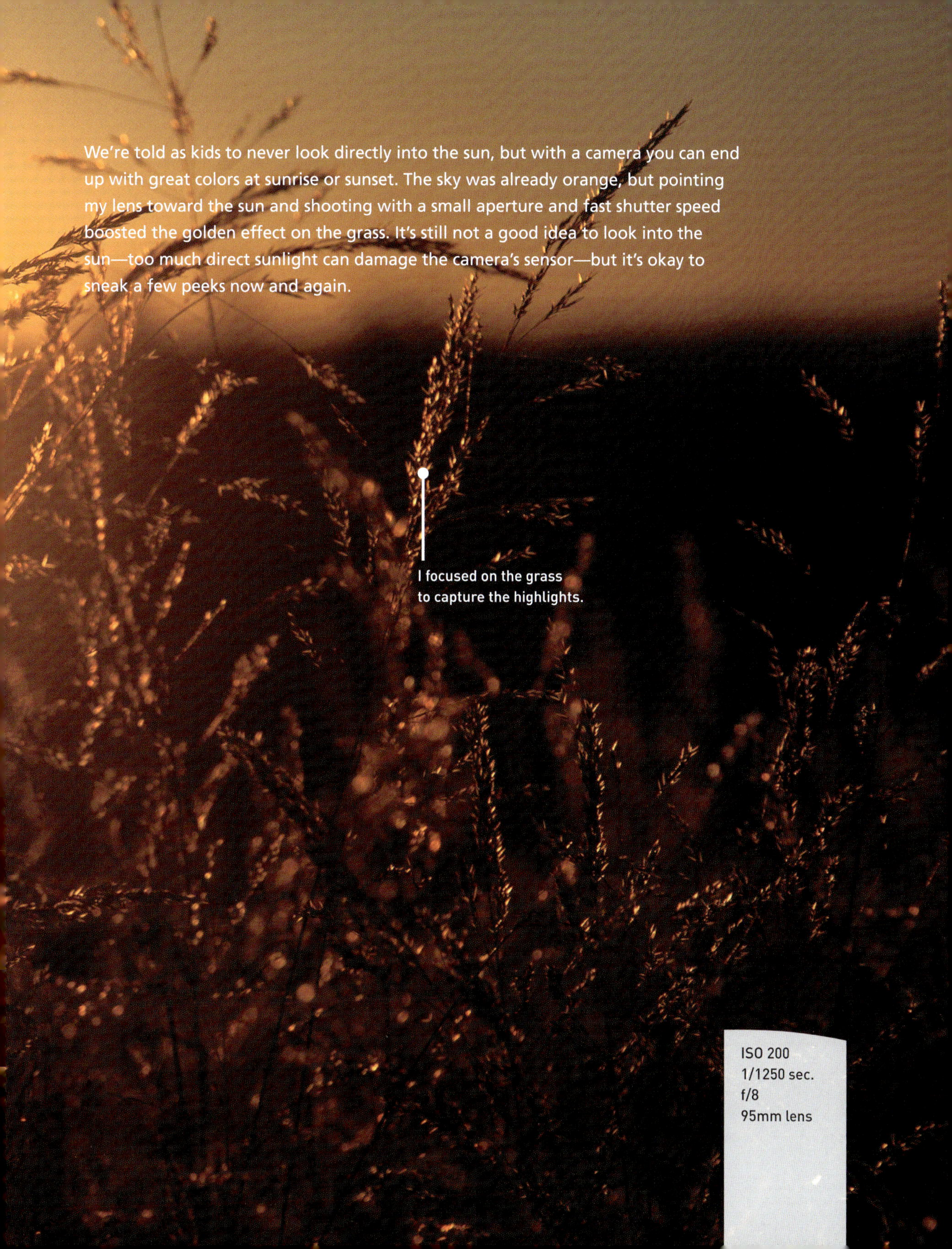

We're told as kids to never look directly into the sun, but with a camera you can end up with great colors at sunrise or sunset. The sky was already orange, but pointing my lens toward the sun and shooting with a small aperture and fast shutter speed boosted the golden effect on the grass. It's still not a good idea to look into the sun—too much direct sunlight can damage the camera's sensor—but it's okay to sneak a few peeks now and again.

I focused on the grass to capture the highlights.

ISO 200
1/1250 sec.
f/8
95mm lens

SPOT METER FOR MORE EXPOSURE CONTROL

Generally speaking, Evaluative metering mode provides accurate metering information for the majority of your photography. It does an excellent job of evaluating the scene and then relaying the proper exposure information to you. The only problem with this mode is that, like any metering mode on the camera, it doesn't know what it is looking at. There will be circumstances where you want to get an accurate reading from just a portion of a scene and discount the remaining area. To give you greater control of the metering operation, you can switch the camera to Spot metering mode. This allows you to take a meter reading from a very small circle in the center of the viewfinder, while ignoring the rest of the viewfinder area.

So when would you need to use this? Think of a person standing in front of a very dark wall. In Evaluative metering mode, the camera would see the entire scene and try to adjust the exposure information so that the dark background is exposed to render a lighter wall in your image. This means that the scene would actually be overexposed and your subject would then appear too light. To correct this, you can place the camera in Spot metering mode and take a meter reading right off of—and only off of—your subject, ignoring the dark wall altogether.

Other situations that would benefit from Spot metering include:

- Snow or beach environments where the overall brightness level of the scene could fool the meter
- Strongly backlit subjects that are leaving the subject underexposed (**Figures 10.1** and **10.2**)
- Cases where the overall feel of a photo is too light or too dark

SETTING UP AND SHOOTING IN SPOT METERING MODE

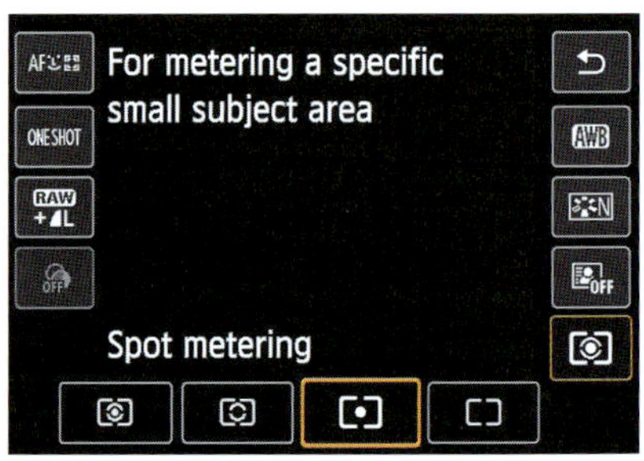

A

1. Press the Q button to bring up the Quick Control screen, and then tap the Metering Mode button.
2. Tap, or rotate the Main dial, to select the Spot metering icon (**A**), and then press the shutter release button halfway to return to shooting mode.
3. Point the center focus point at the subject that you wish to use for the meter reading.
4. Press the ✱ button to enable the AE Lock, which will hold the exposure value while you recompose, and then take the photo.

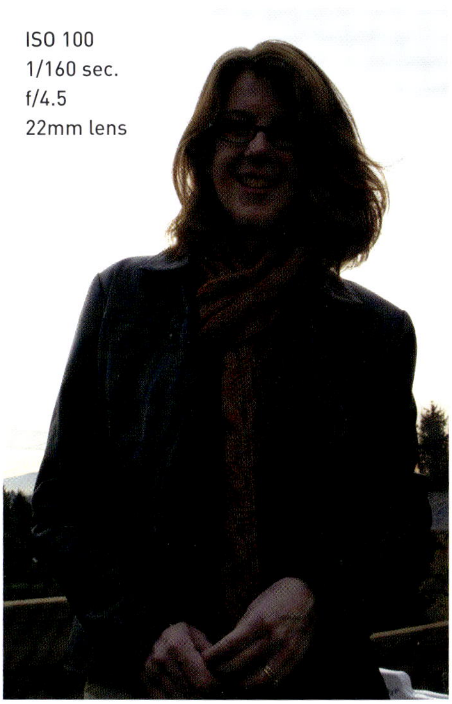

FIGURE 10.1
The sun in the background is fooling the meter into underexposing the image.

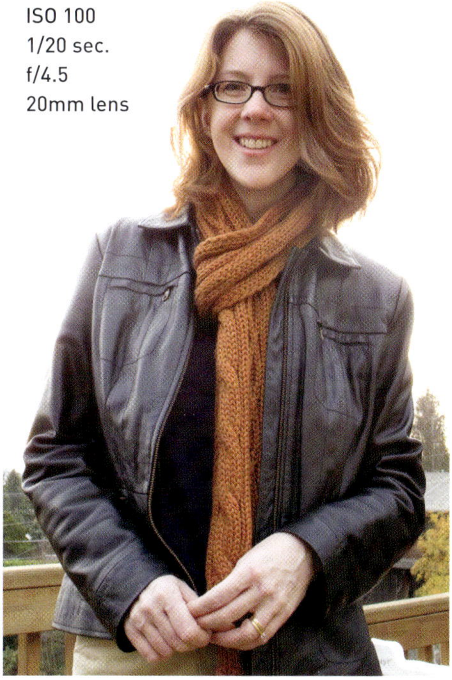

FIGURE 10.2
A spot meter reading on the face improves the exposure, but at the expense of losing background detail. The next thing to try would be to adjust the Exposure Compensation to regain the texture of the sky.

When using Spot metering mode, remember that the meter believes it is looking at a medium gray value, so you might need to incorporate some exposure compensation of your own to the reading that you are getting from your subject. This will come from experience as you use the meter.

METERING FOR SUNRISE OR SUNSET

Capturing a beautiful sunrise or sunset is all about the sky. If there is too much foreground in the viewfinder, the camera's meter will deliver an exposure setting that is accurate for the darker foreground areas but leaves the sky looking overexposed, undersaturated, and generally just not very interesting. To gain more emphasis on the colorful sky, point your camera at the brightest part of it and take your meter reading there. Use the AE Lock and then recompose. The result will underexpose the foreground but provide a darker, more dramatic sky (**Figure 10.3**).

FIGURE 10.3
By taking the meter reading from the brightest part of the sky, you will get darker, more colorful sunsets.

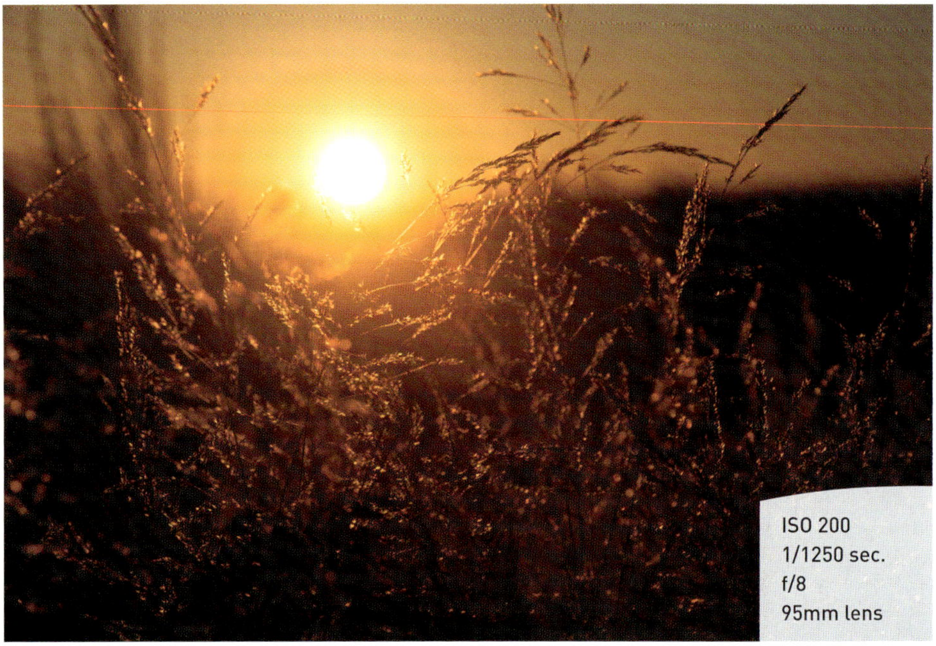

ISO 200
1/1250 sec.
f/8
95mm lens

MANUAL MODE

Probably one of the most advanced and yet most basic skills to master is shooting in Manual mode. With the power and utility of most of the automatic modes, Manual mode almost never sees the light of day. I have to admit that I don't select it for use very often, but there are times when no other mode will do. One situation that works well with Manual is studio work with external flashes. I know that when I work with studio lights, my exposure will not change, so I use Manual to eliminate any automatic changes that might happen from shooting in P, Tv, or Av mode.

Since you may not be too concerned with studio strobes at this point, I'll concentrate on one of the ways in which you will want to use Manual mode for your photography: long nighttime exposures.

BULB PHOTOGRAPHY

If you want to work with long shutter speeds that don't quite fit into one of the selectable shutter speeds, you can select Bulb. This setting is available only in Manual mode, and its sole purpose is to open the shutter at your command and then close it again when you decide. I can think of two scenarios where this would come in handy: shooting fireworks and shooting lightning.

If you are photographing fireworks, you could certainly use one of the longer shutter speeds available in Tv mode, since they are available for exposure times up to 30 seconds. That is fine, but sometimes you don't need 30 seconds' worth of exposure and sometimes you need more. If you open the shutter and then see a great burst of fireworks, you might decide that that is all you want for that particular frame, so you click the button to end the exposure (**Figure 10.4**).

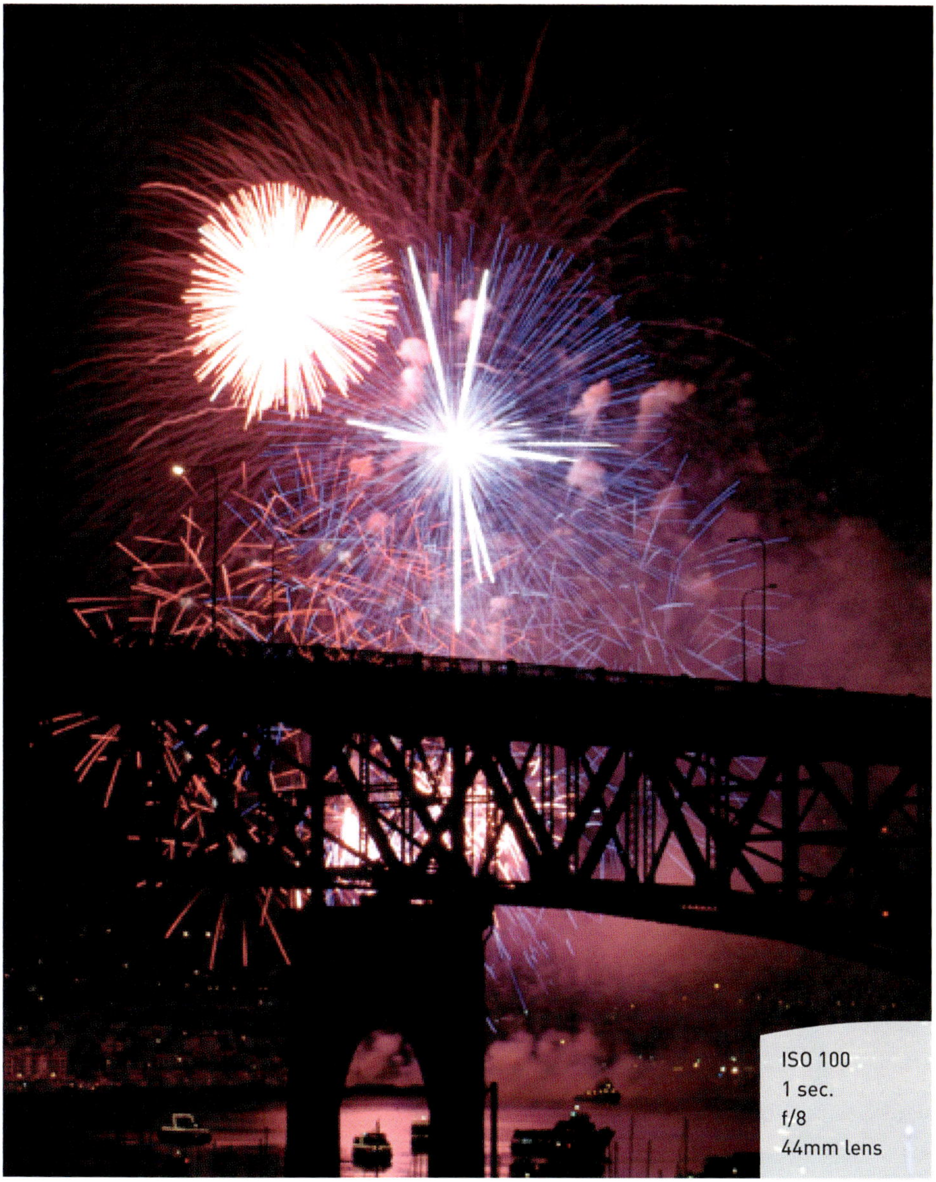

ISO 100
1 sec.
f/8
44mm lens

FIGURE 10.4
A great use for the Bulb setting is capturing fireworks.

The same can be said for photographing a lightning storm. Lightning can be very tricky to capture (and dangerous—a tripod can act like a lightning rod!), and using the Bulb setting to open and then close the shutter at will allows for more creativity, as well as more opportunity to get the shot.

SWITCHING TO BULB SHOOTING

1. Switch to Manual shooting mode.
2. Press the Q button to bring up the Quick Control screen, and then tap the Shutter Speed button. Or, press the Right cross key to select the Shutter Speed button.
3. Tap, or rotate the Main dial, to select the Bulb option at the far left edge.
4. Press the shutter release button halfway to return to shooting mode.
5. To begin an exposure, press the shutter release button fully *and hold it down*. A timer appears in the lower-right corner of the screen.
6. Stop pressing the shutter release button to complete the exposure.

When you're using the Bulb setting, the shutter will stay open only for the duration that you are holding down the shutter button. You will also see a counter on the lower-right portion of the LCD screen that will count off the seconds that the shutter is open. You can use this counter to either add or subtract time for your next shot. You should also be using a sturdy tripod or shooting surface. I want to point out that using your finger on the shutter button for a bulb exposure will definitely increase the chances of getting some camera shake in your images. To get the most benefit from the Bulb setting, I suggest using a remote control such as the Canon RC-6. You'll also want to turn on the Long Exposure Noise Reduction, as covered in Chapter 7.

BULB

If you are new to the world of photography, you might be wondering where in the world the *bulb* shutter function got its name. After all, wouldn't it make more sense to call it the Manual Shutter setting? It probably would, but this is one of those terms that harkens back to the origins of photography. Way back when, the shutter was actually opened through the use of a bulb-shaped device that forced air through a tube, which, in turn, pushed a plunger down, activating the camera shutter. When the bulb was released, it pulled the plunger back, letting the shutter close and ending the exposure.

USING THE SUN CREATIVELY

Have you ever seen photographs where the sun is peeking through a small hole and it creates a very cool starburst effect (**Figure 10.5**)? There is actually a little trick to pulling it off, and it's fairly easy once you know how. The real key is to be shooting at f/22 (or whatever your smallest aperture is). Then you need to have just a small bit of the sunlight in your frame, peeking either over an edge or through a small hole. The other thing you need to do is make sure that you are properly exposing for the rest of your scene, not the bright bit of sunlight that you are allowing in. With a little practice, you can really make some very cool shots.

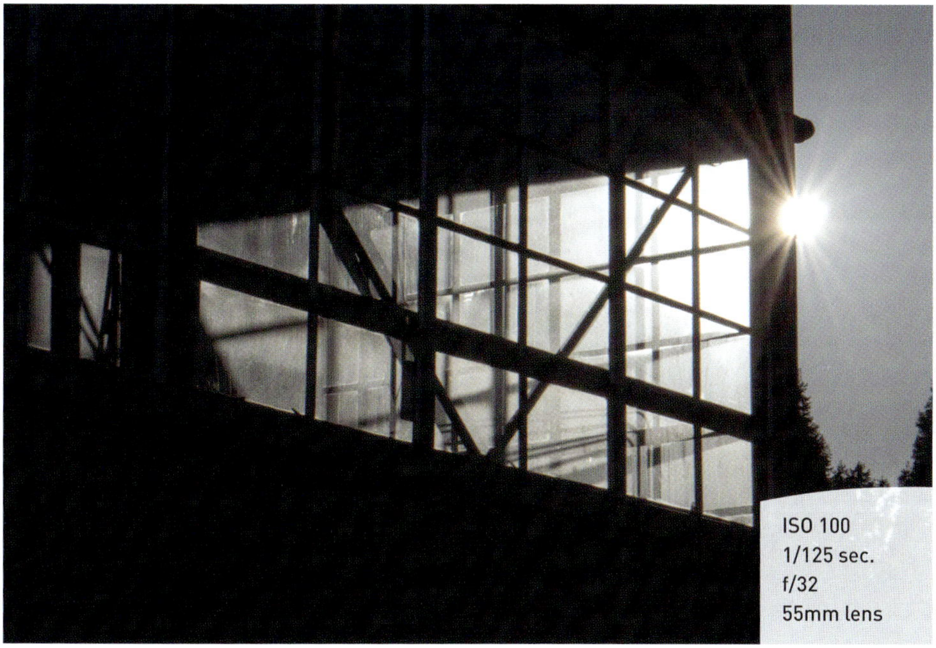

ISO 100
1/125 sec.
f/32
55mm lens

FIGURE 10.5
By letting the sun peek into my shot and using f/32, I was able to capture this cool starburst.

AVOIDING LENS FLARE

Lens flare, which appears as bright circles on the image, is one of the problems you will encounter when shooting in the bright sun (**Figure 10.6**). The flare is a result of the sun bouncing off the multiple pieces of optical glass in the lens and then being reflected back onto the sensor. Lens flare is especially frequent when using wide-angle lenses, because of their greater angle of coverage. You can avoid the problem using one of these methods:

- Try to shoot with the sun coming from over your shoulder, not in front of you or in your scene.
- Use a lens shade to block the unwanted light from striking the lens. You don't have to have the sun in your viewfinder for lens flare to be an issue. All it has to do is strike the front glass of the lens to make it happen.
- If you don't have a lens shade, just try using your hand or some other element to block the light.

BRACKETING EXPOSURES

So what if you are doing everything right in terms of metering and mode selection, yet your images still sometimes come out too light or too dark? You can use a technique called *bracketing*, which will help you find the best exposure value for your scene by taking a normal exposure as well as ones that are over- and underexposed. When I am out shooting, I typically shoot with my camera set to an exposure compensation of –1/3 stop to protect my highlights. If I am dealing with a subject that has a lot of different tonal ranges from bright to dark, I will often bracket by one stop over and one stop under my already compensated exposure. That means I will have exposures of –1 1/3, –1/3, and +2/3.

You can set the amount of exposure bracketing from as little as a third of a stop to as much as two stops per exposure (this is the setting I use for creating HDR images, which we discussed in Chapter 7). You can also dial in the amount of exposure compensation that you might need. You can adjust the compensation as much as five stops in either direction, depending on the range of your bracketed exposures. Either way, bracketing will help you zero in on that perfect exposure, and you can just delete the ones that didn't make the grade (**Figures 10.7** through **10.9**).

The camera will take the normal image first, then the underexposed image, then the overexposed image. Don't forget to take all three. The Auto Exposure Bracketing feature will reset itself when the camera is turned off and then on again.

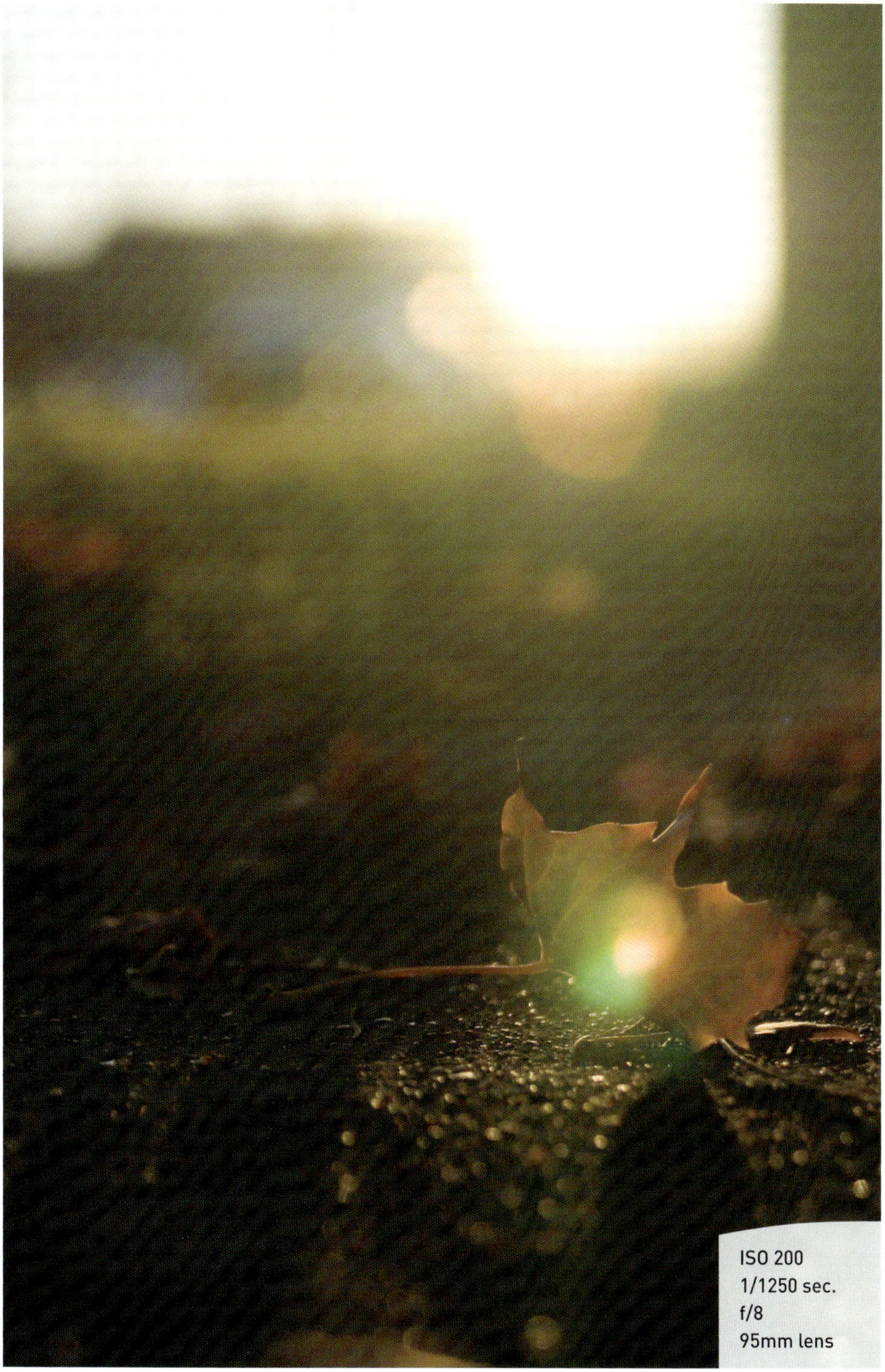

FIGURE 10.6 The bright sun in the upper portion of the frame has created flare spots that are visible as colored circles radiating down through the image.

FIGURE 10.7
One stop of exposure below normal.

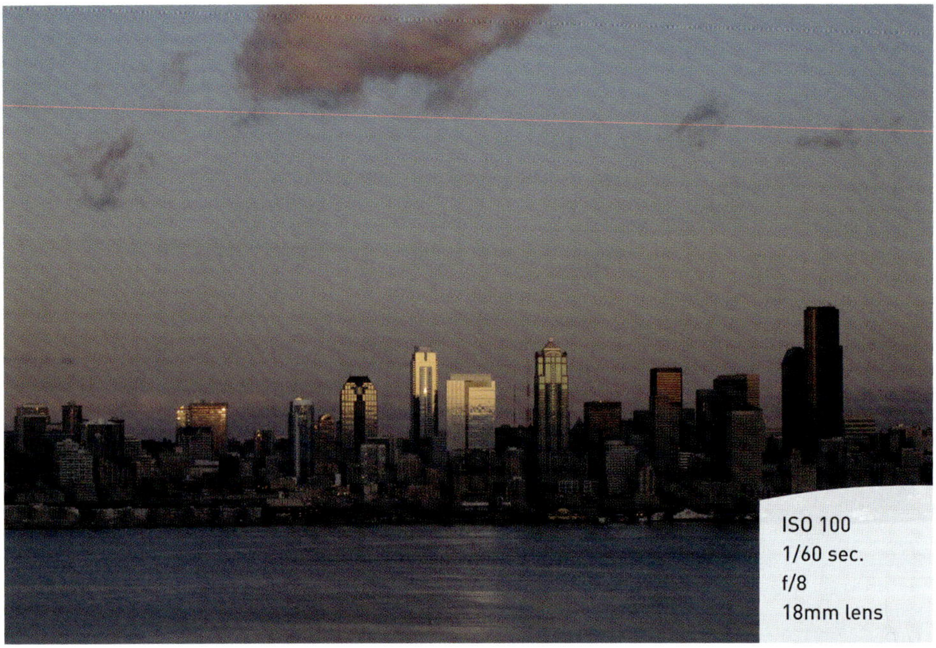

FIGURE 10.8
The normal exposure as indicated by the camera meter.

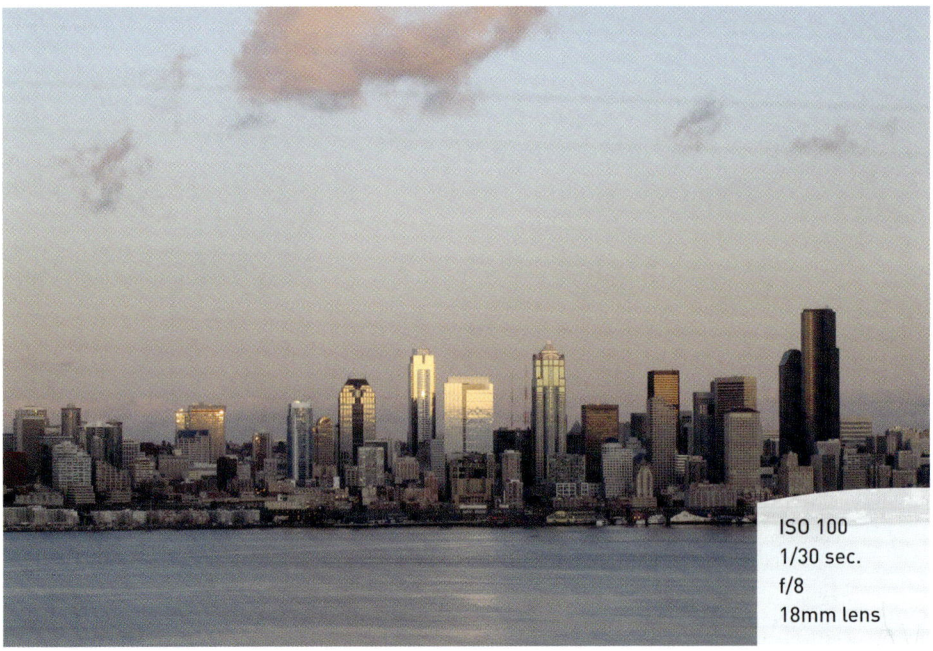

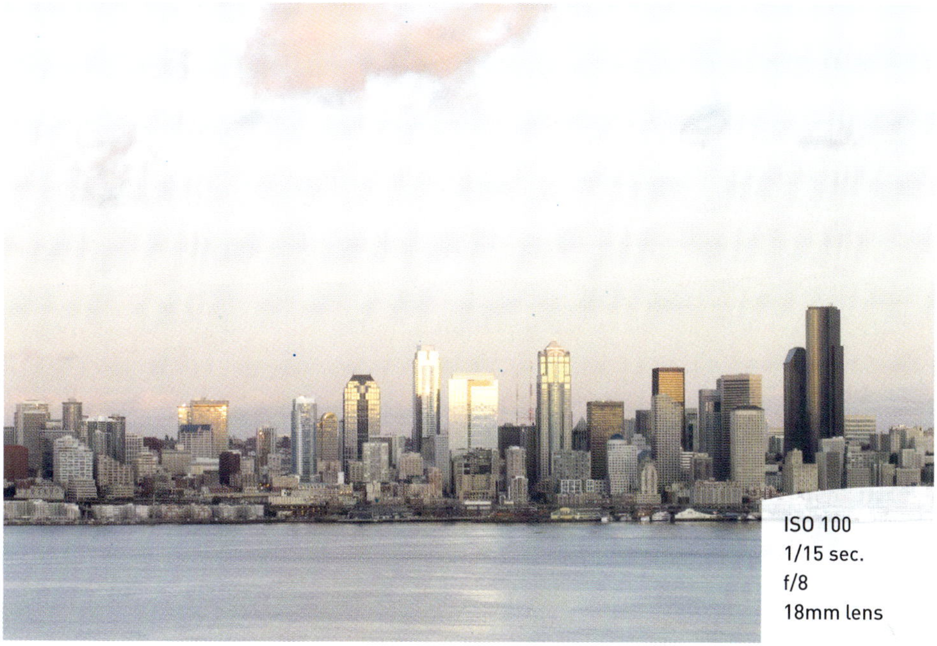

FIGURE 10.9
One stop of exposure above normal.

ISO 100
1/15 sec.
f/8
18mm lens

SETTING AUTO-EXPOSURE BRACKETING

1. Press the Info button until you're viewing just the settings without an image preview (**A**).
2. Tap the Exposure Compensation/AEB setting button.
3. Use the Main dial to set the amount of over- and underexposure that you desire (**B**).
4. If you want the "normal" exposure to be a little over- or underexposed, you can adjust that with your Left/Right cross keys.

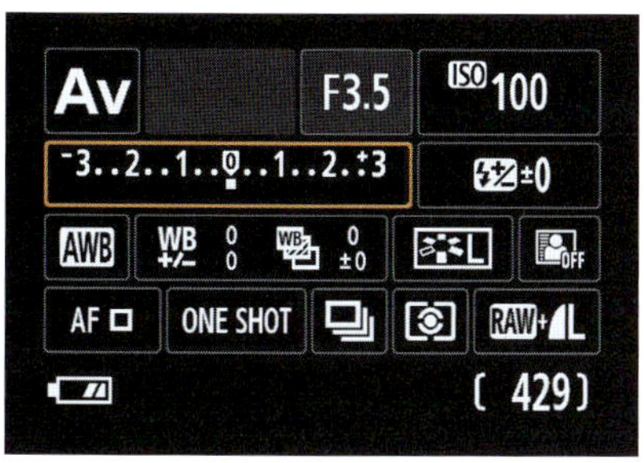

A

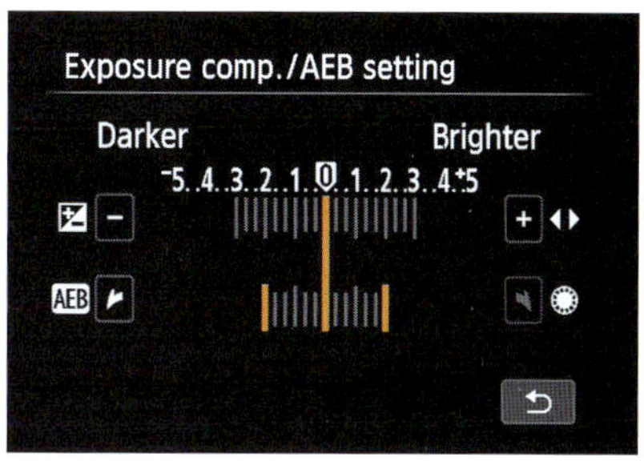

B

HDR BACKLIGHT CONTROL

Earlier in the book I explained the process for creating HDR images using three separate images that need to be combined using special software. There is, however, a special feature on your camera that will let you take three images and combine them right in your camera for improved highlight and shadow details. It's a mode called HDR Backlight Control.

When you switch to HDR Backlight Control mode, the camera will take three consecutive photos with a single click of the shutter button. After the photos have been taken, the camera will combine the images to give you an image with greater detail in the highlights and shadows (**Figure 10.10**).

There are limitations to using this setting. First, you should always have your camera on a stable surface or a tripod when taking photos. Second, you should only use it on non-moving subjects, because you can get ghosting if there is movement during the exposure process.

AUTO LIGHTING OPTIMIZER

Did you know that your camera provides a function that can automatically make your pictures look better? It's called Auto Lighting Optimizer. It works this way: The camera evaluates the tones in your image and then lightens any areas that it believes are too dark or lacking in contrast (**Figures 10.11** and **10.12**). This is different than the HDR Backlight Control because it is working on only a single exposure and boosting the shadows while pulling the exposure down slightly to darken the highlights. This optimization is applied automatically in the shooting modes of the Basic zone.

You can choose from four levels: Disable, Low, Standard, and High. You will need to evaluate the strength of the effect on your images and change it accordingly. I typically leave it set to Standard so that I have brighter, more detailed shadow areas in my photographs. If you are using exposure compensation to darken your image, you might find that your image is too bright with this option turned on. Also, you should disable it if you are using flash exposure compensation since it will try to work against you when you alter the flash strength.

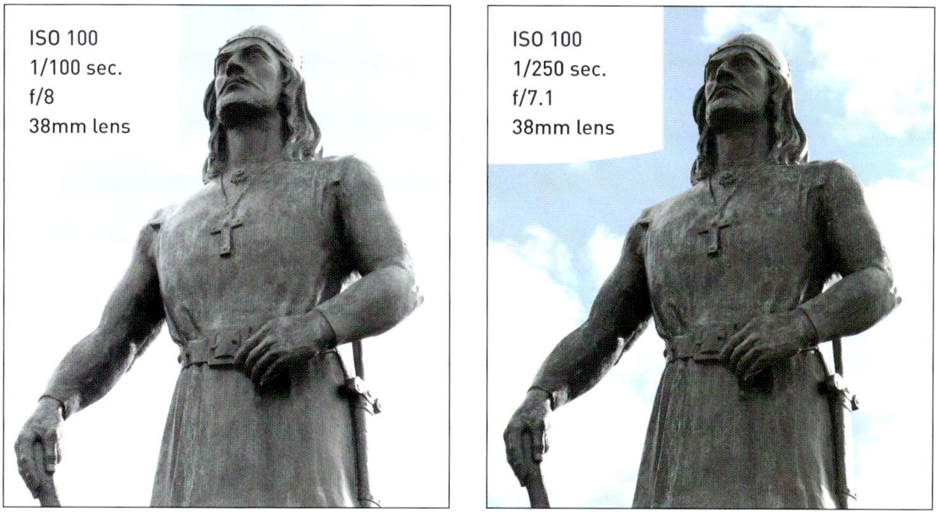

FIGURE 10.10
The HDR Backlight Control mode darkened the background but also retained detail in the foreground.

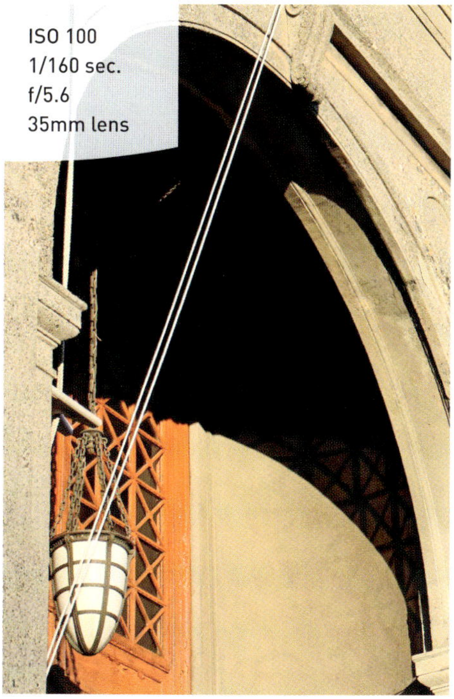

FIGURE 10.11
Without the Auto Lighting Optimizer, the shadows are dark and contrasty.

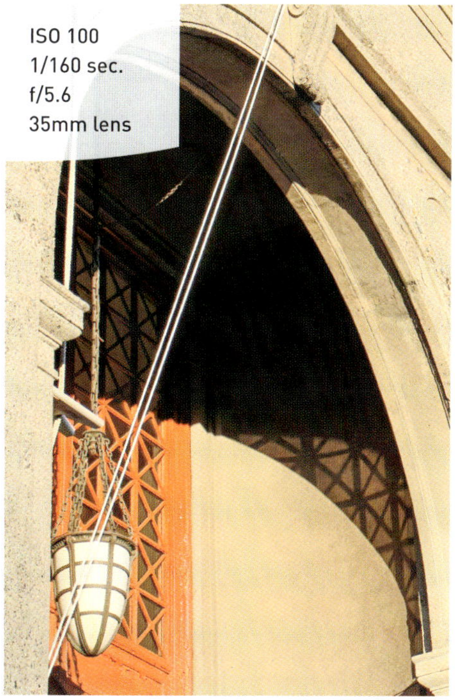

FIGURE 10.12
Although the exposure hasn't changed, the shadows are brighter after changing the Optimizer to the High setting.

SETTING UP THE AUTO LIGHTING OPTIMIZER

1. Press the Quick Control button, tap the Auto Lighting Optimizer, and press the Set button (**A**).
2. Use the cross keys to select the level of optimization that you prefer, and press the Set button to lock in the change.

A

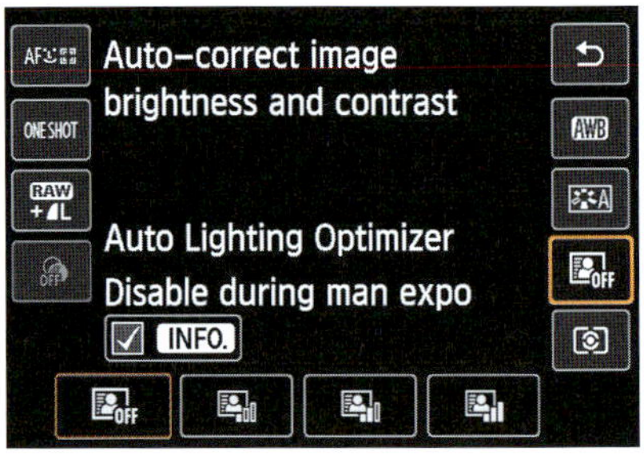

HANDHELD NIGHT SCENE

Another great little automatic feature in the EOS M is the Handheld Night Scene mode. This is yet another Basic shooting mode, and it acts in a similar fashion to the HDR mode except it is made for getting a sharp image in low-light or night scenes, where handholding a camera usually isn't possible. To do this, the camera fires off four consecutive frames and then processes them in-camera to create one sharp, properly exposed image (**Figure 10.13**).

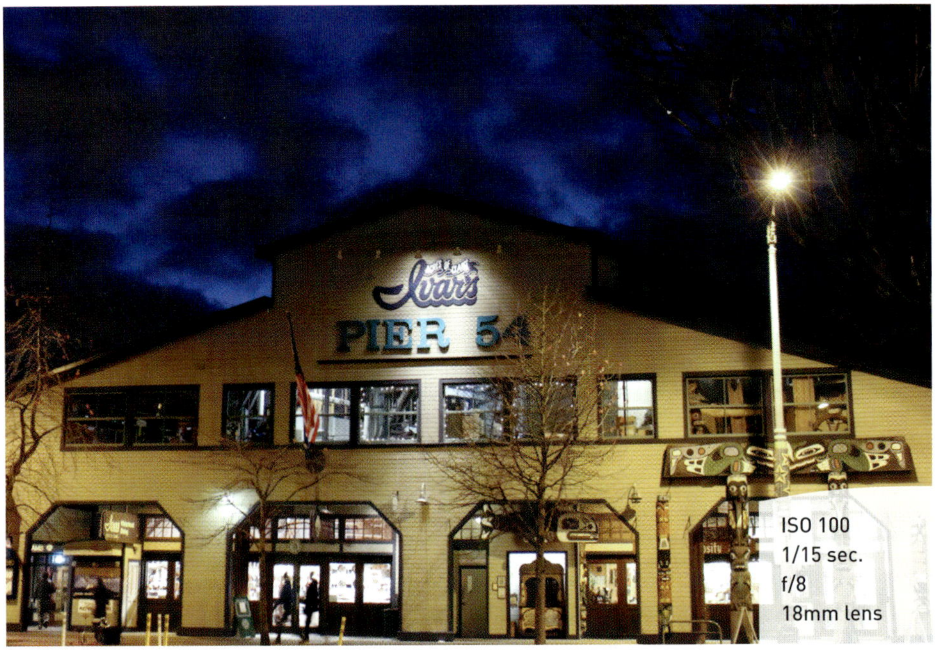

FIGURE 10.13
Handheld Night Scene combines your photos to give you one sharp, noise-free image.

THE MY MENU SETTING

There are a lot of items in the menu that you can change, but some are used and changed more frequently than others.

The My Menu function allows you to place six of your most-used menu items in one place so that you can quickly get to them, make your changes, and get on with shooting. You can see what I have in my My Menu in **Figure 10.14**.

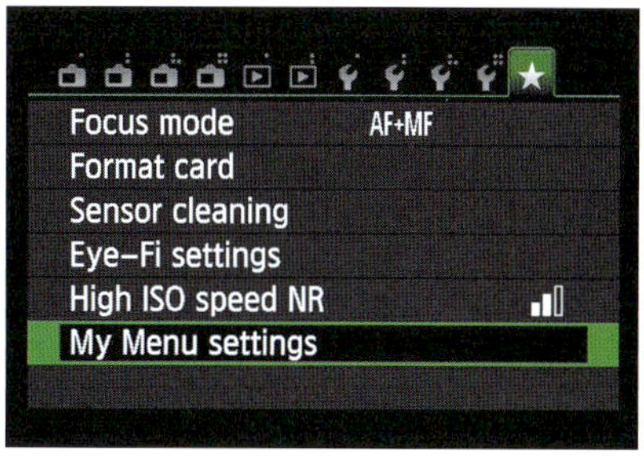

FIGURE 10.14
The functions I've stored in My Menu

CUSTOMIZING YOUR MY MENU SETTING

1. Press the Menu button, and use the cross keys to select the tab with the star.
2. Select My Menu settings, and press Set (**A**).
3. Highlight Register to My Menu, and press Set (**B**).
4. Scroll through the available menu items, and select one you want to add. Press the Set button (**C**).
5. When asked if you want to register the item, highlight OK and press Set (**D**).
6. Continue adding the items that you want in the list until you have selected your favorites (up to six of them).

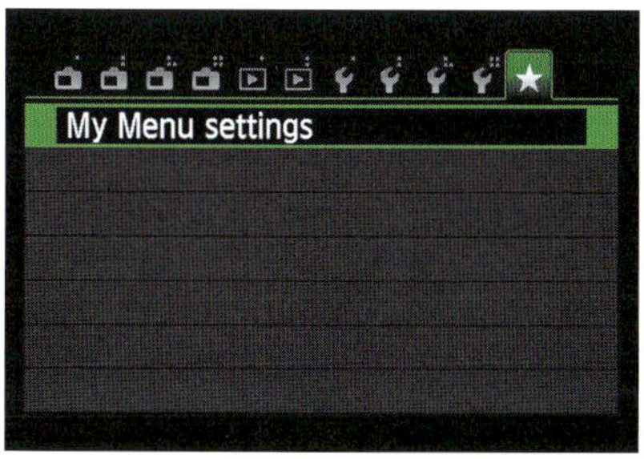

A

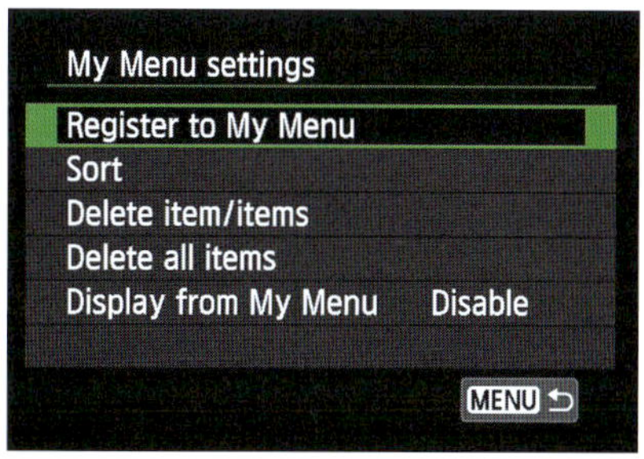

B

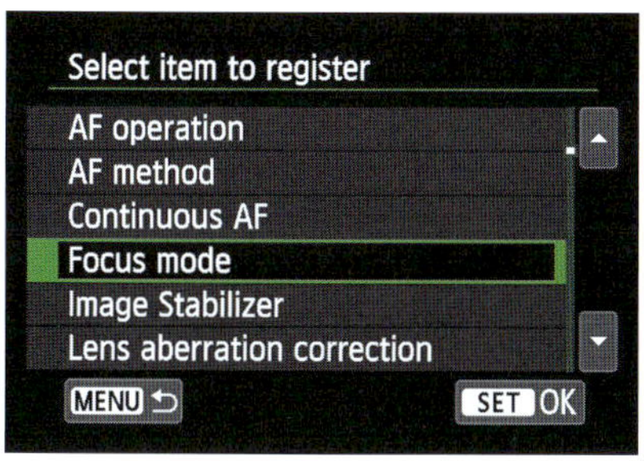

C

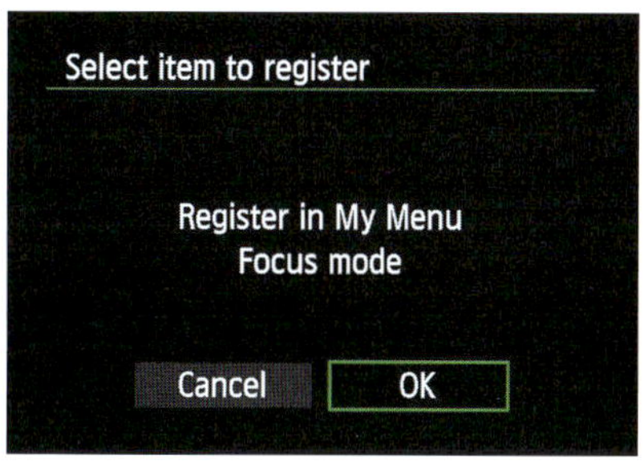

D

CUSTOMIZE YOUR WHITE BALANCE

Previous chapters have addressed the issue of setting your white balance, but what if you are in a situation that doesn't fall neatly into one of the existing categories like Daylight or Tungsten? You might want to consider creating a custom white balance. This is especially helpful if you have more than one kind of light source shining on your subject. A perfect example might be indoors with fluorescent lighting fixtures overhead and daylight coming through a window. To ensure that you are getting the best possible results in a situation like this, perform a quick white balance customization by using the Custom White Balance option. Don't worry, though—it's easier than you might think. Typically, the only thing you will need is a piece of white paper.

CREATING A CUSTOM WHITE BALANCE

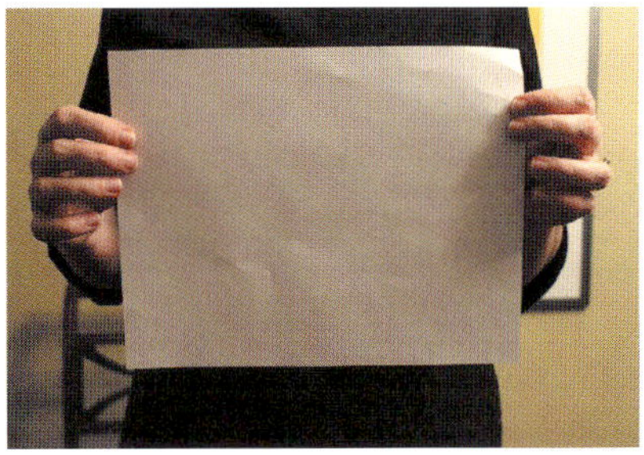

A

1. Begin by having your subject hold a piece of white paper, and then take a picture of it. You can have the camera set on any white balance preset for this (**A**).
2. Next, press the Menu button, navigate to the second shooting menu, highlight Custom White Balance, and press the Set button (**B**).
3. The camera should then display the photo that you took of the white paper. If it is the correct image, press the Set button. If it is not, use the Left/Right cross keys to locate the image first (**C**).

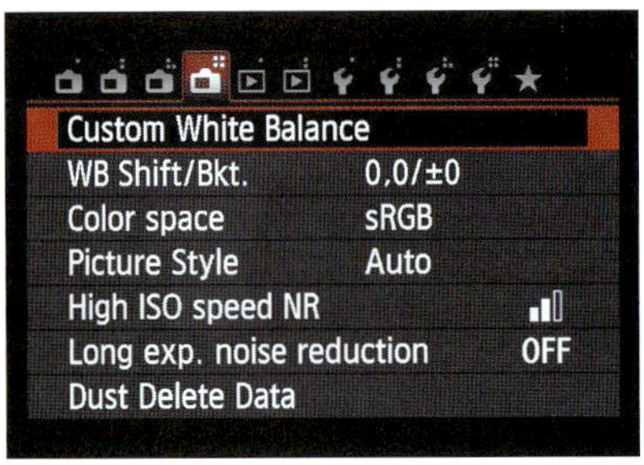

B

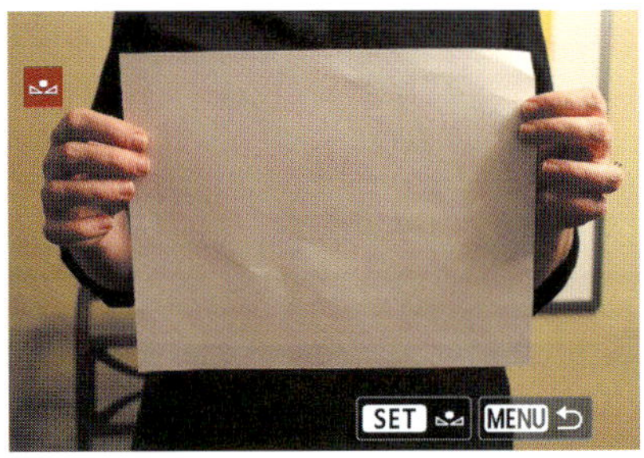

C

4. Confirm that this is the image you want to use by highlighting the OK option and pressing Set (**D**).
5. Click OK to set your camera to the Custom White Balance setting.
6. Press the shutter button halfway to return to shooting mode.
7. To shoot with the new white balance setting, press the Quick Control button, tap the White Balance icon, and choose the Custom button (**E**).

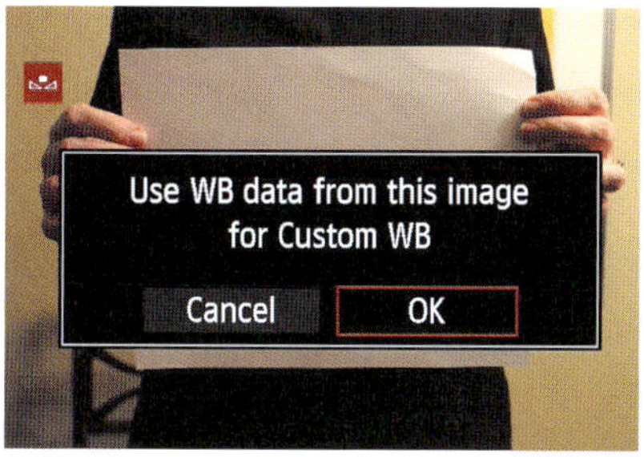

D

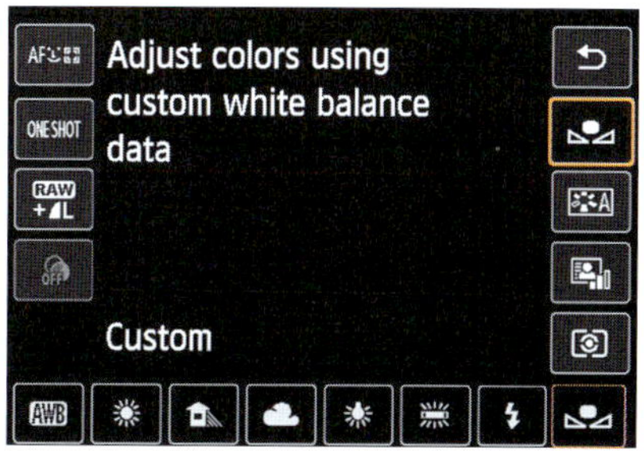

E

You are now ready to take images with much more accurate color for the environment where you are shooting.

Chapter 10 Assignments

Many of the techniques covered in this chapter are specific to certain shooting situations that may not come about very often. This is even more reason to practice them so that when the situation does present itself you will be ready.

Adding some drama to the end of the day

Most sunset photos don't reflect what the photographer saw, because they weren't metered correctly. The next time you see a colorful sunset, pull out your camera, take a meter reading from the sky, and take a photo. Then take a photo without a meter reading, and see what a difference it makes.

Making your exposure spot-on

Using the Spot metering mode can give accurate results, but only when the camera is pointed at something that has a middle tone. Try adding something gray to the scene and taking a reading off it. Now switch back to your regular metering mode and see if the exposure isn't slightly different.

Using the Bulb setting to capture the moment

This is definitely one of those settings that you won't use often, but it's pretty handy when you need it. If you have the opportunity to shoot a fireworks display or a distant storm, try setting the camera to Bulb and then playing with some long exposures to capture just the moments that you want.

Bracketing your way to better exposures

Why settle for just one variation of an image when you can bracket to get the best exposure choice? Set your camera up for a 1/3-stop bracket series, and then expand it to a one-stop series. Review the results to see if the normal setting was the best or perhaps one of the bracketed exposures was even better.

Share your results with the book's Flickr group!

Join the group here: flickr.com/groups/eosmfromsnapshotstogreatshots

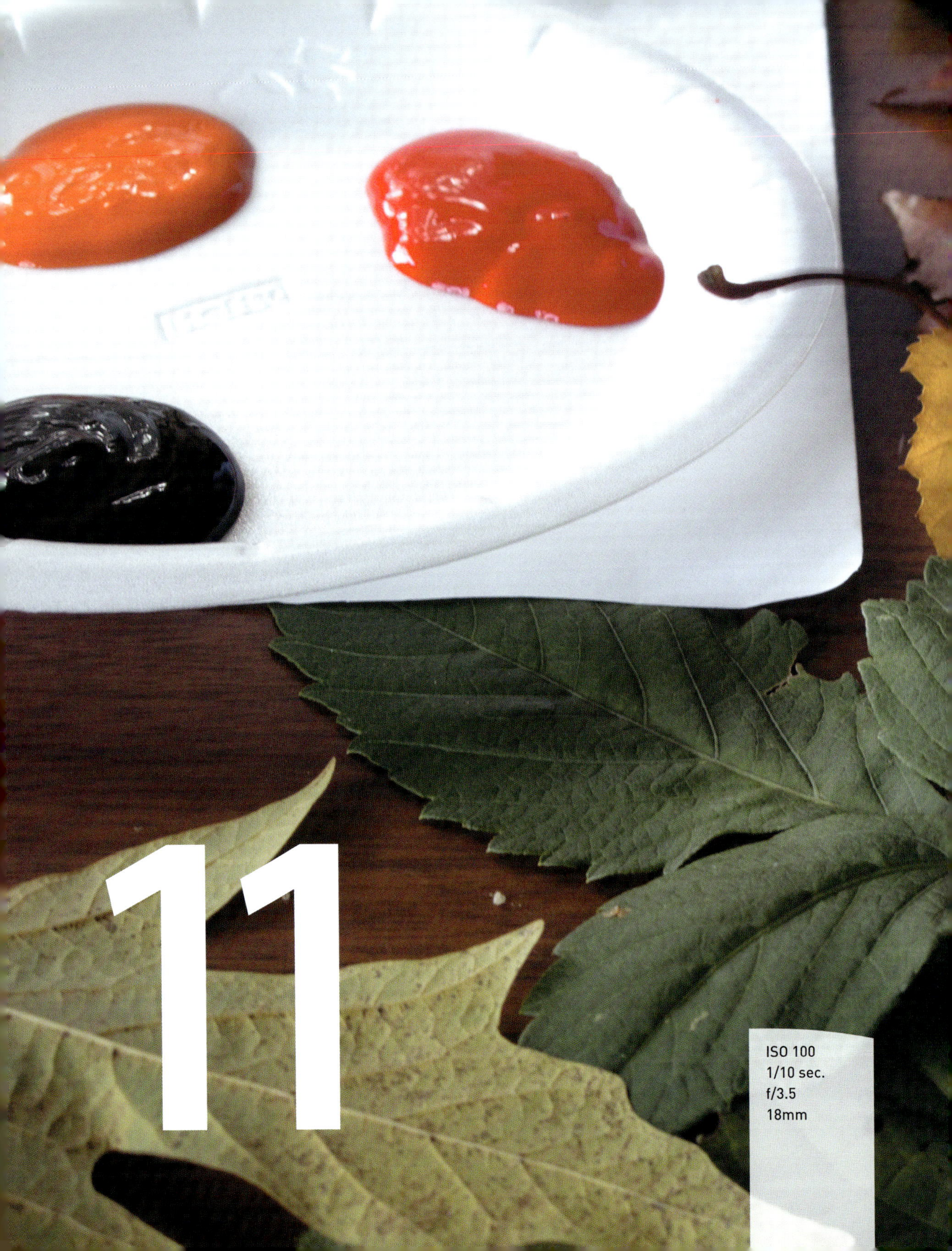

11

ISO 100
1/10 sec.
f/3.5
18mm

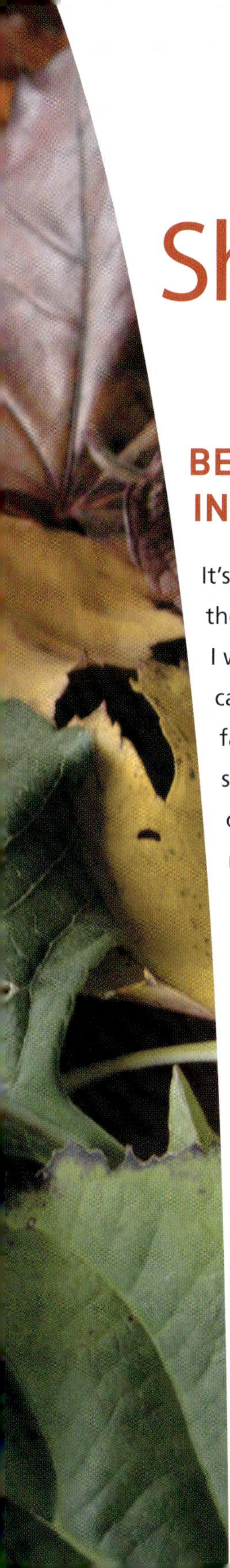

Shooting Video

BECAUSE EVERYTHING IN FRONT OF THE LENS IS MOVING

It's now rare to find a digital camera that does *not* record video, and in the case of the EOS M, the high-definition (HD) video is quite impressive. I wouldn't go so far as to say you could completely replace a digital camcorder with it for some situations, but the EOS M is currently my favorite video-recording device for grabbing clips on the go or capturing short projects. Capturing video entails most of the same techniques covered in this book, but as you'll discover, wrangling moving pictures requires a few extra considerations that I cover in this chapter.

SHOOTING VIDEO

To get started, turn the Mode dial to the Movie shooting position (**Figure 11.1**). Just as with shooting still photos in Auto mode, the camera attempts to make adjustments automatically before starting to record video. Some aspects—such as manual focus and, to a limited extent, exposure—can be adjusted before you start recording. Just don't expect to wield the same degree of control over video that you enjoy over still photos.

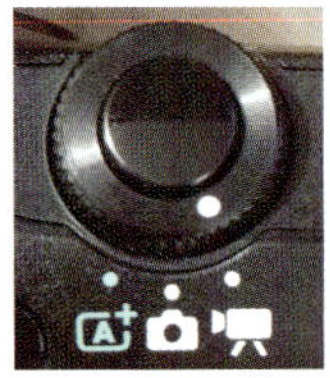

FIGURE 11.1
Movie mode

CAPTURING VIDEO

1. Compose your shot, and then tap an area of the screen to set the focus. You can also press the shutter button halfway to lock focus.
2. If you're not happy with the camera's light meter reading of the scene, use the Exposure Compensation control to brighten or darken the shot.
3. Press the Movie Start/Stop button to begin recording. A red indicator ● appears to let you know you're recording live, along with a count of the time elapsed (**Figure 11.2**).
4. To stop the video recording, press the Movie Start/Stop button a second time.

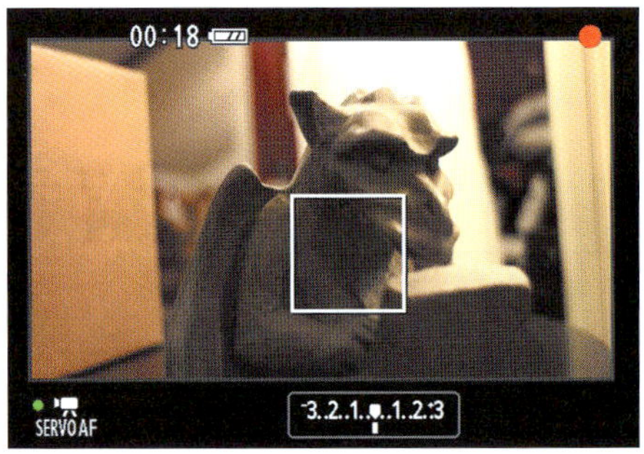

FIGURE 11.2
The EOS M takes a no-frills approach when actually recording video.

MEMORY CARDS FOR SHOOTING VIDEO

For the best performance when capturing video, buy SDHC cards that are rated Class 6 or higher. They can transfer data faster and come in larger capacities (which is good for shooting stills, too). According to Canon, a 4 GB card will hold approximately 25 minutes of HD video, whereas a 16 GB card will hold about 1 hour 43 minutes' worth. The 4 GB capacity is important to remember, because the EOS M will stop recording automatically once the clip nears that limit; you'd need to start recording a new clip to continue.

VIDEO QUALITY

The highest-quality video setting on your EOS M will render high-definition video with a resolution of 1920 x 1080, also referred to as 1080p; it will also capture at 1280 x 720 pixels, known as 720p. The "1080" and "720" represent the height of the video image in pixels, and the "p" stands for progressive, which is how the camera records/draws the video on the screen. A lower-resolution video setting, 640 x 480, is also available, which requires less storage space on a memory card. Unless you have a specific need to shoot in the lower quality, I recommend sticking to the HD sizes; you can always downsize the video on a computer later.

The other thing to consider when selecting a quality setting is the capture frame rate. At the 1920 x 1080 size, you have two frame rates to choose from: 30 frames per second or 24 frames per second (fps). The 30 fps setting is more of a TV standard and complies with the NTSC video standards used in the United States. This should be your choice for most of your video recording. If you are going to use the video for DVD or for movies with a "Hollywood" look, you should go with the 24 fps option.

The 60 fps on the 1280 x 720 option should render smooth video sequences, but they might also look a little like slow motion. One reason for using this frame rate is that it helps with fast movement of the camera or subject.

SETTING THE MOVIE QUALITY

1. Press the Quick Control button.
2. Tap the Movie record size option (**A**).
3. Select the desired movie quality setting by tapping one of the options or pressing the Left or Right cross key (**B**).
4. Press the Set button to return to Movie mode.

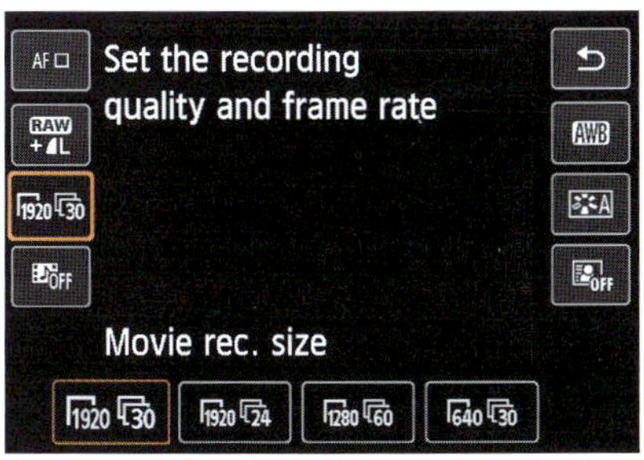

A

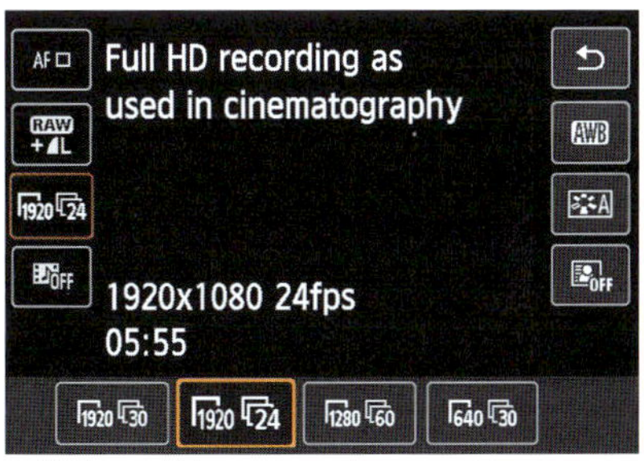

B

SOUND

The EOS M can record audio to go along with your video, but there are a couple of things to keep in mind when using it. The first is to make sure you don't block the microphones on the top of the camera, to the left of the hot shoe (**Figure 11.3**).

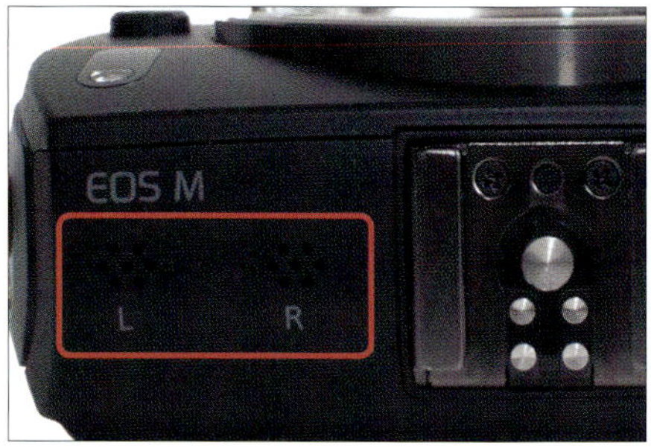

FIGURE 11.3
The EOS M's built-in microphones

The next thing you need to know about the sound is that because the microphone is part of the camera, any noise that the camera makes, such as when it's focusing the lens, will be audible in your movies. If you find that the lens focus noise is distracting or you plan to add your own soundtrack to the video at a later time, you can turn the audio recording off.

TURNING OFF THE SOUND

1. Press the Menu button and navigate to the movie-shooting tab.
2. Highlight Sound recording and press the Set button (**A**).
3. Select the Disable option, and press Set to lock in the change (**B**). Press the Menu button to return to recording mode.

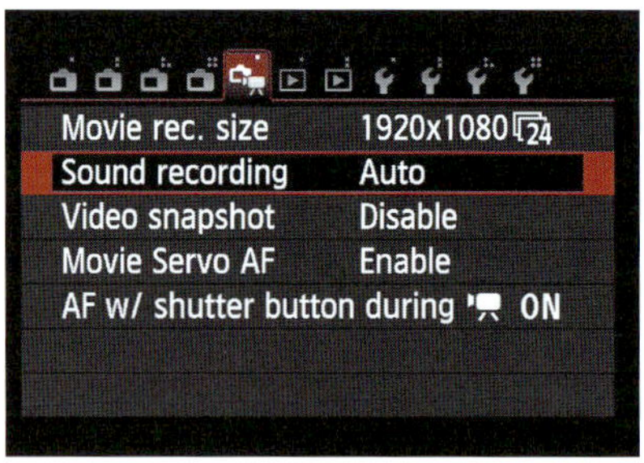

A

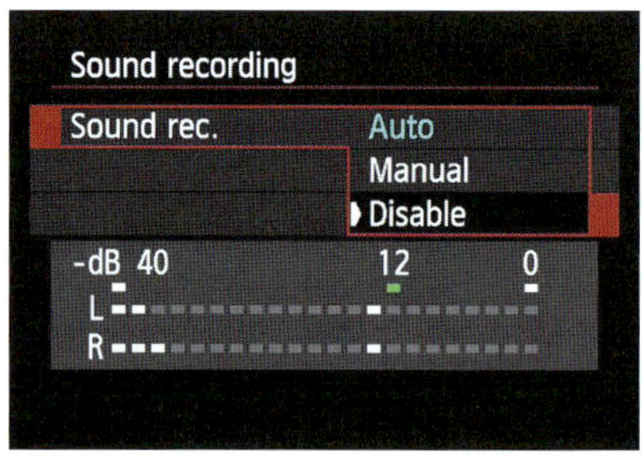

B

That same menu also allows you to manually adjust the sound input, which can be helpful if the surrounding audio is too loud or soft. Watch the audio levels—if they're consistently yellow or red, you'll want to reduce the overall volume. You can also enable a wind filter and attenuator to bring levels in line; these options are available in both the Auto and Manual sound-recording modes.

BETTER SOUND FOR YOUR MOVIES

If you want to eliminate the camera noise that comes with recording sound with your camera, consider using an external microphone. You gain much more control over the quality of the audio because the mic is separate from the camera body and its sole purpose is to record audio. There is a growing market of microphones for DSLR cameras, including mics with hot shoe adapters that allow you to mount the mic to the camera so you can record without having to hold it.

Another advantage of using external microphones is that you can use ones that are designed to do a better job of recording directional audio, such as that coming from subjects in front of the camera. Most of these microphones are long and slender and are referred to as shotgun mics.

FOCUSING THE CAMERA

The EOS M uses a focusing system it calls Movie Servo AF, which can refocus the scene during recording. If your subject moves closer to or farther from the camera position, it will be necessary for you to refocus in order to maintain sharp focus. Tap an area on the LCD to specify the focus point—I recommend using the FlexiZone – Single focus mode for better control. If you don't specify a focus point, the camera will continually maintain focus on wherever the focus box is placed.

However, that can be problematic when recording video, because the image "bounces" as the camera adjusts the lens to find focus. So even if you're shooting a stationary subject, small changes (a person leans slightly forward or back, for example) could cause a distracting refocus. If that's the case, tap the Servo AF button in the lower-left corner to temporarily turn the feature off.

Movie Servo AF can be disabled in the menus (under the movie-shooting tab). When it is disabled, the only ways to focus while recording are with a half-press of the shutter button or by switching to manual focus (MF) mode and using the focus ring on the lens.

CAPTURING VIDEO SNAPSHOTS

So, what if you don't need more than a short video clip, say, 4 seconds or so? Or perhaps you want a longer sequence that is made up of smaller video clips. Well, you might want to consider setting up the Video Snapshot feature. When this is activated, you can be in Movie mode and then press the Record button to grab a small snippet of video (2, 4, or 8 seconds in length). Once the camera has completed recording, you can save the clip to an album. You can add additional video snapshot clips to the album to create one longer video from the snapshots. This feature allows you to make some very creative video sequences right in your camera.

ACTIVATING VIDEO SNAPSHOTS

1. Press the Menu button and navigate to the movie-shooting tab.
2. Use the Down cross key to select Video snapshot, and press Set (**A**).
3. Select Video snapshot, press the Set button, and then select Enable (**B**) (if it's not already selected) and press Set.
4. Select Album settings (**C**), and press Set.

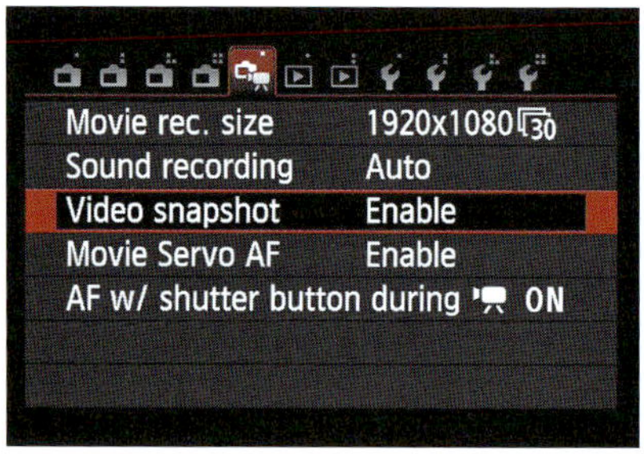

A

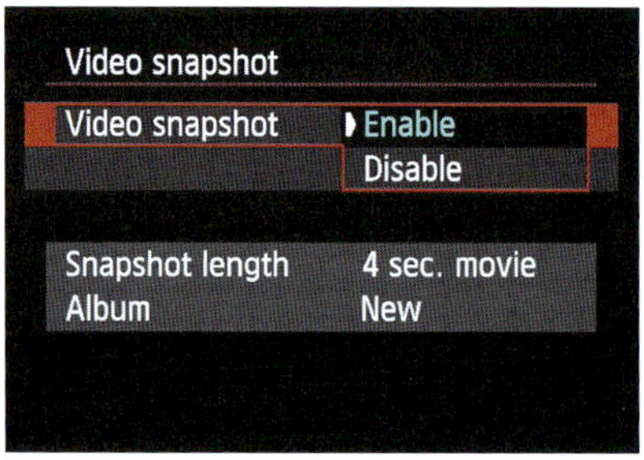

B

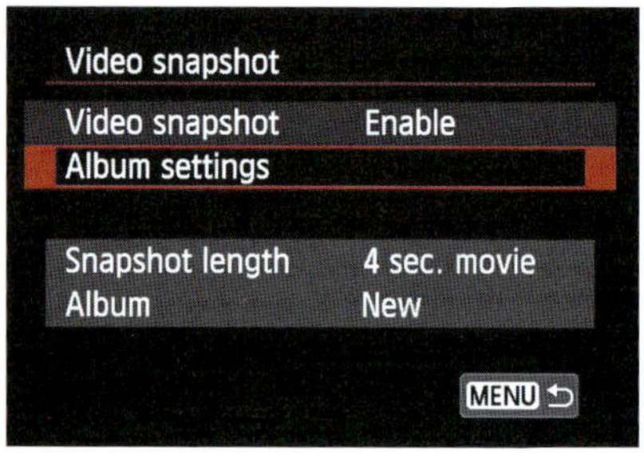

C

5. Select Create a new album, and press Set.
6. Press the Set button to view the Snapshot length options, and choose a clip length of 2, 4, or 8 seconds (**D**). Select OK and press Set.
7. Exit the menu by pressing the Menu button or pressing the shutter button halfway.
8. Set up your movie shooting just like you normally would, and press the Record button to begin the recording process. The video recording will cease once the time limit has been reached.
9. Now you can add the clip to your album, save it as a new album, play back the video, or delete it without saving (**E**).

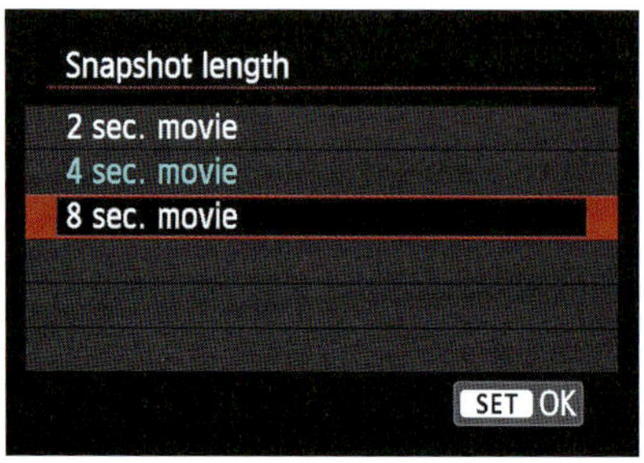

D

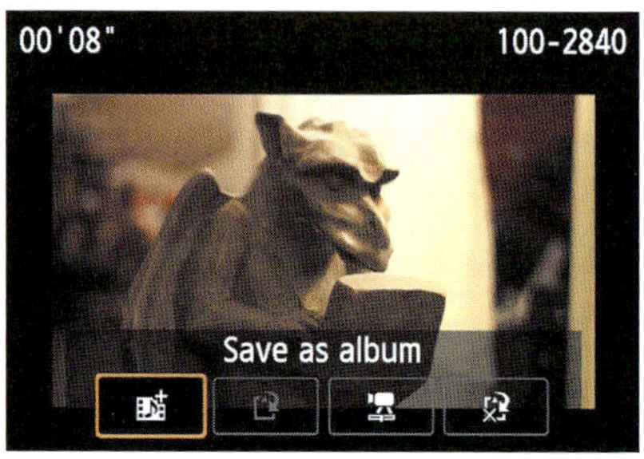

E

LOCKING THE EXPOSURE LEVEL

Not everything is automatically locked once you begin recording. The camera tries to dynamically compensate for exposure fluctuations (moving from bright to shaded areas, for example) as you record, which can often be a distraction. Fortunately, you can manually adjust and lock the exposure level before recording.

SETTING THE EXPOSURE

1. With the camera in Movie mode, press the ✱ AE Lock button when the exposure level is to your liking.
2. Press the shutter button to begin recording, or press the ✱ AE Lock button again to disable the lock.
3. Once you do start recording, you can tap the Exposure Compensation button and adjust the exposure manually by pressing the Left/Right cross keys or tapping the + and – buttons that appear.

MOVIE MANUAL EXPOSURE

If you want more control over the video shooting settings, tap the Mode button and choose Movie manual exposure. Doing so lets you set a shutter speed, aperture, and ISO value instead of handing those over to the camera.

CAPTURING STILLS WHILE RECORDING

As you record video, pressing the shutter button fully captures a still image without halting the video recording. The photo is saved as a separate file, but there's a catch: The camera pauses recording while processing the image, so when you watch the video you'll find a 1-second freeze-frame of the event. Personally, I find that makes the feature useless.

VIDEO SHOOTING TIPS

From a technical standpoint, shooting video with the EOS M isn't that much different from capturing stills. Instead, shooting video requires a slightly different mind-set.

SHOOTING SMOOTH, NOT JERKY

My best advice is to, as much as possible, take your time and be calm while shooting. If you whip the camera around like a caffeinated toddler, you'll end up with blurry, nausea-inducing footage. Be deliberate about holding the camera steady and panning slowly and smoothly. Your viewers will thank you.

If possible, set the camera on something when you need to move as you shoot. It's possible to buy or make rail systems for making smooth dolly moves (a Web search will reveal lots of solutions), but don't discount anything on wheels you may have at hand (**Figure 11.4**).

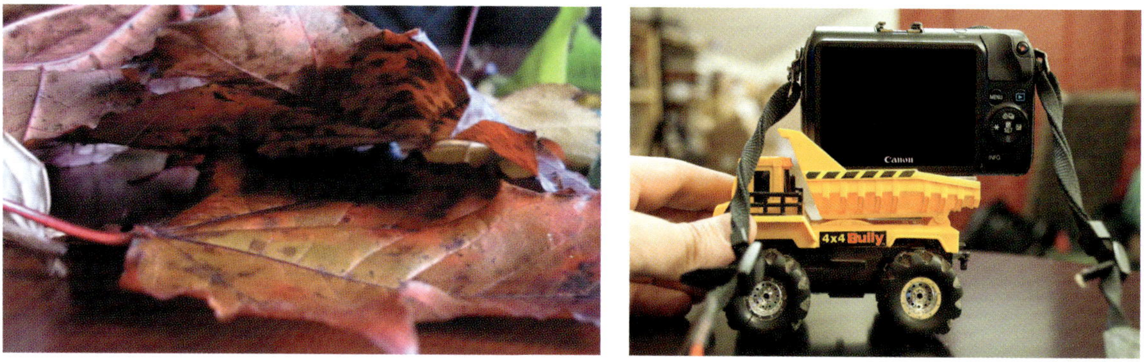

FIGURE 11.4
To pan across a scene, I pressed into service one of my daughter's toy cars.

A TRIPOD BECOMES MORE IMPORTANT

Speaking of shooting smooth footage, a tripod can be even more important for capturing video than for capturing stills. With video, the motion of the camera is as noticeable as what's in the frame. A tripod also gives you the opportunity to make sure the camera is level with the horizon. If a tripod isn't available, I highly recommend activating the EOS M's onscreen grid (found in the menus).

SHOOTING EXTRA FOOTAGE

I'm assuming that you plan to edit your footage later, so here's another essential tip: Shoot lots of video. Not just of the event happening in front of you, but of what's going on around it. When my wife and daughter were painting leaves last autumn, I made a point to capture footage of visually appealing things nearby (**Figure 11.5**). A shot of a lone leaf against the blue sky became a nice place to put a title, for example, and an overhead clip of the leaves and paints provided an establishing shot when segueing between gathering the leaves and painting them. These types of supplemental clips add flavor and texture to your movie.

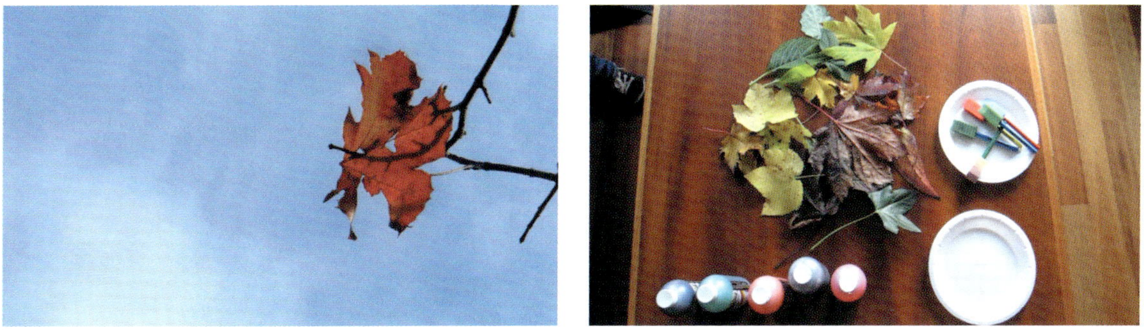

FIGURE 11.5
Shoot plenty of extra video so you can add visual interest to your movie when editing it.

WATCHING YOUR VIDEOS

There are a couple of options you can use to review your video once you have finished recording. The first is probably the easiest: Press the Playback button to bring up the recorded image on the LCD, and then press the Set button to start playing the video. The Left/Right cross keys act as the video controller and allow you to rewind and fast-forward as well as stop the video altogether.

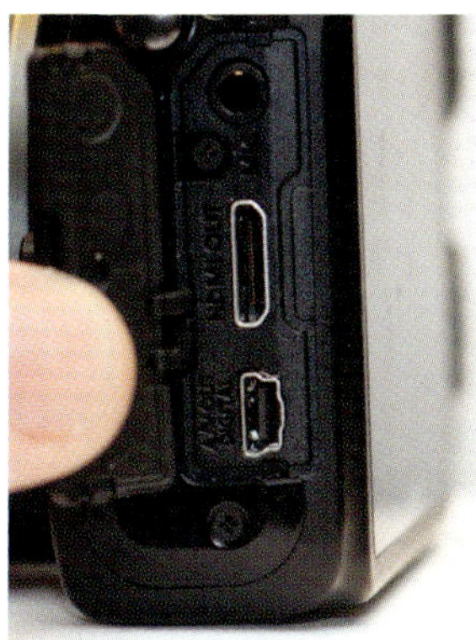

FIGURE 11.6
The video ports on the EOS M

If you would like to get a larger look at things, you will need to either watch the video on your TV or move the video files to your computer. To watch on your TV, you can use the video cable that came with your camera and plug it in to the small port on the side of the camera body (**Figure 11.6**). This will let you watch low-resolution video on your TV.

To get the full effect from your HD videos, you will need to purchase an HDMI cable (your TV needs to support at least 720 HD and have an HDMI port to use this option). Make sure you purchase a Mini-HDMI-to-HDMI cable, since the camera does not use a standard-sized HDMI jack for outputting video. Once you have the cable hooked up to your TV, simply use the same camera controls that you used for watching the video on the LCD.

If you want to watch or use the videos on your computer, you will need to download the images by using the Canon software or by using an SD card reader attached to your computer. The video files will have the extension ".mov" at the end of the file name. These files should play on either a Mac or a Windows PC, using software that came with your operating system or that can be downloaded for free (Apple's QuickTime for Mac and Windows is available at www.apple.com/quicktime/download/). If you are using an SDXC card, make sure that you have a compatible card reader to attach to your computer.

Manual Callout

You can check out all of the video features of your camera by turning to page 177 of the EOS M owner's manual.

Chapter 11 Assignments

Shooting video is fun and makes you stretch your photographer's mind-set in ways you don't when capturing still photos.

Recording some video clips

Set the video quality to 1920/30 (1920 x 1080 at 30 fps) and record a short sequence, and then try it with the 1920/24, 1280, and 640 settings.

Recording video snapshots

Enable the Video Snapshots feature and record a few 2-, 4-, or 8-second clips. Add them all to the same album and play back the result.

Locking the exposure

Shoot a scene with the EOS M in its automatic video mode, and then shoot the same scene using the AE Lock feature to see how the exposure levels change.

Grab extra footage

Spend some time intentionally shooting anything but the main focus of the video to see what kinds of footage you can bring to your editing software later.

Watch and enjoy

Open the video clips on your computer or hook the camera up to your TV, review the different video clips to see how the quality settings affect the video, and compare them to how they appear on the camera's LCD.

Share your results with the book's Flickr group!

Join the group here: flickr.com/groups/eosmfromsnapshotstogreatshots

INDEX

A

G

H

I

J

K

L

M

N